New Developments in International Finance

Edited by
Joel M. Stern
and
Donald H. Chew Jr

D1028654

Basil Blackwell

Copyright © This collection and all editorial matter
Joel M. Stern and Donald H. Chew, Jr 1988

First published 1988
Reprinted 1988, 1989

Basil Blackwell Inc.
432 Park Avenue South, Suite 1503
New York, NY 10016, USA

Basil Blackwell Ltd
108 Cowley Road, Oxford OX4 1JF, UK

Library of Congress Cataloging in Publication Data

New developments in international finance.
  Bibliography: p.
  Includes index.
  1. International finance.   I. Stern, Joel M.
II. Chew, Donald H.
HG3881.N398   1986   332'.042   86—3615
ISBN 0—631—15115—X
      0—631—15204—0 (pbk)

British Library Cataloguing in Publication Data

New developments in international finance.
  1. International finance
  I. Stern, Joel M.   II. Chew, Donald H.
332'.042   HG3881
ISBN 0—631—15115—X
      0—631—15204—0 (pbk)

Printed in Great Britain at the University Press, Cambridge
All articles reprinted with permission from
Midland Corporate Finance Journal
and the *Chase Financial Quarterly*

Contents

Preface

New Developments in International Finance is intended as a companion volume to *The Revolution in Corporate Finance* (Basil Blackwell, 1986). *The Revolution in Corporate Finance* is a collection of 45 articles which apply principles of "modern finance"— that is, market efficiency and its various corollaries— to current issues of financial management in a domestic, or single-country, setting. This book presents 17 articles which explore the practical implications of recent research on world capital markets for *multinational* financial management.

In the field of domestic corporate finance, the "revolution" in theory seems largely over, the governing principle of market efficiency commands a broad consensus (in the academic world, at least), and extensions and adaptations of the theory are abundantly evident in the "real world" of practicing corporate executives. In the international area, however, the evolution of the theory is in an earlier phase of development, and thus corporate applications have been few and tentative.

Donald Lessard, M.I.T.'s distinguished international finance scholar, sums up the present relationship between theory and practice as follows:

International finance is in the same position today as the entire field of financial management was a decade ago. On the one hand there exists a body of capital market theory that has had little practical impact; on the other, there exists a substantial body of institutional knowledge and normative theory that has not yet been linked to a positive economic base. This situation is both exciting and frustrating. It is exciting because there is great scope for advancement in the field and important conceptual breakthroughs are possible. It is frustrating because many of the practical problems at hand remain beyond the reach of existing theoretically based approaches. Further, the standard of rigor that has been applied in recent years in the field of finance often is unattainable in the international area at its current, relatively early level of development. (International Financial Management: Theory and Applications *(2nd Edition, Wiley & Sons, 1985), p. v)*

To put the case more bluntly, there seems as yet a conspicuous absence of theoretical justification

(and, thus, sound economic motive) for many of the current practices of multinational corporations, especially in the following three areas: (1) the measurement and management of foreign exchange risk; (2) the evaluation of the underlying (exchange-adjusted) profitability of foreign operations; and (3) the evaluation of international investment and, to a lesser extent, financing opportunities. (In areas like international financing and tax planning, however, international economists are working hard just to stay in the wake of corporate practitioners.)

This book aims to help narrow the breach between the theory and much of the current practice of international financial management by presenting a collection of articles addressed principally to the above three issues—exchange risk management, performance measurement, and international financing and investment. Each of these three issues, especially in recent years, has become critical for multinational corporations, and each accordingly is made the focus of one of this book's five sections; the other two consist of an introductory overview of the changing role of the finance function under global competition and, at the end, a brief consideration of issues of international banking—most notably, country risk analysis.

Overview: The Finance Function in a Multinational Setting

We begin with Donald Lessard's ambitious survey of the field entitled "Finance and Global Competition: Exploiting Financial Scope and Coping with Volatile Exchange Rates." Lessard's thesis is that the rise of global competition, combined with the greater integration of international capital markets, is now in the process of transforming the finance function within the multinational corporation. In the older days of what Lessard (following Michael Porter) calls "multidomestic competition," corporate decisions to invest abroad were made on an individual basis, generally with a view toward exploiting only local market opportunities; and thus the standard behavior of MNCs was to treat international subsidiaries as largely independent operating units. Today, by contrast, a much greater proportion of corporate operating functions are coordinated globally, including parts of marketing and manufacturing. As a result, decisions to invest overseas are less likely to be made on a purely individual basis. Instead, the aim of multinational strategic planners has increasingly become the design of a single, comprehensive plan to serve a *world* market.

In helping to execute such a global plan, the corporate treasury and planning staffs still perform the same tasks: capital budgeting, funding, performance measurement, tax planning, and risk management. But the adoption of a global perspective fundamentally changes most of them. For example, whereas MNCs once raised capital principally at home (while sometimes seeking out local overseas financing to hedge asset exposures and take advantage of subsidies), the treasurers of MNCs now compete aggressively on a worldwide basis to undercut their global competitors' cost of capital. Witness, for example, the enormous growth of currency swaps and the Euromarkets. MNCs also appear to have become fairly adept at devising worldwide tax planning schemes which shift profits from higher- to lower-tax regimes through the use of transfer pricing and a variety of financing practices.

But if corporate treasurers, with the help of their investment bankers, have adapted with remarkable speed to the new financing environment, other aspects of the corporate finance function appear to be evolving much more slowly—most notably, exchange risk management. MNCs are only beginning to address the problem of coping with large operating exposures (which affect the profitability of not only MNCs, but of domestic companies with global competitors). The conventional practice of exchange risk management continues to concern itself largely with the hedging of transaction exposures (that is, identifiable contractual revenues and liabilities), a practice which in many cases accentuates rather than reduces an MNC's real economic exposure to currency shifts. As Lessard comments, "Current methods of managing exchange risk are unlikely to help firms compete effectively and, indeed, are likely to provide misleading signals. In fact, as now practiced, corporate exchange risk management differs little from staking the assistant treasurer with a sum of money to be used to speculate on stock op-

tions, pork bellies, or gold."

Besides calling for a change of the hedging focus from transaction and translation exposures to operating profits, Lessard also argues that foreign exchange risk management should take a more anticipatory or "proactive" stance. That is, the expected effect of currency shifts on profits should be factored into budgeted standards and compensation plans, and operating responses to exchange rate shifts should be rehearsed. But this will require not only major changes in conventional accounting-based corporate perspectives, but "far more and better dialogue between operating and financial management." (This theme is later sounded and explored more thoroughly in articles by Brad Cornell and Alan Shapiro ("Managing Foreign Exchange Risks") and by Christine Hekman ("Don't Blame Currency Values for Strategic Errors").)

Another area where there is considerable room for improvement is that of performance measurement. The volatility of exchange rates has greatly complicated the task of evaluating the underlying profitability of overseas operations—both for purposes of compensating operating management and longer-range strategic planning. In the past, MNCs have typically chosen to evaluate overseas performance either in terms of local currency standards (while placing the responsibility for managing currency exposure entirely within the corporate treasury) or in terms of the home currency. Lessard, however, maintains that neither of these alternatives is appropriate in a global environment. Instead operating success should be judged relative to a flexible standard which adjusts to reflect the competitive effects of exchange rate changes. "A failure to incorporate such a standard within the control system," Lessard argues, "is likely to lead managers to 'leave money on the table' when they are favored by exchange rates, and to sacrifice too much market share by attempting to hold constant dollar margins when exchange rates work against them."

Exchange Risk Management

We begin this section with "The Nature and Management of Exchange Risk," in which Niso Abuaf provides a somewhat "macro" perspective on the corporate problem of dealing with exchange risk. After reviewing the behavior of exchange rates since the initiation of floating rates in 1973, Abuaf then goes on to evaluate current forecasting techniques and risk management strategies. He argues that the "dismal" forecasting performance of econometric models, as well as the very limited horizon of technical models, supports the notion of an efficient market for foreign currencies. Purchasing power parity, moreover, although a reasonably good guide to exchange rate movements over the long run, is nevertheless a poor predictor in the short to intermediate range. Large deviations from PPP, which have lasted for periods as long as five years, represent changes in *real* exchange rates which, unlike expected nominal changes, impose significant currency risks on corporations.

In the next piece, "Managing Foreign Exchange Risks," Brad Cornell and Alan Shapiro provide a comprehensive approach for coping with the consequences of unexpected changes in exchange rates. The authors begin by discrediting the conventional corporate practice of attempting to hedge accounting earnings—regardless of whether translated according to FAS #8 or FAS #52 principles. In accordance with principles of modern finance, exchange risk is defined as the variability in expected *cash flows* caused by changes in *real* exchange rates; that is, by changes in the *relative prices* of a firm's inputs and outputs. A brief case study, involving a hypothetical Swedish subsidiary of an American multinational, is used to illustrate the potential difference between accounting measures and real, economic measures of currency exposure.

Cornell and Shapiro then go on to dismiss most of the conventional hedging techniques as "vastly overrated." Contrary to much current corporate practice, exchange risk should not be managed exclusively by the corporate treasurer nor by a staff of (generally autonomous) currency traders. Effective planning instead should involve the participation of marketing and production executives, whose operating decisions should be coordinated with the treasurer's expectations about currency changes. Purely financial hedging is recommended only as a strategy of last resort, a means of hedging the "residual" operating exposure that remains after the appropriate marketing and production strategies have been put into place.

In "Don't Blame Currency Values for Strategic Errors," Christine Hekman warns executives against attributing substandard operating results solely to currency changes. Poor performance may also reflect a general deterioration of competitive position which, unlike the effects of temporary currency shifts, must be addressed by changes in pricing or sourcing and, perhaps, by major strategic revision. Dr. Hekman offers the outlines of a method for assessing a company's real currency exposure. Such a measurement technique is designed to be used by financial management to filter out the effects of currency changes on performance, thereby providing a clearer picture of underlying profitability and competitive position.

"A Practical Method of Assessing Foreign Exchange Risk" differs from the other articles in this book in two ways: it represents a collaboration between a finance scholar and a practicing financial executive, and it demonstrates in some detail the successful application of modern finance theory in a specific corporate setting. Kent Garner, Treasurer of Vulcan Materials Company, and Alan Shapiro collaborate in recounting how Vulcan's management used the concept of economic exposure to formulate its policy for managing exchange risks.

The question Vulcan faced was how to finance its British operation, whether in pounds sterling or dollars, in order to minimize the exposure of its overseas operating cash flows to fluctuations in the sterling-dollar exchange rate. Vulcan's investment banker and other financial advisors argued that because the revenues and expenses generated by its U.K. subsidiary were denominated in pounds, the operations should be financed with sterling borrowings. Garner and Shapiro, however, used correlation analysis of historical operating flows and exchange rates to determine that the dollar cash flows from Vulcan's U.K. investment were not consistently affected by changes in the pound-sterling rate. Consequently, they concluded that funding the English subsidiary with sterling borrowings was actually creating a "short" pound exposure for Vulcan, and that funding in dollars offered the best risk-minimizing strategy.

Ian Giddy's article on "The Foreign Exchange Option as a Hedging Tool" should prove useful for those multinationals facing currency risk associated with specific transactions. Giddy attempts to distinguish between the appropriate uses of currency *futures*, and the uses of the relatively new currency options that have been provided by several international banks and are available, on a limited basis, on the Philadelphia Exchange. These new tools appear to increase the hedging flexibility of multinational treasurers in two important ways: (1) they allow for the hedging of so-called *quantity risk*, i.e., those cases in which there is uncertainty about whether a future transaction will go through, or about the currency in which payments will be made; and (2) speculation on the *volatility*, as distinguished from the *direction*, of future currency movements.

Performance Measurement

Fluctuating exchange rates, besides affecting multinationals' real operating profitability (and thus causing exchange risk), also complicate the evaluation of the operating performance of foreign subsidiaries. To do the best possible job of allocating capital among overseas operations and of compensating overseas managers, corporate headquarters requires a reliable measure of the year-to-year profitability of its foreign operations.

We begin this section with "FAS #52 —Measuring the Performance of Foreign Operations," a discussion by Bryan Carsberg of the current accounting treatment of international earnings. In December of 1981 the U.S. Financial Accounting Standards Board adopted the current rate method of currency translation, replacing Statement No. 8 with No. 52. Around the same time, the U.K. Accounting Standards Committee also issued its first prescription for currency translation, and it too endorsed the current rate method. In this article, Carsberg provides a concise exposition of the differences between the new and old accounting standards, assessing their relative strengths and their implications for performance measurement. In a nicely-crafted series of illustrations, he explains the expected improvements, as well as the major remaining shortcomings, of the current rate method.

In "A Proposal for Measuring International Performance," Bennett Stewart proposes an alternative accounting framework for internal corporate uses such as evaluating existing foreign operations and local country operating management. It is designed to overcome the two most important limitations of FAS #52 and its British counterpart: their reliance on historical cost accounting and their vulnerability to short-run deviations of exchange rates from purchasing power parity. Stewart's article suggests that multinationals, in evaluating foreign operations for internal purposes, should first attempt to write up assets to current values (and the article contains a proposal for inflation adjustments that should be of interest to purely domestic as well as multinational companies), and then translate assets and income

into the home currency.

In the translation process, however, management should be using neither the historical rate prescribed by the old FAS #8 nor the current rate prescribed by FAS #52, but instead a current exchange rate that has been "normalized" to reflect long-run purchasing power parity—one that incorporates only the long-run difference in rates of inflation between the two countries concerned. Stewart' proposal is based on the assumption that exchange rates are forced to conform to PPP, at least over the long run, and that local operating managers should neither be rewarded nor penalized for the effects on translated results of more or less temporary, reversible exchange rate "distortions."

The following article, "Measuring the Performance of Operations Subject to Fluctuations," by Donald Lessard and David Sharp, is conceived in large part as an answer to Stewart's proposal. Lessard and Sharp argue that Stewart's proposal solves the problem of evaluating international performance only under a restrictive set of conditions: namely, when the international subsidiary being evaluated is a so-called "balanced" operation acquiring inputs from sources and producing output for consumers *strictly within* the country of operations, and facing no significant cross-border competition.

Arguing that in the 1980s such conditions have become the exception rather than the rule, the authors propose a flexible (their word is "contingency") budgeting scheme which makes the performance standards a direct function of the exchange rate that actually materializes. Although overseas operating managers are evaluated in local currency terms, thus insulating their performance from translation effects, the budgeted performance goals incorporate operating managers' *expected* response—that is, changes in marketing, sourcing, and production—to currency changes. Such an evaluation method, besides ridding performance measures of currency distortions, provides the added benefit of requiring local operating managers to take an active role in the budgeting process; in so doing, they are forced to plan well in advance their response to a range of possible exchange rate changes.

Alan Shapiro's "The Evaluation and Control of Foreign Affiliates" offers a number of general recommendations for dealing with certain international complications in measuring international performance. The usefulness of such performance measures depends, of course, on the use for which the measures are intended; and Shapiro discusses various alternative measures for the three distinct purposes of (1) multinational capital budgeting, (2) evaluating current subsidiary performance, and (3) compensating subsidiary management.

Especially interesting, we think, is Shapiro's suggestion that a measure of a foreign affiliate's value from the perspective of corporate headquarters may differ significantly from a fair measure of local managers' *operating* efficiency. Translated accounting results for subsidiaries typically do not allow headquarters to distinguish between good (or bad) operating management and good (or bad) luck. Shapiro argues that the ideal scheme for evaluating managers of foreign affiliates would remove the effects on translated financial statements of variables beyond local management's control (for example, local GNP growth rates, unexpected local inflation, and unexpected foreign exchange fluctuations).

Two alternatives are proposed: (1) remove the effect of unanticipated exchange rate changes by translating results into the home currency *using a projected rather than the actual end-of-period exchange rate* (that is, the corporate treasury should be held responsible for hedging *unanticipated* exchange rates); or (2), more ambitious, devise a *flexible budgeting scheme* in which "floating" performance objectives are expressed as a function of variables like local GNP, local inflation, and exchange rates. Under such a scheme, local managers are not penalized for the effects of an unexpected devaluation or downturn in the local economy; nor are they rewarded when artificially high exchange rates cause translated profits to be overstated. (Flexible budgeting schemes also would be useful, of course, for highly cyclical domestic operations as well.)

In the final article in this section, "Treasury Performance Measurement," Professors Ian Cooper and Julian Franks of the London Business School propose a set of guidelines for evaluating the performance of corporate treasury staffs in three key areas: borrowing, cash management, and risk management. Sophisticated, *market-based* measurement techniques have long been used to evaluate the performance of investment fund managers. But, performance evaluation of the corporate treasury, to the extent it is even attempted in any systematic way, continues to remain in "a primitive state"—while the importance and complexity of the corporate finance function seems to have increased dramatically in recent years. Such performance evaluation schemes as

do exist are typically tied to the accounting system of the firm. Indeed, as the authors maintain, "The major criterion (whether implicit or otherwise) by which corporate treasurers are judged by headquarters is the measurable effect of their decisions on reported earnings."

In place of the typical accounting-based criteria, this article offers *market-based* measures which quantify the economic returns from various treasury decisions (for example, the decision to hedge currency exposures) *relative* to the risks taken to achieve those returns. It is especially in the area of risk measurement that the future of treasury performance evaluation seems most promising. For, as the rising volatility of exchange rates (and of interest rates and commodity prices as well) exposes corporations to ever greater financial risks, current management methods for evaluating and managing such risks are coming to seem all the more inadequate.

The International Investment and Financing Decisions

This section begins with Alan Shapiro's "International Capital Budgeting," an ambitious attempt to incorporate some of the complexities of international finance within the standard DCF valuation framework. Shapiro reaches a number of somewhat surprising conclusions: for example, the popular practice of raising discount rates to reflect international risks only obscures the effect of such risks on the expected returns on foreign investment. From the point of view of well-diversified investors in multinational corporations, international investment—especially in lesser-developed countries—is, if anything, less risky than investments at home. Modern finance thus suggests that while purely domestic corporate diversification does not add value, multinational corporate diversification may offer significant benefits to investors.

In "Guidelines for Global Financing Choices," Donald Lessard and Alan Shapiro offer a broad framework for evaluating overseas financing decisions. The major objectives of a global financing strategy are three: (1) tax minimization; (2) the management of political, exchange, and commodity risks; and (3) the exploitation of overseas financing bargains. Tax minimization is the major source of value added by appropriate financing decisions, but distortions in financial markets caused by foreign exchange controls and special credit subsidies also provide opportunities for gains. Finally, the authors argue that structuring financing decisions so as to reduce commodity and foreign exchange risks is likely to be valuable because the risks of volatile cash flows and profitability, although perhaps not a major concern of well-diversified international investors, affects other corporate constituencies such as employees, suppliers, customers, and management (especially to the extent its compensation is tied to conventionally translated earnings) itself.

In "An International Perspective on the Capital Structure Puzzle," Janette Rutterford of the London School of Economics discusses the question of optimal capital structure in an international context. According to OECD statistics, Japanese firms tend to rely most heavily on debt financing, while French and German companies are somewhat less levered. U.S. and U.K. companies, by comparison, seem to have a preference for equity financing. While acknowledging the difficulty of comparing ratios among countries with different reporting systems, Ms. Rutterford considers the basic differences in the tax structures and contractual arrangements which could give rise to these differences in aggregate leverage ratios. She then goes on to suggest that the higher leverage ratios found in Japan—and to a lesser extent in Germany and France—are the result of special contractual ties between corporations and institutional lenders which reduce the conflict of interest (known as "agency costs") that typically exists between borrower and lender.

International Banking

In "International Banking and Country Risk Analysis," Alan Shapiro notes that international lenders are also subject to currency risk—a recognition which international bankers have only recently been forced to come to grips with. Perhaps the principal currency risk faced by lenders is the tendency of governments facing hard times to fix their exchange rates at artificially high levels. In this sense the failure of nominal exchange rates to adjust to changing economic fortunes is a sign of problems ahead. Other indications of trouble are highly variable terms of trade, price controls, interest rate ceilings, trade restrictions, and other government-imposed barriers to the smooth adjustment of the economy to changing relative prices.

Bluford Putnam's "Perspectives on Country Risk" applies principles of corporate finance and monetarist economics to the troublesome task of evaluating overseas credits and investments. The article begins by showing that conventional "current account" analysis—the primary focus of attention for many international lending institutions—provides an unreliable indication of a country's economic prospects or the strength of its currency. Also, the remedies prescribed for developing countries with current amount deficits—"competitive" devaluations, import substitution, and trade and capital controls—are seen as ineffectual if not actually destructive. In place of current account analysis, Putnam argues that attention must be focused on the entire balance of payments—that is, on capital as well as trade flows. Such an approach stresses the critical role of central banks in conducting monetary policy and influencing international capital flows.

In "The International Banking System: Measuring the Risks," Putnam offers an assessment of the condition of our international banking network. Grounded in economic realism, Putnam's affirmation of the resourcefulness and fundamental resilience of the international funding mechanism provides a forceful statement of the case for a free-market solution to the "crisis" in international lending.

In Closing

All of the articles in this book were previously published (within the past four years) in the *Midland Corporate Finance Journal*. For those unfamiliar with the aims of the journal, the purpose of the *MCFJ* has been to bring to the attention of senior corporate management the practical import of theoretical developments in finance for a wide range of corporate decisions: capital budgeting, dividend policy, capital structure planning, domestic and international performance measurement, merger and acquisition pricing, restructuring, and risk management. What success the journal has achieved, and whatever value this book will prove to have, is largely the result of the efforts of our Advisory Board and other contributing academics. Joel and I extend our thanks to all those involved, especially to Don Lessard and Alan Shapiro, whose names occur repeatedly throughout the Contents page.

Donald H. Chew, Jr.
New York City
January 30, 1987

Part I Overview

Finance and Global Competition: Exploiting Financial Scope and Coping with Volatile Exchange Rates[*]

Donald R. Lessard,
Massachusetts Institute of Technology[**]

Two major shifts over the last decade have radically changed the battle for competitive advantage among corporations and, with it, the potential contribution of the finance function to that advantage. The first is the shift toward global competition. Multinational corporations (MNCs) not only participate in most major national markets, but they are also increasingly integrating and coordinating their activities across these markets in order to gain advantages of scale, scope, and learning on a global basis.[1] The second major change is the globalization of financial markets, which has been accompanied by the increased volatility of exchange rates and other key international financial variables.

The emergence of global competition represents a major threat, as well as an opportunity, to those European and American companies that gained competitive advantage under an older mode of multinational competition. Labeled "multidomestic" competition by Michael Porter, this now passing phase in the development of international business was characterized by large MNCs with overseas operations which operated for the most part independently of one another.[2] What centralization existed in this stage of the evolution of the MNC was typically restricted to areas such as R & D and finance. With global competition, a much larger proportion of value added is coordinated globally, including aspects of manufacturing, important aspects of marketing, and virtually all of R & D.

The emergence of global competition reflects the merging of previously segmented national markets caused by a variety of forces, including reductions in trade barriers, a convergence of tastes, and the introduction of new corporate strategies and structures. These new strategies and structures, spearheaded primarily by the Japanese, have been successful in exploiting new competitive opportunities provided by placing both domestic and foreign markets in a global context. This adoption of a global perspective is reflected in large part in the increasing proportion of value added in many industries in the form of "up-front" intangibles, such as product and process design and software. The multidomestic era, in contrast, was characterized by transfers of fixed capital outlays and by recurring unit manufacturing costs. New global strategies also take advantage of changes in information technology and in-

*Adapted, with permission, from a paper of the same title forthcoming in Michael Porter, ed., *Competition in Global Industries*, Harvard Business School Press, 1986.

**I am grateful to Carliss Baldwin, Gene Flood, Sumantra Ghoshal, Bruce Kogut, John Lightstone, Tom Piper, Michael Porter, David Sharp, Mark Trusheim, and Lou Wells for comments on earlier drafts; Alberto Boiardi, Yongwook Jun, Chartsiri Sophonpanich, David Sharp, and Mark Trusheim for allowing me to draw on their unpublished thesis research; and to Don Chew for his excellent editorial suggestions.

1. By scale economies I refer to reductions in unit costs and/or product enhancements resulting from increases in production volume in a single location. Scope economies, in contrast, are reductions in unit costs and/or product enhancements associated with current production volume in related facilities and include the benefits of coordination of multiple facilities. Learning, or experienced-based, gains are unit cost reductions or quality improvements resulting from cumulative volume in one location or in related facilities.

2. See Porter [1986] for a number of perspectives on global competition. Full citations for all references are provided at the end of this article.

Volatile exchange rates distort traditional measures of current and long-term profitability, creating illusions that depend on the currency in which strategic alternatives are weighed and operating managers' performance evaluated.

creased organizational sophistication to improve coordination among geographically dispersed operations.

This new competitive and financial environment places important demands on the corporate finance function. Broadly conceived, the role of the finance function under global competition is to:
(1) provide the appropriate yardstick for evaluating both current operations and strategic alternatives;
(2) raise the funds required for these operations and, in so doing, minimize the firm's cost of capital;
(3) minimize taxes; and
(4) manage the risks inherent in the firm's activities. The larger stakes associated with world-scale operations require greater financial resources and flexibility. Further, global competition in product and factor markets reduces the ability of companies to pass through to their customers any financing or tax costs in excess of those facing the lowest-cost producers. And this means that global competition affects not only MNCs with international operations, but also those largely domestic firms which face global competitors in their home goods and factor markets.

Especially critical and difficult, however, is the task of coping with volatile exchange rates in the new competitive environment. Volatile exchange rates create much greater challenges for a firm facing global competition than one operating in a largely multidomestic mode. Under global competition, exchange rate fluctuations not only change the dollar value of the firm's foreign profits and foreign currency-denominated contractual assets and liabilities (such as accounts receivable and debt), they also alter the firm's competitive position and often call for changes in operating variables such as pricing, output, and sourcing. These decisions are complicated by the fact that volatile exchange rates distort traditional measures of current and long-term profitability, creating illusions that depend on the currency in which strategic alternatives are weighed and operating managers' performance evaluated.

A firm wearing "dollar-colored" eyeglasses or, for that matter, "yen-colored" eyeglasses will have a distorted view of its competitive position and is likely to make costly mistakes. A firm that sees through these effects will be in a much better position to judge its evolving competitive strengths. As a result, it will be more likely to make appropriate pricing, output, and sourcing choices in response to exchange rate shifts. It will also be in a better position to measure management's contribution to current performance

by taking account of the effects of macroeconomic events beyond management's control.

These views are borne out by the experiences of 1978 and 1979, when the weak dollar favored global competitors with U.S. production facilities, and of the period from 1981 through the end of 1985, when the strong dollar had the opposite effect. In the first period, many American firms were lulled into a false sense of security; their margins were "holding up" in the face of increasing foreign competition when in fact they should have been doing much better than the norm. As a result, they were poorly prepared for the shift in competitive position vis-a-vis their foreign competitors caused by the "dollar shock" of late 1980.

While it is impossible to forecast exchange rate movements, it is likely that extreme shifts such as these will reoccur, again altering international competitive positions and requiring major adjustments by firms. To make the proper adjustments to such changes, however, will require major changes in conventional corporate financial perspectives as well as considerably more and better dialogue between operating and financial management.

In this paper, I begin by describing changes in financial markets that have accompanied the shift to global competition. Second, I describe the changing role of finance in the context of global competition, and contrast it with the finance function under multidomestic competition. Third, I explore in greater depth the implications for the finance function of volatile exchange rates coupled with global competition. In so doing I argue that adoption of a global financial perspective critically affects a company's ability to maintain or strengthen its competitive position. Such a perspective must be incorporated into the firm's performance measurement scheme, its method of evaluating strategic alternatives, and its incentive compensation plan for local operating managers.

The Changing Financial Environment

The emergence of global competition has coincided with and, to some extent, has given rise to major changes in the international financial environment. National financial markets have been linked into a single global market. At the same time, governments have continued or increased their use of fi-

*In the short run, the volatility of exchange rates obscures longer-term
trends in the international competitive position of particular industries.*

nancial instruments in pursuit of various policy
goals, with the result that the world economy has become more volatile as reflected in the behavior of
exchange and interest rates.

**Increased International Linkage of Finan-
cial Markets.** The increased linkage of national
money and capital markets has been caused by a variety of factors.[3] These include the dismantling of
many restrictions on financial flows across national
borders,[4] the deregulation of financial institutions
both at home and abroad,[5] financial innovations that
allow a separation of the choice of currency and
other attributes of contracts from the jurisdiction in
which they take place,[6] and increased corporate
awareness of the intricacies of international finance.[7]

This increased integration of financial markets
implies, of course, an evening of the cost of funds in
various countries and a consequent reduction in the
benefits accruing to a firm from spanning national
financial markets.[8] At the same time, however, global
competition puts more pressure on MNCs to take advantage of the remaining gains from global financial
scope.

**Increased Financial Intervention in
Domestic Economies.** Counteracting this trend
toward a level international financial playing field is
the increased use by governments of financial intervention to favor home firms or home production.
Credit allocation, with its implicit subsidies to firms
with access to credit, continues in several industrialized countries and is the rule in most developing
countries. Many governments also offer concessional loans and explicit or implicit guarantees,
to the point that these have become a major source
of contention in international trade. Finally, most
governments modify their basic tax structures by
providing tax holidays, special deductions or credits,
or the ability to issue securities exempt from person-

al tax to favor particular activities.[9] (While much of
this intervention has been scaled back by the recent
tax reforms in the U.S. and the U.K., it is too early to
tell whether these changes will last.)

Such intervention has led to intense "shopping"
for tax and financing benefits by MNCs and increasing competition among governments for projects.[10]
In many cases, access to these financial benefits is
linked to performance requirements such as the location of the plant or the level of employment or exports.[11] However, the value of such incentives to an
MNC often depends on how it arranges its internal
and external finances. For example, a firm with no
need for borrowing in a country with cheap credit
can shift its interaffiliate accounts so as to increase its
apparent local borrowing requirements, while a
firm investing in a start-up venture that will not break
even for several years in a country offering a tax holi-
day can use transfer prices to shift profits from related operations to the tax-sheltered unit. Similarly, a
firm engaged in overseas oil exploration may obtain
a tax benefit from having operations in the U.S. because it can deduct these expenses from taxable
profits in the U.S., but not from profits in most other
countries.[12] Later I will show that the ability of an
MNC to exploit these conditions will depend on how
many options it has for shifting funds or profits
among subsidiaries across national boundaries,
which in turn will depend on the number of places it
operates and on the volume and complexity of the
ongoing real and financial interactions among its
component corporations. For this reason alone, a
firm's international financial scope is likely to be an
important factor in its competitiveness.

Exchange and Interest Rate Instability. A
major characteristic of the current world economy
involving both the financial and real spheres is the
extreme volatility of exchange and interest rates.

3. For an overview of recent evidence on financial market integration see
Kohlhagen [1983].

4. For recent studies of border controls and their effects on financial markets
see Dooley and Isard [1980] and Otani and Tiwari [1981].

5. The deregulation of financial institutions first took the form of an escape
from national regulations by banks operating "offshore" as described by Dufey
and Giddy [1981], Grubel [1977], Kindleberger [1974], Tschoegl [1981] and
others. Subsequently, partly in response to this offshore competition and partly
to shifts in domestic considerations, it has taken the form of reduced regulation
of financial intermediation within individual national markets.

6. For a review of recent financial innovations see Dufey and Giddy [1982]
and Antl [1984].

7. This integration of financial markets, however, is as yet far from complete.
Many less-developed countries, in response to foreign exchange crises brought
about by their own external borrowing coupled with the world recession, have
imposed new or tighter exchange controls and other measures that isolate the
domestic financial markets from world markets. As a result, private firms based in

these countries have seen their access to international financial markets cut back
to pre-1970 levels. Nevertheless, financial markets are considerably more integrated on balance than they were in 1970. For a review of exchange restrictions
see International Monetary Fund [1985]. Rosenberg [1983] discusses the
(in)effectiveness of these controls given the mechanisms firms can use to circumvent them.

8. For overviews of the benefits to a firm of spanning national financial
markets see Robbins and Stobaugh [1973] and Lessard [1979].

9. These include the ability to make use of tax-exempt bond issues, "80/20"
offshore financing in the U.S. and similar measures in most other industrialized
countries.

10. These two points are discussed in Baldwin [1986] and Encarnation and
Wells [1986], respectively.

11. See Guisinger and Associates [1985].

12. This has been given as one explanation of BHP's (Australia) recent
acquisition of a U.S. exploration company.

This volatility is inextricably linked to differing degrees of integration internationally of finance, industry, and politics. Because of the high degree of integration among financial markets in major industrialized countries, factors influencing interest rates are readily transmitted across national boundaries. Given the lesser degree of integration in markets for goods and real factors of production, and the almost total lack of coordination in macroeconomic policies among nations, the result has been a high degree of volatility in nominal and real exchange rates.[13] This volatility, in turn, has led to sharp swings in the competitiveness of production facilities based in different countries.

In the short run, the volatility of exchange rates obscures longer-term trends in the international competitive position of particular industries. Over time, though, given that changes in exchange rates tend to offset cumulative differences in rates of inflation among countries,[14] the competitive effects of exchange rate changes are likely to be swamped by microeconomic factors such as the firm's productivity growth compared to that of its host economy.[15]

This long-run tendency for exchange rates and inflation differentials to offset each other is illustrated in Exhibit 1. Cumulative changes in the nominal exchange rate—the dollar price of the foreign currency—are depicted on the vertical axis, while changes in the real exchange rate—defined as changes in the nominal exchange rate relative to cumulative inflation differences—are shown on the horizontal axis.[16] Over relatively long periods, from 1973 until 1980 (points represented by open rectangles) or 1985 (triangles), for example, the spread of cumulative movements in real rates is much less than that of nominal rates.

In the short term of from six months to as long as two or three years, though, when inflation differentials are small, both real and nominal exchange rates move together. Between December 1980 and June 1982, for example, the dollar strengthened against most currencies in real terms and reduced the competitiveness of U.S. producers. From June 1982 to December 1983, there was a further

strengthening of the dollar relative to major currencies. By September 1986, however, this appreciation had been partially reversed in most cases, and more than completely reversed in the case of the yen.

This volatility of real exchange rates, as I shall later show, gives rise to an exaggerated variability in corporate operating margins. This variability in turn creates two problems: (1) a potentially significant currency operating exposure and (2) great difficulty in evaluating the real profitability of overseas operations, both for purposes of strategic planning and compensating operating management.

Resulting Threats and Opportunities. Global competition, together with an increasingly integrated and volatile financial environment, gives rise to both threats and opportunities for firms whose activities span real and financial markets in various countries. A major threat is the exposure to exchange rate volatility and its impact on the firm's competitive position. A closely related threat, which is more subtle and therefore more difficult to address, is the potential for management error due to illusions associated with short-run movements in exchange rates.

On the positive side, exchange rate volatility provides an opportunity to exploit relative price shifts, but this requires production flexibility that is costly and organizational flexibility that is difficult to sustain.[17] For example, in order to be able to switch sources to exploit changes in wage rates, a firm or its suppliers would have to invest in excess capacity; managers would have to devise (and, perhaps, rehearse) alternative sourcing and marketing responses that would be undertaken only in the case of major exchange rate shifts; and those geographic units within the firm whose competitive position is undercut by exchange rate shifts would have to be willing to concede market share to units that were favored by the change.

In addition to its effects on operations, exchange rate volatility combined with less than complete integration of financial markets and the significant degree of government intervention also results in new challenges for firms' financial activities. The treasurers of

13. For recent views of the determinants of exchange rates see Dornbusch [1983], Frenkel and Mussa [1981], and Stockman [1980].

14. This tendency, known as purchasing power parity, was first outlined by Cassel [1923]. For a recent review of its various meanings see Shapiro [1983]. For evidence on who well it holds see Roll [1979], Frenkel [1981], and Adler and Lehman [1983].

15. For a discussion of the strategic implications of purchasing power parity

in the long run, see Kiechel [1982].

16. The real exchange rate, therefore, is a statistical construct that measures the relative price of a composite of goods in the U.S. relative to a similar composite in the foreign country. In this particular case, wholesale price indices are used as measures of the prices of composite goods in the two countries.

17. See Baldwin [1986] and Kogut [1983].

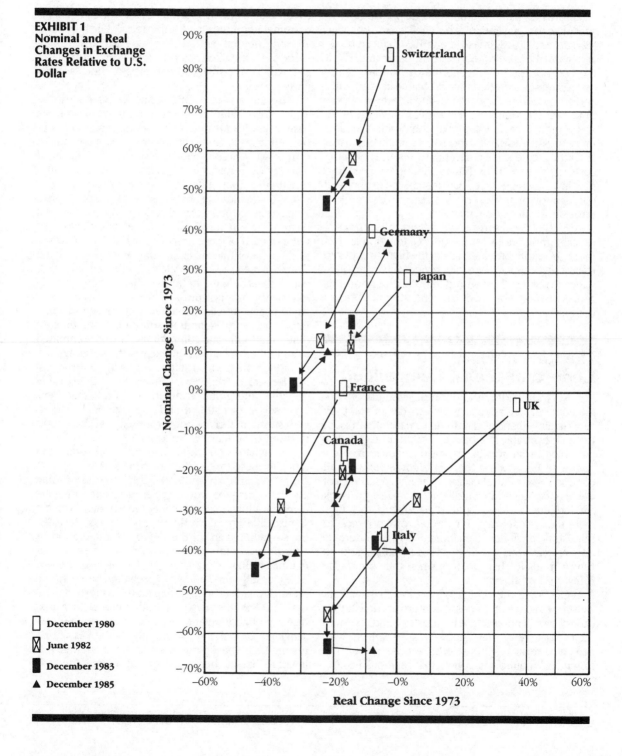

EXHIBIT 1
Nominal and Real Changes in Exchange Rates Relative to U.S. Dollar

Nominal Change Since 1973 (y-axis): 90%, 80%, 70%, 60%, 50%, 40%, 30%, 20%, 10%, 0%, −10%, −20%, −30%, −40%, −50%, −60%, −70%

Real Change Since 1973 (x-axis): −60%, −40%, −20%, −0%, 20%, 40%, 60%

Switzerland
Germany
Japan
France
UK
Canada
Italy

December 1980
June 1982
December 1983
December 1985

MNCs are now daily confronted with opportunities to speculate or engage in arbitrage across financial markets and tax regimes via internal financial transactions. At the same time, they also face greater risks if they do not carefully hedge their positions. While there is reason to believe that profitable cross-border and cross-currency speculative and arbitrage opportunities are becoming scarcer as financial markets become more integrated, global competition creates more pressure to exploit those that remain because it shifts the incidence of differential taxes and financing costs to the firm. Thus, finance not only comes into play in addressing issues that arise because of global competition in product markets, but also becomes a direct factor in that competition.

Each of these threats and opportunities has significant implications for the finance function and its interaction with other aspects of the firm. In order to trace these implications we review the role of finance in the corporation and then consider how this role is or should be changed in the context of global competition.

The Role of Finance in the Context of Global Competition

Notwithstanding the periodic attempts of conglomerateurs or asset strippers to create value by repackaging financial claims, finance derives most of its value from the real business operations it makes possible. In an idealized world characterized by complete information, perfect enforceability of all contracts, and neutral taxation, the principal roles of the finance function would be to provide a yardstick for judging business options to ensure that they meet the "market test" for the use of resources, to raise sufficient funds to enable the firm to undertake all projects with positive present values, and to return funds to shareholders when they cannot be reinvested profitably.

Of course, the world does not match this idealization. Managers often possess information that they cannot or will not disclose to investors, and investors often disagree among themselves as well as with managers regarding future prospects. As a result, defining and monitoring contractual relationships between managers and various classes of claimants is extremely complex and imperfect.[18] Further, taxes are not neutral and access to particular capital markets is often restricted in a discriminatory fashion. As a result, financial contracts at times are not fairly priced.

In such an environment, finance can contribute to the firm's value in several ways in addition to its basic role of evaluating and funding investment opportunities.[19] Finance can add value by allowing the firm to (1) exploit pricing distortions in financial markets, (2) reduce taxes, (3) mitigate risks and allocate them among different parties in order to maximize diversification benefits, create appropriate managerial incentives, and reduce costs of financial distress. The nature and potential contribution to value of each of these functions will differ according to the type of international strategy pursued by the firm. For the sake of simplicity, I will view all multinationals as falling into three stylized categories: (1) international opportunists—firms that focus primarily on their domestic markets but engage in some international sales and/or sourcing from time to time; multidomestic competitors—firms committed to a number of national markets with substantial value added in each country, but with little cross-border integration or coordination of primary value activities; and global competitors—firms that focus on a series of national and supranational markets with substantial cross-border integration and coordination of primary value activities.

To what extent, then, does the finance function differ in these three different contexts?

The nature and potential contribution of some aspects of finance would appear to depend on the firm's multinationality—that is, the extent to which it spans different currency areas or tax jurisdictions—rather than on the degree of integration or coordination of the firm's primary activities such as manufacturing or marketing. Other aspects, however, especially those related to exchange rate risk, will differ dramatically depending on the pattern of competition. For this reason, a multinational firm may have a global orientation in finance but not in other activities. On the other hand, merely the fact of having multinational operations does not guarantee that it will realize the benefits of global scope in finance.

---

18. Myers [1984] and Barnea, Haugen, and Senbet [1981] discuss the impact of these agency effects on financing choices.

19. Here we refer to the warranted (present discounted) value of the firm's shares, the most complete financial measure of a firm's performance.

EXHIBIT 2
Implications of Global Competition for Finance Function

| Function | Nature of Competition | | |
	International Opportunist	Multidomestic	Global
Investment Evaluation	Domestic perspective, few "foreign" considerations	Yes/no decision to enter market or change mode to serve local market	Mutually exclusive global choices, currency and tax issues central
Funding Operations*	Meet domestic norms	Meet local norms	Match global competitors' cost of capital
Exchange Risk Management	Focus on exposure of foreign currency contracts	Focus on exposure of converting foreign profits into dollars	Focus on exposure of home and foreign profits to competitive effects of exchange rate shifts
Output/Pricing Responses to Exchange Rate Movements	No change in home currency price	No change in local currency price	Change in home and local price to reflect global competitive position
Performance Measurement	Measure all operations in dollars at actual rates	Measure foreign operations in local currency	Measure all operations relative to standard that reflects competitive effects of exchange rate

*The entries in this row reflect typical behaviors of firms. Clearly, firms can and some do pursue global cost-minimizing financing strategies regardless of degree of global linkage of operations.

Nevertheless, there are many reasons why the nature and potential contribution of the multinational financial function will differ in the context of global competition.

Exhibit 2 provides an overview of the changing nature of the finance function and its linkages to the firm's overall competitive position under international, multidomestic, and global competition. It classifies firms into these three categories according to their method of dealing with a number of tasks assigned to the corporate treasury and planning staffs: evaluation of new investment, funding, performance measurement, and exchange risk management. I also include tactical pricing and output changes to exchange rate changes—not typically thought of as finance functions—because they are closely linked to exchange risk management and strongly influenced by a firm's currency perspective.

In the remainder of this section I review the implications of increased global competition together with the increased integration of financial markets for each of the major finance functions identified in Exhibit 2.

Evaluating Investment Opportunities. A clear implication of the current competitive and financial environment is an increase in the complexity of investment opportunities and the corresponding increase in the potential for management error. The estimation of incremental benefits from resource outlays must take into account increased international interdependence among the various activities of the firm in terms of the benefits of scale, scope, learning and, hence, future opportunities.

In analyzing alternative plant locations, for example, the firm must evaluate not only differences in the direct costs of operating in each location, but also the impact of different choices on other strategic factors such as access to particular markets and the scale and experience "platforms" that each alternative provides for future operations. Consider the case of the Korean consumer electronics companies whose U.S. operations appear to break even at

What is needed is a closer linkage of competitive analysis and DCF techniques, not a surrender of quantitative techniques to more subjective approaches.

best.[20] This poor financial performance is often offered as evidence of uneconomic behavior on the part of Korean firms or, alternatively, of extensive Korean government subsidies of its firms' operations abroad. Another explanation, however, is that the financial performance of their U.S. operations is only one component of their contribution to Korean firms' value. Others include the effect of unit cost reduction due to the scale made possible by entering the U.S. market on the profits of these firms in Korea (where they are oligopolists with substantial market power), and the benefits of learning from present U.S. operations on future investment opportunities both in the U.S. and elsewhere. Choices among alternative product and marketing programs are even more complex because gains in some product market segments will result in erosion in others; in still other cases there may be positive carryover from success in one segment to others.

Given the varying patterns of government intervention, management must make choices among strategic alternatives that are further complicated by the need to trade off such direct and indirect benefits against alternative packages of investment incentives and performance requirements. Such decisions must be made on the basis of calculations of the present value of each package, which in turn will depend on the corporation's anticipated (worldwide) cash flow and its tax position in various jurisdictions. While similar complications existed under multidomestic competition, in general there were fewer interdependencies to contend with; each decision influenced only whether a firm should enter a particular national market rather than which of a number of (mutually exclusive) alternatives should be chosen as the best way of serving a world market.

A further complication is the problem of the "bent measuring stick."[21] Unless the firm conducts all interaffiliate transactions at arms' length, the profits (incremental cash flows) of any activity to any corporate unit will not equal the incremental flows to the corporation as a whole. There are many reasons, such as the desirability of reducing taxes, why a firm will not choose to adopt arms-length transfer pricing (even provided it is able to produce accurate estimates of such prices). Under global competition, this problem is exacerbated not only by the increased interdependencies among companies' operations, but by the overwhelming impact of exchange rate fluctuations on revenues, costs, and profits. In projecting future profits and cash flows, firms must see through the short-term effects on profits of currency movements to focus on their evolving competitive position assuming "normal" exchange rates. I return to this point in the next section.

These complexities have contributed to a general view that discounted cash flow (DCF) techniques are no longer valid and that their use by U.S. management has contributed to the decline of America's competitive position.[22] Nothing could be farther from the truth. It is probably true that U.S. managers' overreliance on short-term return on investment (ROI) goals, coupled with a simplistic use of DCF techniques, does result in a bias against projects with indirect, future benefits.[23] When properly employed, however, DCF measures provide a powerful framework for combining the effects of scale, scope, and learning on present and future activities.[24] What is needed is a closer linkage of competitive analysis and DCF techniques, not a surrender of quantitative techniques to more subjective approaches.

Funding Business Requirements. The increased scope of the competitive arena implies larger stakes for most major business gambles.[25] But the increased integration of financial markets in different countries has enhanced MNCs' external financing capacity as well, especially for those based in

20. This discussion draws on Jun [1985].

21. This term was coined by Robbins and Stobaugh [1973] in their pathbreaking study of the multinational finance function.

22. This theme is developed by Hayes and Abernathy [1980] and echoed by Hout, Porter, and Rudden [1982]. Donaldson [1972] provides an earlier indictment of DCF techniques, but also indicates where the problems lie and suggests ways to overcome them.

23. Surveys by Schall, Sundem, and Geijsbeck [1978], Wicks [1980] and Oblak and Helm [1980] show that managers continue to favor DCF-rate of return calculations in spite of the clear superiority of additive present value calculations when a projects gives the firm access to significant future growth options. Hodder and Riggs [1985] discuss how methodological biases distort decisions. Hodder [1984] finds substantial differences between the capital budgeting practices of U.S. and Japanese firms. U.S. firms appear to be more "number driven," but devote much less attention to alternative scenarios and strategic options.

24. One line of development of DCF techniques that is capable of taking many of these effects into account is the valuation by components method. Under this approach, cash flows are segregated into equity equivalents, debt equivalents and option equivalents and each component is valued using techniques most appropriate to its characteristics. Developed by Myers [1974], it has been extended to the international context by Lessard [1979, 1981]. Recent work on valuing option equivalents in investment decisions by Brennan and Schwartz [1985] and Myers and Majd [1984] is particularly promising in the treatment of future options to invest, abandon, or receive various forms of government support. Booth [1982] and Lessard and Paddock [1984] discuss the advantages of valuation by components relative to more traditional single discount rate approaches.

25. Vernon [1981] argues that, in contrast to the 1960's, a much larger proportion of new product launches will be on a global scale with correspondingly larger outlays.

Opportunities for financial arbitrage or speculation, although rare, do exist from time to time, especially in capital markets that are distorted and isolated by controls on credit and exchange market transactions.

smaller countries with isolated capital markets.[26] Firms that consider themselves global competitors are broadening their funding bases to ensure that they will not find themselves at a competitive disadvantage in this regard.[27] Even a multidomestic competitor is not safe; the emergence of a firm with a global financing advantage will alter the terms of competition in much the same way as the emergence of a firm with globally-integrated production in an industry hitherto characterized by production only on a national scale.

Exploiting Financing Bargains. To the extent that financial markets are not fully integrated or that financing concessions differ among countries, MNCs' ability to span these markets will increase not only their ability to fund global operations, but also the likelihood that they can identify and exploit financing bargains. If a firm can identify financial investment or borrowing opportunities that are mispriced, it can add value by engaging in arbitrage or speculation. In general, opportunities for such gains are rarer than for gains arising from real market advantages; whereas real advantages are typically protected by barriers to entry, there are likely to be fewer and far less formidable barriers to financial transactions. Nevertheless, such opportunities do exist from time to time, especially in capital markets that are distorted and isolated by controls on credit and exchange market transactions. Exxon, for example, was able to issue zero-coupon bonds at a rate lower than the U.S Treasury yield on the comparable maturity, defease the issue by buying an offsetting portfolio of Treasuries, and pocket a profit of nearly $20 million—largely because of differences in the Japanese tax code and restrictions on Japanese foreign investment.[28]

Because they are at once domestic and foreign, multinationals are more likely to encounter such exploitable distortions in financial markets than firms operating in single countries. They often can circumvent the credit market and exchange market controls that create these profit opportunities.[29] The internal financial networks of MNCs provide them with considerable latitude in the timing of interaffiliate transfers as well as in the choice of channels through which they transfer cash or taxable profits among their various national corporate components.[30] For example, a firm can advance funds to a subsidiary through an injection of funds in the form of equity or a loan, through a transfer of goods (or intangibles such as technology) at less than an arms-length price, or by providing it with a guarantee that enables it to borrow locally. Depending on how the subsidiary is funded, the firm then has a similar array of channels through which it can withdraw funds. It can accelerate or delay transfers by leading or lagging interaffiliate settlements relative to their scheduled dates or, if such behavior is prohibited, by shifting the timing of the shipment of goods within the corporation.

This discretion over the channels and timing of remittances among related corporations is of little value within a single tax and monetary jurisdiction because transfers among units typically involve little cost and have no tax consequences. But when the firm operates across jurisdictions, certain channels may be restricted by virtue of exchange controls, and the use of others will trigger additional tax liabilities. Under these circumstances, the firm benefits from "internalizing" these transactions.[31]

The increase in global competition is likely to increase the pressure on firms to pursue such gains because they are less able to pass through to their customers financing costs in excess of those facing the industry cost leaders. In a multidomestic context, in contrast, the competitive impact of these costs depends only on the relative position of firms in each country.

Reducing Taxes. By appropriately "packaging" the cash flows generated by business operations, firms often can substantially reduce the present value of governments' tax take.[32] The

26. An interesting case in point is the Danish firm Novo whose entry into U.S. equity markets is chronicled by Stonehill and Dullum [1982]. Firms such as Schlumberger and Ciments LaFarge also have shifted their funding from small home markets to integrated world markets; and, most recently, Jardine-Mathieson is shifting its "window" on world capital markets from Hong Kong to Bermuda. (NYT, March 29, 1984). Adler [1974] and Agmon and Lessard [1979] discuss the basis for such capital market-seeking behavior of firms.

27. Hitachi, for example, recently announced the creation of five offshore financing centers for its worldwide business.

28. See the discussion of this transaction by John Finnerty, "Zero Coupon Bond Arbitrage: An Illustration of the Regulatory Dialectic at Work," *Financial Management* (Winter 1985).

29. For a discussion of the relationship between credit market and exchange controls and pricing distortions in financial markets, see Dooley and Isard [1980] and Otani and Tiwari [1981].

30. The source of profit shifting in this case comes from manipulating the transfer prices among affiliates. See Brean [1985] for an in-depth discussion of financial transfer prices.

31. The concept of internalization has been extended to many other aspects of multinational firms' activities. See in particular, Buckley and Casson [1976], Hennart [1982], and Rugman [1981]. Robbins and Stobaugh [1973], studying a set of multidomestic multinationals, showed that the potential gains from exploiting internal financial systems were often significant. They also found, however, that larger firms tended not to fully exploit this potential because of external constraints (or self-policing to avoid sanctions) and organizational limitations.

simplest example in a single country setting is the use of debt as a way to reduce corporate income taxes. Firms operating internationally may be in a position to shift income into jurisdictions with relatively low rates or relatively favorable definitions of income. While some of these profit shifts occur through transfer prices of real inputs and outputs, the pricing of interaffiliate financial transactions often provides the greatest flexibility.[33]

In the current global competitive environment, though, a new factor is coming into play. As governments seek actively to manipulate their fiscal systems for nationalistic or distributional gains, MNCs "shop" fiscal regimes and bargain over the distribution of rents resulting from a given activity. This is especially true of facilities on a world scale such as, for example, a plant to produce automobile engines located in a country with a relatively small local market. Such investments, by definition, are not premised on access to any single market. In these cases, tax system arbitrage becomes an area of active bargaining as well as gaming of passive fiscal systems.[34]

A final way that an international firm can reduce (the present value of expected) taxes is to structure interaffiliate commercial and financial dealings—as well as hedging the risks of individual units through external transactions—so as to minimize the chance that any of its corporate components will experience losses on its tax accounts and, as a result, have to carry forward some of its tax shields. Virtually all corporate income tax regimes are asymmetric in that they collect a share of profits but rebate shares of losses only up to taxes paid in the prior, say, three years. Otherwise, the losses must be carried forward with an implied reduction in the present value of the tax shields.[35]

As with financing costs, global competitors will be under much greater pressure than multidomestic competitors to match the lowest tax burden obtainable by any firm in the industry while, at the same time, increasing their flexibility in where to locate

and how to coordinate value-adding activities. Thus, tax and financial management aimed at minimizing the firm's cost of capital, once an optional activity pursued by a handful of sophisticated firms, has become an integral element of global competitive strategy.

Managing Risks. A final, often critical, role of finance is to offset particular risks inherent in the firm's undertakings and/or shift them to other firms or investors. Global competition, for example, increases firms' exposure to exchange rate volatility, but the firm can to a large extent lay off this risk through hedging transactions such as currency futures, swaps, options, or foreign currency borrowing. Some aspects of exchange risk can also be shifted to suppliers or customers through the choice of invoicing currencies. Alternatively, the firm can retain this risk and, in effect, pass it on to its shareholders.

An important insight of modern financial theory is that in an idealized capital market, the allocation of risk among firms, as well as the form in which it is passed on to investors, does not affect the value of the firm's securities. The reasoning is that sophisticated investors, simply by holding diversified portfolios, can manage most risks just as efficiently as corporate management. Under these circumstances, hedging by the corporation does not add to the value of a company's shares; and, as long as hedging prices are "fair," contractual risk-sharing with suppliers or customers is of no consequence.

In practice, however, firms devote a great deal of effort to risk allocation in the form of hedging and risk sharing. While much of this behavior can be traced to attempts by managers to "look good" within imperfect control systems, several recent analyses provide a rigorous basis, consistent with shareholder value maximization, for hedging under some circumstances. In particular, as we have seen above, it can reduce the (present value) of taxes. It can also increase diversification benefits, improve managerial incentives, and reduce the probability (and thus the expected costs) of financial distress.[36]

---

32. Packaging can involve setting up tax-minimizing ownership chains as discussed by Rutenberg [1970] or choosing the nature of the parent's financial claim — equity, debt, or a claim on royalties — as discussed by Horst [1977] and Adler [1979].

33. Examples of the impact of interaffilate financial transactions of a firm's taxes are presented by Horst [1977] and Brean [1985].

34. The industry studies in Guisinger and Associates [1985] confirm that fiscal incentives are most important when several alternative sites provide access to the same (common or world) market.

35. As explained by Smith and Stulz [1985], the tax authorities effectively hold a call option on profits. As a result, the expected tax rate is an increasing function of the variability of the taxable profits of each entity that comprise the firm.

36. See for example, Barnea, Haugen and Senbet [1985], Shapiro and Titman [1985], and Smith and Stulz [1985].

Volatile earnings and cash flows may reduce a firm's ability to compete by distorting management information and incentives, hindering access to capital markets, and threatening the continuity of supplier and customer relationships. In the case of risks which, although outside the control of individual firms, affect many companies, such as the effects of variable exchange rates or relative prices of key commodities, firms with large specific exposures will benefit by laying off these risks to other firms or investors that have smaller or perhaps even opposite exposures. To the extent that the risks affecting particular business undertakings are at least partially controllable by one or more potential participants, risk allocation to create appropriate strategic stakeholdings is likely to reduce risk.

Although capital markets are becoming more integrated, there are barriers to cross-border investment in the form of taxes, controls on foreign investment, and political risks that have different effects on domestic and foreign investors, particularly transfer risks. Because of these barriers, investors in various countries will differ in their scope for diversifying particular risks and, hence, will place different values on particular securities.[37] They also may differ in their ability to mitigate those risks that are at least in part the result of choices by governments or other firms.[38] A firm may exploit this comparative advantage in risk-bearing by issuing securities either directly or indirectly (that is, by contracting with a firm with a different set of investors) to the investor group which will value them most highly. A global firm will not limit itself to any particular capital market base and, hence, will exploit this potential to the fullest.

Organizational Implications. Global competition results in a blurring of the boundaries between finance and operations. Investment choices involve tax and financing considerations that depend on the firm's overall cash and profit position. Exchange rate impacts, typically the realm of the treasury function, are critical factors in the shifting competitiveness of the firm's operations. Operating profitability cannot be separated from financing considerations and must be judged relative to the macroeconomic environment.

Further, just as global competition blurs national product market boundaries, it also blurs national boundaries in finance. The use of finance to offset exchange exposures and to exploit distortions in financial markets requires a high degree of global coordination and centralization of decision-making. It may interfere with the management of operations sensitive to local conditions, especially in cases where global optimization reduces the profits of a local affiliate. Already bent, measuring sticks used in evaluating the performance of operations in a multi-domestic context will be further distorted.

A further consequence of global management of the finance function is that it may require affiliates to act in conflict with local national interests, especially given MNCs' ability to bypass financial controls by using their internal networks.[39] In recent years, governments of major industrialized countries appear to have conceded the battle over the control of international capital flows and, as a result, have found themselves severely constrained in terms of policies to stabilize currency values. The battle is still being fought on fiscal terrain, but the advent of global competition and the resultant aggressive tax shopping by firms and fiscal promotion by particular countries is transforming the conflict from one between firms and nation-states to one among states.

The Bottom Line. Many of the differences between the finance function under global and under multidomestic competition are differences of degree rather than kind. Because of the ability it provides to span national financial markets, multinationality confers financial benefits on firms whether they compete globally or multidomestically. However, the ability of the firm to pass on differential financing costs and taxes is reduced by global competition. Thus, to compete effectively, MNCs will have to match their competitors' "cost of capital." As a result, the value of an effective finance function to a global firm will be overwhelming.

Furthermore, the greater currency volatility of the current period and its greater proportionate effect on firms' cash flows and profits, given global competition, increase the importance of effective foreign exchange management, both in terms of limiting risks and providing management information for tactical and strategic choices. The biggest differences appear to lie in this latter area, the role of finance in evaluating business options. The boundaries between finance and competitive behavior are blurred, and appear to becoming even more so.

37. For an introduction to the impact of cross-border barriers on the valuation of securities see Stulz [1985].

38. See Blitzer et al [1984].

39. See Robbins and Stobaugh [1973] for an early discussion of this point.

The ability of the firm to pass on differential financing costs and taxes is reduced by global competition. But, to compete effectively, MNCs will have to match their competitors' "cost of capital."

Coping with Exchange Rate Volatility

Given the vital importance of exchange rate volatility in the new global environment, it is necessary to examine in greater depth how exchange rate volatility affects firms engaged in global competition and how these firms cope with this volatility. We focus on three specific issues arising from the coincidence of volatile currencies and global competition. These are (1) the impact of exchange rate fluctuations on competitive position, (2) corporate management of exchange risk, and (3) the effect of firms' currency perspectives on their strategic and tactical choices.

The Impact of Exchange Rate Shifts on Competitiveness

A major difference between multidomestic and global competition is the impact of exchange rates on the competitiveness and underlying profitability of an MNC. Under multidomestic competition, markets are national in scope and, typically, a substantial proportion of value added is local. In this case, exchange rate shifts do not significantly change the relative costs of operating in a particular market. As a result, revenues and costs move together in response to shifts in exchange rates and profits from foreign operations, when converted into dollars, move roughly proportionally with exchange rates.[40]

In contrast, under global competition prices in various national markets are more closely linked and larger proportions of firms' value added are likely to be concentrated in particular countries as they seek to exploit scale economies.[41] Therefore, unless all firms in a given industry have the same geographic patterns of value added, shifts in exchange rates will change their relative costs and profit margins. With the increased importance of Japanese and European firms in many industries, such exchange rate effects on operating profits are becoming the rule rather than the exception.[42]

The responsiveness of operating profits to shifts in exchange rates is comprised of two effects: a *conversion* effect and a *competitive* effect. The conversion effect is the proportional adjustment of foreign currency operating profits into dollars. By definition, it applies only to foreign operations. The competitive effect, in contrast, is the response of local currency operating profits to exchange rate shifts resulting from the interaction of the various competitors' supply and price responses. It applies to domestic as well as overseas activities.

Whereas financial exposure is caused by the sensitivity of the parent currency value of its money-fixed assets and liabilities to exchange rate movements, competitive or operating exposure is measured by the sensitivity of a firm's operating profits (margins) measured in the parent currency. Unlike financial exposures, which are sensitive to changes in nominal exchange rates, operating profit margins are exposed only to changes in *real* exchange rates (that is, exchange rate changes adjusted for offsetting inflation differentials). In further contrast to financial exposure, the extent of operating exposure depends on the structure of the markets in which the firm operates and not necessarily on the country or currency in which the firm purchases or sells its product.

Consider the case of Economy Motors, a hypothetical U.S. manufacturer of small cars.[43] Economy produces components and assembles its products in the Midwest and sells them throughout the U.S. Its products sell in direct competition with Japanese imports, which dominate the market and are the price leaders. The shifting competitive position of Economy under different real exchange rate scenarios is illustrated in Exhibit 3.

In the base year, when the yen and dollar are "at parity," the Japanese set U.S. prices so that they (and Economy) earn normal margins. In some later year, if the yen strengthens in line with the difference in inflation between the two countries, Economy remains on par with the Japanese. But, if the yen weakens while Japan's inflation remains below that of the U.S. (that is, the yen depreciates in real terms),

---

40. In more technical terms, given a change in the real exchange rate, the demand and supply curves facing the firm will remain unchanged in the local currency (adjusted for inflation). Hence the optimal output and local currency price will remain unchanged, as will local currency profit. From a dollar perspective, of course, both curves will shift by the same amount, and the dollar profit will change in proportion to the change in the exchange rate.

41. An exception may be IBM, which, because of its very large scale and its responsiveness to national goals, is able to balance global scale production of specific products with a matching of value added and sales in most major markets.

42. Under these circumstances, a change in the real exchange rate will result in a *relative* shift of demand and supply curves, regardless of the reference currency of the firm. This implies that the optimal price and volume will change as well.

43. This example is drawn from Lessard and Lightstone [1986].

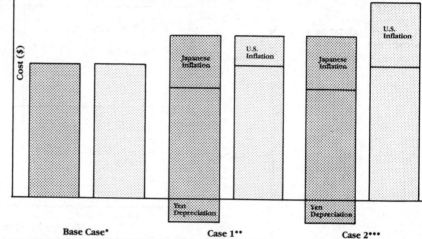

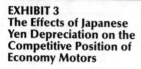

EXHIBIT 3
The Effects of Japanese Yen Depreciation on the Competitive Position of Economy Motors

Cost ($)

Japanese Inflation

U.S. Inflation

Japanese Inflation

U.S. Inflation

Japanese Inflation

Yen Depreciation

Yen Depreciation

Dollar Equivalent Cost of Japanese Manufacturers

Dollar Cost of Economy Motors

Base Case*   Case 1**   Case 2***

* Dollar equivalent costs of Economy Motors and its Japanese competitors are equal with exchange rates at parity
** A change in the nominal exchange rate with no change in the real exchange rate does not change competitive position
*** A change in the real exchange rate changes competitive position

the Japanese firms will have lower dollar costs, they will cut prices to gain share, and Economy will face lower profit margins.

The reason Economy faces an operating exposure, even though it operates entirely in its domestic market, is that the market in which it sells its output is much more integrated globally than the markets in which it purchases its inputs.

The sensitivity of a firm's profits to shifts in exchange rates under global competition may be greater than one for one. Extending the Economy Motors example, assume that the operating margin under normal (parity) conditions is 15 percent, that all costs are in U.S. dollars, but that a one percent change in the *real* yen/dollar rate results in a .5 percent change in dollar prices of small cars in the U.S. In this case, assuming that the optimal response to exchange rate changes involves matching price and holding volume constant, the sensitivity of profits would be 3.33 to 1.[44] In other words, a 10 percent

change in the real exchange rate would result in a 33 percent change in operating profits!

A useful way to think of the price effects of exchange rate changes is to determine the currency habitat of each product or input. This currency habitat is defined as the currency in which the price of the good tends to be most stable.[45] The determinants of the currency habitat can be summarized along the two dimensions illustrated in Exhibit 4: (1) the geographical scope of the product market (that is, whether national or global) and (2) the relative influence on price of both producer costs and consumer demand in a given market (that is, are prices determined largely by costs or demand?).

The geographic scope of the market will depend on the ability of the firm—or, in the case of inputs, its suppliers—to segment national markets, either by limiting transshipment or by differentiating the products it sells in various markets. As product markets become more globally integrated,

44. If volume does not change, the sensitivity of operating profits can be defined as:
sensitivity (profits) =
$$\text{sensitivity (revenues)} \cdot \frac{\text{revenues}}{\text{profits}} - \text{sensitivity (costs)} \cdot \frac{\text{costs}}{\text{profits}}$$
See Levi [1982] and Flood and Lessard [1986] for a fuller explanation.
45. The term currency habitat is introduced by Flood and Lessard [1986]. It

also has been defined as the "currency of price (cost) determination." It may differ from the currency in which prices are quoted, invoices issued, or transactions settled. For example, the prices of various products are quoted in particular currencies, e.g. crude oil in dollars, certain chemicals in DM, etc. and as shown by Grassman [1973], and Magee [1974], certain currencies are favored in invoicing, but the prices of the products in these currencies are not necessarily independent of the exchange rate.

In those cases where transshipment cannot be barred—whether because of the portability of the product, the inability of manufacturers to control distribution channels, or the power of key customers—prices will tend to a single world level.

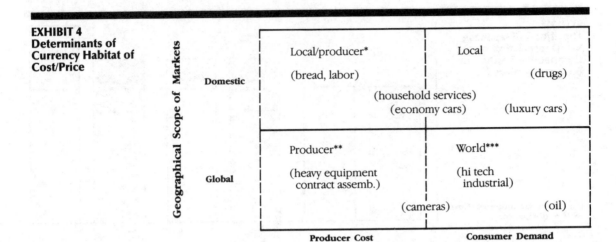

EXHIBIT 4
Determinants of Currency Habitat of Cost/Price

Geographical Scope of Markets (vertical axis): Domestic, Global
Marginal Pricing Factor (horizontal axis): Producer Cost, Consumer Demand

Domestic / Producer Cost:
Local/producer*
(bread, labor)

Domestic / Consumer Demand:
Local
(drugs)
(household services)
(economy cars)   (luxury cars)

Global / Producer Cost:
Producer**
(heavy equipment contract assemb.)

Global / Consumer Demand:
World***
(hi tech industrial)
(cameras)   (oil)

* Local if recurring costs of production are local.
** Currency of marginal firm/price leader depending on industrial structure.
*** Basket weighted by relative importance (income and elasticity) of consumers. As a first approximation, this is the basket comprising special rights (SDRs).

prices in various national markets tend toward a world price.

The second dimension, the marginal pricing factor, captures the relative importance of supply and demand considerations which reflect, among other things, the competitive structure of the industry, the price elasticity of demand, the existence of complements and substitutes, and the structure of costs—in particular the level of nonrecurring costs.[46]

The two dimensions are not entirely independent because firms with significant market power will be able to discriminate among national market segments by "bundling" local services (e.g., warranties) with products or otherwise precluding transshipment by distributors or customers. For example, the recent collaboration of Mercedes Benz and other luxury auto manufacturers with the U.S. government in requiring the stamping of various component parts, although ostensibly intended to reduce theft, was squarely aimed at stamping out the gray market. The same effect was also intended by MBZ's ads stressing that, while they stood behind all their cars, they could only promise exceptional service to owners who had purchased their cars from authorized U.S. dealers. Quotas have performed the same role for Japanese manufacturers, preventing American importers from arbitraging the difference in the price of Toyotas in Japan and in the U.S.

In the case of local markets (as shown in the upper half of Exhibit 4), the currency habitat will clearly be the local currency if costs are locally determined as well; in such cases international supply and demand will play little or no role. The more interesting cases, however, are those in which a significant proportion of value added is global in nature—that is, cases where the degree of global configuration and coordination is high, but producers have sufficient market power to engage in some price discrimination across borders. Because such firms can effectively segment national markets through their own market power and with the collaboration of regulatory authorities, they face local currency-denominated marginal revenue curves. If recurring costs are low, therefore, they will tend to maintain constant local prices in the face of exchange adjustments. If these costs are high, in contrast, they will adjust both local price and volume.

---

46. If nonrecurring costs, e.g., "up front" capital investment including R & D and capital equipment, are a large proportion of total costs, then the marginal unit costs of production will be small and pricing will be dictated primarily by demand considerations.

As currently practiced, corporate exchange risk management differs little from staking the assistant treasurer with a sum of money to be used to speculate on stock options, pork bellies, or gold.

Manufacturers of patented drugs with local currency habitats, for example, represent one extreme in this regard; they are able to segment national markets, and thus maintain market power and high margins, with the help of national regulations of the drug industry. In contrast, the price habitat of mid-range autos such as Toyota and Nissan, in the absence of quotas, would involve a combination of local and producer currencies. The currency habitat for luxury cars, which face less elastic demand because of greater product differentiation, and with higher margins of sales price over recurring costs, will also involve a mix of local and producer currencies, but with a much greater weight on the local currency.

In those cases where transshipment cannot be barred—whether because of the portability of the product, the inability of manufacturers to control distribution channels, or the power of key customers—prices will tend to a single world level (lower half of Exhibit 4). The camera industry is a case in point, with gray marketeers denying manufacturers the ability to fully segment national markets. The same is true of industrial equipment and components that are sold to sophisticated buyers which themselves are multinational. The currency habitat of these world prices will depend on the weighted importance of demand from various countries and the currency habitat of the costs incurred.

Foreign Exchange Risk Management Under Global Competition[47]

Exposure to exchange rate movements is a serious problem for firms in the current environment, especially those that are global competitors.[48] Unfortunately, current corporate methods of managing exchange risk are unlikely to help firms compete effectively and, indeed, are likely to provide misleading signals. In fact, as currently practiced, corporate exchange risk management differs little from staking the assistant treasurer with a sum of money to be used to speculate on stock options, pork bellies, or gold.

There are two reasons for this. First, foreign exchange risk management is concerned primarily with deciding whether to hedge or retain particular exposures arising from operations. Instead of this residual or reactive approach, management should take a more anticipatory or "proactive" stance, seeing to it that operating exposures and their expected effect on profits are factored into operating decisions. The second shortcoming of conventional corporate practice is that it tends to focus on exposures that lead to identifiable foreign exchange gains or losses—that is, on effects on contractual items instead of operating profits.

Foreign exchange exposure can be defined as the sensitivity to shifts in exchange rates of a number of variables but, for hedging purposes, the choice comes down to two alternatives: reported profits or operating cash flows. While the cash flow perspective makes more economic sense, the reporting perspective also matters to the extent that it affects managerial decisions or financial market reactions.[49]

Exhibit 5 shows the major categories of foreign exchange exposures on these two dimensions: earnings and cash flow. Accounting impacts are classified in terms of their recognition in accounting reports. Under FAS 52, transaction gains or losses are separately identified in earnings, translation adjustments bypass earnings and go directly to net worth, while operating impacts are mixed in with all other sources of variation in profits. Cash flow effects are classified in terms of the nature of the cash flows in question, whether they are contractually fixed in some currency or depend on competitive interactions. The fictitious category refers to those accounting adjustments that have no cash flow counterpart.

The category that differs most under global, as opposed to multidomestic, competition is the operating/noncontractual cell; it reflects the effect of exchange rate fluctuations on operating profits via adjustments in revenues and costs that have not been contracted for. This is what we refer to as operating exposure; and it consists of both a conversion effect and a competitive effect. The conversion component is readily identifiable. The competitive component, however, is much more difficult to isolate because it is mixed in with a host of other variables, both macroeconomic and microeconomic, that affect local operating profits. As a result, few firms have fully incorporated it into their foreign exchange management function. Furthermore, they often do not take

---

47. This section draws substantially on Lessard and Lightstone [1986].

48. For a discussion of why a firm should concern itself with managing foreign exchange risk see Logue and Oldfield (1977), Wihlborg [1980], Dufey and Srinivasulu [1984], Lessard and Shapiro [1984], and the references cited in note 36 above.

49. There is no clearcut evidence on the financial market reactions to alternative approaches for reporting exchange rate impacts. For one attempt, and reasons why one should not expect definitive findings, see Dukes [1980] and the accompanying discussion by Lessard.

EXHIBIT 5
Types of Foreign
Exchange Exposures

Accounting Exposures		Contractual	Noncontractual	Fictitious
	Transaction	Contracts including accts payable, receivable, and debt "closed out" during period	not applicable	not applicable
	Translation	Contracts on books at end of period	not applicable	fixed assets
	Operating	Gains/losses on "unbooked" contractual items incl. backlogs, purchase contracts	gains/losses on items not contracted for (e.g. future revenues, expenses)	not applicable

Cash Flow Exposures

into account the effects of these exposures on current and projected operating profits in making strategic and tactical choices. I review each of these points in turn below.

Measuring Operating Exposures. While most firms are aware of their operating exposures, it appears that few have defined or estimated them very carefully or developed explicit procedures for dealing with them. In reviewing the 1982 and 1983 annual reports of 30 firms, Mark Trusheim found that while 22 mentioned the impact of the strong dollar, 16 of them focused on the reduced dollar value of foreign revenues and only six discussed the impacts of the strong dollar on their margins or overall competitive position.[50]

While these external reports do not provide a full picture of internal procedures, they do show that the treatment of operating exposure by U.S. firms is less than complete. This is corroborated by more detailed reviews of the practices of a few firms. In in-depth interviews with three firms, Alberto Boiardi found that all three had a rough notion of their operating exposures, but none had acted on this estimate.[51] In discussions with six firms, we have found the same thing—a growing awareness of the general concept, but little or no progress in addressing it.[52] One reason for this is the relative difficulty of assessing operating exposures. The second is the difficulty of managing them appropriately in the typical firm.

Managing Operating Exposures. Firms have both business and financial options for reducing exchange rate exposures. Three kinds of business options are available for managing operating exposure: (1) configure individual businesses to have the flexibility to increase production and sourcing in countries that become low-cost producers due to swings in exchange rates; (2) configure individual businesses to reduce operating exposure by matching costs and revenues; and (3) select a portfolio of businesses with offsetting exposures.

The first option, configuring operations to increase flexibility, can actually increase a firm's expected operating profits while reducing their variability. The other two can at best reduce variability with no reduction in expected operating profits, but they are more likely to result in some reduction in expected operating profits. In the case of configuring individual businesses to match revenues and costs (or the currency habitats), such matching typically will require some departure from the optimal configuration in terms of scale and locational advantages. In the case of selecting a portfolio of businesses with offsetting exposures, reduced profits are likely to result from the increased administrative costs and reduced efficiency associated with managing diverse businesses without other synergistic linkages.

50. See Trusheim [1984].
51. See Boiardi [1984].

52. The same point is made by Waters [1979] and several corporate finance officers interviewed in "Coping with Volative Currencies: Multinationals Go For Safety First," *Business Week*, January 30, 1984.

*After having considered and exhausted its business options, the firm can
then hedge its remaining exposure using the available financial options.*

After having considered and exhausted its business options, the firm can then hedge its remaining exposure using the available financial options. These include long-dated forwards, swaps, or borrowing in foreign currencies as well as long-dated currency options. None of these provides an exact hedge because they are keyed to nominal rather than real exchange rates. But they do have the advantage that, when competitively priced, they reduce the variability of operating profits with little or no reduction in the anticipated level of such profits.[53]

Given the magnitude of operating exposures and the fact that they do not necessarily have even the same sign as contractual exposures, firms that hedge only their contractual exposures may actually increase their total exposures.[54] If a firm doesn't understand its operating exposure, its best policy is not to hedge at all.

Strategic and Tactical Responses to Exchange Rate Volatility

Volatile exchange rates create havoc for operations in a globally competitive industry. Shifts in rates require decisions regarding pricing, output, and sourcing. Such decisions will typically involve a balancing act between vaguely understood limits to sustainable price differentials across countries and the impact of local currency price shifts on demand and hence profits. Further, given the emergence of global oligopolies in many industries, pricing decisions must reflect anticipations of competitor actions or reactions. Estimating these reactions is likely to be complicated by the fact that competitors differ significantly in the currency composition of their costs and, perhaps more importantly, in the currency "eyeglasses" they wear.

Currency fluctuations also introduce noise into measures of current performance, reducing the firm's ability to monitor its evolving competitive position and distorting its results-based managerial incentives. If these distortions are significant, and if many key decisions are made on a decentralized ba-

sis, the firm's choices are likely to be distorted as well. Finally, the impact of currency fluctuations on the accounting-based performance of current operations is likely to distort management's perception of the long-term profitability of strategic choices.

The finance function plays a key role in terms of the perspective it can provide on these choices (though, again, this does not involve finance in the classic sense of raising funds). This financial perspective on operating choices, and the rules of thumb that follow from it, are part of a firm's culture. The perspective is the result of corporate experience and is unlikely to change rapidly. Thus, given the drastic change in the competitive and financial environment over the last ten years, we expect that this perspective is only now catching up with the new reality. This is clearly borne out in the relatively slow evolution of corporate management of exchange risk; and we expect it to have major operational implications as well.

Currency Illusions and Pricing/Output Choices. A perennial pricing error that results from a currency illusion is the practice of setting foreign currency prices by multiplying the domestic price by the spot rate and, perhaps, adding an "uplift" for the extra costs of doing business overseas. The illusion is that the foreign currency proceeds can be converted into dollars at the spot rate. In fact, the prices quoted are for future payment and, hence, can be converted only at the forward rate (or expected future spot rate) corresponding to the time of cash payment.[55] Foreign currency receivables are often "booked" at spot rather than forward rates with the result that operating profits are initially over(under)stated in the case of depreciating (appreciating) currencies, and subsequently exposed to potentially large transaction gains or losses that on average will offset the initial error. Depending on when and at what rate these receivables are "handed off" to treasury, the true profitability of one or both functions will be misstated and, as a result, management decisions based on such measures are likely to be misguided.[56] If operating managers are held responsible for the ultimate exchange gains or losses, their contribution

---

53. Lessard and Lightstone [1986] describe an alternative hedge that is keyed to real exchange rates and, hence, is more appropriate for operating exposures.

54. This is especially likely for firms facing global competition that hedge their transactions as well as transaction exposures because under FASB 52 foreign plant often is classified as a foreign asset, without regard to whether the prices of its inputs and outputs are determined locally, the prices of its inputs are determined locally but its outputs are priced internationally, or vice versa. While this contradiction can be resolved to some extent by clever choices of functional

currencies, it is unlikely that any translation scheme will capture the exposure of a firm's future operating profits that is so important in the context of global competition.

55. For a recent example, See Hintz-Kessel-Kohl, a Harvard Business School case prepared by Professor Thomas Piper.

56. See Lessard and Lorange [1977] and Lessard and Sharp [1984] for further discussion of this point.

Shifts in rates require decisions regarding pricing, output, and sourcing. Such decisions will typically involve a balancing act between vaguely understood limits to sustainable price differentials across countries and the impact of local currency price shifts on demand and hence profits.

is likely to be buried in the noise created by exchange rate movements; if they are not, their contribution will be systematically misstated.

This illusion can be readily overcome by valuing all contracts at forward rates, but this requires an explicit recognition that generally accepted accounting rules are misleading and requires a shift in procedures.[57] While many firms have changed procedures to do this, it is surprising how many have not. A survey of corporate practices found, for example, that 55 percent of all firms included transaction gains and losses in measures of managers' performance.[58] This illusion affects all international transactions and is not unique to global competition. It does illustrate, however, how traditional perspectives can interfere with appropriate choices in a changing environment.

With global competition, the problem is compounded by the fact that pricing not only must take into account the relative value of future claims in various currencies, but also the possibly asymmetric impact of exchange rate shifts on the firm's costs and prices relative to competitors'. If prices in local currencies are left unchanged subsequent to an exchange rate shift, prices will differ across countries inviting transshipment and entry by competitors in "high-priced" markets. On the other hand, if prices in the parent currency are maintained by "passing through" the exchange rate variations to local customers, sales volumes may react abruptly (as Volkswagen discovered when the DM strengthened in the early 1970s, and as Caterpillar later discovered in 1980).

Therefore, even with full information and a "rational" economic perspective, pricing adjustments to exchange rates will be extremely complex. In practice, though, we expect that choices will be strongly influenced by the firm's view of the world. The easiest response to a change with complex implications is to do nothing. Doing nothing, however, can be defined in many different ways. In the case of pricing responses to exchange rate changes, it could mean either maintaining parent currency (dollar) prices or maintaining local prices. Active responses, in turn,

could involve either maintaining market share or adjusting both price and volume to maximize long-term profit.

Under multidomestic competition, with its largely autonomous national operating units, the likely choice is for the firm to "do nothing" by maintaining local prices (although the parent currency, as I argue below in discussing control systems, may play a role as well). But with global competition, firms' activities are more integrated or coordinated across national boundaries; and, therefore, such companies are more likely to "do nothing" in terms of maintaining parent currency prices. This may be a reasonable approximation to the correct response for a firm that dominates world markets, but it will not be for a member of a global oligopoly with players based in several different countries and with different currency perspectives and exposures.

The heavy construction equipment industry, once dominated by a handful of U.S. firms but now including major Japanese and European players in global markets, is an excellent case in point. A study by David Sharp found that distributor prices of construction equipment sold in the U.K. by U.S. firms tended to remain stable in dollars through 1980, when they shifted abruptly in response to Japanese inroads and subsequently appeared to be sensitive to the dollar-yen relationship as well.[59] Sharp's finding of different pricing responses to exchange rate changes for virtually identical products produced and sold in the U.K. by a U.S.- and a U.K.-based firm supports the view that at least some of this effect can be traced to organizational factors rather than to technical demand or cost considerations.

An ironic example of this type of pricing is the reported satisfaction of many U.S. firms with their ability to hold their own and maintain dollar prices during the 1978-1979 period. In fact, given the general weakness of the dollar in that period, they should have been able to raise dollar prices. And U.S. firms are not alone in their susceptibility to this kind of illusion. The Swedish auto firms, especially Volvo, nearly priced themselves out of U.S. markets in this same period. They apparently attempted to pass

57. Strictly speaking, valuing contracts at forward rates only makes them comparable to contracts for future payment in the home currency. Both should still be discounted to reflect the time value of money measured in that currency.

58. See Czechowitz, Choi, and Bavishi [1982]. The question asked does not quite address the issue we raised, since transaction gains/losses include anticipated gains/losses and surprises. We would contend, however, that neither component should be included in a manager's evaluation. See Lessard and Sharp [1984] for further discussion.

59. See Sharp [1984]

If operating managers are held responsible for the ultimate exchange gains or losses, their contribution is likely to be buried in the noise created by exchange rate movements; if they are not, their contribution will be systematically misstated.

through to U.S. customers most of the appreciation of the kroner, while they should have maintained relatively stable dollar prices.[60]

The picture is not all bleak, of course. Sharp's findings do suggest an awakening of U.S. firms to the realities of global pricing; and Boiardi found that pricing decisions were consistent with market structures, although two of the three firms he studied faced multidomestic product market competition.

Interaffiliate Pricing. A large proportion of the production of firms engaged in global competition moves through interaffiliate sales on its way to the final customer. Apart from their effect on taxes and tariffs, the transfer prices on these sales have no economic impact except through their effect on the behavior of managers. These behavioral impacts, though, are often substantial and represent a key determinant of the firm's pricing of final sales. Firms with strong, centralized (or coordinated) production units often apply transfer pricing rules based on standard costs measured in the parent currency, imposing the full impact of currency swings on the downstream stages of the value-added chain. The shift to global competition strengthens this effect because the pursuit of global scale and scope economies requires greater integration and coordination of production.

There are several different ways to address this problem. The first is to create a mechanism whereby transfer prices are negotiated to approximate arms-length prices, in essence forcing production and marketing to share the exchange rate impact. This clearly is most feasible where there are alternative sources of supply. The second is to leave the transfer prices as they are, but adjust the performance standards (margin or ROI) of the marketing units to reflect the baseline effect of the exchange rate shifts. This requires substantial prior analysis of exchange rate impacts and appropriate operating responses at the corporate and business unit levels. A third is to substitute narrower performance standards (e.g. market share or some measure of production efficiency) for profits at one or more stages in the value-added chain. This approach, however, presupposes that the firm can specify such standards appropriately, which may be as complex as solving the cross-unit

profit conflicts. This clearly is one the most challenging issues arising in global competition and is likely to push key operating responsibilities up to higher levels within the firm.

Measurement of Current Performance. Currency fluctuations clearly have an impact on measured performance, and these measures presumably feed back to a host of operating choices. While there are many technical issues in measuring performance in the face of fluctuating exchange rates, the debate among practitioners appears to be centered on whether performance should be measured in local currency or parent currency terms. Under conditions of global competition, neither is appropriate.

An ideal performance measurement system should hold managers responsible for those aspects of performance over which they have substantial control, but should limit responsibility for performance shifts due to factors largely beyond their control. Of course, this ideal is seldom met because, for example, fluctuations in aggregate demand are inextricably linked with managerial success in producing and selling a product. The emphasis of many firms on market share, however, is an attempt to separate these two effects. In the case of currency fluctuations, some aspects of the problem are easily separable while others are not. Gains or losses on accounts receivable due to currency surprises, for example, are outside the control of operating managers and can be split out by transferring these claims to treasury at forward rates. If this is done, treasury's contribution through "selective hedging" (that is, speculation in the form of market timing) is measured fairly as well.

In contrast, with the competitive component of operating exposures, such a clear separation is not possible because managers can and should react to exchange rate shifts by altering prices, output, and sourcing. However, so long as there is some degree of global competition it should be recognized that profits in either local or parent currency should fluctuate in line with real exchange rates. A failure to incorporate this in the control system is likely to lead managers to "leave money on the table" when they are favored by exchange rates, and to sacrifice too much market share by attempting to hold constant

---

60. The reason why the dollar/kroner relationship should have had little or no impact on dollar prices of Saabs and Volvos was that transshipment was limited and demand, presumably, relatively price elastic. Further, the effect of the ex-change rate on short-run variable costs measured in dollars was quite small given that under Sweden's labor policies, wages are a fixed cost in the short run, and most inputs are internationally sourced.

An ideal performance measurement system should hold managers responsible for those aspects of performance over which they have substantial control, but should limit responsibility for performance shifts due to factors largely beyond their control.

dollar margins when exchange rates work against them. What is required is a budgetary standard that adjusts for exchange rate impacts. The process of developing such a budget should involve a joint exploration by corporate and business unit managers of the impacts of and appropriate responses to exchange rate movements, thus providing a dress rehearsal of future tactics as well as a standard against which future performance can be judged.[61]

The controller of a U.S firm's U.K. plant, in an interview with Sharp, stated that he would have no trouble in meeting his firm's goal of "cutting real dollar costs by x percent" because in the period since the program was announced the pound had already fallen by a large fraction of that amount relative to the dollar. His response would have been quite different if the corporation had demanded an x percent cut relative to costs normalized for exchange rate circumstances.

Assessment of Strategic Options. Just as currency fluctuations affect current performance, they alter the attractiveness of the firm's strategic options. The long-run profitability of a given business unit will depend on its evolving competitive advantage, but in the short-run this advantage can be swamped by exchange rate impacts. In some cases, the firm will be able to enhance its average profitability over time by building a degree of flexibility that allows it to shift sourcing and value-added activities as exchange rates move.[62] In general, though, it will have to look past the current circumstances to assess its long run competitiveness. This requires a multi-stage procedure:
(1) assess future expected cash flows conditional on purchasing power parity, concentrating on micro-competitive factors such as the firm's likely experience gains relative to anticipated wage increases;[63]
(2) assess how these (conditional expected) cash flows would differ under alternative exchange rate scenarios; and
(3) estimate expected cash flows across scenarios given their relative probability.
In general, management should choose the alternative with the highest (net present value of) expected cash flows, without regard for exposure to exchange

rate movements, because as noted above these exposures can be offset by financial hedges that have little or no cost in present value terms.

While there have been several recent surveys of capital budgeting practice,[64] none have focused on this issue; so I do not know whether academic observers are lagging behind practice or whether practice is lagging behind changes in the competitive environment. I suspect some of both.

Summary and Conclusions

The emergence of global competition, coupled with both an increased integration of financial markets and continued exchange rate volatility, represents a major threat and challenge to corporations that have been accustomed to world market leadership under conditions of multidomestic competition.

In this paper I have argued that the finance function plays a critical role in such firms' ability to respond to this challenge, both because of the demands it places on the finance function per se and its requirement for a much more sophisticated financial perspective on strategic and tactical choices. Because a company's financial eyeglasses are part of its culture, these changes in outlook inevitably lag changes in the competitive environment. Nonetheless, it does appear that many firms are rapidly moving down the "financial learning curve" and changing their standard operating procedures to accommodate the economic realities of global competition. Within the traditional realm of finance—which includes primarily the treasury functions of raising funds externally and maneuvering them efficiently within the corporation—companies will find that, in order to compete globally, they must fully exploit the benefits of multinational financial scope to match their competitors' costs of capital and effective rates of taxation. The structure of external financing will have to become more global; the corporate convention of home currency borrowing at the parent level and local currency borrowing on the part of foreign subsidiaries must give way to a more

---

61. Lessard and Sharp [1984] discuss alternative ways that this recognition of exchange rate effects can be incorporated in the control system.

62. This point is discussed by Kogut [1983, 1984] and Baldwin [1986].

63. As might be expected, there is no unambiguous measure of purchasing power parity. An instructive attempt to estimate parity rates, though, is provided by Williamson [1983]. A further issue that has not been resolved in the literature is whether real exchange rates tend to return to parity or to move randomly. The results of Adler and Lehman [1983] and Roll [1979] support the latter view, but the macroeconomic models of Dornbusch [1983] and others suggest that there must be some type of adjustment over time.

64. See note 23.

complex pattern which recognizes the interaction between three distinct objectives: minimizing taxes, exploiting financial incentives and distortions in financial markets, and offsetting exchange rate exposures.

Even greater changes will be required in areas where finance interacts more closely with operations, most notably in the area of the management of foreign exchange exposures. Financial managers, with their knowledge of the dynamics of foreign exchange, must assist operating managers in configuring operations to cope with exchange rate volatility and in responding to shifts as they occur. The corporate treasury should also provide internal hedging facilities (or contingent performance standards) to insulate operating managers from the inevitable exposures resulting from strategic bets to the fullest extent consistent with maintaining incentives for proper operating responses. At the same time, they must expand the scope of exchange risk management to deal with operating exposures—a task which multinationals are only beginning to address.

Another important area where there is great room for improvement is performance measurement for overseas operating units. Each unit's performance should be measured relative to a standard that takes into account key changes in the macroeconomic environment, especially the exchange rate. Further, the measures employed must capture trade-offs that improve corporate profits at the expense of the one unit in question. To do this, firms will have to redefine business units along the dimensions where greatest coordination is required. But because no structure can simultaneously capture geographic, product, and stage of value-added leverage points, they will also have to create more effective processes for mediating conflicts among units. This will involve, among other things, the substitution of relatively narrow measures of business performance such as market shares and unit costs for the "bottom line" measures of financial profitability now favored by most U.S. firms.

References

Adler, Michael (1974). "The Cost of Capital and Valuation of a Two-Country Firm." *Journal of Finance* 29, 119-37.

Adler, Michael (1979). "U.S. Taxation of U.S. Multinational Corporations." In M. Sarnat and G. Szego (eds.), *International Trade and Finance*, Vol. 2., Cambridge, MA., Ballinger.

Adler, Michael and Bernard Dumas (1983). "International Portfolio Choice and Corporate Finance: A Survey." *Journal of Finance* 38, 1471-87.

Adler, Michael and Bruce Lehman (1983). "Deviations from Purchasing Power Parity in the Long Run." *Journal of Finance* 38, 1471-87.

Agmon, Tamir and Donald Lessard (1977). "Financial Factors and the International Expansion of Small Country Firms," in Agmon and Kindleberger (eds.), *Multinationals from Small Countries*, Cambridge, MA.: MIT Press.

Antl, Boris (1984). *Swap Financing Techniques*. London: Euromoney Publications.

Baldwin, Carliss (1986). "The Capital Factor: The Impact of Home and Host Countries on the Global Corporation's Cost of Capital," in Michael Porter, ed., *Competition in Global Industries*. Cambridge, Mass.: Harvard Business School Press.

Barnea, Amir, Robert A. Haugen and Lemma W. Senbet (1981). "Market Imperfections, Agency Problems, and Capital Structure: A Review," *Financial Management* 10 No. 2 (Summer), 7-22.

Barnea, Amir, Robert A. Haugen and Lemma W. Senbet (1985). "Management of Corporate Risk," *Advances in Financial Planning and Forecasting* JAI Press, Vol. 1, 1 -2345.

Blitzer, Charles, Donald Lessard and James Paddock (1984). "Risk-Bearing and the Choice of Contract Forms for Oil Exploration and Development." *The Energy Journal 5*, 1-28.

Boiardi, Alberto (1984). "Managing Foreign Subsidiaries in the Face of Fluctuating Exchange Rates." Unpublished master's thesis, MIT Sloane School of Management.

Booth, Lawrence D. (1982). "Capital Budgeting Frameworks for the Multinational Corporations." *Journal of International Business Studies 8*, No. 2, 113-23.

Brean, Donald J.S. (1985). "Financial Dimensions of Transfer Pricing," in Rugman and Eden, eds., *Multinationals and Transfer Pricing*. London and Sydney: Croom Helm.

Brennan, Michael J. and Eduardo S. Schwartz (1985). "Evaluating Natural Resource Investments." *Journal of Business 58*, No. 2, 135-158.

Buckley, Peter and Mark Casson (1976). *The Future of Multinational Enterprise*. London: Macmillan.

Carsberg, Bryan (1983). "FAS # 52—Measuring the Performance of Foreign Operations." *Midland Corporate Finance Journal 1, No. 2, 47-55.*

Cassell, Gustav (1923). *Money and Foreign Exchange after 1914*. London: Macmillan.

Caves, Richard (1986). "Entry of Foreign Multinationals into U.S. Manufacturing Industries," in Michael Porter, ed., *Competition in Global Industries*. Cambridge, Mass.: Harvard Business School Press.

Chesowitz, James, Frederick Choi, and Vinod Bavishi (1982). *Assessing Foreign Subsidiary Performance: Systems and Practices of Leading Multinational Companies*. New York: Business International.

Cornell, Bradford and Alan C. Shapiro (1983). "Managing Foreign Exchange Risk." *Midland Corporate Finance Journal 1*, No. 3 (Fall).

Donaldson, Gordon (1972). "Strategic Hurdle Rates for Capital Investment." *Harvard Business Review 50*, (March-April, 50-55).

Dooley, Michael and Peter Isard (1980). "Capital Controls, Political Risks and Deviations from Interest Rate Parity." *Journal of Political Economy 88*, 370-84.

Dornbusch, Rudiger (1980). "Exchange Rate Economics: Where Do We Stand? *Brookings Papers on Economic Activity 1*, 143-85.

Dornbusch, Rudiger (1983). "Equilibrium and Disequilibrium Exchange Rates." *Zeitschrift fur Wirtschafts—und Sozial Wissenschaften 102*, 573-99.

Dufey, Gunter and Ian Giddy (1978). *The International Money Market*. New York: Prentice-Hall.

Dufey, Gunter and Ian Giddy (1981). "Innovation in the International Financial Markets." *Journal of International Business Studies 7*, No. 2, 33-52.

Dufey, Gunter and Ian Giddy and S. L. Srinivasulu (1984). "The Case for Corporate Management of Foreign Exchange Risk." *Financial Management 12*, No. 4.

Dukes, Roland (1980). "Forecasting Exchange Gains (Losses) and Security Market Response to FASB 8," in Levich and Wihlborg (eds.) *Exchange Risk and Exposure*. Lexington, MA.: Heath Lexington.

Encarnation, Dennis and Louis T. Wells (1986). "Negotiating Global Investments: A View From the Host Country," in Michael Porter, ed., Competition in Global Industries. Cambridge, Mass.: Harvard Business School Press.

Finnerty, John (1985). "Zero Coupon Bond Arbitrage: An Illustration of the Regulatory Dialectic at Work," *Financial Management* (Winter 1985).

Flood, Eugene (1985). "Global Competition and Exchange Rate Exposure," Research Paper # 837, Graduate School of Business, Stanford University (September).

Flood, Eugene and Donald Lessard (1986). "On the Measurement of Operating Exposure to Exchange Rates: A Conceptual Approach. " *Financial Management*, Vol. 16, No. 1 (Spring).

Frenkel, Jacob A. (1981). "The Collapse of Purchasing Power Parities During the 1970's." *European Economic Review 16*, 145-65.

Frenkel, Jacob A. (1983). "Flexible Exchange Rates, Prices and the Role of "News": Lessons from the 1970's." *Journal of Political Economy*.

Frenkel, Jacob A. and Michael Mussa (1980). "The Efficiency of Foreign Exchange Markets and Measures of Turbulence." *American Economic Review 70*, 374-381.

Grassman, Sven (1973). "A Fundamental Symmetry in International Payment Patterns." *Journal of International Economics* (May).

Grubel, Herbert (1977). "A Theory of International Banking." Banca Nazionale del Lavoro Quarterly Review.

Guisinger, Steven E. and Associates (1985). *Investment Incentives and Performance Requirements: Patterns of International Trade, Production, and Investment*. New York: Praeger.

Hayes, Robert and William Abernathy (1980). "Managing Our Way to Economic Decline." *Harvard Business Review 58*, No. 4, 67-77.

Hennart, Jean-Francois (1982). *A Theory of Multinational Enterprise*. Ann Arbor: University of Michigan Press.

Hodder, James E. (1984). "Evaluation of Manufacturing Investments: A Comparison of U.S. and Japanese Practices," Technical Report 84-8, Department of Industrial Engineering and Engineering Management, Stanford University, November.

Hodder, James E. and Henry E. Riggs, Pitfalls in Evaluating Risky Projects." *Harvard Business Review 85*, No. 1 (January - February), 128-135.

Horst, Thomas (1977). "American Taxation of Multinational Firms." *American Economic Review 67*, 376-89.

Hout, Thomas, Michael Porter and Eileen Rudden (1982). "How Global Companies Win Out." *Harvard Business Review 60*, No. 5, 98-108.

Ijiri, Yuji (1983). "Foreign Exchange Accounting and Translation," in R. J. Herring (ed.) *Managing Foreign Exchange Risk*, New York: Cambridge University Press.

International Monetary Fund (1985). *Annual Report on Exchange Arrangements and Exchange Restrictions.*

Jun, Yong Wook (1985). "The Internationalization of the Firm: The Case of the Korean Consumer Electronics Industry." Unpublished Ph.D. Thesis.

Keichel, Walter, 3rd (1981). "Playing the Global Game." *Fortune 104*, (November 16), 111-126.

Kindleberger, Charles P. (1969). *American Business Abroad.* New York: Yale University Press.

Kindleberger, Charles P. (1974). *The Formation of Financial Centers: A Study in Comparative Economic History.* Princeton Studies in International Finance, No. 36.

Kindleberger, Charles P. (1985). "Plus Ca Change — A Look at the New Literature," in Kindleberger, ed., *Multinational Excursions.* Cambridge, MA.: M.I.T. Press.

Kogut, Bruce (1983). "Foreign Direct Investment as a Sequential Process." In Kindleberger and Audretsch (eds.), *The Multinational Corporation in the 1980's.* Cambridge, MA.: M.I.T. Press.

Kogut, Bruce (1985). "Designing Global Strategies: Profiting from Operating Flexibility." *Sloan Management Review.* Fall issue, 27-38.

Kohlhagen, Steven (1983). "Overlapping National Investment Portfolios: Evidence and Implications of International Integration of Secondary Markets for Financial Assets," in R. Hawkins, R. Levich, and C. Wihlborg (eds.), *Research in International Business and Finance*, Greenwich, CT: JAI Press.

Lessard, Donald (1979a). "Transfer Prices, Taxes and Financial Markets: Implications of Internal Financial Transfers within the Multinational Firms," in R. B. Hawkins (ed.), *Economic Issues of Multinational Firms. Greenwich, CT: JAI Press.*

Lessard, Donald (1979b). "Evaluating Foreign Projects: An Adjusted Present Value Approach," in D. R. Lessard (ed.), *International Financial Management.* New York: Warren, Gorham, and Lamont.

Lessard, Donald (1981). "Evaluating International Projects: An Adjusted Present Value Approach," in R. Krum and F. Derkindiren (eds.), *Capital Budgeting under Conditions of Uncertainty.* Hingham, MA: Martinus Nijhoff.

Lessard, Donald and John Lightstone (1986). "Coping with Exchange Rate Volatility: Operating Financial Responses." *Harvard Business Review*, July/August 1986.

Lessard, Donald and Peter Lorange (1977). "Currency Changes and Management Control: Resolving the Centralization/Decentralization Dilemma." *Accounting Review 52*, No. 3, 628-37.

Lessard, Donald and James Paddock (1980). "Evaluating International Projects: Weighted-Coverage Cost of Capital versus Valuation by Components." Unpublished manuscript.

Lessard, Donald and David Sharp (1984). "Measuring the Performance of Operations Subject to Fluctuating Exchange Rate." *Midland Corporate Finance Journal 2*, No. 3, 18-30.

Lessard, Donald and Alan Shapiro (1984). "Guidelines for Global Financing Choices." *Midland Corporate Finance Journal 1*, No. 4, 68-80.

Levi, Maurice (1982). *International Finance.* New York: McGraw-Hill.

Logue, Dennis and George Oldfield (1977). "Managing Foreign Assets when Foreign Exchange Markets are Efficient." *Financial Management 7*, No. 2, 16-22.

Magee, Stephen (1974). "U.S. Import Prices in the Currency Contract Period." *Brookings Papers on Economic Activity*, No. 1, 303-23.

Magee, Stephen and Ramesh Rao (1980). "Vehicle and Nonvehicle Currencies in Foreign Trade." *American Economic Review 70*, 368-73.

Mason, Scott and Robert C. Merton (1985). "The Role of Contingent Claims Analysis in Corporate Finance," in Altman and Subrahmanyan eds., *Advances in Corporate Finance*, New York: Dow Jones Irwin.

Myers, Stewart (1974). "Interactions of Corporate Finance and Investment Decisions." *Journal of Finance 29*, 1-25.

Myers, Stewart (1984). "The Capital Structure Puzzle." *Journal of Finance 39*, 575-92.

Myers, Stewart and Saman Majd (1983). "Calculating Abandonment Value Using Option Pricing Theory." M.I.T. Sloan School of Management, Working Paper # 1462-83, August.

Oblak, David J. and Roy J. Helm, Jr. (1980). "Survey and Analysis of Capital Budgeting Methods Used by Multinationals," *Financial Management 9*, No. 2, 37-40 (Winter).

Otani, Ichiro, and Siddarth Tiwari (1981). "Capital Controls and Interest Rate Parity: The Japanese Experience 1978-1980." *Staff Papers 28*, 798-815.

Porter, Michael (1986. "Competition in Global Industries: A Conceptual Framework," in Michael Porter, ed., *Competition in Global Industries.* Cambridge, MA.: Harvard Business School Press.

Robbins, Sidney and Robert Stobaugh (1973). *Money in the Multinational Enterprise.* New York: Basic Books.

Roll, Richard (1979). "Violations of Purchasing Power Parity and Their Implications for Efficient International Commodity Markets," in Sarnat and P. Szego (eds.) *International Finance and Trade.* Vol 2, Cambridge, MA: Ballinger.

Rosenberg, Michael (1983). "Foreign Exchange Controls: An International Comparison," in A. George and I.

Giddy (eds.), *International Finance Handbook*. Vol. 1. New York: John Wiley.

Rugman, Alan (1981). *Inside the Multinationals: The Economics of Internal Markets*. New York: Columbia University Press.

Rutenberg, David (1970). "Maneuvering Liquid Assets in a Multinational Company: Formulation and Deterministic Solution Procedures." *Management Science 16*, No. 10, B671-84.

Schall, Lawrence D., Gary L. Sundem, and W. R. Geijsbeek, Jr. (1978). "Survey and Analysis of Capital Budgeting Methods," *Journal of Finance 33*, No. 1, 281-287.

Schydlowsky, Daniel (1973). "Simulation Model of a Multinational Enterprise," in S. Robbins and R. Stobaugh, *Money in the Multinational Enterprise*.

Shapiro, Alan (1983). "What Does Purchasing Power Parity Mean?" *Journal of International Money & Finance 2*, 295-318.

Shapiro, Alan and Sheridan Titman (1985). "An Integrated Approach to Corporate Risk Management," *Midland Corporate Finance Journal 3*, No. 2, 41-56.

Sharp, David (1984). "Organization and Decision Making in the U.S. Multinational Firm: Price Management Under Floating Exchange Rates." Dissertation in progress, M.I.T. Sloan School of Management.

Smith, Clifford W. Jr., and Rene Stulz (1985). "The Determinants of Firms' Hedging Policies, *Journal of Financial and Quantitative Analyses 20*, No. 4 (December) (forthcoming).

Sophonpanich, Chartsiri (1984). "Exchange Rates and Corporate Performance." Unpublished master's thesis. M.I.T. Sloan School of Management.

Stockman, Alan (1980). "A Theory of Exchange Rate Determination." *Journal of Political Economy 88*, 673-98.

Stonehill, Arthur and Kare Dullum (1982). Internationalizing the Cost of Capital. New York: John Wiley.

Stulz, Rene (1985). "Pricing Capital Assets in an International Setting: An Introduction," Journal of International Business Studies, 15, No. 3, 55-73.

Tobin, James (1978). "A Proposal for International Monetary Reform." Cowles Foundation Discussion Paper 506, Yale University.

Trusheim, Mark (1984). "An Exploration of Foreign Exchange Operating Expense." Unpublished master's thesis. M.I.T. Sloan School of Management.

Tschoegl, Adrian (1981). *The Regulation of Foreign Banks: Policy Formation in Countries Outside the United States*. NYU Monograph series in Finance and Economics (1981-2).

Vernon, Raymond (1979). "The Product Cycle Hypothesis in a New International Environment." *Oxford Bulletin of Economics & Statistics 41*, 4.

Waters, Somerset (1979). "Exposure Management is a Job for all Departments." *Euromoney* (December 1979) 79-82.

Wicks, Marilyn E. (1980). *A Comparative Analysis of Foreign Investment Evaluations Practices of U.S.—based Multinational Companies*. New York: McKinsey and Co.

Wihlborg, Clas (1980). "Economics of Exposure Management of Foreign Subsidiaries of MNCs." *Journal of International Business Studies 6*, No. 3, 9-18.

Williamson, John (1983). *The Exchange Rate System*. Washington, D.C.: Institute for International Economics.

Part II Exchange Risk Management

The Nature and Management of Foreign Exchange Risk

Niso Abuaf,
*Chase Manhattan Bank**

Since the 1970s, exchange rate volatility has increased markedly and, with it, the levels of foreign exchange risk. In fact, fluctuations in financial variables such as exchange rates and interest rates have produced capital gains and losses so large as to swamp many companies' operating results. In response, many financial managers have turned to hedging as well as to more active risk management strategies in the foreign exchange markets. In this article, I review the theoretical and practical issues involved, while citing actual market experience since 1973. With this as background, I then go on to discuss current forecasting techniques and risk management strategies.

Before the main issues are addressed, however, let me offer a few definitions of key terms. First, care should be exercised when using the term "risk." In popular usage, risk is the possibility of an outcome that is less favorable than expected. This is not the definition used either in the finance literature or in this article. Here risk is defined as the dispersion of possible values, favorable or not, around those values that are expected. Foreign exchange risk is the chance that fluctuations in the exchange rate will change the profitability of a transaction from its expected value.

Second, *real* exchange rate risk should be considered apart from *nominal* exchange rate risk. Fluctuations in exchange rates that are not matched by offsetting changes in price levels at home and abroad are changes in the real exchange rate (or, alternatively, deviations from purchasing power parity (PPP)). It is only changes in real exchange rates that affect a country's international competitive position and the underlying profitability of its businesses. As such, they are crucial in both corporate and governmental decisions.

The Recent Foreign Exchange Experience

Many economists have been surprised by the recent volatility of foreign exchange rates and by the persistence of deviations from purchasing power parity (which they call "misalignment"). Milton Friedman, for example, has argued that exchange rates should be unstable only if fundamental economic variables—most notably, national monetary policies, economic growth rates, interest and inflation rate differentials, and current account imbalances—are also unstable. But such arguments have overlooked the extent to which exchange rates behave like asset prices. The prices of financial assets are extremely sensitive to news; they adjust very quickly to reflect new information about the intrinsic value of the underlying asset. The variability of this news by itself increases the volatility of financial asset prices. Moreover, because financial assets, unlike goods, can be almost costlessly stored or traded, their prices are more volatile than those of goods. Exchange rates, accordingly, have been more volatile than goods prices.

This section summarizes well-documented

*I would like to acknowledge the support of the Chase Manhattan Bank, where this research was carried out. I also wish to thank R.L. Slighton, C.W. Slighton, J.R. Zecher for helpful comments, criticisms, and suggestions; D. Chew and C.B. Pantuliano for editorial assistance, and K. Holmes for research support.

Past monthly changes [in exchange rates] are not useful in forecasting future monthly changes, and the expected change in the monthly exchange rate is thus zero.

observations of exchange rate movements, most of which are consistent with this "asset market" view of exchange rate determination.

Volatility Has Been High Compared to Market Fundamentals and Is Increasing.

The most striking observation about exchange rates since 1973 is that monthly exchange rate changes have been more volatile than changes in the observed values of the fundamental determinants. Monthly changes in exchange rates have been within ± 6 percent, with a few approaching ± 12 percent, while reported inflation differentials have not exceeded ± 2 percent.[1]

Moreover, the daily volatility of most currencies, with the exception of the Japanese yen, had increased until the September 1985 "Group of Five" meeting. Due to coordinated intervention, there has been a marked decline in volatility since then—with a few exceptions.[2] Though the reasons for this increase in volatility are not completely clear, part of the explanation may be the increasing deregulation and integration of the financial markets, along with increased uncertainty about the international financial system. By contrast, the daily volatility of the Japanese yen seems to have declined since 1984, especially when compared to the volatilities of other currencies. This is probably due to day-to-day smoothing operations by the Japanese authorities.

There is Almost No Correlation Between Successive Changes in Exchange Rates.

Along with the increased volatility since 1973, monthly changes in exchange rates have been uncorrelated over time and have tended to average zero. This absence of statistically detectable trends suggests that past monthly changes are not useful in forecasting future monthly changes, and that the expected change in the monthly exchange rate is thus

zero. The econometric evidence also shows that weekly changes are uncorrelated. Daily changes, however, appear to be weakly correlated. This could happen if news that affects exchange rates takes a few days to be fully absorbed by the markets (or if central banks intervene to attempt to reverse market trends).

Spot and Forward Rates Move Together.

Spot and forward rates tend to move together. In fact, a regression of the change in the DM/$ forward rate on the change in the DM/$ spot rate results in a coefficient estimate of 0.98, with a standard error of 0.01 and an adjusted R^2 of 0.98.[3] The statistical properties of changes in spot rates, the fact that these changes cannot be predicted by lagged forward rates or discounts, and the high correlation of these changes with changes in forward rates support the hypothesis that most exchange rate changes are unexpected and are thus the result of market adjustments to new information.[4]

Deviations From Purchasing Power Parity Persist For Long Periods.

Along with a weaker short-run link with the fundamentals since 1973, there have been persistent deviations from purchasing power parity (PPP) that have lasted, on average, about five years. One possible explanation is that exchange rates react to shocks quickly while price levels adjust slowly. In the long run, however, both exchange rates and price levels will tend to adjust to absorb shocks. The best available estimate of this rate of adjustment is 2 to 4 percent per month.

Deviations from PPP, as mentioned earlier, are changes in real exchange rates. The real exchange rate can be defined as:

$$E = SP^*/P \tag{1}$$

where S is the nominal exchange rate in terms of home currency per foreign currency, P^* is the foreign price level and P is the home price level. If PPP

1. In fact, some analysts argue that exchange rate changes have more frequent outliers than changes in their fundamental determinants. Formally, academics characterize exchange rate changes as having "fat tails," that is, as compared to the normal distribution function.

2. Volatility may be defined in various ways. Here, it is simply defined as the absolute value of the daily percentage changes times 15.8, the square root of 250, which is the approximate number of trading days in a year. The constant 15.8 annualizes the daily volatility calculations.

3. The residuals do not signal any autocorrelation or other econometric problems. The data are monthly from February 1975 to March 1985.

4. If changes in spot rates had been expected, then such changes would be highly correlated with lagged forward premiums and discounts, and uncorrelated with contemporaneous changes in forward rates. Since this is not so, we infer that spot and forward rates jointly respond to the same news.

It is clear that substantial deviations from PPP do happen; further, they have lasted, on average, five years during the period of floating rates.

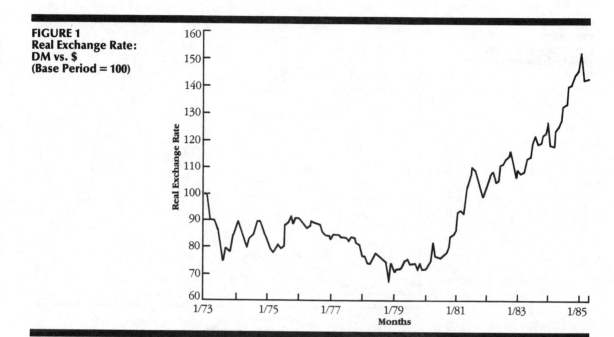

FIGURE 1
Real Exchange Rate:
DM vs. $
(Base Period = 100)

holds, then a change in P*/P should be exactly offset by a change in S, yielding a constant E.

In the short run, movements in real exchange rates reflect primarily changes in the nominal exchange rate rather than changes in relative inflation differentials. Hence, real exchange rate risk in the short run is difficult to distinguish from the risk of changes in nominal exchange rates.

To demonstrate this relationship between real and nominal exchange rate changes, Figure 1 plots the real exchange value of the mark against the dollar. By definition, an upward movement in the index implies that the mark is depreciating in real terms, and a downward move implies a real appreciation. If the years between 1973 and 1977 are taken as the base period, the dollar has been clearly overvalued with respect to PPP in the early 1980s.

In PPP calculations, however, the choice of the base period is always difficult. In this case, for example, if the 1950s were instead chosen as the base period, then the dollar in the early 1980s would not be considered overvalued. To illustrate this point, Figure 2 plots the trade-weighted real exchange value of currencies of the major U.S. trading partners *vis-a-vis* the dollar. (Note that an upward movement in this graph implies a real *depreciation* of the dollar.)

Regardless of the choice of the base period,

however, it is clear that substantial deviations from PPP do happen; further, they have lasted, on average, five years during the period of floating rates. That is, as can be seen in a graphical analysis of various real exchange rates, the real exchange rate tends to wander away from some agreed-upon base level for approximately five years on average. This average embodies both the magnitude of past shocks and the speed of adjustment towards PPP. As such, the predictive ability of this average is quite limited.

There are several reasons for deviations from PPP. Actual or expected changes in central bank reactions and monetary and fiscal policies are predominant. Differential productivity growth in various countries also result in deviations from PPP. And under certain conditions, such as the imposition of capital controls, these deviations can become permanent.

Correlations with Market Fundamentals Are Unstable and Sometimes Curious.

Explanations for movements in exchange rates are hampered by the extremely weak and unstable relationship over the past decade between changes in exchange rates and the major macroeconomic

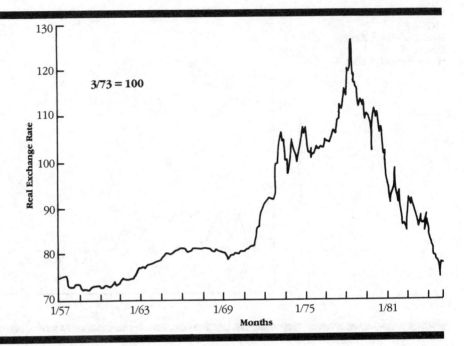
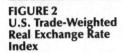

**FIGURE 2
U.S. Trade-Weighted
Real Exchange Rate
Index**

3/73 = 100

Real Exchange Rate

Months

variables. Some of this may be due to the inconsistency of economic relationships over time; some may be due to the role of swiftly changing expectations.

For example, contrary to theoretical arguments by monetarist economists, the actual correlation between relative changes in the money supply and in exchange rates has been almost nonexistent in the monthly data of the industrialized countries. The correlation does seem to hold, however, for countries subject to extremely high inflation. In such cases, high monetary growth seems to be a reliable predictor of a sharply depreciating currency.

Another weak, though often asserted, correlation is that between relative current account balances and exchange rate changes. Most models maintain that an improvement in the home current account implies an appreciation of the home currency and, conversely, that large trade deficits cause depreciations. The gist of the argument is that a current account surplus increases domestic holdings of foreign exchange reserves, thereby raising the price of the home currency. That is, for domestic residents willingly to own a greater proportion of foreign assets, the relative price of those assets must fall.

Figure 3 plots the quarterly percentage changes

in the DM/$ rate against changes in the difference between the ratio of the current account to GNP for the U.S. and the same ratio for Germany over the period 1973-1985. If the theory posited above were true, we would expect larger relative current account surpluses (deficits) to be reflected in an appreciating (depreciating) currency. This expectation is not borne out in Figure 3.

Similarly, attempts to find a stable relationship between interest rates (whether daily, weekly or monthly), oil prices, and exchange rate changes have failed. Table 1, which lists the elasticities of various exchange rates with respect to oil price changes, illustrates the instability of some econometric relationships. Except in the case of Britain, signs of oil prices changes driving exchange rate movements are visible in 1983, not at all in 1982, and only faintly detectable in 1984 and 1985. In 1982, the stability of oil prices may explain the inability of statistical tests to pick up a relationship. As for 1984, it is possible that most countries learned how to hedge their oil exposures while Britain did not because of the size of its oil endowment. Countries that are oil poor relative to the U.S. should experience an appreciation of their currencies when oil prices decrease. (In Table 1, this relationship would appear as a positive

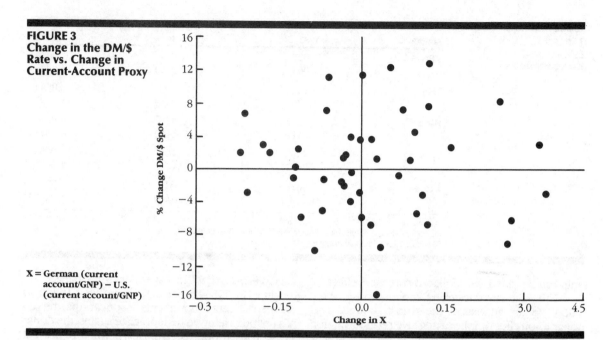

FIGURE 3
Change in the DM/$
Rate vs. Change in
Current-Account Proxy

X = German (current
account/GNP) − U.S.
(current account/GNP)

% Change DM/$ Spot

Change in X

TABLE 1
Foreign Exchange Rate
Elasticities with Respect
to Oil Price Changes

Sample	1982	1983	1984–85
DM/$	.0166	−.0874[c]	−.0809
	(.0915)	(.0428)	(.0739)
YEN/$	.0459	−.0754[b]	−.0524
	(.1172)	(.0434)	(.0467)
SF/$	.0489	−.1563[c]	−.0931[a]
	(.1171)	(.0479)	(.0671)
BP/$	−.0144	−.1268[c]	−.1190[b]
	(.0888)	(.0449)	(.0699)
FF/$	−.0165	−.0672[a]	−.0980[a]
	(.0876)	(.0452)	(.0720)
LIT/$	.0535	−.0825[c]	−.0639
	(.1753)	(.0407)	(.0666)

Standard errors are in parentheses.
Data are daily. The 1985 sample ends on February 6.
DM, YEN, SF, BP, FF and LIT, respectively, stand for the German mark, Japanese yen, Swiss franc, British pound, French franc and Italian lira.
[a,b,c] Denote significance at the 10, 5 and 2.5% levels for a two-tailed t-test.

number because of the way exchange rates are defined.) The converse is true for the U.K. because it is endowed with oil (and would be shown as a negative number in Table 1). Let us call this the "oil-to-currency" effect.

Yet, the fact that oil is priced in dollars introduces

a complication. When the dollar appreciates (and, thus, foreign currencies depreciate relative to the dollar), oil producers may be prompted to reduce their dollar oil prices to foreign buyers to keep local currency oil prices more or less constant (thus giving rise to a negative number in Table 1). This relation-

There is good reason to believe that U.S. monetary policy is more unstable than its German counterpart. Hence, the dollar might be a riskier asset than the DM. This suggests that the DM/$ forward rate would overvalue the DM compared to the expected future spot rate.

TABLE 2 Estimates of Currency Betas	Sample	1982	1983	1984–85
	YEN/$	1.027 (.0496)	.8044 (.0390)	.0436 (.0241)
	SF/$	1.134 (.0356)	.9727 (.0385)	.8544 (.0191)
	BP/$	.7272 (.0412)	.5179 (.0589)	.9012 (.0321)
	FF/$	.9533 (.0412)	.9525 (.0657)	.9650 (.0090)
	LIT/$	.9629 (.0790)	.8519 (.0264)	.9015 (.0170)

Data are daily: The 1985 data end on March 28.
All coefficients are significant at least at the 2.5% level (two-tailed test).
See Table 1 for additional notes.

ship can be called the "dollar-to-currency" effect.

The oil-to-currency effect implies a positive relationship for all except the British pound. The dollar-to-oil effect implies a negative relationship for all. Table 1 suggests that, contrary to conventional wisdom, the dollar-to-oil effect dominates. Even for the pound, it might be argued that were it not for the dollar-to-oil effect, the pound would not be as sensitive to oil price changes as it seems to be. Note that both the first and second effects for the pound are in the negative direction. For the other currencies, the effects tend to cancel out.

Correlations Across Rates Are Often Unstable.

Movements in one exchange rate are not independent of movements in another. Such relationships, however, are not stable. Correlations among currency movements can be measured using the concept of "beta (β)," a regression coefficient, which is formulated as follows:
$$\Delta S = \beta \, \Delta S_{DM/\$}$$
where Δ is the percentage change, S is the exchange rate in foreign currency units per dollar, $S_{DM/\$}$ is the DM/$ exchange rate and β is a constant. Note that the DM/$ rate is chosen as the anchor only for convenience. Table 2 presents estimates of various currency betas over several periods.

As exhibited in the cases of SF and yen, betas are

unstable over time. In particular, the Japanese authorities in 1984-85 seem to have been trying to dampen currency movements. It appears that the yen has not been allowed to depreciate against the dollar as much as European currencies, possibly to prevent trade sanctions against Japan by the U.S. or even Europe. The mildness of this depreciation is made up when the dollar depreciates, for then the yen is not allowed to appreciate against the dollar by as much as the European (EMS) currencies. Casual observation suggests that the betas of other EMS currencies are roughly around 1.0 for DM/$ changes of no more than 10 percent in absolute value. For larger changes, EMS betas drop below 1.0.[5]

Forward Rates May Have Stable or Fluctuating Biases.

Forward rates may continuously under- or overpredict future spot rates. These biases may be due to the risk characteristics of the underlying economies. For instance, there is good reason to believe that U.S. monetary policy is more unstable than its German counterpart. Hence, the dollar might be a riskier asset than the DM. This suggests that the DM/$ forward rate would overvalue the DM compared to the expected future spot rate. In fact, most recent econometric evidence, discussed in more detail later, suggests that forward rates are actually biased predictors of future spot rates. If the riskiness of the

---

5. It is interesting that the Swiss beta is lower in 1984-85 than in 1982. The explanation for the previously larger Swiss beta was that the SF market was not as deep as the DM market and produced larger swings. Apparently, this is no longer true, either because of central bank intervention or deeper markets.

It is important to remember that the volatility of exchange rates, even though high, is not significantly different from that of the prices of other financial assets.

underlying economies fluctuates, so would the bias in the forward rate.

There is an additional source of fluctuating biases. Currencies that are not allowed to float freely, such as the Mexican peso, exhibit a special statistical characteristic that has come to be known as the "peso problem." When the market expects the peso to be sharply devalued, but does not know the exact date of the devaluation, the forward discount on pesos is not as large as the expected devaluation. Hence, the forward peso continuously undervalues the peso through a series of negative forecast errors for dates preceding the devaluation. And for dates subsequent to the devaluation, the forward rate overvalues the peso through a large positive forecast error. Thus, a series of small negative forecast errors followed by a large positive forecast error, or its converse, has come to be called the peso problem.

Biases similar to the peso problem may also exist for the exchange rates of more or less freely floating currencies. This is especially true when there is uncertainty about both the timing and actual occurence of major economic or political events—for example, the unexpected election of a political candidate likely to change a country's monetary and fiscal policies.

The Implications

Just as in the stock market, foreign exchange analysts use various techniques alleged to provide an edge in forecasting financial prices such as exchange rates and stock prices. If such techniques did prove to be effective forecasting tools, it would imply that the users of such techniques could generate profits above the fair market rate of return. While this sometimes may occur, it generally does not. And there is good reason to be skeptical about apparent free lunches: it is not rational to share successful forecasting methods with others because doing so would reduce per-capita profits.

In this section we discuss the efficient markets hypothesis (EMH)—loosely, the notion that there is no free lunch—and its implications for foreign exchange forecasting. In the critical light of EMH, we then assess the usefulness of the technical and econometric analyses that are currently used to forecast exchange rates.

There Is No Free Lunch: The Efficient Markets Hypothesis

The dismal forecasting performance of econometric models, as well as the very limited horizon of technical models, add further credence to the efficient markets hypothesis. In its so-called "strong" form, the EMH states that financial asset prices, such as exchange rates, fully reflect *all* information. Investors therefore cannot consistently earn extraordinary profits by exploiting any sources of information, even that of insiders. Less extreme versions of the hypothesis state that only *publicly* available information, including all past price performance, is already reflected in the current price.

The strong form of the hypothesis is based on the observation that financial assets can be easily traded by numerous well-informed traders who make decisions continuously.[6] For this reason, financial prices are extremely sensitive to news and immediately adjust to reflect all available information about the major determinants of an asset's value. In turn, the strength of these expectations affects the volatility of the financial asset's price.

In the long run, financial prices do turn out to be consistent with market fundamentals. In the short run, however, financial prices are rather "noisy," whether because of shifts in expectations, institutional movements in and out of the market, or other unsystematic factors. Nevertheless, it is important to remember that the volatility of exchange rates, even though high, is not significantly different from that of the prices of other financial assets.

For reasons discussed previously, efficient market theorists contend that the apparent departures from market fundamentals do not necessarily imply that the market is inefficient. Such departures do not offer consistent opportunities to earn extraordinary profits (on a risk-adjusted basis).

In judging the efficient markets hypothesis, it is perhaps better to think of market efficiency as the description of a process rather than a static condition of the market at each point in time. It is, in fact, almost impossible for investors to make extraordinary profits using only publicly available information. Those who do make such profits possess superior forecasting skills and their economic return may be viewed as a "monopoly rent." Aside from these ex-

---

6. It also assumes that these assets can be stored without cost.

ceptions, many other traders invest in information gathering and processing; and they make economic profits on their positions if their judgments are borne out. Such traders help ensure that the market reflects all available information.

A corollary of the EMH is the validity of the random walk model (or some variant thereof). The model holds that the best predictor of future asset prices is the current asset price, perhaps with some adjustment for the expected growth of the asset. There are two types of random walk models: those with and those without "drift." Drift stands for the expected growth of the asset in question.

Are Current Rates Adjusted for Interest Differentials the Best Forecasters of Future Spot Rates?

Price changes have two components: the expected and the unexpected. In the case of equities, stock prices move at a rate appropriate to their risk class (the expected component) together with a random term (the unexpected component). The unexpected component can only be random because new information, by definition, arrives randomly. From this, it follows that stock prices behave according to the random walk model with a drift term (which reflects, again, an expected rate of growth in the asset's price).[7]

This model is also applicable to the foreign exchange market. One can either invest a dollar at home or, alternatively, convert it to foreign currency, invest it abroad, and repatriate it at the end of the investment period. The functioning of arbitrageurs who are indifferent between holding domestic and foreign assets ensures that the above two investment strategies produce the same rate of return. That is, we would expect the home currency to depreciate by an amount approximately equal to the difference between domestic and foreign interest rates.[8] For example, if home interest rates are 200 basis points below foreign rates, then one expects the home currency to appreciate by 2 percent.

This relationship is known as the *uncovered interest rate parity* theorem. In essence, it is the ran-

dom walk model with drift, in which the drift (or expected) term is the differential between home and foreign interest rates. The unexpected term is the arbitrageurs' judgmental error.[8]

Aha, the Corresponding Forward Rate Is the Best Forecaster of Future Spot Rates!

One twist in the foreign exchange markets that must be accounted for is the forward market. In the absence of capital controls, arbitrage dictates that the home currency must be at a forward discount that is approximately equal to the difference between home and foreign interest rates.[9] For instance, if foreign annual interest rates are 300 basis points above home rates, then the foreign currency must be at a 3 percent annual forward discount. Otherwise, there would be arbitrage opportunities through the forward market.

Because speculators take forward positions which reflect their views, it can be argued that forward rates should be unbiased predictors of future spot rates.[10] In fact, some authors have coined the term "forecasting efficiency" to indicate that forward exchange rates are the best available forecasters of the future spot rate.

Or Maybe the Best Forecaster of Future Spot Rates Is the Current Rate.

Unfortunately, the most satisfying simple model of exchange rate movement turns out to be the random walk model without drift, which implies that the best forecaster of all future spot rates is the current spot rate. The forecasting superiority of the spot rate over the forward rate is especially prominent in the short run, but gradually disappears as the forecasting horizon is lengthened.

What Really Forecasts Future Spot Rates Best?

There is increasing evidence that forward rates, and hence the random walk model with drift, are not unbiased predictors of future spot rates. This may be due to the existence of a risk premium that arises from restrictions on the free substitution of home

---

7. Expressed in the form of an equation, the random walk model with drift is as follows: $s_t = u + s_{t-1} + e_t$, where s is the natural log of the underlying asset price, subscripts t and t-1 denote the time at which a variable is measured, u is the drift term (expected component) and e (unexpected component) is a normally, independently distributed error term with mean zero and constant variance. Note that since s_t and s_{t-1} are in logs, their difference is the expected growth rate of the asset. And e represents the unexpected growth of the asset.

8. The uncovered interest rate parity theorem, which is simply a reworking of the equation for the random walk model with drift, can be formulated as follows: $s_{t+1} = (i - i^*) + s_t + e_{t+1}$, where s_{t+1} and s_t are the logs of the exchange

rate in terms of home currency per unit of foreign currency at times t+1 and t, respectively; i and i* are the home and foreign interest rates; and e_t, the unexpected component, is a normally, independently distributed error term with mean zero and constant variance.

9. In equation form, $f_{t+1} - s_t = i - i^*$, where f_{t+1} is the log of the forward rate set at time t for delivery at time t+1.

10. This assumes there is no risk premium in international capital markets—either because of risk neutrality or because assets can be readily substituted.

and foreign assets, or from investors' demand for a higher expected return for holding more risky currencies. The evidence is that current exchange rates predict future spot rates better than do forward rates; forecast errors, as measured by the mean absolute errors for example, are smaller when current rates are used.

Further, there is evidence that the random walk model without drift has better forecasting performance than such models, even when econometric models use actual values for the independent variables. This is well documented for forecasting horizons of up to a year. Hence, the empirical evidence suggests that the best simple predictor of future spot prices is the driftless random walk model.

This finding poses a problem because the driftless random walk model is extremely unsatisfactory from a theoretical perspective. In fact, this implies a money-making strategy (which I discuss later) and is inconsistent with long-term PPP.

Technical Analysis May Work in the Very Short Run.

Technical analysis is a vague term but is here defined as a body of analysis for forecasting the price of a financial asset solely on the basis of that asset's own price history. Common forms of technical analysis include models with names such as "momentum," "slope," "moving average," and "head and shoulders." Most of these models forecast only the direction of price movements.

A momentum model is based on the idea that a price, such as an exchange rate, will continue to move up if it has been rising in the past, and vice versa. Another theory defines a peak as a resistance area. If the market again approaches a peak, after having moved down from it, it is said to be "testing" the resistance area. If it "pierces" the resistance area, it is likely to move up for a while. If it backs away, it is likely to go down some more. Resistance areas are also formed on the downside.[11]

Technical analysis can be successful only if successive price changes are correlated. There is some support for technical analysis from a number of mechanisms that cause price changes to be positively autocorrelated. These include mass psychol-

ogy, in the form of price changes feeding upon themselves, and the slow spread of new information. The existence of central banks that "lean against the wind" is another such mechanism. When central banks attempt to dampen price changes that would otherwise take place, they make exchange rate behavior look like the slow spread of new information.

For example, if there is market pressure for the exchange rate to move by 10 percent and the central bank instead allows only a series of 2 percent changes in stages, these small changes would be positively autocorrelated, whereas a once-and-for-all 10 percent jump does not have to be correlated with subsequent changes. Furthermore, technical analysis may pick up certain factors that escape classical statistical methods. For instance, technical analysis might be better at signaling certain discrete "jumps," such as a European Monetary System realignment.

Indeed, there is evidence that technical models have predictive power, especially in intra-day trading. However, their predictive power for periods of a month or longer does not seem strong. If information spreads in a few days, and if information in technical models is quickly disseminated, it is possible to have daily but not monthly autocorrelations.

If a technical model signals that a market will go up—and if enough people act on this signal—the market will go up by an amount corresponding to the information embodied in the technical signal. But because financial markets react quickly to news, it is unlikely that any worthy news will take a month or longer to be disseminated. Thus, the very use of technical models in the short run invalidates their use in the longer run.

Econometric Analysis Has Been Disappointing In The Short To Medium Run.

The exchange rate is an asset price that equilibrates various markets. When asset holders' expectations change with respect to the factors that affect those markets, the exchange rate also adjusts to reflect the new expectations. Attempts to uncover this process have produced several theoretical models of exchange rate determination, ranging from simple monetary theories to more complex portfolio bal-

---

11. There are also less common forms of technical analysis. Sophisticated econometric techniques such as Box-Jenkins analysis that use a price series' own history for forecasting are philosophically no different from the more traditional forms of technical analysis. However, Box-Jenkins-like autoregressive methods forecast the magnitude of change as well as the direction of change.

Given the current state of the art, econometric models are not very useful for forecasting exchange rates in the short to medium term—that is, up to five years—though forecasting performance improves with the length of the horizon.

ance formulations. Econometric analysis is generally used to substantiate the superiority of one model over another. Thereafter comes forecasting.

With econometric forecasting of exchange rates, however, a number of problems arise. First, we do not have a satisfactory theory to explain the formation of expectations. Moreover, we cannot accurately measure expectations—not surprisingly, since expectations are not directly observable (that is, when we are unable to measure accurately the variables that go into an econometric forecasting model, we cannot place much faith in the forecast itself). Second, any knowledge embodied in an econometric or technical model should already be embodied in the market price of a financial asset. Thus, the use of a model should not give its user an edge over other market participants. Third, the true underlying model that drives the world has not yet been uncovered. And fourth, the data needed to build econometric models of foreign exchange rates are inadequate. Statistics collected for this purpose usually are not timely or of the desired frequency. They are often inaccurate and generally do not reveal enough about institutional factors such as interventions and financial flows. Institutional factors may not be important in the determination of foreign exchange rates in the long run. Nevertheless, a large jump in the demand for foreign exchange by a large corporation on any given day will move the exchange rate on that day. And for traders whose profitability hinges on intra-day movements, that is important.

On balance, then, given the current state of the art, econometric models are not very useful for forecasting exchange rates in the short to medium term—that is, up to five years—though forecasting performance improves with the length of the horizon. Still, the longer-run forecasting capabilities of econometric modeling may be useful for other purposes, if only for focusing management's attention on the likely economic consequences of future exchange rate changes.

Risk Management Strategies

Though faced with ever greater exchange rate risk, financial managers can nevertheless reduce their exposure to such risk. Some of the available means for managing exchange risk are the consolidation of foreign exchange receivables and payments, hedging, and diversification.

Consolidate Receivables and Payables

The obvious first step in the management of foreign exchange exposure is to consolidate foreign currency receivables and payables. This gives management a clearer picture of foreign exchange exposures and avoids unnecessary covering costs.

In addition, correlations among currency movements can be exploited. Suppose, for example, that the current spot rates are 2.00 DM/$ and 150 yen/$, with receivables consisting of 200,000 DM and payables consisting of 15,000,000 yen in matched maturities. At current exchange rates, the yen payables are offset by the DM receivables. If management does not expect exchange rates to change, then no hedging transactions are necessary.

This would also be true if exchange rates change and the yen Beta equals one; that is, if changes in the yen were accompanied by the same percentage change in the value of the DM. If, however, the yen Beta is less than one, the DM receivables do not fully hedge the yen payables when the dollar appreciates because the depreciation of the DM exceeds the depreciation of the yen. Put differently, the yen has appreciated against the DM. Conversely, if the dollar depreciates, the mark receivables more than fully hedge the yen payables. In fact, it can be shown that one can be fully hedged by altering the DM position by the amount y, where:

$y = x (1 - Beta)$ and where x is the expected change in the DM/$ exchange rate. That is, if x equals 0.10 (that is, the dollar appreciates by 10 percent), and Beta is 0.5, the DM position should be increased by 5 percent (y = .05).

Hedging Is Relevant.

The second step in foreign exchange exposure management is assessing and, if necessary, hedging the remaining exposure to exchange risk. The selection of an appropriate risk management strategy depends on management's view of what constitutes risk. The prevailing view, among practitioners at least, is that the primary purpose of exchange risk management is to reduce the variability of the firm's profits—whether measured by cash flows or conventionally reported dollar earnings—caused by changes in exchange rates. Financial academics, however, have long argued that reducing the variability of a company's returns, while leaving the expected level of those returns unchanged, should

Reducing the overall risk profile of the firm is relevant to shareholders if only because risk affects the perceptions and behavior of other corporate stakeholders such as employees, managers, lenders, and suppliers.

have little effect on the value of the firm. This view of risk management focuses on risk in the equity markets and considers a security or a firm's operations risky only to the extent that the firm's activities move in tandem with the market as a whole. Well-diversified international investors, so the argument goes, should not be willing to pay a premium for corporate hedging activities which they can easily duplicate for themselves simply by adjusting their portfolios. According to this view, although hedging to reduce overall variability of profits may be important to executives compensated on the basis of short-term earnings, it is largely a matter of "irrelevance" to shareholders.

I take issue with this argument, first of all, because it underestimates the importance of information, transaction costs, and other sources of friction in the operation of markets. These factors may make it costlier for market participants to hedge certain risks than for the firm to do so. In this article, I begin with the assumption that hedging does have value for shareholders (in part because it is so widely observed). Reducing the overall risk profile of the firm—stemming from fluctuations in commodity prices, high fixed costs, high financial leverage, as well as exchange rate swings—is relevant to shareholders if only because risk affects the perceptions and behavior of other corporate stakeholders such as employees, managers, lenders, and suppliers.[12] By reducing the total risk or variability of the firm, hedging transactions reduce the exposure of a range of corporate constituencies; and this in turn may increase the value of shareholders' claims.

Use Passive Strategies If You Cannot Forecast Nominal Rates.

For protection against the risk arising from currency volatility, there are a number of passive strategies that either totally or partially hedge a firm's foreign exchange exposure. These strategies are particularly useful when management has little confidence in its ability to forecast. In general, these strategies try to avoid risk at almost all cost. By contrast, active strategies—those which entail participation in the foreign exchange market based on a view of currency

movements—require some appetite for risk.

Some passive strategies ensure a minimum level of profits and, at the same time, allow the opportunity for more. But at the least, passive strategies are beneficial because they insure positions and insulate the firm's income from undesirable foreign exchange moves. These strategies, with the exception of using futures, also avoid the costs involved in managing positions.

Passive strategies use a variety of financial instruments, including forwards, futures, swaps, and options. Other widely used techniques are leading and lagging, borrowing and lending, currency matching, and commodity hedging. (Only a few examples are illustrated below, but the pros and cons of each technique are outlined in the Appendix to this article.) Because the characteristics of foreign exchange risk tend to differ by time horizon, the appropriate strategies for the short, medium, and long term also vary.

Use Readily Available Instruments in the Short Term.

The evidence presented above suggests that in the short term (less than one year), most movements in nominal exchange rates are largely unanticipated. Moreover, prices at home and abroad do not adjust quickly to offset nominal exchange rate changes (thereby causing deviations from PPP). And finally, nominal interest rate differentials across countries are not matched by subsequent and offsetting exchange rate changes.

This evidence implies that there is *real* foreign exchange risk in the short term. In turn, this leads directly to business risk by affecting both unhedged monetary and nonmonetary positions arising out of commercial transactions and dividend flows. This type of currency risk is sometimes referred to as "transaction" risk.

Because foreign exchange forecasting is so unreliable in the short term, transaction risk should be (and is easily) hedged by using the available financial instruments and techniques mentioned above. Of course, there is a cost attached to these procedures. For example, the cost of forward covering is best represented as the difference between the bid-ask spread in the forward contract and in the spot markets.[13]

---

12. For an extensive discussion of this point, see Alan Shapiro and Sheridan Titman, "An Integrated Approach to Corporate Risk Management," *Midland Corporate Finance Journal*, Vol. 3 No. 2 (1985).

13. This, however, is a controversial matter. Some authors argue for the difference between the current spot and the forward rate. Others believe cost should be viewed as the difference between the forward contract and the spot

In order for FASB 52 to provide an accurate representation of true economic value, all items on the balance sheet must be marked to market.

Match Assets and Liabilities in the Medium Term and Use Actual or Synthetic Instruments.

In the medium term—say, one to five years—foreign exchange risk encompasses both transaction and translation risks. Translation risk relates to the effects of nominal exchange rate changes on balance sheet exposures. Firms try to manage such exposures by matching assets and liabilities in a particular currency as well as by using the above-mentioned techniques and instruments. Nevertheless, such efforts have limited effectiveness because of transaction costs and various constraints.

An understanding of translation exposure requires knowledge of accounting rules and regulations such as FASB 8 and FASB 52. For instance, the more recent, and more relevant, FASB 52 rule states that all translation must be carried out at the prevailing spot rates when the accounting statements are prepared. By contrast, FASB 8 translates monetary items at the exchange rate on the reporting date and nonmonetary items at the exchange rates prevailing at the time of acquisition. Another difference between the two rules concerns the separation of foreign exchange income from operating income. FASB 8 reports translation gains and losses in current income, blurring the distinction between operating income and foreign exchange income. FASB 52, on the other hand, incorporates foreign exchange gains and losses in an equity account (except for certain aspects of the operations of foreign subsidiaries that use a certain "functional" currency as reported in FASB 8).

For the purpose of judging a firm's economic value, FASB 52 is incomplete unless it is accompanied by thorough inflation accounting at home and abroad. In order, then, for FASB 52 to provide an accurate representation of true economic value, all items on the balance sheet must be marked to market. To illustrate, consider a foreign subsidiary located in an inflationary environment where price increases are fully matched by local currency depreciation (such that PPP is maintained). To the extent that the fixed assets of the subsidiary are valued at historical book value and translated at current exchange rates, translation according to FASB 52 will understate the value of these fixed assets. Because share prices are likely to reflect real economic performance rather than that indicated by translated accounting earnings, it might be argued that accounting exposure should not be a matter of concern. Nonetheless, translation exposure can have some important effects. Accounting conventions affect tax payments, royalty payments, executive compensation, and various other contractual obligations.

Try to Forecast Real Exchange Rates in the Long Term.

Long-term exchange risk (more than five years), also known as "real" or "economic" exchange risk, arises from permanent secular changes in real exchange rates and from permanent differences in real returns across countries. Such changes influence the profitability of various production locations around the globe and are critical to decisions about foreign production and investment.

It is very difficult to hedge real exchange risk in the marketplace with any precision. Explicit instruments for such operations are either nonexistent or thinly traded. Nevertheless, there are some, admittedly crude, approaches to hedging economic exchange risk. For example, a U.S. multinational sourcing some of its components in Brazil will face reduced profitability if the real exchange value of the cruzado appreciates—that is, if Brazilian prices (wages and other costs) rise faster than the rate of cruzado depreciation. To protect itself, the company can construct a hedge by buying Brazilian cruzados forward, together with forward contracts of Brazilian commodities. Or it can buy forward cruzados and Brazilian real assets.

The problem with these strategies, however, is that long-dated forward markets for the cruzado and for Brazilian commodities are probably extremely thin. One alternative is to borrow in the U.S. and lend in Brazil. But these sets of transactions are too cumbersome to be economical. Yet another alternative is to attempt to forecast real exchange rates, particularly since long-term real exchange rates are probably easier to forecast than short-term rates.

Under certain assumptions, an improvement in overall home productivity points to a real appreciation of the home currency. This suggests that when

rate at maturity. Still others vote for the difference between the forward rate and the expected future spot rate. Ultimately, though, the cost of the forward cover is the income of units that provide this cover. This income is the bid-ask spread, and it is this cover that has to be compared to the alternative of transacting in the spot market.

Despite persuasive arbitrage arguments, real rates of interest may be consistently different across countries, even after adjusting for exchange rate changes. Perhaps the reason is that there is risk associated with being long in a certain country.

TABLE 3 Spot and Forward Rates for the BP and SF on 3/22/85	Sample	Spot	30 Days	90 Days	180 Days
	$/BP	1.1740	1.1692	1.1623	1.1594
	$/SF	.3663	.3674	.3696	.3743

multinationals produce abroad, they should invest in industries with higher than average expected productivity growth. Such a strategy helps to ensure that the cost of the components sourced in these countries remains competitive.

Use Active Strategies If You Have A View.

At the opposite end of passive strategies in the risk-management spectrum are those that maximize expected value regardless of risk. Examples of some active management strategies, which are geared toward achieving a profit target at the expense of incurring some risk, are discussed below.

Borrow Low, Lend High.

As shown above, the current spot rate may be a better predictor of future spot rates than the corresponding forward or futures rates (as predicted by the random walk model). Although even this relationship is not precise, it can be exploited if investors are willing to bear some risk. The strategy is to make buy or sell decisions in the forward markets based on the assumption that, on average, the current spot rates will prevail in the future.

To illustrate, consider the spot and forward rates for the British pound (BP) and the Swiss Franc (SF) in Table 3. Note that the pound is at a discount and the SF is at a premium throughout the forward horizon of 30 to 180 days. For the 180-day horizon, the forward rates imply that the pound is at a 2.48 percent per year discount, and the SF is at a 4.36 percent per year premium. Under the above strategy, which essentially bets on the current spot rate against the forward rate, the company should take a long forward position in pounds and a short forward position in SFs. In essence, this means taking a long forward position in BPs because forward BPs are incorrectly cheaper than spot BPs. That is, in the relevant future, the spot BP will not be as cheap as the forward rates indicate but, instead, will be just as expensive as the current spot rate. The converse is true for the SF. The strategy expects to make profits of .0048c/BP, .0117c/BP and .0146c/BP on the 30-, 90- and 180-days contracts, respectively.

Such a strategy, incidentally, is virtually identical to borrowing in countries with low interest rates and lending in countries with high interest rates. Borrowing in Switzerland is the same as being short Swiss bonds. At maturity, SFs must be bought to pay one's liabilities; and this is thus identical to shorting forward SFs. Similarly, lending in the U.K. means that one is long British bonds, which is equivalent to being long in forward pounds.

Under these circumstances, it is no wonder that international arbitrage and the figures given in the table indicate that annualized British and Swiss interest rates are approximately 248 basis points higher, and 436 basis points lower, than U.S. rates, respectively. Another example: when 15-year interest rates were 8 percent for the SF and 17 percent for the US$, the World Bank was funding some of its operations in the Swiss franc. The Bank calculated that the breakeven point would occur at a 9 percent annual rate of appreciation for the SF vis-a-vis the dollar. Over 15 years, this would compound to a 364 percent appreciation, or a change to $1.75/SF from the 48c/SF prevailing at the time. Since the World Bank reasoned that this was an unlikely outcome, they accepted the risk and funded in SFs.

But let me offer one caveat in betting against the forward rate. In doing so, one maintains naked positions in the forward markets. Put differently, the expected return of this strategy may be viewed as a reward to the risk associated with the strategy. Despite persuasive arbitrage arguments, real rates of interest may be consistently different across countries, even after adjusting for exchange rate changes. Perhaps the reason is that there is risk associated with being long in a certain country. This risk can be mitigated in two ways: first, by using foreign exchange options, which put a limit on losses; and, second, by using a portfolio approach to currency management.

Use the Portfolio Approach to Exploit Correlations, or Lack Thereof, among Currency Movements.

The portfolio approach takes advantage of the correlations, or lack thereof, among various exchange rate changes. For example, we know that movements in the Dutch guilder (DG) and the German mark (DM) are highly correlated vis-a-vis the dollar. If Dutch interest rates suddenly go up, the portfolio approach suggests that one should borrow marks and lend guilders. This is a less risky strategy than borrowing dollars and lending guilders because it involves uncertainty in only one exchange rate—that is, the DM/DG. By contrast, borrowing US$ and lending DG entails uncertainty in two exchange rates: the $/DM and DM/DG. (Here, it is useful to think of the DM as a price leader and the DG as a price follower.)

While it is useful to exploit high degrees of co-movements, managers can reduce overall variability when there are low degrees of co-movement between returns on different assets or markets. This can be done by diversifying away from a single market or asset toward several markets or assets. For example, if returns on French securities, after accounting for exchange rate changes, have almost no correlation with returns on Australian securities, a U.S. investor could reduce the overall variability of his portfolio by holding both French and Australian securities. This is similar to selling life insurance to a diverse group of people.

International portfolio diversification pays off if national financial markets are sufficiently segregated. If they are, arbitrage relationships such as PPP may not hold while returns, measured in the home currency of the investor, may be uncorrelated. The risk of this approach is that correlations among the returns of various assets may be unstable over time. Even so, the evidence suggests that international portfolio diversification does pay off by reducing risk when an expected return is the main goal, or by increasing expected return when a specific level of risk is kept under control.

Concluding Comments

The facts about exchange rate behavior summarized in this article suggest that it is difficult to forecast exchange rates with any degree of confidence. The reason is that exchange rate movements are largely unanticipated and are more volatile than market fundamentals. In addition, correlations with market fundamentals and among rates are unstable. Though there is a gradual move towards purchasing power parity—at an average of about 4 percent a month—this is nonetheless not a very useful forecasting paradigm, given the volatility of foreign exchange rates. Even forward rates may not be accurate forecasters because of built-in biases and because of the rapidity with which new information hits the markets.

Because of this difficulty in forecasting exchange rates, corporate treasurers are well advised to hedge net exposures by using readily available (or synthetically constructing) hedging instruments such as forwards, swaps, and options. The markets for these instruments are usually very deep for tenors of one to two years, and are deepening for maturities of up to 15 years—especially in the major currencies. It is noteworthy that these instruments can also allow corporate treasurers to exploit borrowing or investment "windows" across the globe while reducing foreign exchange risk.

In managing longer-term, economic exposures, however, there is more room for economic analysis and perhaps even forecasting—despite the risks. For instance, if exchange rates are misaligned according to most PPP calculations, then treasurers might want to position themselves so as to benefit from a shift of rates back toward PPP. Similarly, interest rate differences might indicate certain borrowing or lending strategies even after accounting for possible exchange rate adjustments. It also might be wise to reduce production costs by sourcing overseas in industries where the expected productivity growth of the sourced component is higher than the overall rate of productivity growth in the source country. More adventurous corporate treasurers can attempt to exploit correlations among currency movements and to benefit from the insights provided by some of the more esoteric econometric techniques—although these should also be used with caution.

Instruments	Description	Pros	Cons
Forwards	An almost custom-made contract to buy or sell foreign-exchange in the future, at a presently specified price.	Maturity and size of contract can be determined individually to almost exactly hedge the desired position.	Use up bank credit lines even when two forward contracts exactly offset each other.
Futures	A ready-made contract to buy or sell foreign exchange in the future, at a presently specified price. Unlike forwards, futures have a few maturity dates per year. The most common contracts have maturity dates in March, June, September, or December. But, these contracts are almost continuously traded on organized exchanges. Contract sizes are fixed.	No credit lines required. Easy access for small accounts. Fairly low margin requirements. Contract's liquidity guaranteed by the exchange on which it is traded.	Margin requirements cause cash-flow uncertainty and use managerial resources.
Options	A contract that offers the right but not the obligation to buy or sell foreign exchange in the future, at a presently specified price. Unlike forwards and futures, options do not have to be exercised. Available on an almost custom-made basis from banks or in ready-made form on exchanges.	Allow hedging of contingent exposures and taking positions while limiting downside risk and retaining upside potential for profit. Also permit tradeoffs other than risk versus expected return.	Since an option is like insurance coupled with an investment oportunity, its benefits are not readily observable, leading some to conclude that it is "too expensive."
Swaps	An agreement to exchange one currency for another at specified dates and prices. Essentially, a swap is a series of forward contracts.	Versatile, allowing easy hedging of complex exposures.	Documentation requirement might be extensive.

Techniques	Description	Pros	Cons
Borrowing and lending	Creates a synthetic forward by borrowing and lending at home and abroad. For example, a long forward foreign-exchange position is equivalent to borrowing at home, converting the proceeds to foreign exchange and investing them abroad. The converse holds for a short forward foreign-exchange position.	Useful when forwards, futures or swaps markets are thin—particularly for long-dated maturities.	Utilizes costly managerial resources. May be prohibited by legal restrictions.
Commodity hedging	Going short (long) a commodity contract denominated in a foreign currency to hedge a foreign-exchange asset (liability).	Commodity markets are usually deep, particularly for maturities up to a year.	Price changes of commodities, in terms of home currency, may not exactly offset price changes in the asset (liability) to be hedged. Commodity hedging may not be possible for maturities of over one year.
Leading and lagging	Equating foreign-exchange assets and liabilities by speeding up or slowing down receivables or payables.	Avoids unnecessary hedging costs.	Appropriate matches may not be available. Utilizes costly managerial resources.
Matching	Equating assets and liabilities denominated in each currency.	Avoids unnecessary hedging costs.	Appropriate matches may not be available.

Managing Foreign Exchange Risks

by Bradford Cornell, *University of California, Los Angeles*
and Alan C. Shapiro, *University of Southern California*

Since the introduction of the floating-exchange rate regime in 1973, foreign exchange risk has become of increasing concern to firms doing business internationally. With their integrated cross-border production and market operations, multinational corporations (MNCs) continually face devaluation or revaluation worries somewhere in the world. Hardly a day passes without a multinational announcing a foreign exchange gain or loss. And although the recent adoption of FAS #52 may do much to reduce the wild swings in the translated earnings of overseas subsidiaries, the problem of coping with volatile currencies remains essentially unchanged. Those MNCs which hedged FAS #8 earnings in the past will doubtless abandon their previous hedging strategies (which, as we shall argue, were misguided in the first place). But, fluctuations in exchange rates will nevertheless continue to have "real" effects on the cash profitability of foreign subsidiaries, complicating overseas selling, pricing, and buying decisions.

Many MNCs have responded to increased currency volatility, and the resulting greater uncertainty, by devoting more resources to the management of foreign exchange risk. Most existing corporate programs, however, lack a coherent and theoretically sound approach to the problem. The development of an effective strategy for managing currency risk should proceed in three distinct stages. First, management should determine what is at risk, and this requires an appropriate definition of foreign exchange risk. Second, it must clearly identify the ob-

jectives of its exchange risk management program. This step is important not only because success can only be measured relative to objectives, but because in practice the fundamental purpose of exchange risk management is often lost sight of or subordinated to other concerns: hedging specific transactions, reducing the variability of translated earnings, and even speculating on foreign currencies. Third, having determined the extent of its exposure to currency risk and defined its objectives, management can then design a set of company-wide policies to achieve its objectives.

This article attempts to guide management's thinking through each of these stages of development. The first section discusses the nature and origins of exchange risk. The second develops a theory of the "economic," as distinguished from the accounting, consequences of currency changes on a firm's value. The third evaluates current hedging practices and goals, concluding with a statement of our own view of the proper objective of multinational currency risk management. The fourth section offers suggestions for a comprehensive strategy for managing exchange risk—one designed to cope with both anticipated and unanticipated currency changes. Unlike the conventional recommendations of financial advisors, which generally focus exclusively on financial hedging, our proposed strategy for managing exchange risk calls for the integration of marketing and production decisions with more traditional financial responses.

44

The change in accounting net worth produced by a movement in exchange rates often bears little relationship to the change in the value of the firm.

Foreign Exchange Risk and Exposure

As a result of its investment, production, and other operating decisions, a firm generates both a current structure of assets and liabilities, and a stream of expected future cash flows. A comprehensive program for managing exchange risk should attempt to incorporate expectations about changes in exchange rates into *all* basic corporate decisions affecting cash flow and financial structure. Once having assessed the effects of possible currency changes on the cash generation and financial structure of the firm, management is then in a position to decide whether to "self-insure" the risks of unanticipated (and largely diversifiable) currency fluctuations or to "lay them off" to financial markets.

Prior to making this decision, then, management must begin by determining what is at risk. Throughout this article, we will define exchange risk as the variability in the value of a firm—as measured by the present value of its expected future cash flows—caused by uncertain exchange rate changes. Thus, exchange risk is viewed as the possibility that currency fluctuations can alter the expected amounts or variability of the firm's future cash flows.

In choosing a definition of exchange risk based on market value, we are assuming that management's goal is to maximize the value of the firm. Whether management actually behaves in this fashion has been vigorously debated. Clearly, some managers will prefer to pursue other objectives. In fact, many, if not indeed most, multinational financial managers probably consider the reduction of the variability of translated earnings as the principal function of exchange risk management. Such a concern was clearly behind the earlier widespread practice of hedging FAS #8 earnings. Nevertheless, the assumption that management attempts to maximize (risk-adjusted) after-tax cash flow remains standard in much of the finance literature. Moreover, the principle of stockholder wealth maximization provides a rational guide to financial decision-making.

The companion to value maximization is market efficiency. If the capital market did not rationally price the firm's securities, managers would be hard pressed to design a foreign exchange strategy which could be expected to maximize firm value. Fortunately, there is strong evidence that capital markets are relatively sophisticated in responding to publicly available information. Most of the large body of research on financial markets suggests that when accounting numbers diverge significantly from cash flows, changes in security prices generally reflect changes in cash flows rather than reported earnings.

Our definition of exchange risk is very different from that employed by accountants, who rely on a balance sheet approach to measure exposure to exchange rate changes. Those who use an accounting definition—whether FAS #8, FAS #52, or some other method—divide the balance sheet's assets and liabilities into those accounts that will be affected by exchange rate changes and those that will not. The value of assets and liabilities are then translated back into the domestic currency.

The problem with this accounting approach is that book values and market values typically differ, so that the change in net worth produced by a movement in exchange rates often bears little relationship to the change in the value of the firm. And even if management focuses on the real instead of the accounting effects of currency changes, it still faces another problem. No matter how careful it is in measuring the true economic consequences of currency changes, management still has a fundamentally flawed picture of the firm's actual exposure unless it takes into account two key equilibrium relationships observed in international financial markets: Purchasing Power Parity and the International Fisher Effect.

The theory of purchasing power parity (PPP) maintains that changes in the ratio of domestic to foreign prices will cause offsetting changes in the exchange rate so as to maintain the relative purchasing powers of the currencies involved. Although purchasing power parity does not hold exactly, a large portion of exchange rate changes over the long run are explained by equal and opposite changes in national price levels.

The International Fisher Effect says that returns on assets held and the costs of liabilities incurred (should) implicitly incorporate anticipated currency changes. In other words, the difference in interest rates between countries (holding risk constant) should equal the expected change in the exchange rate during the term of the loan. For example, if the one-year U.S. interest rate is 10 percent while the equivalent English interest rate is 15 percent, the International Fisher Effect says that the pound is expected to decline by about 5 percent during the year. Of course, after the fact, interest rates adjusted

Without relative price changes, a multinational company faces no real operating exchange risk.

for currency changes usually diverge from such expectations. This is because unexpected exchange rate changes occur. However, it is impossible, by definition, to expect to profit consistently from changes that are unexpected. All that the International Fisher Effect predicts is that, over time, exchange gains or losses on debt denominated in currencies likely to appreciate will be offset by lower interest rates and, on debt denominated in currencies likely to depreciate, by higher interest rates. This prediction appears to be borne out by the available empirical evidence.

Only by explicitly recognizing the implications of these equilibrium relationships for the estimation and valuation of future cash flows can we hope to come to grips with the problems of determining a firm's true economic exposure.

Accounting Vs. Economic Exposure

Accounting exposure arises from the need, for purposes of reporting and consolidation, to convert the results of foreign operations from local currencies (LCs) to the home currency (HC). When an exchange rate changes, this translation or restatement of the various accounts denominated in the foreign currency leads to a new accounting measurement of the dollar value of the firm's investment in the foreign subsidiary (or in the asset or liability itself). If translation gains and losses are recorded on the income statement, then this also results in a change in reported earnings. The possible size of this change in earnings is known as *translation exposure* to foreign exchange risk.

It has become clear, however, that retrospective accounting techniques, no matter how refined, cannot truly account for the economic effects of devaluation or revaluation on the value of a firm. The inevitable result of using an inappropriate definition of exposure is that the impact of exchange rate changes, as recorded on a firm's balance sheet and income statements, is so distorted as to make accounting results of little use to either investors or corporate managers. Because of this accounting distortion of economic reality, many multinational firms are now taking a longer-term look at their degree of exchange risk. This involves focusing on the firm's economic exposure.

Economic exposure to exchange risk, which we defined earlier as the extent to which the firm's value will be affected by changes in exchange rates, can in turn be separated into two components:

transaction exposure and real operating exposure. *Transaction exposure* is the possibility of incurring exchange gains or losses, upon settlement at a future date, on transactions already entered into and denominated in a foreign currency. Some of these unsettled transactions, including foreign currency-denominated debt and accounts receivable, are already listed on the firm's balance sheet. But other obligations, such as contracts for future sales or purchases, are not. Although transaction exposure is often included under accounting exposure, it is more properly a cash flow exposure and, hence, part of economic exposure.

Real operating exposure is the possibility that currency fluctuations, together with price changes, can alter the expected amounts or variability of a company's future revenue and cost streams—in short, its operating cash flows. Measuring operating exposure requires a longer-term perspective, one which views the firm as an ongoing operation whose cost and price competitiveness will be affected by exchange rate changes.

The measurement of economic exposure is made especially difficult because it is impossible to assess the effects of an exchange rate change without simultaneously considering the impact on cash flows of the underlying relative rates of inflation in each currency. It is also necessary to consider the extent to which exchange rate changes cause *relative* price changes—that is, changes in the ratio of prices of individual goods, like oil, to the general level of prices. For example, in 1974 the price of gas fuels rose by 33.6 percent while the wholesale price index increased by only 8.0 percent. Thus, the year was characterized both by general inflation and by an increase in the relative price of oil. As you might expect, the press frequently confused the two events and attributed the effects of an increase in the relative price of oil to inflation.

The distinction between inflation and relative price changes is important because both affect exchange rates, but they have vastly different implications for exchange risk. As we shall show, a dramatic change in an exchange rate accompanied by an equal change in the price level will not alter real cash flows as long as relative prices remain constant.

Inflation and Exchange Rates

Let's begin by holding relative prices constant and looking only at the effects of general inflation. This means that if the inflation rate is 10 percent, the

Real long-run exchange risk is largely the risk associated with relative price changes brought about by currency changes.

price of every good in the economy rises by 10 percent. In addition, we initially assume that all goods are traded in a competitive world market without transaction costs, tariffs, or taxes of any kind. Given these conditions, economic theory tells us that the law of one price must prevail; that is, the price of any good, measured in a common currency, must be equal in all countries.

If the law of one price holds, and if there is no variation in the relative prices of goods or services, then the rate of change in the exchange rate must equal the difference between the inflation rates in the two countries. Purchasing power parity does not imply that exchange rate changes will necessarily be small or easy to forecast. If a country has high and unpredictable inflation, like Argentina, then the country's exchange rate will also fluctuate randomly.

Nonetheless, without relative price changes, a multinational company faces no real operating exchange risk. As long as the firm avoids contracts fixed in foreign currency terms, its foreign cash flows will vary with the foreign rate of inflation. Because the exchange rate also depends on the difference between the foreign and the domestic rates of inflation, the movement of the exchange rate exactly cancels the change in the foreign price level, leaving dollar cash flows unaffected.

Of course, the above conclusion does not hold if the firm enters into contracts fixed in terms of the foreign currency. Examples of such contracts are fixed-rate debt, long-term leases, labor contracts and rent. However, the risk introduced by entering into fixed contracts is not exchange risk; it is inflation risk. For instance, an Argentine firm with fixed-rate debt in pesos faces the same risk as the subsidiary of an American firm with peso debt. If the rate of inflation in Argentina declines, the real interest cost of the debt rises and the real cash flow of both companies falls. The solution to the problem of inflation risk is to avoid writing contracts fixed in nominal terms in countries with unpredictable inflation. If the contracts are indexed, and if purchasing power parity holds, exchange risk is eliminated.

Relative Prices and Exchange Rates

In general, exchange rate changes occur in conjunction with relative price changes. But unless exchange rate changes are themselves the cause of relative price changes, what is usually termed "exchange risk" may be just the risk of relative price changes within and between countries. For exam-

ple, the revaluations of the mark and the yen in the late 1970s are often blamed for shifting the export mix of West German and Japanese companies toward more technologically sophisticated and capital-intensive products. It is more likely, however, that these changes were dictated by technological advances in Germany and Japan which reduced capital costs relative to labor costs. By making German and Japanese goods more competitive, such advances were largely responsible both for the shift in exports and for the appreciation of the yen and mark.

The above example notwithstanding, changes in exchange rates can cause relative price changes. During the late 1970s worldwide demand for Swiss franc-denominated assets caused the Swiss franc to appreciate against the dollar by more than the inflation differential between the two countries. As a result, Swiss watchmakers were squeezed. Because of competition from Japanese companies, Swiss firms could not significantly raise the dollar price of watches sold in the United States. Yet, at the same time, the *dollar* cost of Swiss labor was rising because the franc wage rate remained unchanged, while the franc was appreciating against the dollar.

Real long-run exchange risk, then, is largely the risk associated with relative price changes that are brought about by currency changes. Such relative price changes are most likely to occur when a government intervenes to control prices and/or wages. For example, devaluations are generally accompanied by the imposition of price controls. These controls can benefit a multinational corporation that has a foreign subsidiary producing locally for export; the cost of wages and other local inputs remains largely unchanged while the devaluation makes exports more competitive, or even allows the subsidiary to raise prices abroad. By contrast, a subsidiary with extensive domestic sales will likely be hurt by price controls. For instance, following the recent floating of the peso, the Mexican government threatened "price gougers" with jail sentences. In this circumstance, price gougers were domestic and foreign businessmen raising prices to offset the effect of the devaluation on their cash flow.

To summarize, the economic impact of a currency change on a firm depends on whether the exchange rate is fully offset by the difference in inflation rates or whether, because of price controls, a shift in monetary policy, or some other reason, the exchange rate change results in relative price changes. It is these relative price changes that ultimately affect the value of the firm.

Measuring Economic Exposure

A hypothetical example illustrates our proposed procedure for measuring economic exposure to currency risk.[1] It also shows how the conventional accounting measure of translation exposure fails to represent real operating exposure.

Spectrum Manufacturing AB is the wholly-owned Swedish affiliate of a U.S. multinational industrial plastics firm. It manufactures patented sheet plastic in Sweden. Sixty percent of its output is currently sold in Sweden and the remaining 40 percent is exported to other European countries. Spectrum uses only Swedish labor in its manufacturing process, but sources its raw material both locally and overseas. The effective Swedish tax rate on corporate profits is 40 percent. The annual depreciation charge on plant and equipment is Skr 900,000. In addition, Spectrum AB has Skr 3 million in debt outstanding, with interest payable at 10 percent annually.

Based on the current exchange rate of Skr 4 = $1, Spectrum's projected sales, costs, after-tax income, and cash flow for the coming year are presented in Exhibit 1. All sales are invoiced in kronor.

EXHIBIT 1
Summary of Projected Operations for Spectrum Manufacturing AB: Base Case

	Units (hundred thousand)	Unit Price (Skr)	Total (Skr)
Domestic sales	6	20	12,000,000
Export sales	4	20	8,000,000
Total revenue			**20,000,000**
Local labor (man-hours)	1.5	40	6,000,000
Local material	8	3	2,400,000
Imported material	6	4	2,400,000
Total operation expenditure			**10,800,000**
Net operating income		Skr	9,200,000
Overhead expenses			3,500,000
Interest on krona debt (@ 10%)			300,000
Depreciation			900,000
Total other expenses			**4,700,000**
Net profit before tax		Skr	4,500,000
Income tax @ 40%			1,800,000
Profit after tax		**Skr**	**2,700,000**
Add back depreciation			900,000
Net cash flow in kronor		Skr	3,600,000
Net cash flow in dollars (Skr 4 = $1)		**$**	**900,000**

1. This example is based on a more extensive one presented in Alan C. Shapiro, *Multinational Financial Management* (Boston: Allyn & Bacon, 1982) pp. 132-140.

Accounts receivable equal one-fourth of annual sales; i.e., the average collection period is ninety days. Inventory is carried at direct cost, valued on a last-in, first-out (LIFO) basis, and also equals 90 days' worth of sales. Accounts payable average 10 percent of sales while cash equaling 50 percent of sales is typically held. Spectrum's balance sheet (before any exchange rate change) is as shown in Exhibit 2.

EXHIBIT 2 **Balance Sheet for Spectrum Manufacturing AB (Skr): Base Case**	Assets		Liabilities	
	Cash	1,000,000	Accounts payable	2,000,000
	Accts Rec.	5,000,000	Long-term debt	3,000,000
	Inventory	2,700,000	Total liabilities	5,000,000
	Net fixed assets	10,000,000	Equity	13,700,000
	Total assets	**18,700,000**	**Total liabilities & equity**	**18,700,000**

Spectrum's accounting exposure. To contrast the economic and accounting approaches to measuring exposure, let's assume that the Swedish krona devaluates 20 percent, from Skr 4 = $1 to Skr 5 = $1. According to the current rate method of accounting for currency translation, as mandated by FAS #52, Spectrum would have to recognize a loss of $935,000. (See Exhibit 3.)

EXHIBIT 3 **Impact of Krona Devaluation on Spectrum AB's Financial Statements**	Assets and Liabilities	Kronor	U.S. dollars before krona devaluation (Skr 4 = $1)	U.S. dollars after krona devaluation (Skr 5 = $1)
	Cash	1,000,000	250,000	200,000
	Accounts	5,000,000	1,250,000	1,000,000
	Inventory	2,700,000	675,000	540,000
	Net fixed assets	10,000,000	2,500,000	2,000,000
	Total assets Skr	**18,700,000**	**$4,675,000**	**$3,740,000**
	Accounts payable	2,000,000	500,000	400,000
	Long-term debt	3,000,000	750,000	600,000
	Equity	**13,700,000**	**3,425,000**	**2,740,000**
	Total liabilities plus equity Skr	18,700,000	$4,675,000	$3,740,000
	Translation gain (loss)			**$(935,000)**

Spectrum's economic exposure. On the basis of the information currently available, it is impossible to anticipate the economic impact of the krona devaluation. Therefore, two different scenarios have been constructed, and Spectrum's economic exposure has been calculated under each. These two scenarios are based on the following assumptions:

1. All variables remain the same.
2. Partial increases in prices, costs, and volume.

Scenario 1: All variables remain the same.

If all prices remain the same (in kronor) and sales volume does not change, then Spectrum's krona cash flow will stay at Skr 3,600,000. At the new exchange rate, this equals 3,600,000 x .2 dollars, or $720,000. Then the net loss in dollar operating cash flow the first year can be calculated as follows:

First-year cash flow (Skr 4 = $1)	$900,000
First-year cash flow (skr 5 = $1)	720,000
Net loss from devaluation	**$180,000**

Moreover, this loss will continue until relative prices adjust. Part of this loss, however, will be offset by the $150,000 gain that will be realized at the end of year 3 when Skr 3 million loan is repaid (3 million x .05)[2] If a three-year adjustment process is assumed, then the present value of the economic loss from operations associated with the krona devaluation, using a 15 percent discount rate, equals $312,420 as follows:

reduction in dollar profits. Note, however, that the economic loss of $312,420 contrasts markedly with the accounting recognition of a $935,000 loss under FAS #52.

Scenario 2: Partial increases in prices, costs, and volumes.

In reality, of course, prices, costs, volumes, and the input mix are likely to adjust somewhat. It is assumed here that the sales price at home rises by 10 percent to Skr 22 while the export price is raised to Skr 24, still providing a competitive advantage in dollar terms over foreign products. This results in a 20 percent increase in domestic sales and a 15 percent increase in export sales.

Total input prices are assumed to go up by 15 percent while the dollar price of imported material stays at its earlier level. This leads to some substitution of imported for domestic goods. Overhead expenses rise by only 10 percent because some components of this account, such as rent and local taxes, are fixed in value.

The net result of all these adjustments is an operating cash flow of $1,010,800, a *gain* of $110,800 over the predevaluation level of $900,000. (Ex. 4.)

From this translated operating cash flow of $1,010,800 must be subtracted, in the first year, the $388,890 cash outflow associated with higher working capital requirements. (The derivation of this figure is presented in Exhibit 5.) Inventory requirements increase to reflect the combination of an 18

Present Year	Postdevaluation cash flow		Predevaluation cash flow		Change in cash flow		15% Present value factor		Value
	(1)	–	(2)	=	(3)	x	(4)	=	(5)
1	$720,000		$900,000		-$180,000		.870		-$156,600
2	720,000		900,000		- 180,000		.756		- 136,080
3	870,000[a]		900,000		- 30,000		.658		- 19,740
Net loss									**-$312,420**

[a] Includes a gain of $150,000 on loan repayment.

This loss is primarily due to the inability of Spectrum to raise its sales price. The resulting constant krona profit margin translates into a 20 percent

percent higher unit sales volume and a 17 percent increase in unit costs, for an overall increase of 21 percent in krona terms (.18 x 1.17), or Skr 568,449.

2. For a systematic approach to calculating the after-tax costs of borrowing in foreign currencies, see Alan C. Shapiro (1975), "Evaluating Financing Costs for Multinational Subsidiaries," *Journal of International Business Studies*, Fall, pp. 25-32.

EXHIBIT 4
Summary of Projected Operations for Spectrum Manufacturing AB: Scenario 2

	Units (hundred thousand)	Unit Price (Skr)	Total (Skr)
Domestic sales	7.2	22	15,840,000
Export sales	4.6	24	11,040,000
Total revenue			**26,880,000**
Local labor (man-hours)	1.77	46	8,142,000
Local material	10.62	3.45	3,664,000
Imported material	6.2	5	3,100,000
Total operation expenditure			**14,906,000**
Net operating income		Skr	11,974,000
Overhead expenses			3,850,000
Interest on krona debt (@ 10%)			300,000
Depreciation			900,000
Total other expenses			**5,050,000**
Net profit before tax		Skr	6,924,000
Income tax @ 40%			2,769,000
Profit after tax		**Skr**	**4,154,000**
Add back depreciation			900,000
Net cash flow in kronor		Skr	5,054,000
Net cash flow in dollars (Skr 5 = $1)		**$**	**1,010,800**

EXHIBIT 5
Working Capital Requirements (Skr): Scenario 2

	Predevaluation	Postdevaluation	Net Change
Cash (5% of Sales)	1,000,000	1,344,000	344,000
Accounts receivable (25% of sales)	5,000,000	6,720,000	1,720,000
Inventory (25% of direct cost)	2,700,000	3,268,449[a]	568,449
Accounts payable	2,000,000	2,688,000	688,000
Net working capital	**Skr 6,700,000**	**Skr 8,644,449**	**Skr 1,944,449**
Increase in working capital, in dollars (Skr 5 = $1)			$388,890

[a] Sales volume rises by 180,000 units requiring an additional 45,000 units of inventory at a cost of Skr 568,449.

Even in cases where significant exchange risk exists, it may not be in shareholders' interest to hedge.

Over the next three years, Spectrum's cash flows and its economic value will change as follows:

Year	Postdevaluation cash flow	Predevaluation cash flow	Change in cash flow	15% Present value factor	Present Value
	(1) −	(2) =	(3) x	(4) =	(5)
1	$ 621,910[a]	$900,000	−$278,090	.870	−$241,938
2	1,010,800	900,000	110,800	.756	83,765
3	1,160,800[b]	900,000	260,000	.658	171,080
Net gain					**$12,907**

[a] Includes $388,890 working capital outflow.
[b] Includes $150,000 gain on loan repayment.

Thus, under the latter scenario, the economic value of the firm actually *increases* by $12,907 as a result of the devaluation. The gain on loan repayment and on operating cash flows just manages to offset the additional investment required in working capital.

These two scenarios demonstrate the sensitivity of a firm's economic exposure to assumptions about its price elasticity of demand, its ability to adjust the input mix as relative costs change, its pricing flexibility, its use of local currency financing, and its ratio of net working capital to sales. Most important, though, this example makes clear the potentially large disparity between accounting-based measures of exchange gains or losses and the real impact of currency changes on a firm's value.

The Hedging Decision

The preceding analysis implies that real economic exposure to exchange risk occurs under two general sets of circumstances:

1. Some cash flows are fixed in foreign currency terms.
2. Exchange rate changes cause relative price changes.

Of the two sources of risk, the second is the more significant. For one thing, in countries with high and variable inflation, fixed currency contracts are avoided as a matter of course; even taxes are indexed. Second, most of the month-to-month variation in exchange rates is unrelated to differential inflation rates. On the basis of a detailed study of 23 pairs of countries, Richard Roll reported that less than 10 percent of the monthly variation in any ex-

change rate is due to inflation. The 10 percent figure, furthermore, is for pairs of countries like the United States and Argentina, where the annual inflation differential is close to 100 percent. For pairs like the United States and Germany, where the inflation differential is small, inflation typically accounts for less than 2 percent of the monthly variation in exchange rates. In other words, there is a very strong relationship between exchange rate changes and relative price changes. Although Roll's work does not allow him to determine whether exchange rate changes cause relative price changes or vice versa, it seems clear that currency appreciations or depreciations are likely to affect relative prices—at least in the short run.[3]

To apply our theory of exchange risk to the individual firm requires a forecast of the relation between exchange rates, relative prices, and the company's real cash flow. Management should begin by considering possible future currency changes that would affect its business. For example, a U.S. firm selling products in West Germany might examine the possibility of a deutsche mark revaluation or a dollar devaluation. (Incidentally, such a firm might find that a devaluation of the French franc would affect its sales as strongly as would a change in the dollar-deutsche mark exchange rate, since France is West Germany's major trading partner.) Next, for each scenario, the projected effect of the devaluation or revaluation on relative prices and hence on the company's sales, costs, and capital requirements should be estimated, thus enabling management to derive an estimate of cash flow.

Then, by assigning probabilities to each of the scenarios, the expected level of cash flow and its variability can be estimated. Finally, the manager should evaluate how a foreign government is likely

3. See Richard Roll, "Violations of the Law of One Price and Their Implications for Differentially Denominated Assets," in Marshall Sarnet and George Szego, eds. *International Finance and Trade* , Vol. I, (Cambridge, Mass: Ballinger, 1979).

to respond to a devaluation or revaluation of its currency. Will price controls be imposed? If controls are introduced, will they be general or will certain goods be exempted? Will the local government act to prevent repatriation of profits, thereby reducing the parent's cash flow?

Obviously, the range of possible scenarios is infinite and the costs of gathering the required information can be substantial. Consequently, in selecting scenarios to evaluate, management should concentrate its efforts on those scenarios that have a high probability of occurrence and would also have a major impact on the firm.

The Value of Hedging

Given a forecast of the future relation between real cash flows and exchange rates, management must next decide whether to hedge or take other action to reduce exchange risk. As shown earlier, the real impact of nominal currency changes will probably be less severe than is generally supposed, primarily because of the offsetting effects of inflation. Even in cases where significant exchange risk exists, however, it may not be in shareholders' interest to hedge for several reasons. First, shareholders can reduce the risk of currency fluctuation by holding well-diversified portfolios. Second, shareholders may actually prefer that a portion of their returns be denominated in a foreign currency. If an investor purchases Japanese goods, his overall risk will be reduced by having yen inflows to match his yen outflows. Finally, hedging is expensive. Steven Kohlhagen estimates that a simple strategy of forward hedging in the major currencies costs about 0.65 percent per year.[4] And borrowing in local currency, when points and other fees are considered, is likely to be even more costly than forward cover. Of course, there is often no alternative to local borrowing because active forward markets exist in less than a dozen currencies.

It is also important to recognize that management cannot hedge against *anticipated* movements in exchange rates. Studies by Cornell and others show that the anticipated change in the exchange rate is reflected in the forward premium and the interest rate differential.[5] In the case of Mexico, for instance, the one year forward discount in the fu-

tures market was close to 100 percent just before the peso was floated.

Local borrowing and forward covering are not the only means of reducing exchange risk. Other standard techniques for hedging against possible devaluation are these:

- Reducing levels of local currency cash and marketable securities.
- Delaying payment of accounts payable.
- Invoicing exports in foreign currency and imports in local currency.
- Tightening trade credit in local currency.

Such techniques, however, are vastly overrated. If a devaluation is unlikely, they are costly and inefficient ways of doing business. If a devaluation is expected, as in the recent case of Mexico, then the cost of using the techniques, like the cost of local borrowing, rises to reflect the anticipated devaluation. Just prior to the Mexican devaluation, for example, every company in Mexico was trying to delay peso payments. Of course, this cannot produce a net gain because one company's payable is another company's receivable. As another example, if one company wants peso trade credit, another must offer it. Assuming that both the borrower and the lender are rational, a deal will not be struck until the interest cost rises to reflect the expected decline in the peso.

A company can benefit from the above strategies only to the extent that it can estimate the probability and timing of a devaluation with greater accuracy than the general market. Attempting to profit from foreign exchange forecasting, however, is speculating, not hedging. The hedger is well-advised to assume that the market knows as much as he does. Those who feel that they have superior information will choose to speculate, but this activity should not be confused with hedging.

Under some circumstances it is possible for a company to benefit at the expense of the local government without speculating. If exchange controls are not imposed to prevent capital outflows and if hard currency can be acquired at the official exchange rate, then money can be moved out of the country via intercompany payments. For instance, a subsidiary can speed payment of intercompany accounts payable, make immediate purchases from other subsidiaries, or speed remittances to the par-

4. See Steven W. Kohlhagen, "Evidence on the Cost of Forward Cover in a Floating System," *Euromoney* (September, 1975), pp. 138-141.

5. See Bradford Cornell, "Spot Rates, Forward Rates and Market Efficiency," *Journal of Financial Economics* 5, (1977), pp. 55-65.

Most companies earn their keep because of their superior marketing, production, organization, and technological skills.

ent. Unfortunately, governments are not unaware of these tactics. During a currency crisis, when hard currency is scarce, the local government can be expected to block such transfers, or at least make them more expensive.

Hedging Objectives

Management's decision about the specific financial hedging tactics and strategy to pursue will largely be determined by its objectives. These objectives, in turn, should reflect management's view of the world, particularly its beliefs about how markets work. Before setting its own hedging objectives, management should ask itself the key question posed by Gunter Dufey: "Could we profitably exist as a purely financial institution?"[6] Honest introspection would reveal that most companies earn their keep because of their superior marketing, production, organization, and technological skills.

There are two principal implications of this doctrine of "comparative advantage" for exchange risk management:

1. *The principal exposure management goal of financial executives should be to arrange their firm's financial affairs in such a way as to minimize the real (as opposed to accounting) effects of exchange rate changes, subject to the costs of such rearrangements.*
2. *The major burden of exchange risk management must fall on the shoulders of marketing and production executives. They deal in imperfect product and factor markets where their specialized knowledge provides them with a real advantage; that is, they should be able consistently to outperform their competitors in the markets in which they operate because of their superior knowledge.*

Managing Exchange Risk

As we argued earlier, in order for a devaluation or revaluation to significantly affect a firm's value, it must lead to changes in the relative prices of either the firm's inputs, or the products bought or sold in various countries. To the extent that exchange rate changes do bring about relative price changes, the firm's competitive situation will be altered. As a result, management may wish to adjust its production process or its marketing mix to accommodate the new set of relative prices. Conceptually, this is no different than the adjustment to changing relative prices within a country—for example, the adjustment to higher energy costs.

By making the necessary marketing and production revisions, the firm can either counteract the harmful effects of, or capitalize on the opportunities presented by, a currency appreciation or depreciation. To show how, we introduce the concept of the real exchange rate. The *real* exchange rate is defined as the *nominal*, or actual, exchange rate adjusted for relative inflation rates. Thus, if changes in the nominal rate are fully offset by changes in the relative price levels between the two countries, the real exchange rate remains unchanged. Only deviations from PPP result in a change in the real rate.

This distinction between the nominal exchange rate and the real rate has important implications for those marketing and production decisions that bear on exchange risk. As we saw, nominal currency changes that are fully offset by differential inflation (and thus do not lead to relative price changes between economic sectors) do not entail a material degree of real exchange risk for a firm, unless that firm has major contractual agreements in the foreign currency. A real devaluation or revaluation of a particular currency, however, can strongly affect the competitive positions of local firms and their foreign competitors.

The appropriate response to an anticipated or an actual change in a real exchange rate depends crucially on the length of time that real change is expected to persist. For example, following a real home currency revaluation, an exporter has to decide whether and how much to raise its foreign currency prices. If the change were expected to be temporary, and if regaining market share would be expensive, the exporter would probably prefer to maintain its foreign currency prices at existing levels. While this would mean a temporary reduction in unit profitability, the alternative—raising prices now and reducing them later when the real exchange rate declined—could be even more costly. A longer-lasting change in the real exchange rate, however, would probably lead the firm to raise its foreign currency prices, at the expense of losing some export sales. Assuming a still more permanent shift, management might choose to build production facilities overseas.

6. "Corporate Financial Policies and Floating Exchange Rates," a paper presented at the meeting of the International Fiscal Association in Rome, October 14, 1974.

In the absence of government intervention in the foreign exchange markets, most real exchange rate changes are likely to be transitory. Permanent changes in real exchange rates are usually due to the pegging activities of central banks. Hence, in selecting appropriate exchange risk management strategies, the focus must be on the present and anticipated objectives and policies of the central banks in question. Predicting a government's likely response requires an evaluation of the key political decision-makers, their often conflicting economic goals, the economic consequences of a currency change on these goals, the ruling party's ideology, and internal and external political pressures. A persistent problem for forecasters in a system of "managed floating" such as currently exists is that there is no certainty about the desired currency level. In fact, government officials often deliberately maintain confusion in order to increase the uncertainty facing currency traders and thereby prevent or defer speculative "attacks" on their currencies.

The lack of clear-cut exchange rate objectives is due primarily to conflicting economic goals. Devaluation may stimulate exports and temporarily increase employment, but it is also likely to fuel inflation. On the other hand, a revaluation, while reducing the competitiveness of exports, also helps to reduce inflation by lowering the home currency cost of imported goods and services.

In the remainder of this section, we offer a set of currency management policies for dealing with those changes in nominal exchange rates that lead to relative price changes within or between countries.

Marketing Management of Exchange Risk

One of the international marketing manager's tasks should be to identify the likely effects of an exchange rate change and then act on them by adjusting pricing, product, credit, and market selection policies. Unfortunately, multinational marketing executives have generally ignored exchange risk management. Marketing programs are almost always "adjusted" only *after* changes in exchange rates. Yet the design of a firm's marketing strategy under conditions of home currency (HC) fluctuation presents considerable opportunity for gaining competitive leverage.

Market selection. Major strategic questions for an exporter are the markets in which to sell and the relative marketing support to devote to each market. From an exposure point of view, a key consideration is the impact of currency changes on the revenue to be gained from future sales in individual countries. Marketing management must take into account its economic exposure and selectively adjust the marketing support, on a nation-by-nation basis, to maximize long-term profit.

It is also necessary to consider the issue of market segmentation within individual countries. A firm that sells differentiated products to more affluent customers may not be harmed as much by a foreign currency devaluation as a mass marketer. On the other hand, following a currency devaluation, a firm that sells primarily to upper income groups may find it is now able to penetrate mass markets abroad.

Market selection and market segmentation provide the basic parameters within which a company may adjust its marketing mix over time. In the short term, however, neither of these two basic strategic choices can be altered in reaction to actual or anticipated currency changes. Instead, the firm must select certain tactical responses such as adjustments of pricing, promotional and credit policies. In the long run, if deviations from PPP persist, the firm will have to revise its marketing strategy.

Pricing strategy. A firm selling overseas should follow the standard economic proposition of setting the price that maximizes dollar (HC) profits (by equating marginal revenues and marginal costs). In making this determination, however, profits should be translated using the forward exchange rate that reflects the true expected dollar (HC) value of the receipts upon collection.

In the wake of a foreign currency devaluation, a firm selling in that market should consider opportunities to increase the foreign currency prices of its products. The problem, of course, is that producers in the country whose currency has devalued will now have a competitive cost advantage. They can use that advantage to expand their market share by maintaining, or increasing only slightly, their local currency prices. In any event, the existence of local competitors will limit an exporter's ability to recoup dollar profits by raising foreign currency selling prices.

At best, therefore, an exporter can raise its product prices by the extent of the devaluation. At worst, in an extremely competitive situation, the exporter is forced to absorb a reduction in home currency revenues equal to the percentage decline in the exchange rate. In the most likely case, foreign currency prices can be raised somewhat and the exporter will make up the difference through a lower profit margin on its foreign sales.

Under conditions of a real home currency devaluation, it follows that exports will gain a competitive price advantage on the world market. However, a company does not have to reduce export prices by the full amount of the devaluation. Instead, it has the option of increasing unit profitability (price skimming) or expanding its market share (penetration pricing). The decision is influenced by such factors as whether this change is likely to persist, economies of scale, the cost structure of expanding output, consumer price sensitivity, and the likelihood of attracting competition if high unit profitability is obvious.

The greater the price elasticity of demand, the greater is the incentive to hold down prices and thereby expand sales and revenues. Similarly, if significant economies of scale exist, it is generally worthwhile to hold down price, expand demand, and thereby lower unit production costs. The reverse is true if economies of scale are nonexistent or if the price elasticity is low.

In the case of pricing after devaluation, a domestic firm facing strong import competition may have much greater latitude in pricing. It then has the choice of potentially raising prices consistent with import price increases, or of holding prices constant in order to improve market share. Again, the strategy depends on such variables as economies of scale and consumer price sensitivity.

In early 1978, for instance, General Motors and Ford took advantage of price increases on competitive foreign autos to raise prices on their Chevette and Pinto models. The prices of those small cars had previously been held down, and even reduced, in an attempt to combat the growing market share of West German and Japanese imports. However, the declining value of the U.S. dollar relative to the deutsche mark and yen led the West German and Japanese auto makers to raise their dollar prices. The price increases by the U.S. manufacturers, which were less than the sharp rise in import prices, were expected to improve profit margins while keeping U.S. cars competitive with their foreign rivals.

Of course, if a domestic firm is operating with weak or nonexistent import competition, then it will have little chance to adjust its prices after devaluation and its pricing latitude will be restricted. To improve its competitive position *vis-a-vis* other domestic producers, the firm would have to substitute local for imported materials and services.

Advance planning in pricing is particularly important if price controls are expected to follow a devaluation. Foreign firms are especially susceptible to such controls because they face subtle pressures to be "good corporate citizens."

Several options are available to a firm to counteract these expected controls. One possibility is to set prices at an artificially high level and accept the resulting loss of market share. If devaluation occurs and price controls are imposed, the firm is then in a better position to continue operating profitably.

An alternative approach is to raise list prices but continue selling at existing prices—in effect, to sell at a discount. This mitigates the problem of competing with higher prices before a devaluation or a similar change in the pricing environment (such as increased inflation). Price controls can be avoided by eliminating part or all of the discount.

Another common means of circumventing price controls is to develop new products that are only slightly altered versions of the firm's existing goods, and then sell them at higher prices. This method is particularly convenient for a multinational company already dealing in a range of different products with a continual stream of updated or new merchandise.

Such anticipatory or "preactive" planning is especially important for firms that are heavy users of imported materials. Companies unable to raise their prices when production costs increase will have the unpleasant choice of producing inferior merchandise, cutting back on service, sustaining considerable losses, or dropping unprofitable product lines.

Promotional strategy. Promotional strategy should similarly take into account anticipated exchange rate changes. A key issue in any marketing program is the size of the promotional budget for advertising, personal selling, and merchandising. Promotional decisions should explicitly build in exchange risks, especially in allocating budgets among countries.

A firm exporting its products after a domestic devaluation may well find that the return per dollar expenditure on advertising or selling is increased as a function of the product's improved price positioning. The exporter may also find it has improved its ability to "push" the product based on the option of greater distribution margins or consumer dealing.

Devaluation may well be the time to reevaluate the mix of advertising, personal selling, and merchandising because the firm has more market leverage. A foreign currency devaluation, on the other hand, is likely to reduce the return on marketing expenditures and requires a more fundamental shift in the firm's product policy.

Product strategy. Exchange rate fluctuations may affect the timing of the introduction of new products. In periods of currency uncertainty, distributors may be reluctant to accept the risks associated with introducing new products, which involves up-front investment in marketing costs, especially for inventories and advertising. The firm must devise a strategy for new product introduction and market selection as a function of its relative exposure in different markets. Because of the competitive price advantage, the period after a home currency devaluation or foreign currency revaluation may be the ideal time to develop a brand franchise.

Similarly, decisions to eliminate products, as products become obsolete or fall into consumer disfavor, may be influenced by exchange risk considerations. Indeed, companies may continue manufacturing marginally profitable goods domestically if a home currency devaluation is expected. Conversely, they might stop producing those goods if a home currency revaluation or foreign currency devaluation is likely.

Exchange rate fluctuations also affect *product line decisions*. Related to the issue of market segmentation, a firm pursuing foreign markets after a home currency (HC) devaluation will potentially be able to expand its product line and cover a wider spectrum of consumers in the foreign market. Following devaluation, a domestic firm facing import competition in its local market may have the option to emphasize and place greater marketing support behind the top of its line (which generally has a higher margin) because it will be at a competitive price advantage.

Following a foreign currency devaluation or home currency revaluation, a firm may have to reorient its product line completely and target it to a higher-income, more quality-conscious, less price-sensitive constituency. Volkswagen, for example, achieved its export prominence on the basis of low-priced, stripped-down, low-maintenance cars. Its product line was essentially limited to one model: the relatively unchanging "Bug." The appreciation of the deutsche mark relative to the dollar in the early 70s, however, effectively ended Volkswagen's ability to compete primarily on the basis of price. The company lost over $310 million in 1974 alone attempting to maintain its market share by lowering deutsche mark prices.

To compete in the long run, Volkswagen was forced to revise its product line and sell relatively high-priced cars from an extended product line to middle-income consumers on the basis of quality and styling rather than cost.

Production Management of Exchange Risk

The adjustments discussed so far involve attempts to alter the dollar value of foreign currency revenues. Forward-looking exchange risk management should also consider the possibility of changing the firm's production and product sourcing strategies to reduce its dollar costs.

Input mix. A primary reason for devaluation is to make domestically produced goods more competitive both at home and abroad. A well-managed firm should be searching for ways to substitute domestic for imported inputs, depending on the relative prices involved and the degree of substitution possible. In fact, plants can sometimes be designed to provide added flexibility in making substitutions among various sources of goods. Maxwell House, for instance, can blend the same coffee by using coffee beans from Brazil, the Ivory Coast, and other producers. The added design and construction costs must, of course, be weighed against the advantages of being able to respond to relative price differences among domestic and imported inputs.

Plant location. A firm exporting to a competitive market whose currency has devalued may find that these short-term adjustments are not enough. Unit profitability could decrease so drastically that the firm would have to locate new plants abroad. In many cases, third-country plant locations are a viable alternative. Volkswagen, for example, began producing in Brazil before establishing U.S. production facilities.

Before making a major commitment of resources, however, management should attempt to assess the length of time a particular country will retain its cost advantage. If the local inflationary conditions that led to a nominal exchange rate change are expected to persist, a country's apparent cost advantage may soon reverse itself. In Mexico, for example, the wholesale price index rose 18 percent relative to U.S. prices between January 1969 and May 1976. This led to a 20 percent devaluation of the peso in September 1976. Within one month, though, the Mexican government allowed organized labor to raise its wages by 35 to 40 percent. As a result, the devaluation's effectiveness was nullified and the government was forced to devalue the peso again in less than two months.

Planning. Thus far, the marketing and production strategies advocated are based on knowledge of exchange rate changes. Even if exchange rate changes are unpredictable, however, contingency plans can be made. The first step is to take the currency scenarios described earlier and analyze the the effect on the firm's competitive position under each set of conditions. Using the results of the analysis, the firm should set forth strategies to deal with each of the possibilities. Then, if a currency change actually occurs, the firm is able to quickly adjust its marketing and production strategies in line with the plan. It can immediately begin to redirect its marketing efforts toward those markets in which it has become more competitive. It can also begin to shift its production sourcing and input mix in the directions management has determined would be most cost-effective under the circumstances. If new plant locations are required, planning in advance reduces the lead time involved in site selection, labor recruitment, and contractor and supplier selection.

Financial Management of Exchange Risk

Even after the requisite marketing and production initiatives have been taken, there usually is some residual operating exposure. This cash flow exposure, if it seems large enough to warrant hedging, must be offset by forward contracts or other financial commitments. (In the case of the Spectrum AB subsidiary considered earlier, the residual exposure is probably small enough to call for a "passive" financial approach.) As mentioned earlier, the aim of financial hedging should be to structure the firm's balance sheet in such a way that a reduction in asset earnings due to exchange rate changes is matched by a decrease in the cost of servicing liabilities.

One possibility is to finance the portion of a firm's assets used to create export profits so that any shortfall in operating cash flows due to an exchange rate change is offset by a reduction in the debt service expenses. For example, a firm that has developed a sizable export market should hold a portion of its liabilities in the currency of that country. The portion to be held in the foreign currency depends on the size of the loss in profitability associated with a given exchange rate change. No more definite recommendations are possible because the currency effects will vary from one company to another.

As a case in point, Volkswagen, to hedge its operating exposure, should have used dollar financing in proportion to its net dollar cash flow from U.S. sales, or sold forward the present value of these future net dollar cash flows, or used some combination of the two methods. This strategy would have cushioned the impact of the deutsche mark revaluation which almost brought VW to its knees. But even this strategy would not have provided a perfect hedge. In VW's case, the shifting of some production facilities to a lower-cost country was probably the best solution.

The implementation of a hedging policy is likely to be quite difficult in practice, if only because the specific cash flow effects of a given currency change are hard to predict. Estimating these effects requires an intimate knowledge of the MNC's sales breakdown—domestic versus exports—and the import content of its inputs, along with an understanding of the firm's ability to choose between domestic and foreign input sources and its capacity to shift its market focus. Trained personnel are required to implement and monitor an active hedging program. Consequently, hedging should be undertaken only when the effects of anticipated exchange rate changes are expected to be significant.

Summary and Conclusions

The foregoing analysis leads to three principal conclusions. First, exchange risk cannot be measured in terms of accounting numbers. The proper way to measure exchange risk is to *forecast* the relation between changes in exchange rates and changes in the expected level and variability of real cash flow to the firm. Moreover, in measuring the degree of exchange risk, it is necessary to realize that currency risk and inflation risk are intertwined. For multinationals incurring costs and selling products in foreign countries, the net effect of worldwide devaluations and revaluations may be offset by price level changes in the long run.

Second, traditional hedging techniques are overrated as a means of reducing exchange risk. The cost of routine hedging is high, and last-second attempts to hedge are fruitless because prices will reflect anticipated changes in exchange rates. In addition, because investors can individually manage exchange risk by internationally diversifying their own portfolios, it may not be in the interest of shareholders to hedge.

The third, and perhaps most important, conclusion of this article is that currency risk affects all facets of a company's operations and, therefore, should not be the concern of financial managers alone. Operating managers, in particular, should develop marketing and production initiatives that help to ensure profitability over the long run. They should also devise anticipatory or "preactive" strategic alternatives in order to gain competitive leverage internationally.

The key to effective exposure management is to integrate currency considerations into the general management process. One approach used by a number of multinationals is to establish a committee concerned with managing foreign currency exposure. Besides financial executives, such committees should—and often do—include the senior officers of the company, such as the vice president-international, top marketing and production executives, the director of corporate planning, and the chief executive officer. The most desirable feature of this arrangement is that top executives are exposed to the problems of currency risk management. They can then incorporate exchange rate expectations into their own nonfinancial decisions.

Another way to encourage this process is to hold subsidiary and other operating managers responsible for net operating income targets expressed in the home currency. In this kind of integrated exchange risk program, the role of the financial executive would be threefold: to provide local operating management with forecasts of inflation and exchange rates, to structure evaluation criteria such that operating managers are not rewarded or penalized for the effects of unanticipated real currency changes, and to estimate and hedge whatever real operating exposure remains after the appropriate marketing and production strategies have been put in place.

References

Cornell, Bradford., "Spot Rates, Forward Rates and Market Efficiency." *Journal of Financial Economics* 5, (1977).

Dufey, Gunter., "Corporate Financial Policies and Floating Exchange Rates," a paper presented at the meeting of the International Fiscal Association in Rome, October 14, 1974.

Kohlhagen, Steven W., "Evidence on the Cost of Forward Cover in a Floating System." *Euromoney* (September, 1975).

Roll, Richard., "Violations of the Law of One Price and Their Implications for Differentially Denominated Assets," in Marshall Sarnet and George Szego, eds. *International Finance and Trade* , Vol. I. Cambridge, Mass: Ballinger, 1979.

Shapiro, Alan C., *Multinational Financial Management.* Boston: Allyn & Bacon, 1982.

Shapiro, Alan C., "Evaluating Financing Costs for Multinational Subsidiaries," *Journal of Interntional Business Studies* . Fall, 1975.

Don't Blame Currency Values for Strategic Errors:

Protecting Competitive Position by Correctly Assessing Foreign Exchange Exposure

Christine R. Hekman,
The Claremont Graduate School

One consequence of the progressive globalization of product and financial markets is that large and rapid changes in the international financial environment have become permanent parts of the economic landscape. The heightened volatility of exchange rates is especially disconcerting. In fact, preserving the viability of strategic objectives in the face of constantly shifting currency values is now perhaps corporate management's most formidable challenge.

This challenge presents itself in two ways—one obvious and the other subtle. First is the task of managing currency risk directly. Risk—the possibility that operating and financial results might exceed or fall short of budget—strains management incentives and the planning and evaluation processes. Providing effective insulation of corporate profitability against exchange rate shocks requires major changes in both the measurement and management of currency risks. As I shall argue later, local operating management must be made to participate to a far greater extent in the process, becoming in effect the "front line" of defense by anticipating and responding appropriately to currency shifts.

The second, much less straightforward, challenge is to coordinate the management of currency risk and responses to competitive change. When currency markets are volatile, it is especially difficult to distinguish between losses which are due to temporary currency misalignment and those which signal a more fundamental and permanent loss of competitive position.

Accurate Assessment of Exposure to Foreign Exchange Rate Changes is Central to the Management of Change

The problem is that unexpected financial or operating results which coincide with changes in currency values may either be short-lived and self-correcting, or they may reflect changes in the long-term fundamentals of the business. The larger the swings in the financial markets, the greater the difficulty in distinguishing between the two. By obscuring permanent changes in economic structure and environment, market volatility also obscures the need for strategic response to those changes. Failure to make the proper strategic response is likely to cause competitive failure.

Consider the many U.S. companies—Caterpillar, Upjohn, Archer-Daniels-Midland, and Weyerhauser, to name just a few—which attributed much of their competitive weakness in the first half of the 1980s to the strength of the U.S. dollar. This assumption was often joined to the expectation that dollar decline was imminent and would bring with it improved competitive conditions.

In retrospect, we know that events in the currency markets were, in many cases, partly concealing the beginnings of dramatic shifts in fundamental competitive advantage. If properly recognized, these competitive threats and increased market risks could have been countered by the rapid and complete recognition of losses and the abandonment of old sourcing strategies in favor of lower-cost or more flexible programs. Instead, these companies and many others responded by cutting costs and margins in hopes of protecting their markets—and then simply waited for the dollar's value to fall. Many delayed more fundamental action in hopes of recouping losses when the currency markets returned to "normal."[1] Finally, as dollar strength and operating losses continued, some of these companies realized that the shifts in competitive conditions were permanent and began to transfer production to overseas facilities.

However, the emigration of manufacturing operations was evidently too little and too late. Even as the dollar's decline brought more appropriate currency valuation (although at the price of substantial government intervention), the deterioration in the trade balance continued. To some extent, all of the companies mentioned above have failed to recapture markets lost prior to March 1985, the peak of dollar strength. For example, as a recent *Fortune* article described Caterpillar's performance, "After years of loudly advertising the need for a weaker dollar, the company finally got one—and got clobbered anyway."[2]

The implication is that executives of many U.S. companies exaggerated the effects of dollar strength on operating results and corporate value. Management's failure to assess the true sensitivity of corporate returns to exchange rate changes, and thereby detect changes in the underlying economics of their businesses, has resulted in major strategic miscalculations.

Distinguishing between the effects of exchange rate changes and the effects of shifts in business fundamentals requires more accurate measures of exchange rate effects on corporate operating results and, hence, on market value. An accurate and comprehensive measure of currency effects must accomplish two things: first, it must explicitly incorporate expectations about both near-term and long-term effects of exchange rate levels on corporate performance and competitive position; second, it must reflect operating management's ability, or lack thereof,

to respond to currency shifts within a given industry and competitive environment. (This degree of managerial responsiveness will also depend in large part on the organizational structure and incentives within the firm itself, and should also be taken into account by headquarters in devising a measure of exposure.)

In the pages that follow I shall propose a measurement system which attempts to meet both of these objectives. It assumes that management's primary objective is to maximize the market value of the company (or the price of its shares) by maximizing the present value of future after-tax cash flows. This framework meets the first criterion by capturing the effects on value of the timing and risk of expected cash flows; it thus provides a longer-term as well as a near-term perspective on underlying operating profitability. It meets the second objective by accommodating specific competitive, industry, and organizational factors—information that must be obtained in part from knowledgeable and appropriate sources *outside* of the corporate treasury.

Not surprisingly, the measurement technique will provide an accurate measure of real economic exposure only if it is used correctly. For example, the ability to distinguish between relevant time frames depends on obtaining the right inputs, which translates into asking the right questions. Recognition of competitive and industry constraints requires that information and estimates be obtained from the appropriate personnel—and this means extensive participation by operating and marketing managers. Because exposure to foreign exchange risk is continuously changing, non-financial management must be continually involved in the process of risk assessment and management. Undoubtedly the most effective means of bringing about this involvement would be to incorporate a measure of market value exposure into budgeting, incentive, and compensation systems.

The aim of this article, then, is to offer the outlines of a method for assessing a company's real currency exposure. Having presented this method, I go on to show that this measurement technique can be used by financial management to filter out the effects of currency changes on corporate performance, thereby providing a clearer picture of underlying profitability and competitive position. In this sense,

---

1. This widespread response to dollar strength was reflected in the aggregate deterioration, from 1980 to 1985, of the U.S. international trade deficit from $25 to $124 billion. These numbers represent U.S. manufacturers' losses, in spite of cost and margin cutting efforts, in both domestic markets and hard-won export markets.

2. "Caterpillar's Triple Whammy," *Fortune*, October 27, 1986.

Management's failure to assess the true sensitivity of corporate returns to exchange rate changes, and thereby detect changes in the underlying economics of their businesses, has resulted in major strategic miscalculations.

the identification of currency exposure is the essential first step in a process which leads to a more reliable assessment of current performance and may end with a revision of strategic plans.

Divide and Conquer: Disaggregating Corporate Value into Distinct Components of Risk

Foreign exchange exposure is the sensitivity of a company's market value—that is, the present value of its expected future cash flows—to changes in currency values. Measurement of exposure thus requires a quantification of the extent to which changes in currency values are expected to change the firm's operating cash flow profitability. As suggested above, however, a company's real operating exposure depends critically on how management is able to respond to and offset the effects of currency shifts on profitability. Consequently, a patchwork of corporate responses to changes in currency values must be incorporated within the measure of exposure.

The result of this measurement process is a single measure of the total corporate value which is effectively exposed. It is this exposure that remains to be managed (most likely hedged with financial instruments) *after* the appropriate marketing and operating responses have been made.

More specifically, the method I propose focuses on assessing the *proportion* of a company's total *market* value which is exposed. This proportion, which I call the "aggregate exposure coefficient," captures the relationship between percentage changes in corporate market value and percentage changes in currency values.[3] This exposure coefficient is then applied to total market value, as follows, to yield a measure of total exposure:

Exposed Market Value =
Exposure Coefficient × Total Market Value
The aggregate exposure coefficient of a corporation can be thought of as the weighted sum of the exposure coefficients of each of the individual corporate

assets (with weights that correspond to the proportion of each asset's value to the corporate total). In theory, one could attempt to determine an exposure coefficient for each specific asset or, alternatively, for each cash flow stream expected to be generated by an asset. Because this would clearly be impracticable, my proposed technique follows balance sheet conventions and groups together assets and liabilities with common exposure characteristics (for example, "marketable securities," "inventories," "plant & equipment"). It then assesses the exposure of, and assigns an exposure coefficient to, each of the component groups.

Before turning to the question of how to estimate exposure coefficients for the components, let me first illustrate the final output of such a procedure. Exhibit 1 displays the components of market value exposure of the British subsidiary of a hypothetical U.S. company. The sensitivity of each component of the subsidiary's value is estimated by its exposure coefficient. This coefficient is then applied to an estimate of the total market value to yield a measure of the value of each component which is effectively exposed. The end result for International Manufacturing, as shown in Exhibit 2, is that only $19 million (or 13 percent) of the $150 million market value of the subsidiary's equity is effectively exposed; and thus its aggregate exposure coefficient is .13.

Using the Concept of Natural Hedges to Identify Common Exposure Characteristics

At the first stage, assets are grouped by sector—along lines of either business activity or managerial responsibility. This classification recognizes that basic currency exposure is determined, and is likely to be managed most effectively, at the level of business operations.

Within each division or subsidiary, assets (or associated cash flow streams) can be classified by the degree of their sensitivity to changes in currency values. Assets may be fully exposed, completely unexposed, or partially exposed. In other words, dollar values of the assets may rise and fall in direct propor-

---

3. The approach is similar to the exposure measurement method implied by the Capital Asset Pricing model. There the beta coefficient captures the corporate and environmental complexities which determine the sensitivity of corporate returns to aggregate market activity.

A company's real operating exposure depends critically on how management is able to respond to and offset the effects of currency shifts on profitability.

EXHIBIT 1
Market Value Exposure:

International Manufacturing, Inc.—U.K. Subsidiary Consumer Products Division

	Exposure Coefficient	Book Value	Market Value	Exposed Market Value
Assets				
Cash*	1.0	$ 3.0	$ 3.0	$ 3.0
Marketable Securities*	1.0	8.0	8.0	8.0
Accounts Receivable*	1.0	17.0	17.0	17.0
Inventories**	.5	19.0	22.0	11.0
Value of Market Position, Operating Capacity, and Option on Future Opportunities	.2	53.0	150.0****	30.0
Total Assets		$100.0	$200.0	
Liabilities				
Accounts Payable*	1.0	$ 20.0	$ 20.0	$20.0
Accrued Liabilities*	1.0	6.0	6.0	6.0
Debt*	1.0	24.0	24.0	24.0
Net Worth		50.0	150.0 ***	
Total Liabilities and Net Worth		$100.0	$200.0	

* Assumes book and market values are approximately equal and that these assets and liabilities are nominally determined in sterling.
** Market value of inventories is $22 million.
*** Market value of the equity is $150 million. This may be approximately derived from the market value of equity shares (when available or may be separately valued.
**** Book value of residual assets (plant and equipment) is $53 million. Market value of operating capacity is also a residual; it is total corporate market value ($200) less the market value of other assets ($50).

EXHIBIT 2
Aggregate Market Value Exposure

Value Component	Exposed Market Value
Cash	$ 3.0
Marketable Securities	8.0
Accounts Receivable	17.0
Inventories	11.0
Value of Market Position, Operating Capacity, and Option on Future Opportunities	30.0
Less Financing Offsets	
Accounts Payable	(20.0)
Accrued Expenses and Other	(6.0)
Debt	(24.0)
Net Aggregate Market Value Exposure	$19.0

Note: Component exposures are derived on Exhibit 1.

tion to changes in exchange rates; they may be totally insensitive to changes in exchange rates; or, like most non-financial assets, they may fall somewhere in between.

Consider one extreme—an asset which is completely exposed. A subsidiary's investment in deutschemark C.D.s is a prime example. Changes in the dollar value of this investment correspond in-

versely to changes in the dollar value of the deutschemark. When the dollar value of the deutschemark rises by 10 percent, the dollar value of this investment declines by 10 percent, and vice versa.

An investment in precious metals is an example at the other extreme. The dollar value of a British subsidiary's investment in precious metals is completely insensitive to changes in the dollar value of

The extent to which cash flows can be adjusted in response to currency changes is determined by several factors. Competitive position, sourcing patterns, management organization and incentive systems, and technologies are among the most important.

the pound sterling. Because the prices of metals are typically set in world markets, any decline in the dollar value of sterling should be accompanied by an offsetting increase in the value of the investment in sterling. If the increase in the sterling price fully offsets the reduction in the value of the currency, the dollar value is unchanged, and the investment is thus free of devaluation risk. I call such pricing offsets "natural hedges" because this protection of value follows the natural workings of the global marketplace.

The fundamental difference between these investments is the indirect effect of the change in exchange rates on the prices of the assets in sterling or deutschemarks. The Certificate of Deposit is a nominal or financial asset and is fully exposed because its value is fixed in deutschemarks. The investment in a precious metal is a real asset whose pound sterling value increases to offset completely declines in the dollar value of the British currency. The dollar value of this investment is "naturally hedged" because the sterling prices of these metals conform to a standard global price.

These extreme examples of exposure suggest a natural scheme for grouping cash flows and assets according to common exposure characteristics.

The most obvious group includes nominal or financial investments and liabilities—that is, those components with fixed foreign currency values. Cash, marketable securities, accounts receivable and payable, short-term credit, and fixed-rate bonds are all fully exposed. (Of course, the net exposure of these nominal contracts is the excess of such assets over liabilities.)

The market value of these obligations is the value attached to the expectation of future cash flow. In most cases the market value of this fully exposed group need not be estimated independently, and book value can be used as a proxy. Assuming that market value is close to book value and that these contracts are fully exposed (i.e., the exposure coefficient equals 1.0), exposed market value is equal to book value.

Thus, the gross but useful distinction between financial and real assets assigns an exposure coefficient of unity to several value components. Consequently, coefficients of 1.0 for nominal assets and liabilities are entered on Exhibit 1.

The remaining assets, claims, or obligations are "real" as opposed to financial. This distinction implies that the dollar values of the claims may be stabilized,

to some degree, by a "natural hedge." That is, foreign currency prices, costs, cash flows, and returns may adjust to offset the effect of changes in the dollar's foreign exchange value. The potential for adjustment or price offset implies that these flows may be effectively insensitive or unexposed to exchange changes. They may be totally exposed; or they may be partially exposed and partially hedged. They may even exhibit a reverse exposure in which the dollar value of the asset rises as the dollar strengthens.

Evaluating the Natural Hedging Capacity of Real Assets and Cash Flows—Operating Exposure

The extent to which an asset is naturally hedged depends on the indirect adjustment of cash flow or returns to changes in currency values. This adjustment is a potential offset to changes in the exchange value of the currency. At the aggregate level, this adjustment represents the potential restoration of purchasing power parity. At the corporate level, the adjustment is the potential for maintaining margins or returns (translated into the home currency) in spite of a local currency depreciation.

The extent to which cash flows can be adjusted in response to currency changes is determined by several factors. Competitive position, sourcing patterns, management organization and incentive systems, and technologies are among the most important.

Exhibit 3 illustrates the interplay of these factors by displaying both the operating budgets and the results of operations of six hypothetical British subsidiaries of U.S. companies in an unexpectedly strong dollar environment. The variation in translated operating results demonstrates the effects of the interactions among cost structure, cost exposure, and marketing flexibility.

The first three companies share the same initial budget. They are characterized by relatively low margins and a relatively high proportion of production cost relative to operating expense. The last three companies share a high margin, low production cost profile. Six-month budgets for these companies were set as of June 30, and the deviation of operating results from budget is displayed under each column.

Between June and December, the operating performance of each subsidiary is affected differently by unexpected dollar strength. The budget incorporates a forecast that sterling will weaken and

EXHIBIT 3
Exposure of
Operating Results

	Budget, June 30*	Results, December 31**		
		Grocery Importers, Ltd.	Neighborhood Restaurants, Ltd.	Steel Fabrications, Ltd.
Revenue	£80,000	£80,000	£80,000	£84,211
Costs of Goods Sold	48,000	50,526	48,000	50,526
Gross Margin	32,000	29,474	32,000	33,684
Operating Expenses	15,000	15,000	15,000	15,789
Other Expenses	8,000	8,000	8,000	8,421
Net Income Before Tax	9,000	6,474	9,000	9,474
Tax Expense	4,500	3,237	4,500	4,737
Net Income	£4,500	£3,237	£4,500	£4,737
Target Dollar Income	$6,214	$6,214	$6,214	$6,214
Exchange Rate	$1.3810	$1.3119	$1.3119	$1.3119
Realized Dollar Income		$4,246	$5,904	$6,214
Deviation from Budget		$1,968	$311	$0
(Percent deviation)		31.7%	5.0%	0.0%

	Budget, June 30*	Specialty Chemicals, Ltd.	Domestic Services, Ltd.	Technology Consulting, Ltd.
Revenue	£80,000	£80,000	£80,000	£78,476
Costs of Goods Sold	30,000	31,579	29,429	31,579
Gross Margin	50,000	48,421	50,571	46,897
Operating Expenses	15,000	15,000	14,429	14,429
Other Expenses	8,000	8,000	7,695	7,695
Net Income Before Tax	27,000	25,421	28,448	24,773
Tax Expense	13,500	12,711	14,224	12,387
Net Income	£13,500	£12,711	£14,224	£12,387
Target Dollar Income	$18,643	$18,643	$18,643	$18,643
Exchange Rate	$1.3810	$1.3119	$1.3119	$1.3119
Realized Dollar Income		$16,675	$18,660	$16,250
Deviation from Budget		$1,968	($17)	$2,393
(Percent deviation)		10.6%	−0.1%	12.8%

*Exchange rate forecast June 30 for December 31 is $1.3810; inflation is forecast at 5%.
**Exchange rate realized December 31 is $1.3182; realized inflation rate is 5%.

that British inflation will proceed at a rate of 5 percent. The pound sterling operating targets reflect this inflation forecast; the translated dollar results reflect the currency forecast.

Contrary to forecast, sterling is assumed to weaken by 10 percent, rather than 5 percent, over the intervening six months. At the same time, forecasts for British inflation are assumed to be right on target at 5 percent. (Note that aggregate purchasing power parity is violated in this assumed economic scenario: Sterling weakens by 10 percent externally even though domestic price inflation would suggest external deterioration of only 5 percent.)

The mixed corporate responses to this purchasing power "disequilibrium" are summarized in Exhibit 4. They range between a dollar budget deficit of 31.7 percent for Grocery Importers and a slight budget surplus of 0.1 percent for Domestic Services. Operational sensitivities to unexpected exchange changes, stated as exposure coefficients, range between 6.34 and − .02.

Steel Fabrications' response is especially interesting. With results which are completely insensitive to sterling's decline, it conforms perfectly to the academic Purchasing Power Parity relationship, even though changes in exchange rates and aggregate

EXHIBIT 4
Measures of
Operating Exposure

	Budget Deficit	Unexpected Currency Deterioration	Operating Exposure Coefficient*
Grocery Importers, Ltd.	31.7%	5%	6.34
Neighborhood Restaurants, Ltd.	5.0%	5%	1.00
Steel Fabrications, Ltd.	-0-	5%	-0-
Specialty Chemicals, Ltd.	10.6%	5%	2.12
Domestic Services, Ltd.	−.1%	5%	−.02
Technology Consulting, Ltd.	12.8%	5%	2.56

* The exposure coefficient relates the unexpected change in the local currency's foreign exchange value to the surplus or deficit from operating budget.

price levels do not.

Exhibit 4 also summarizes the results shown in Exhibit 3 by attaching an exposure coefficient to each company's operations. These coefficients represent the proportional relationships between the extent to which dollar strength exceeded expectations (5 percent, in this case) and the percentage deviations from the dollar budget. Grocery Importers' performance was 31.7 percent under budget as a consequence of the 5 percent component of sterling's depreciation which was unexpected. Stated in proportional terms, the company's operating exposure coefficient is 6.34 (31.7/5), reflecting a large sensitivity to the value of the pound sterling. The coefficient implies that changes in the exchange value of sterling are magnified by 6.34 times in the company's returns.

These various results are functions of the assumed responses of costs and revenues to changes in currency markets. The differences in response are, in turn, reflections of underlying differences in the pricing, marketing, production, and sourcing responses that are available to local management. The assumed differences in these characteristics, together with a brief description of the market or operating conditions consistent with each, are outlined on Exhibit 5.

The operating results of Neighborhood Restaurants and Steel Fabrications differ because of their contrasting orientations to global and domestic economic conditions. The restaurant chain's orientation is primarily domestic. Product price, production costs, and operating expenses all mirror the realized rate of British inflation and, thus, come in at budget. As a result, 100 percent of all unexpected exchange rate changes are reflected in the dollar equivalent of the company's income—as captured in an exposure coefficient of 1.0.

In contrast, Steel Fabrications' results are completely determined by the global economy and are independent of domestic conditions. Prices, costs, and expenses reflect the decline of sterling's external exchange value rather than domestic inflation. In fact, this company's returns conform to purchasing power parity because its costs and prices are effectively set outside the domestic economy. This insensitivity to exchange rate fluctuation is reflected in an exposure coefficient of zero.

The exposure characteristics of Grocery Importers are an unfortunate hybrid of those of Neighborhood Restaurants and Steel Fabrications. Production costs conform to purchasing power parity, but output prices do not. Grocery Importers is attempting to introduce a line of imported food items into a traditionally domestic market sector. With branding power and product identification not yet sufficiently strong, product prices are still determined by the company's entrenched competition. Consequently, the prices of Grocery Importers' products conform to budget and to U.K. inflation because they are determined by competitors that source domestically. However, because the company's products are imported, its costs are determined by global economic conditions. Thus, Grocery Importers performs poorly when sterling is unexpectedly weak relative to realized British inflation, but can be expected to outperform its budget at times when sterling is strong relative to local inflation.

For Grocery Importers, then, the effect of exchange rate shifts on its operating deficits or surpluses is very strong; unexpected exchange rate changes, as mentioned earlier, magnify deviations from operating budgets magnify by a factor of 6.34. The strength and direction of the company's risk derives from a sourcing pattern which is extremely different from that of the majority of its competitors.

The difference between Grocery Importers and

EXHIBIT 5
Determinants of
Operating Exposure

	Corporate Operating Characteristics	Global/Domestic Orientation
Grocery Importers, Ltd.	High production costs relative to operating expense; relatively low net margins.	Product price increases mirror British inflation (5%); production costs mirror net extent of currency depreciation (10%). Global costs/domestic revenues.
Neighborhood Restaurants, Ltd.	High production costs relative to operating expense; relatively low net margins.	Product prices, production costs and operating expenses all increase in line with domestic inflation (5%). Domestic costs and revenues.
Steel Fabrications, Ltd.	High production costs relative to operating expense; relatively low net margins.	Product prices, production costs and operating expenses mirror extent of external depreciation of currency (10%). Global costs and revenues.
Specialty Chemicals, Ltd.	High proportion of operating costs relative to production costs; relatively high net margins.	Product price increases mirror British inflation (5%); production costs mirror extent of currency depreciation (10%). Global costs/domestic revenues.
Domestic Services, Ltd.	High proportion of operating costs relative to production costs; relatively high net margins.	Product prices increase with domestic inflation; production cost increases reflect only 60% of domestic inflation; operating expenses reflect only 20% of domestic inflation. Lagging domestic costs/domestic revenues.
Technology Consulting, Ltd.	High proportion of operating costs relative to production costs; relatively high net margins.	Product prices increase by only 60% of domestic inflation increase; production costs increase by 100% of inflation; operating expenses increase by 20% of domestic inflation. Lagging domestic costs/lagging domestic revenues.

Specialty Chemicals illustrates the effects of different profit margins on exposure levels. The domestic/global economic orientation and market and cost responses of these companies are identical. Product prices of both rise by 5 percent as budgeted, but costs increase in step with currency depreciation. However, Specialty Chemical's larger margin (34 percent before taxes as opposed to 11 percent) protects its results from a larger percentage deficit relative to budget. This operating cushion is reflected in Specialty Chemical's reduced sensitivity to exchange rate changes and an exposure coefficient of 2.12.

Technology Consulting and Domestic Services illustrate less than complete responses to domestic inflation. Domestic Service's marketing and pricing management is able to increase product prices along with the 5 percent domestic inflation even though production costs and operating costs rise by only 60 percent and 20 percent, respectively, of the inflationary increase. Domestic Services sources from a sector which is relatively immune to inflationary cost increases. However, the fact that product prices mirror inflation increases suggests that the company's competition sources from more inflation-sensitive sectors. This might imply use of a different technology (that is, more capital intensive production) or access to different types of labor or other inputs.

Technology Consulting's position is the reverse.

Its suppliers are able to demand compensation for the full inflationary increase, while industry product prices rise by only 60 percent of the rate of inflation. This suggests that the competition is sourcing from other, more protected sources. One saving grace is that operating expenses increase by only 20 percent of domestic inflation.

The differences between the cost sensitivities of Domestic Services and Technology Consulting explain the difference in their measured operating coefficients. Whereas the former's results are virtually insensitive to exchange rate changes, currency changes are magnified by 2.5 times in the latter's results.

These last two examples demonstrate two very important aspects of exposure. First, effective exposure depends on how sourcing and marketing patterns compare to that of the competition. For most companies, industry prices are set by competitive conditions, and are based on the sourcing patterns of the competition. Companies which cannot protect dollar returns by adjusting prices may have adopted marketing and production strategies with domestic/global orientations which differ from those adopted by dominant competitors.

The second key point is that the extent of a business's integration in both the local and global economies is an important component of the capacity to offset the effects of exchange rate changes on dollar returns. This integration determines whether changes in prices and costs will conform more closely to changes in currency values, to local inflation, or will be relatively insensitive to changes in the financial environment.

Evaluating the Natural Hedging Capacity of Real Assets and Cash Flows—Value Exposure

Operating exposures, as illustrated by the six examples above, play important roles in determining total value exposure. Such examples demonstrate the direct and indirect effects of exchange rate changes on the achievement of short-term expectations. But, of course, it is the expectation of net cash inflows over the longer term that comprises the largest share of the value of most corporations; and the measurement method described here requires that we attach exposure coefficients to this value of future operations.

Fortunately, the lessons learned by studying operating exposure can be transferred to this problem. The size of the exposure coefficient—the extent to which the dollar values of the flows are sensitive to changes in the currency markets—depends on the relative integration of the business with local and global markets, and on competitive relationships. These factors determine management's flexibility and the extent to which changes in dollar cash flows can be partially or fully offset at the level of local sales and operations.

The exposure of nominal financial assets is, of course, the same regardless of the time horizon. However, a useful estimate of the exposure of real assets—primarily inventories and plant and equipment—requires an extension of the concept of short-term operating exposure to the longer term. This extension is based on a recognition that the underlying value of such assets is the capacity for future production and cash flow that they represent. In a sense, their value is based on longer-term operating forecasts—that is, the expectations of future cash flows.

In effect, then, both inventories and fixed capital represent corporate options on cash flows expected to be realized in the future. The difference between the option represented by inventories from that represented by fixed capital ownership is primarily in the time to realization. The potential cash flow represented by physical inventories, though the amount is still uncertain, will be realized relatively quickly—that is, throughout the inventory turn period.[4] In the intervening period, existing inventory will be transformed into receivables, then into cash; and existing operations will provide inventory replacement. Thus, the value that resides in inventory investments will be transformed into cash within the inventory turn period.

The fundamental source of the exposure of inventory is the time constraint which limits management's ability to adjust margins in response to changes in currency conditions. The exposure coefficient assigned to inventories should reflect constraints on this response. The amount of potential

---

4. Of course, to the extent that sales prices or volumes are uncertain, the amount realized in the disposition of inventory is also uncertain.

exposure is the market value of the inventory; and the effective, or natural, exposure can be quantified simply by multiplying the exposure coefficient by the inventory's market value. This effective market value exposure will change in value directly as the exchange rate changes.

To illustrate this process of evaluating inventory exposure, consider again the case of the British subsidiary of International Manufacturing. The market value of the subsidiary's inventory is $22 million at current exchange rates. Because operating management feels that it can offset a 10 percent sterling devaluation with an average price increase of 5 percent within the inventory turn period (taking into account the kind of analysis of competitive operating exposure illustrated in Exhibits 3 and 4), the degree of sensitivity of inventory is assessed at 0.5.[5] Thus, the expected flexibility in pricing—only half of the $22 million market value is effectively exposed—translates into an effective, fully exposed equivalent of $11 million.

Now let's turn to the remaining corporate resource, the stock of fixed capital—property, plant, equipment, etc. These fixed assets represent capacity for future production and thus an option on future investment and production opportunities. Although this option is generally the largest component of corporate value, it is also the least exposed. The longer-term nature of the option, as well as the pricing and sourcing flexibility inherent in greater lead time, serve to increase the potential for offset to changes in currency values.

In our example of International Manufacturing, this greater flexibility and offset potential is represented by the exposure coefficient of 0.2. This measure implies that management judges that it has the flexibility to adjust price and sourcing over the longer term to offset 80 percent of any change in currency value. Thus, only $30 million, or 20 percent, of the $150 million full market value is effectively exposed.

To see the aggregate effect of the individual component exposures, return to Exhibits 1 and 2. Nominal assets (cash, marketable securities, and accounts receivables) are all fully exposed and thus represent a $28 million exposure. Shorter-term results (in this case, inventories) are exposed by the equivalent of $11 million. And the equivalent of $30 million is exposed over the longer term.

These exposures totalling $69 million are offset, however, by the financial liability exposure of $50 million, resulting in a net aggregate market value exposure of $19 million. The "bottom line" of this analysis is that the foreign exchange exposure of the British subsidiary is equivalent to the foreign exchange exposure of an investment of $19 million in pound sterling cash. And it is this $19 million exposure that should accordingly be managed using traditional hedging instruments or one of the variety of new hedging approaches now appearing on the financial horizon.

Accurate and Continuing Exposure Assessment Supports the Evaluation of Corporate Strategy and Success

At the beginning of this article, I identified two important challenges to management's ability to coordinate responses to currency risk with responses to competitive change. First is the challenge to manage operating exposure as well as conventional translation exposure by enlisting the participation of local operating and marketing management. Second is the preservation of strategic objectives in the face of the fluctuating signals from currency markets. Both require a reliable assessment of the exposure of corporate *economic* (as opposed to accounting) value to the risk of changes in currency values. Furthermore, I argued that achievement of these objectives requires the ability to distinguish short-term and temporary effects of currency market volatility from long-run structural changes that are independent of changes in currency values. The measurement method presented here can be used to gain an accurate assessment of exposure. It can also be used as an early warning system to isolate and identify shifts in underlying competitive position.

The key is to separate the actual effects of exchange rate changes on both current and future operations from the effects predicted by the exposure analysis. For example, when sterling depreciates unexpectedly, International Manufacturing's management should anticipate budget deficits from current operations and reductions in budgeted

---

5. This figure reflects an average currency depreciation and price increase over the period.

profits from future operations. In fact, based on the analysis in the last section, when sterling depreciates by 5 percent more than British/U.S. inflation differential, the value of the British subsidiary should be expected to fall by $95,000 (five percent of the $19 million equivalent exposed market value). That is, the 5 percent excess currency depreciation is expected to produce current and future deficits from the existing budget which amount to roughly $95,000 in present value terms.[6]

If actual results fall short of those predicted, however, and budgets for the future must be adjusted downward by more than anticipated, headquarters should suspect that more than currency shifts are at work. Unexpected and unexplained deficits and downward adjustments of future budgets are, by definition, unrelated to international currency markets. They may be caused by fundamental shifts in costs and opportunities for sourcing or marketing, changes in technologies, or changes in competitors' opportunities or actions. They may also represent fundamental changes in flexibility and therefore in currency exposure. In either case, management attention at the strategic level is required. It is likely that either plans for strategic achievement, or the strategy itself, is in need of revision.

Shifts in sourcing or market opportunities may require changes in supply channels, the relocation of production facilities, the development of new marketing approaches, or investment in new technology. Fundamental changes in currency exposure—that is, in management's flexibility of response—may also require a change in strategy. For example, the increase in exposure caused by a competitor's imitation of technology might be reversed by acquisition of alternative supply sources.

In this sense, the exposure measurement system described in these pages could be an important agent of strategic success if incorporated in information and performance evaluation systems on an ongoing basis. It can provide the necessary perspective by which changes in fundamental competitive and business structure are distinguished from changes in corporate returns caused only by changes in currency values.

6. In practice, effective use of the exposure measurement process to distinguish between currency-related and underlying competitive shifts requires that management anticipate the effects of a broad range of possible exchange rate outcomes. These anticipated scenarios may then be compared to actual results given a particular exchange rate outcome.

A Practical Method of Assessing Foreign Exchange Risk

C. Kent Garner, *Vulcan Materials Company* and
Alan C. Shapiro, *University of Southern California*

There is a growing awareness among multinational corporations (MNCs) that the operating consequences of exchange rate changes are more serious than the balance sheet effects. This awareness, combined with the realization that there is no end in sight to seemingly unpredictable currency fluctuations, has prompted many MNCs to examine more closely what constitutes "real" or economic foreign exchange exposure (as distinguished from the accountant's definition) and how to cope with the associated risks.

As one of us argued in a recent article in this journal, economic exposure is concerned with the impact of an exchange rate change on future cash flows. Stated more precisely, real foreign exchange exposure is the extent to which the present value of a firm is expected to change as the result of a given currency's appreciation or depreciation.[1] Exchange *risk* is defined as the variability of a firm's value that is due to *unexpected* exchange rate changes.

Accordingly, economic exposure and its companion, exchange risk, are determined by the difference between inflows and outflows of both domestic and foreign currencies over a specified time period, and by the sensitivity of those projected net flows to exchange rate changes. This includes not only those cash flows already known or contracted for (from maturing receivables and payables, confirmed orders and purchases, or principal, interest and dividend payments), but also those that can be foreseen on the basis of the company's future worldwide investment, sales, and material and labor purchase plans.

This concept of exposure suggests that a sensible exchange risk management strategy is one that is designed to protect the dollar (or home currency) earning power of the company as a whole. To do this, it is necessary to determine how the firm's dollar cash flows will be affected by currency fluctuations. This is a daunting task, to be sure, requiring a singular ability to forecast the amounts and exchange rate sensitivities of future cash flows. Most firms that follow the economic approach to managing exposure must, therefore, settle for a measure of their economic exposure that is often supported by nothing more substantial than intuition.

The purpose of this paper is to show how one firm, Vulcan Materials Company ("Vulcan"), devised a workable approach to determine its true economic exposure. The resulting technique is straightforward in concept, easy to apply, and requires only historical data from the firm's actual operations. (In the case of a *de novo* venture, data from a comparable business would be necessary.)

The first section provides some background information on Vulcan, and presents the exchange risk management dilemma it faced in deciding how to finance a major investment in the United Kingdom. The second section describes the concept of economic exposure in more detail and shows how this concept was applied to determine Vulcan's pound sterling exposure resulting from its U.K. investment. The third section presents the application of this method to Vulcan's situation, the results of the analysis and our interpretation of the results. The fourth section discusses the outcome of this analysis, including the decision reached by Vulcan's management and the reasons for that decision.

---

1. See Bradford Cornell and Alan C. Shapiro, "Managing Foreign Exchange Risks," in *Midland Corporate Finance Journal*, Fall 1983, pp.16-31.

Situation

Vulcan is a U.S. company operating in three basic industries. It is the nation's foremost producer of construction aggregates, a leading manufacturer of chlorinated solvents and other industrial chemicals, and a principal producer of secondary aluminum, detinned steel scrap and tin chemicals. Additionally, Vulcan conducts domestic oil and gas exploration and production operations through its wholly owned subsidiary, Southport Exploration, Inc.

In January 1981, Vulcan acquired Batchelor Holdings (Birmingham) Ltd. ("Batchelor"), the only detinning company operating in the United Kingdom. Batchelor operated two detinning plants, one in south Wales and the other in northeast England, and had been engaged in detinning since 1903.[2]

At the time Vulcan acquired Batchelor, approximately 80 percent of Batchelor's scrap supply was provided by 39 tinplate fabricators, including one fabricator which provided nearly half of Batchelor's scrap feed stock. These fabricators sold their tinplate scrap to Batchelor on a cost-plus basis under quasi-tolling arrangements. These contracts established a pre-tax profit for Batchelor equal to a fixed percentage of the ultimate sales price received for the detinned steel and recovered tin. Under these agreements, essentially all variable costs as well as a specified portion of fixed costs, excluding financing charges, were recovered. These contracts required that the suppliers sell all their scrap to Batchelor and, in return, Batchelor was required to purchase each supplier's entire scrap output. All contracts contained similar terms and conditions. The remaining 20 percent of Batchelor's tinplate scrap requirement was met through open market purchases.

During the years preceding its acquisition by Vulcan, Batchelor had increased its production of detinned steel at a time when the steel industry in the U.K. was contracting. This period saw the closure of several major steel-making facilities and the rationalization of production at others. From 1974 through 1976 only two percent of Batchelor's detinned steel sales revenue came from foreign sales whereas, in 1980, export sales accounted for 33 percent of the company's detinned steel revenues. Batchelor's primary domestic detinned steel customer was British Steel Corporation; its export detinned steel sales were to western Europe. All tin sales were to domestic customers.

The acquisition of Batchelor was effected through Vulcan's newly-formed United Kingdom subsidiary, Vulcan U.K. ("VUK"), which purchased all of the outstanding common and preference shares of Batchelor. Subsequently Batchelor and its primary subsidiaries were liquidated into VUK.

As Vulcan's management considered the alternatives for funding this acquisition, one of its paramount concerns was the possible economic foreign exchange exposure inherent in the U.K. detinning operations. If VUK's value as a firm, defined as the present value of future U.S. dollar after-tax cash flow, was expected to be affected by changes in the U.S. dollar-pound sterling exchange rate, then funding this acquisition in whole, or in part, with pounds sterling would have appeared advisable. In this way, the financing would have served as an economic hedge against the effects of unanticipated exchange rate changes. By definition, however, such changes are unpredictable and, thus, impossible to profit from in advance. To expect otherwise would be to speculate on the future dollar-sterling exchange rate, a course of action Vulcan's management does not believe is in the best interest of its shareholders.

Vulcan's management tested the sensitivity of VUK's income and debt service capacity to likely changes in the dollar-sterling exchange rate by making the following assumptions: the then current (1980's) proportions of pound sterling- and U.S. dollar-denominated sales would remain unchanged and sterling prices would be unaffected by exchange rate changes. Based on these assumptions, the analyses tended to indicate that dollar-denominated earnings and cash flows were sensitive to exchange rate fluctuations. It must be recognized, however, that the assumption that sterling prices would be unaffected by exchange rate changes predetermined this conclusion. At that time, past data were not analyzed to determine whether such an

---

2. Detinning involves the separation and recovery of tin and detinned steel from tinplate scrap. The principal sources of tinplate scrap are the waste cuttings and stampings from the manufacture of tinplate articles by can and bottle cap manufacturers. Other sources include tinplate trimmings and rejects from steel companies which manufacture tinplate for primary fabrication. The steel and tin recovered in this wet chemical process are high-purity, premium metals.

assumption was supported by the historical price record.

Additionally, Vulcan consulted with its investment bankers. The advice of one is reprinted at some length below:

Following our recent conversations, I am writing to give you our thoughts on the appropriate currency Vulcan should utilize for financing the acquisition of Batchelor. You have asked specifically that we review alternatives in pounds sterling, U.S. dollars, Deutsche marks, and Swiss francs.

You have indicated that exports currently account for approximately half of Batchelor's sales tonnage and that, while no one can be certain as to future levels of export sales, you would expect that in 1981 such sales might average around 40% of total sales, which is high when compared to historical export levels. Of these sales, some 40% are to German clients and are billed in Deutsche marks and the bulk of the remainder go to Spanish and Italian clients and are invoiced in dollars.

It is quite common for multinational corporations involved in exporting to price their goods in currencies other than that of the parent company. Oftentimes this is done to enhance the marketing effort in the country of import or because of concerns over having foreign currency receivables in a "weak" currency or from a country where various exchange controls exist. If the reasons for invoicing export sales in a different currency are the ones stated above or similar reasons, then the only currency exposure to the parent is during the period between the setting of the foreign currency sales prices and the collection of the receivables. If, however, the reasons for pricing in foreign currencies are market related (i.e., to be competitive in Germany, one must price one's goods in line with similar German products regardless of the amount received in the parent currency), then there is a different set of circumstances which might result in a different financing strategy for the parent. What one must know then, is whether export sales are invoiced in foreign currencies principally for convenience and if prices are set merely by taking the U.K. sales price, adding transportation and insurance costs, etc., and then converting it into the foreign currency, or whether for competitive reasons prices must be set in foreign currencies and if these markets are well insulated from U.K. markets. One final

point to remember here—Batchelor to date has not had to depend on export sales and has had the option of only participating in those transactions which were profitable.

In the case of Batchelor, one has a company where virtually 100% of the expenses and 60% of the expected 1981 revenues are in sterling, while the remaining 40% of expected 1981 revenues are in dollars and Deutsche marks. If one finds that these export sales are effectively sterling revenues denominated for convenience in a different currency, then our earlier recommendation to finance the acquisition of Batchelor in sterling or a sterling equivalent would still hold. If, however, market forces dictate foreign currency pricing and these foreign currency revenue streams are insulated from the U.K. market, then Vulcan should consider financing a portion of the acquisition price in the appropriate foreign currency. To not do so would expose Vulcan to the possibility of having a somewhat more volatile and a lower average earnings stream.

In doing your research in ascertaining how export prices are determined, we would suggest that in addition to talking with Batchelor personnel, you consider the following:
- *The standard supply contract pricing mechanism, which covers approximately 75% of total scrap unit purchases, currently allows you to flow back to your suppliers X% of any exchange gains or losses. As to the remaining 25% of purchases which are made in the spot market, Batchelor would have full exposure;*
- *Given that scrap is basically a commodity where prices vary daily, it would appear that any major change in the foreign exchange market would be quickly reflected in the sales prices Batchelor receives; and*
- *Future export levels may change.*

Based on the discussions we have had and our understandings of the operations of Batchelor as detailed to us by Vulcan personnel, we believe that financing the acquisition of Batchelor with sterling or a sterling equivalent makes the most financial and business sense. It is sterling revenues and income which Batchelor generates in its daily operations and sterling which Vulcan would then have available to service any debt used for the acquisition. If Batchelor were a substantial exporter or competed in the United Kingdom against firms which set their prices on a dollar basis (e.g., the U.K. computer industry, North Sea Oil, etc.), the appropriate currency might be dollars. Since this is not the case, a financing in dollars places an unnecessary foreign currency exposure burden on Vulcan. Vulcan's primary business is not currency speculation. Since neither you nor we know the future movements of the sterling exchange rate over the next few years and since sterling has been one of the most volatile and least predictable currencies in the world recently, incurring such an exchange risk would, in our opinion, be ill-advised.

Borrowing in the Deutsche mark or Swiss franc markets on an unhedged basis to fund the acquisition makes even less sense for Vulcan since you have no natural exposure in either of these currencies. On a hedged basis, the cost should theoretically be similar to that for the dollar borrowing alternative.

Vulcan also consulted two major international banks regarding the proper funding strategy for this acquisition. To reduce any foreign exchange risk, the banks also recommended that Vulcan borrow pounds sterling to finance Batchelor's acquisition, thereby matching the currency of denomination of Batchelor's revenues and expenses.

To minimize the gains and losses on its investment in Batchelor resulting from fluctuations in the rate of exchange between the U.S. dollar and the pound sterling, Vulcan concluded that the acquisition should be funded entirely in pounds sterling. This decision was based upon the following factors:

(a) all Batchelor's assets would be denominated in pounds sterling;

(b) Batchelor's future revenues and costs would be denominated in pounds sterling or would, with high probability, be determined on a pound sterling-equivalent basis;

(c) Vulcan's projected income and debt service sensitivity analyses;

(d) U.K. and U.S. tax laws and U.K. corporate law; and

(e) the advice of its investment and commercial banks.

Accordingly, in January 1981, Vulcan and VUK borrowed £2,355,000 and £1,137,104, respectively, for 10 years on a floating-rate basis (LIBOR plus a margin) to fund part of the purchase of all the outstanding common and preference shares of Batchelor. The balance of the purchase price was funded by VUK's borrowing under a sterling overdraft facility and its issuance of short-term sterling notes. VUK's obligations were not guaranteed by Vulcan. On the date of these borrowings, the exchange rate was U.S.\$2.4060 = £1.00.

To repeat, Vulcan decided to finance its acquisition of Batchelor with sterling debt to hedge against the effects of unanticipated exchange rate changes, not to profit from the possibility that sterling would devalue by more than the amount already reflected in the sterling-dollar interest rate differential. Pursuing the latter objective would have constituted currency speculation, not hedging. And, again, Vulcan's management believed then, as it does now, that its comparative advantage lies in production and marketing, not in currency speculation.

During April 1983, the average U.S. dollar-pound sterling exchange rate was \$1.5362. Based on quarterly exchange rates between 1981:1 and 1983:1, the nominal, or actual, sterling depreciation against the dollar was 33.6 percent. In real or inflation-adjusted terms, using the implicit price indices in both countries to measure inflation, sterling depreciated 31.0 percent. This significant and rapid depreciation of the pound sterling in both nominal and real terms raised the question: Had the sterling borrowing to finance the acquisition of Batchelor provided an effective hedge of the economic foreign exchange exposure believed to be inherent in its operations? Vulcan's management accordingly decided to reexamine its original conclusion that the acquisition of Batchelor created a "long" pound sterling exposure for Vulcan.

Method

The method developed to estimate VUK's exposure to foreign exchange risk is based on a particular definition of exposure, one that is not subscribed to by all firms. Thus, some background information on exposure follows.

Companies with international operations have foreign currency-denominated assets and liabilities, revenues and expenses. But, because home country investors and the entire financial community are interested in home currency values, the foreign currency balance sheet and income statement accounts must be assigned home currency values. In particular, the financial statements of an MNC's overseas subsidiaries must be translated into home currency

It is important to realize that many exchange rate gains or losses are purely cosmetic; that is, no cash flows are affected.

values before consolidation with the parent's financial statements.

If currency values change, foreign exchange translation gains or losses may result. Assets and liabilities translated at the current (post-change) exchange rate are considered to be exposed, while those translated at an historical (pre-change) exchange rate maintain their historical home currency values. Translation exposure is simply the difference between exposed assets and exposed liabilities.

Accountants continue to debate which assets and liabilities are exposed, and when accounting-derived foreign exchange gains and losses should be recognized. To set this controversy in proper perspective, however, it is important to realize that many of these gains or losses are purely cosmetic; that is, no cash flows are affected.

The current accounting standard for reporting exposure is Financial Accounting Standard Board Statement No. 52, which requires all balance sheet and income items to be translated at their appropriate current exchange rates. Translation gains and losses are placed in a separate equity account, bypassing the income statement.

Exchange rate changes, however, affect all facets of a firm's operations. These effects are primarily prospective in nature and, therefore, cannot be adequately accounted for within the framework provided by historical cost-based accounting systems. This has led to growing dissatisfaction with accounting-derived measures of exposure and to a search for a more meaningful definition of exposure. One outcome of the translation controversy is that, over the past decade, the concept of currency exposure has evolved from an initial focus on the impact of exchange rate changes on the home currency values of foreign currency-denominated assets and liabilities (accounting exposure) to a more proper focus on the effect of currency fluctuations on the home currency values of total corporate cash flows (economic exposure).

Economic exposure can be separated further into transaction exposure and real operating exposure. *Transaction exposure* results from the possibility of exchange gains or losses, upon settlement at a future date, of transactions already entered into and denominated in a foreign currency. Although transaction exposure is often captured by the accounting measure of exposure, it is also a cash flow exposure and hence part of economic exposure. *Real operating exposure* arises because currency fluctuations can alter the firm's future revenue and cost streams.

In opting to use the economic definition of exposure, Vulcan was faced with the necessity of developing a practicable approach for assessing the effects, if any, of a change in the dollar-sterling exchange rate on the dollar value of VUK's cash flows. The analytical method that resulted from this effort was based upon the following considerations: First, Vulcan selected the U.S. dollar as the relevant numeraire currency because, as a U.S. corporation owned almost entirely by U.S. residents, Vulcan's value to its shareholders is determined by its dollar cash flows. (Naturally, a shareholder who was interested in foreign currency purchasing power would be able to convert this holding into the currency of his choice through the foreign exchange markets, or to hedge its value by creating U.S. dollar liabilities.)

Second, as its primary objective, Vulcan's management is committed to maximizing the value of the company's common stock and, hence, the wealth of its shareholders. It also accepts the financial theory and supporting empirical research which hold that financial markets view cash flows, not accounting earnings, as the primary determinant of value and that these markets behave rationally—eventually, if not immediately. Therefore, if the value of VUK—defined as the present value of expected net cash flows—was expected to vary with a change in the dollar-sterling exchange rate, Vulcan's value to its shareholders was exposed to such exchange rate changes. Accordingly, Vulcan's economic foreign exchange exposure through VUK, not its translation or transaction exposure, was management's fundamental concern.

Finally, the original objective of funding VUK's acquisition with sterling borrowings was to reduce the volatility of the value of its investment in VUK resulting from exchange rate changes. Therefore, the final purpose of the analysis was to ascertain whether dollar debt would have been more effective in reducing the volatility of VUK's value.

Measuring a firm's economic exposure, however, is not a trivial task. It requires detailed knowledge about the firm's operations and the sensitivity of their cash flows to exchange rate changes. This task is made especially difficult because it is impossible to assess the effects of an exchange rate change on cash flows without simultaneously considering the impact on revenues and costs of the underlying rates of inflation associated with each currency. If

The effects of exchange rate changes are primarily prospective in nature and, therefore, cannot be adequately accounted for within historical cost-based accounting systems.

the rate of change in the exchange rate just equals the difference between the inflation rates in both currencies—as predicted by purchasing power parity (PPP)—then a firm that avoids contracts fixed in the foreign currency should have no exchange risk; that is, the movement in the exchange rate should exactly offset the change in the foreign price level, leaving dollar cash flows unaffected. Thus if PPP holds, what is usually, and incorrectly, termed "exchange risk" may result from changing business conditions that are independent of currency changes.

An Operational Measure of Currency Exposure

The economic definition of currency exposure suggested to us an operational measure of the exchange risk faced by a foreign affiliate: the extent to which variations in the dollar value of the affiliate's cash flows are expected to be correlated with variations in the nominal exchange rate. The existence of such a correlation can be detected using a statistical technique known as "regression analysis." This technique involves regressing cash flows from past periods, converted into their dollar values, on the average exchange rate during the corresponding period. Specifically, this involves running the regression

(1) $CF_t = \alpha + \beta \, EXCH_t + u_t$

where CF_t is the dollar value of total affiliate cash flows in period t, $EXCH_t$ is the average nominal exchange rate (dollar value of one unit of the foreign currency) during period t, and u is a random error term with mean 0. $EXCH_t$ is the rate used to convert the period t foreign currency cash flow into its dollar equivalent.

The output from such a regression includes three key parameters: 1) the foreign exchange beta (β) coefficient, which measures the sensitivity of dollar cash flows to exchange rate changes; 2) the t-statistic, which measures the statistical significance of the beta coefficient; and 3) the R^2, which measures the fraction of cash flow variability explained by variation in the exchange rate. The higher the beta coefficient, the greater the impact of a given exchange rate change on the dollar value of cash flows. Conversely, the lower the beta coefficient, the less exposed the firm is to exchange rate changes. Similarly, a high t-statistic indicates more exposure and a low t-statistic less exposure.

But even if a firm has a large and statistically

significant beta coefficient, and thus faces real exchange risk, this does not necessarily mean that currency fluctuations are an important determinant of overall firm risk. What really matters is the percentage of total corporate cash flow variability attributable to these currency fluctuations. Thus, the most important parameter, in terms of its impact on the firm's exposure management policy, may well be the regression's R^2. For example, if exchange rate changes explain only one percent of total cash flow variability (as indicated by an R^2 of 0.01), the firm should not devote much in the way of resources to foreign exchange risk management, even if the beta coefficient is large and statistically significant.

Multi-Period Exposure

The usefulness of the regression represented by equation (1) is limited by its implicit assumption that an exchange rate change will have an impact only on current period cash flows. Actually, a given exchange rate change could affect both current and future cash flows; that is, current cash flows might be affected by both the current exchange rate and past exchange rates. This suggests using a modified version of equation (1):

(2) $CF_t = \alpha + \beta_1 \, EXCH_t + \beta_2 \, EXCH_{t-1} + \cdots + \beta_{n+1} EXCH_{t-n} + u_t$

where $EXCH_{t-j}$ is the average exchange rate during period t-j.

How far back one should go to estimate exposure using equation (2) depends on the particular circumstances facing the firm (for example, on how free the firm is to change its prices). As a general rule, however, it seems that one year is sufficient. Beyond this point, prices appear to adjust so as to offset the effects of a currency change. But it is not necessary to trust judgment; one advantage of the regression technique is that one can experiment by including additional periods in the regression to see just how persistent the effects of past currency changes have been.

Limitations

One critical assumption of this method is that the historical sensitivity of cash flows to exchange rate changes is a reasonably good predictor of their future sensitivity. In the absence of additional information, this seems to be a reasonable assumption.

Insignificant correlation between VUK's dollar-equivalent cash flows and the dollar-sterling exchange rate would be indicative of a world market for detinned steel in which the Law of One Price prevails.

But if a firm has reason to believe this will not be the case, then it must modify its use of this method. For example, the nominal foreign currency tax shield provided by a foreign affiliate's depreciation is fully exposed to the effects of currency fluctuations. If the amount of depreciation in the future is expected to differ significantly from its historical values, then the depreciation tax shield should be removed from the cash flows used in the regression analysis and treated separately. Similarly, if the firm has recently entered into a large purchase or sales contract that is fixed in terms of a foreign currency, it might consider the resulting transaction exposure apart from its operating exposure.

Analysis

To determine Vulcan's economic exposure through VUK to dollar-sterling exchange rate changes, an analysis of the dollar-equivalent cash flows from VUK's detinning operations was required. We chose first to analyze VUK's detinned steel results for two principal reasons: (a) during 1978-1982, detinned steel sales contributed 65.6 percent of total revenues, and (b) there is substantial external evidence—primarily well-developed international markets—that tin is a global commodity generally subject to the Law of One Price. This means that exchange-adjusted prices for tin are identical, or nearly so, worldwide and, therefore, no economic exposure exists for tin. (The tin data would also be analyzed, however, if the analysis of the detinned steel data disclosed a significant sterling economic exposure.)

Correlation Analysis

As a first step in assessing VUK's economic exposure, we decided to perform several analyses of the correlation between quarterly cash flows (variously defined) and the average quarterly dollar-sterling (U.S.\$/£) exchange rates from January 1, 1974 through March 31, 1983. A significant positive correlation would indicate VUK's dollar-equivalent cash flows tend to increase as sterling appreciates relative to the dollar. This result would suggest that detinned steel prices are set primarily in sterling and, thus, that the Law of One Price does not hold. If such were the case, then VUK's operations would

face intrinsic economic foreign exchange exposure to the value of the pound sterling. In this circumstance, the economic exposure and resulting potential volatility of VUK's dollar cash flows could be reduced through sterling borrowings.

Conversely, significant negative correlation would result if, for some reason, dollar-equivalent cash flows decrease as sterling appreciates relative to the dollar. This would indicate a negative operating exposure inherent in VUK, one which must be managed. Using sterling finance would only increase Vulcan's "short" position in sterling, increasing its exposure. In this event, the appropriate currency to fund VUK's acquisition would be U.S. dollars. To reduce its negative exposure, Vulcan would have to buy sterling forward.

The third possibility is that there is no significant correlation between dollar-equivalent operating cash flows and exchange rate changes. This result would suggest the absence of any intrinsic economic foreign exchange exposure in VUK's operations. In this case, since Vulcan's home currency is the U.S. dollar, funding VUK's acquisition with pounds sterling would create an unhedged "short" position in sterling. Insignificant correlation between VUK's dollar-equivalent cash flows and the dollar-sterling exchange rate would be indicative of a world market in which detinned steel prices are set on the basis of worldwide supply and demand—the Law of One Price—irrespective of local market conditions and their currency of denomination.

If the last possibility proved to be the case, then it would be counterproductive, for economic hedging purposes, for Vulcan and VUK to maintain their sterling-denominated debt. If management decided that Vulcan and VUK should prepay their sterling borrowings, however, Vulcan would face two problems. First, in view of the substantial depreciation of sterling versus the dollar between January 1981 and April 1983, Vulcan would realize a taxable foreign exchange gain. Second, since VUK did not have sufficient liquidity to prepay its debt, Vulcan would have to provide VUK the funds for prepayment. This, in turn, would result in Vulcan increasing its investment in VUK.

To perform this analysis, we defined four different U.S. dollar cash flow streams from VUK's detinned steel operations. These cash flows were calculated by converting the actual sterling cash flows to their dollar equivalents at the average exchange rates during the periods.

Vulcan's management concluded that very little of the variability of VUK's dollar cash flows is related to dollar-sterling exchange rate changes.

PIT = Operating profit plus depreciation plus/minus the change in working capital but before deducting interest expense, capital expenditures and taxes; quarterly basis from 1974:1 through 1983:1.

PDIT = PIT *minus* depreciation; quarterly basis from 1974:1 through 1983:1.

PT = PIT less actual interest expense; monthly basis from January 1981 through March 1983.

PTE = PIT less the LIBOR-based interest expense which would have been incurred if Batchelor's acquisition had been financed by borrowing Euro-dollars rather than Euro-sterling; monthly basis from January 1981 through March 1983.

PIT was selected as the most appropriate definition of VUK's operating cash flow. This choice was based on the pragmatic assumption that the dollar value of replacement capital spending was independent of the exchange rate. This assumption allowed the cash outflow associated with the replacement of assets to be ignored in the correlation analysis. Otherwise, it would have been necessary to separate nine years' worth of capital spending into replacements and additions. Focusing solely on VUK's economic exposure from operations, we excluded interest income and expense and, consequently, the effects of the original financing decision. Taxes were excluded to avoid the effects of tax law changes on cash flows.

Operating cash flows were calculated as pre-tax operating profits plus the change in the dollar value of working capital. This adjustment for working capital changes is based on the fact that the real (cash flow) impact of currency fluctuations on working capital equals the net increase (decrease) in the dollar value of working capital required following an exchange rate change.

The effect of adding sterling-denominated historical cost depreciation (the dollar-equivalent of which varies one-for-one with the exchange rate) to operating earnings is to magnify any positive sterling exposure faced by VUK. The alternative definition of cash flow set forth above, PDIT, avoids this potential source of bias. Its implicit assumption that depreciation approximates replacement capital spending introduces, however, a potential downward bias in the estimated correlation. The true correlation should lie between the correlations resulting from these two different measures of cash flow.

Therefore, a contemporaneous correlation analysis was performed using both PIT and PDIT. These cash flows were also correlated with lagged exchange rates—that is, PIT_t or $PDIT_t$ versus $EXCH_{t-1,2,3 \text{ and } 4}$ (where the exchange rates are quarterly averages)—to identify any inter-period adjustment process wherein current cash flows respond to prior exchange rate changes.

To test the proposition that sterling-denominated financing as compared with dollar-denominated debt would reduce the volatility of VUK's dollar-equivalent cash flows and, thus, foreign exchange risk, PT and PTE were correlated with average exchange rates. If the standard deviation of PT were less than that of PTE, the volatility of VUK's cash flows would have been reduced by the floating-rate sterling debt. And, which measure of cash flow, PT or PTE, was less correlated with exchange rates would indicate whether sterling or dollar floating-rate debt would result in less economic foreign exchange exposure for Vulcan.

The results of these correlation analyses are set forth in Table 1.

The weak, positive correlations of PIT and PDIT with EXCH indicate that VUK's dollar-equivalent cash flows tend to increase (fall) only slightly and temporarily as sterling strengthens (weakens) against the dollar. Furthermore, this weak correlation, which is statistically insignificant, exists for two quarters but decays rapidly thereafter. The minor increase in the correlation between PIT_t and $PDIT_t$ and $EXCH_{t-1}$, compared to the correlation with $EXCH_t$, might reflect the fact that VUK's quarterly payments for tinplate scrap may be made as much as one month in arrears pursuant to its scrap purchase contracts. The decrease in the correlations thereafter suggests a short adjustment process.

From the statistically insignificant degree of correlation of PIT_t and $PDIT_t$ with $EXCH_{t, t-4}$, Vulcan's management concluded that very little of the variability of VUK's dollar cash flows is related to dollar-sterling exchange rate changes. VUK's dollar cash flows are quite volatile as indicated by the size of their standard deviations relative to their mean values (see Table 1). But, this volatility is caused by factors other than the dollar-sterling exchange rate. Rather, shifts in global supply and demand for steel would appear to be the main causes of fluctuations in cash flows.

An equally important conclusion to be drawn from the near-zero correlations is that detinned

*Detinned steel prices seem to be set in a global market
without regard to any particular currency, which means
that the detinning industry does not involve intrinsic
foreign exchange exposure.*

**TABLE 1
Correlation
Coefficients:
Dollar Cash Flows
and Exchange Rates**

	$EXCH_t$	$EXCH_{t-1}$	$EXCH_{t-2}$	$EXCH_{t-3}$	$EXCH_{t-4}$
PIT_t	0.11	0.12	0.06	0.02	−0.06
$PDIT_t$	0.08	0.09	0.04	0.01	−0.06
PT_t	0.19	0.22	0.13	0.11	0.08
PTE_t	0.06	0.10	0.04	0.02	−0.01

	Mean	Standard Deviation
PIT	658.667	595.584
PDIT	540.222	600.177
PT	112.67	391.88
PTE	62.43	366.53

steel prices seem to be set in a global market without regard to any particular currency. The very low correlations suggest the Law of One Price holds, which means that the detinning industry does not involve intrinsic economic foreign exchange exposure or risk. Management's conclusion, then, was that the acquisition of VUK did not create significant sterling exposure for Vulcan and, consequently, there was no sterling exposure to be hedged.

These conclusions are also supported by the low correlations of PT_t and PTE_t with $EXCH_{t,\ t-4}$. Furthermore, these correlations indicate that dollar-denominated debt would have resulted in marginally lower economic foreign exchange exposure than the sterling debts; that is, PTE was less correlated with EXCH than PT. The higher mean value of PT reflects the windfall gain realized by Vulcan on its sterling-denominated debt as the pound depreciated.

Correlation analyses of PIT_t and $PDIT_t$ with $EXCH_{t,\ t-4}$ were also run using monthly data covering January 1981 through March 1983. These correlations were each approximately 0.10 higher than their quarterly counterparts. This possibly resulted from the 31 percent real devaluation of sterling versus the dollar which occurred over this period. Consequently, purchasing power parity would not have held and VUK's dollar cash flows would have been depressed. Vulcan was, therefore, protected against this real devaluation by its sterling debt. But, in fact, it was *over-protected*, which resulted in a negative sterling exposure. This negative exposure meant that if sterling depreciated, the exchange gain on sterling debt would have exceeded the loss in the dollar value of VUK's operating cash flows. Conversely, if sterling appreciated, the exchange loss on sterling debt would have exceeded the gain in the dollar value of VUK's operating cash flows.

Parenthetically, the substantial volatility of VUK's cash flows has another financing implication. If its borrowings are not supported by Vulcan, VUK should avoid high leverage.

Regression Analysis

Although useful, correlation analysis has important limitations. First, the correlation between two variables indicates only whether the variables are related; it does not provide a precise measure of the relationship. For example, a correlation of 1 indicates that changes in cash flow are directly proportional to changes in the exchange rate; it does not indicate what that factor of proportionality is.

Second, the correlation coefficient does not measure the fraction of cash flow variability attributable to exchange rate changes. A high correlation, in other words, does not necessarily mean that currency fluctuations are an important determinant of overall cash flow variability. Third, a correlation analysis cannot examine the simultaneous effects on cash flows of several variables.

As mentioned earlier, these problems are avoided by using regression analysis. Therefore, we performed the regression analysis described in the previous section, using up to four lagged values of the exchange rate in addition to the contemporaneous exchange rate. The cash flow series used was PIT (000 omitted). The results, which are contained in Table 2, clearly indicate that VUK's exposure to fluctuations in the dollar-sterling exchange rate was slight. The individual beta coefficients are small, indicating that exchange rate changes have only a minimal impact on VUK's dollar cash flows. For example, in the case of Regression 1, the beta coefficient of 0.26 means that a one cent change in

*Vulcan was, in fact, **over-protected** against a sterling devaluation, resulting in a negative sterling exposure.*

TABLE 2 Results of Regression Analysis (CF on EXCH)	Regression Number	Coefficient on					
		EXCH$_t$	EXCH$_{t-1}$	EXCH$_{t-2}$	EXCH$_{t-3}$	EXCH$_{t-4}$	R^2
	1	.260 (.67)*					.013
	2	.177 (.20)	.937 (.10)				.013
	3	.131 (.14)	.459 (.34)	−.357 (−.38)			.018
	4	.092 (.10)	.470 (.35)	−.128 (−.09)	−.226 (−.24)		.020
	5	−.067 (−.07)	.437 (.32)	−.072 (−.05)	.820 (.62)	−1.073 (−1.12)	.059

*t-statistics in parentheses

the price of sterling will lead to a 0.26 percent change in VUK's dollar cash flow. The beta coefficients are also statistically insignificant (financial economists consider a t-statistic below 2 to indicate a coefficient value statistically indistinguishable from 0). Even more important, the maximum R^2 for any of the regressions is just .059, meaning that, at best, exchange rate fluctuations account for less than six percent of the overall variability of VUK's dollar cash flows.

The Decision

On the basis of the foregoing analysis, Vulcan concluded that VUK's value as a firm is not significantly related to the dollar-sterling exchange rate and, therefore, its acquisition did not result in a pound sterling economic exposure for Vulcan. Furthermore, as a consequence of its funding VUK's acquisition with sterling debt, Vulcan had effectively created a "short" sterling position. That position, to be sure, resulted in a windfall economic gain due to sterling's substantial devaluation, but such could not be counted on in the future. For example, if sterling strengthened, Vulcan would realize an exchange loss on its sterling debt which would not be offset by increases in VUK's dollar operating cash flows. Consequently, Vulcan then began to study the various

means by which it could realign its sterling position.

Management identified five methods of eliminating Vulcan's and VUK's sterling debt, thereby reducing its sterling foreign exchange exposure. First, the term loan agreements permitted prepayment of Vulcan's and VUK's sterling debt, in whole or in part, at any time. Second, the loan agreements could be amended, subject to the lender's consent, to permit conversion of the borrowings into Eurodollars. Third, Vulcan and VUK could purchase sterling forward foreign exchange contracts to match the principal repayments of their respective loans. Fourth, U.K. government bonds matching the loans' maturities and amounts could be purchased. Finally, Vulcan's common stock could be exchanged for the term notes. The first and last options would require Vulcan to increase its investment in VUK if its debt were eliminated, as mentioned earlier.

If it chose the first or second option, Vulcan would realize an immediately taxable gain. That gain would equal the excess of the dollar value of the borrowed sterling at the time the loans were received over the dollar value of the sterling at the time the loans were repaid.[3] Although the third and fourth alternatives would defer the incidence of tax until the loans were repaid and the forward contracts settled or bonds matured, these options, nevertheless, would result in the eventual taxation of the foreign exchange gain.

3. Tax counsel advised that the Internal Revenue Service's position regarding the immediately taxable nature of this gain had been approved in many judicial decisions and could not be directly challenged with any substantial hope of success. See *Rev. Rul.* 78-281, 1978-2, C.B. 204. However, counsel noted further that, pursuant to Internal Revenue Code sections 108 and 1917, Vulcan could possibly exclude from its taxable income the foreign exchange gain realized if it made a corresponding reduction in the tax basis of its depreciable assets. Yet, tax counsel advised that the I.R.S. had taken an adverse position regarding application of these sections of the Code as a basis for excluding from tax such income. Counsel noted, however, that the only court decision specifically on this point was favorable. See *Kentucky & Indiana Terminal R.R. Co. v. U.S.*, 64-1 U.S.T.C. ¶ 9374 (CA-6).

Vulcan's objective in evaluating these options was to adjust its sterling exposure at the lowest economic cost to its shareholders. Each of the first four alternatives would entail costs only, but no direct economic gain other than the reduction of Vulcan's economic foreign exchange exposure. These costs would include the loss of the interest tax shield if the debt were prepaid, transaction costs if forward foreign exchange contracts or U.K. government bonds were purchased, and, most important, the tax on the realized foreign exchange gain.

The debt-equity swap, however, presented Vulcan with a unique opportunity not only to reset its sterling exposure but also to realize an economic gain rather than a loss. This gain would equal the present value of the taxes that would otherwise be owed on the foreign exchange gain less transaction costs and the temporary loss of interest tax shield.

To calculate the amount of this gain, Vulcan assumed that it would repurchase any stock exchanged for the sterling notes to restore its original capital structure, and that it would fund such stock repurchases with debt bearing interest at its intermediate term debt rate. Thus, the loss of interest tax shield was temporary only. The cash flows attributable to the tax savings resulting from the exchange were assumed to occur on the notes' original maturity dates. The cash flows, net of transaction costs, were then discounted at Vulcan's estimated after-tax intermediate term debt rate. Vulcan computed the net economic gain on an exchange of stock for its £2,355,000 note to equal approximately $230,000.

Vulcan viewed the other often-mentioned attractions of debt-equity swaps as rather illusory.[4] In any event, some of the supposed advantages—most notably, the reductions in the ratios of the book and market values of debt to equity—were not considerations. Since the debt was foreign-currency denominated, its book value reflected current exchange rates as of each balance sheet date in accordance with FAS Statement No. 52. Additionally, since the debt bore a floating interest rate, its market value was essentially par, in sterling terms. Finally, despite the approximately $1.8 million in book income which would result from this exchange, the real economic benefit to Vulcan's shareholders was con-

siderably less. In particular, prior to this transaction, the foreign exchange gain less the associated taxes had already been realized by Vulcan's shareholders and impounded in its market value. Therefore, the incremental value of the exchange of stock for its sterling note was equal to the present value of the now permanently deferred tax on the foreign exchange gain, less related transaction costs.

In view of the favorable economic effect of a sterling debt-for-equity exchange, Vulcan's tax counsel studied its feasibility. It seemed well established under then current tax law that a corporation would not realize taxable income on exchanging its own stock for outstanding *dollar* debt, even though the value of the stock was less than the face amount of the debt.[5] Would the same result follow if the debt were in a foreign currency, and the original dollar value of the loan were in excess of the value of the stock being issued? At the time, Vulcan and its investment bankers were unaware of any previous foreign currency-denominated debt-for-equity exchanges. Thus, no direct precedent existed. Vulcan's tax counsel advised that, despite the absence of direct authority, there would be a strong case for an affirmative answer to this critical question.[6]

Accordingly, Vulcan entered into negotiations with the holder of its £2,355,000 term note, and on August 5, 1983 exchanged 55,955 shares of its common stock for the note. In accordance with FAS Statement No. 52, Vulcan realized a net, nontaxable gain of $1,846,000. Had the debt been retired by a payment of cash, Vulcan would have realized a taxable gain of $2,068,000, and income taxes payable would have approximated $1,018,000. This transaction was described in the following footnote to Vulcan's 1983 financial statements:

Notes payable in the United Kingdom were reduced in 1983 by the retirement of a term note in the principal amount of £2,355,000 through an exchange of 55,955 shares of the company's common stock. This sterling loan was originally taken to provide an economic hedge for exposure to foreign exchange fluctuations referable to the company's British detinning operations. Management determined in 1983 that this hedge was no longer needed. The retire-

---

4. See Harold Bierman, Jr., "The Debt-Equity Swap," in *Midland Corporate Finance Journal*, Fall 1983, pp. 59-63.

5. See Code sections 108(e)(8) and 1032; Senate Report No. 96-1035 on P.L. 96-589, 1980-2 C.B. 628; *Rev. Rul. 59-222*, 1959-1 C.B. 80; *Tower Bldg. Corp.*, 6 T.C. 125 acq.; *Commissioner v. Capento Securities Corp.*, 140 F.2d 382 (CA-1, 1944).

6. See *National Standard Co.*, 80 T.C. # 27 (1983).

ment of the sterling loan resulted in a $1,846,000 realized foreign currency gain. The remaining United Kingdom note in the amount of $1,380,000 is payable in installments of £135,714 in the years 1984-1990. The interest rate on this obligation is based on the three-or six-month domestic sterling or bank-accepted bill of exchange rate. The interest rate with respect to this obligation is subject to change and may be for longer or shorter periods, as mutually agreed. . . .

Vulcan elected not to repay VUK's own note because to do so would have required Vulcan to increase its direct investment in VUK, since VUK did not have sufficient funds of its own to retire the note. Equally important, no economic gain (tax savings) would have resulted because VUK had realized no foreign currency gain on its debt—a debt denominated in its home currency. Furthermore, Vulcan did not believe a further loss of interest tax shield and reduced leverage were in its stockholders' best interest. If VUK's debt had been retired, Vulcan would have recognized as income, in accordance with FAS Statement No. 52, the previously deferred translation gain.

The alternative of having VUK borrow dollars to repay its sterling debt would not have been tax-effective. Because of a quirk in English tax law, borrowing dollars is more expensive on an after-tax basis, even if the expected costs of borrowing dollars and sterling are equal before tax.[7] The applicable law does not permit the deduction for tax purposes of exchange losses on foreign currency debt principal payments—while the typically higher interest rate on sterling debt, which reflects expected sterling depreciation, is fully tax deductible.

Summary and Conclusions

The most important feature of this case study is that it provides a practicable method for calculating a firm's degree of economic exposure. It avoids the speculative forecasts of future cash flows and their sensitivity to currency movements that are otherwise required.

The case study also offers some lessons to managers concerned about their true economic exposure to currency fluctuations. One is that, depending on one's assumptions, it is possible to come up with very different and plausible estimates of economic exposure. For example, the investment bankers who studied this case focused their attention on the fraction of revenues accounted for by exports. Finding this number to be fairly small, they concluded that Vulcan's U.K. investment was fully exposed to changes in the dollar-sterling exchange rate. In effect, they assumed that the Law of One Price did not hold for tin and detinned steel in the United Kingdom.

This suggests a second lesson: in determining the extent to which its operations are exposed to exchange risks, management should look at its record of operating cash flows. A careful examination of the historical data made it quite clear that, although Vulcan's U.K. investment had highly variable dollar cash flows, less than six percent of that variability could be traced to exchange rate movements.

The final lesson is the importance of tax consequences in international decisions. Even after the decision was made to reduce sterling debt, tax effects were critical in determining how this was accomplished.

7. See Alan C. Shapiro, "The Impact of Taxation on the Currency-of-Denomination Decision for Long-Term Foreign Borrowing and Lending," *Journal of International Business Studies*, Spring/Summer 1984, pp. 15-25.

The Foreign Exchange Option as a Hedging Tool

by Ian H. Giddy, *Columbia University and Claremont Economics Institute*

The Basic Function of Currency Options as a Hedging Tool

Early this year a well-known U.S. electronics firm was asked to bid on a contract to supply the Swiss authority with switching systems. Bids were also to be submitted by French and Japanese firms, both of whose governments were keen on winning the contract. The result of the tender would be known some time during the following two months. Were its bid to be accepted the American firm would receive an initial payment of two million Swiss francs, with the remainder of the payments made in Swiss francs at fixed dates thereafter.

To submit a bid in Swiss francs, our firm could have assumed that the current Swiss franc/dollar exchange rate would remain unchanged and translated the bid at today's spot rate; this is the "no hedge" assumption. The danger, however, was that if the bid was accepted and the franc fell, the profit margin on the deal could easily have been wiped out. Alternatively, the firm could have sold the anticipated Swiss franc receipts in the forward market, at the then current forward exchange rate for two-month and later delivery dates. However, if its bid was *not* selected the firm would then have had a short posi-

tion in Swiss francs and could have lost money.

A third and preferable strategy would have been to purchase an *option* to sell Swiss francs on the payment dates. This would have given the American firm the right to transfer the Swiss francs received at a prearranged exchange rate. If the contract was not won the firm could have allowed the option to expire (even sold the right to someone else) with no further obligation on its part. Note also that even if our firm's bid was accepted, it would have faced no compulsion to exchange any Swiss francs received at the prearranged rate; if the value of the Swiss currency rose, then the firm may have done better by selling the francs in the spot market.

Currency options of this kind can be an extraordinarily valuable addition to the international corporate treasurer's toolbox. All this flexibility, of course, does not come free. So, any company considering this technique must be prepared to evaluate whether the value received warrants the price paid. This article will set out some principles according to which international treasury managers can gauge the usefulness of currency options in hedging specific corporate currency risks.

A foreign exchange option is a rather simple concept: it is a contract conveying *the right to buy or sell a designated quantity of a foreign currency* at a

Forward and futures contracts are sometimes imperfect instruments for hedging certain common exchange risks.

specified price (exchange rate) during a stipulated period under stated conditions. The terminal date of the contract is called the *expiration date* (or maturity date). If the option may be exercised before the expiration date, it is called an *American option*; if only on the expiration date, a *European option*.

The party retaining the option is the *option buyer*; the party giving the option is the *option seller* (or writer). The exchange rate at which the option can be exercised is called the *exercise price* (or strike price). The buyer of the option must pay the seller some amount, called the *option price* or the *premium*, for the rights involved.

A *call option in foreign exchange* is the right to *buy* a specified number of foreign currency units from the option seller at a specified exercise price (in dollars) up to and including the exercise date. A *put option* is the right to sell the foreign currency to the option seller at a specified dollar price, up to the expiration date. Since the right to buy German marks at a known exchange rate is also the right to sell dollars in exchange for German marks at the same exchange rate, it is evident that a foreign exchange put option is simply a call option seen from the other currency's viewpoint.

The key feature of a foreign exchange option is that it provides "asymmetric" risk protection. The purchase of either a put or a call option limits the buyer's loss to the price paid for the option contract (the premium). The option buyer's potential gain, however, is unlimited. It is this feature that differentiates options from forwards or futures, as we shall see below. The asymmetry of currency options has an important sidelight: if you think about it, the holder of a call on, say, one million Deutsche marks would *prefer* that the underlying currency be *more volatile*! The higher the variability of the mark, the more likely it is that the currency will rise substantially above the exercise price, producing a large profit. On the other hand his option risk from downward fluctuations is limited to the loss of the premium should he let the option expire. In essence, therefore, buying (or selling) an option represents a bet on the currency's volatility.

More on this aspect later. Let us now turn to a question asked by many corporate treasurers: when should foreign exchange options be used in preference to more conventional hedging techniques?

Options versus Forward Contracts for Hedging

Few involved in treasury management of international corporations would want to forego the use of currency futures and forward contracts to hedge assets, liabilities, and future cash flows in foreign currencies. Yet it cannot have escaped the notice of these same treasury managers that forward and futures contracts are sometimes imperfect instruments for the hedging of certain common exchange risks faced by multinational firms. The reason is simply that a forward contract is a fixed and inviolable agreement to receive or deliver a currency at a specified price. Yet, in many practical instances, the hedger is uncertain whether the hedged foreign currency cash inflow or outflow will materialize. When an overseas deal falls through or when a bid on a foreign currency contract is accepted, or when a foreign subsidiary's dividend payments exceed (or fall short of) the expected amount, then the international corporate treasurer will find himself partially exposed. The most careful forward hedging cannot protect against such *quantity risk*.

In such cases what is needed is not the *obligation*, but the *right*, to buy or sell a designated quantity of a foreign currency at a specified price (exchange rate). This is precisely what a foreign exchange option provides.[1]

Although options and forwards serve different purposes, they are linked in interesting ways. As may be seen in the box on page 34, the "profit picture" of a currency option is lopsided while that of a forward or futures contract is symmetric. Yet options can be made symmetric, by combining two of them in such a way as to mimic a forward contract, and this provides the fundamental link between options and forwards. A combination of *buying a call and selling a put* at the same exercise price is identical to *buying the currency forward*; you gain if the currency rises above the forward rate and lose if it falls below. A similar link exists between buying a put plus selling a call and selling the currency forward. Arbitrage techniques called conversions and reversals ensure that options and forwards are linked in this fashion continuously. (See the author's article, "Foreign Exchange Options.")

1. For an analogous discussion of the different uses of interest rate futures and options, see Bluford Putnam's "Managing Interest Rate Risk: An Introduction to Financial Futures and Options," *Issues in Corporate Finance* (New York: Stern Stewart Putnam & Macklis, 1983).

A put option, when used alone, is a combined bet on direction and volatility.

Profit Profiles of Forwards and Options

"Profit Profiles" trace the relationship between the *exchange rate at expiration* of the contract and the *net gain* to the trader. These diagrams show how the profit profile of the *holder* and *seller* of a call or put option differs from the profit picture of a conventional forward contract at expiration.

1. Buy Sterling Forward

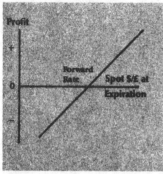

2. Sell Sterling Forward

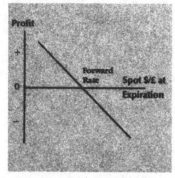

3. Buy a Sterling Call Option

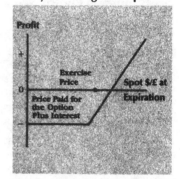

4. Buy a Sterling Put Option

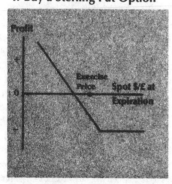

5. Sell a Sterling Call Option

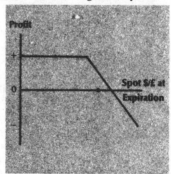

6. Sell a Sterling Put Option

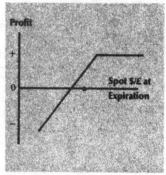

In a *forward contract*, diagrams 1 and 2 show, the long or short position produces a *one-to-one gain or loss* depending on where the spot rate ends up relative to the contracted forward rate.

In an *options contract*, the gain or loss is *asymmetric*. Diagram 3 shows that, for a *call option* on pounds sterling, the loss is limited to the price originally paid for the option, plus interest foregone. As long as the spot rate exceeds the prearranged exercise price, some gain will be made, but the net profit will be positive only when the holder of the call has recouped the price of the option, plus interest. The holder of a *put option* will gain one-for-one only when sterling has fallen below the exercise price by more than the price of the put, plus interest. Again, downside loss is limited. The *seller* of puts or calls has a profit picture that is the upside-down mirror image of the buyer's: the most he can gain is the option price, plus accumulated interest; but the downside loss is unlimited.

The basic rules for distinguishing between the appropriate use of options and the use of forwards for *hedging* purposes can be summarized as follows. Other things being equal:

- **When the quantity of a foreign currency cash outflow is known, buy the currency forward; when the quantity is unknown, buy a call option on the currency.**

- **When the quantity of a foreign currency cash inflow is known, sell the currency forward; when the quantity is unknown, buy a put option on the currency.**

- **When the quantity of a foreign currency cash flow is partially known and partially uncertain, use a forward contract to hedge the known portion and an option to hedge the maximum value of the uncertain remainder.**

The above presupposes the use of both forwards and options as *pure hedging* tools, without regard to the treasurer's expectations about the direction or riskiness of the currency's possible fluctuation. It also presupposes that both forward and options contracts are priced fairly; that is, the prices reflect all available information about the expected value and variability of the exchange rate. These are in effect the "efficient market" criteria for the choice between options and forwards: they assume that the hedger should make no attempt to outguess the market.

When the corporation is selective about its hedging policies—i.e., when the firm tempers its decision to cover an exposure by assessing the extent to which its own currency forecasts agree with those of the market—the story changes. Such firms, indeed most firms, are prepared to take a risk in a currency when conditions are right. Consider three examples.

Options versus Forwards: Three Cases

Corporation X, a Swiss-based publishing company that distributes books printed in the United States, makes large monthly payments in dollars to its U.S. parent. During the early 1980s, the American Board of Directors became concerned about foreign exchange losses incurred on the Swiss franc revenues. These losses resulted from the sharp rise in the dollar during that period. In late 1982 the Board had a meeting with the Swiss treasurer, who persuaded them that the franc would rise significantly in the coming year and that to hedge then would be to lock in a disadvantageous exchange rate. The Board took his advice, warning him, however, to hedge should his forecast change.

This is the kind of situation to which forwards are better suited than options, because the top management of the firm is willing to take a position based purely on the expected value, or point forecast, of the Swiss franc's future value.

Corporation Y, a Chicago commodities firm with considerable experience in speculative trading, felt that signs were accumulating that the Japanese yen was entering a period of great instability—although it was not possible to predict which way the currency would go. Normally the firm's grain exports to Japan were fully hedged; all contractual yen receivables were sold in the Chicago futures market. But this time somebody suggested that the firm buy a put option on yen instead. Holding a put option would enable the firm to sell their yen receipts at the exercise price if the yen fell; and if the dollar/yen exchange rate ended up above the exercise price, the yen receipts could be sold at the higher market price.

Although the suggested strategy sounds appealing, it was not the optimal one for the simple reason that Corporation Y had a view on *volatility* but not on *direction*. A put option, when used alone, is not a bet solely on volatility; it is a combined bet on direction and volatility. To achieve a pure bet on volatility, Corporation Y should have (1) hedged against the unknown *direction* of the currency by selling yen futures as usual or using a forward contract, and (2) taken a bet on their *volatility* forecast—where they felt they had an edge on the market—by buying both a put and a call with a common exercise price equal to the forward exchange rate.

The latter combination is called a "straddle" and allows the firm to gain from increased volatility. If the currency rises above the exercise price, you exercise the call; if it falls below, you exercise the put. For this combination, of course, you have to pay both the put price and the call price; so a net gain is achieved only if the spot exchange rate moves away from the exercise price by more than the sum of the two premia. Since the premia themselves reflect the "market view" of volatility, buying a straddle is in effect a bet that your forecast of volatility exceeds that of the market. Whichever way the currency goes, you can profit, as long as it moves a lot!

The value of an option is a measure of the downside protection it provides, as well as the upside potential it allows.

Corporation Z is a New York-based advertising concern with considerable international operations. Like Corporation X, its foreign earnings had suffered from the dollar's strength in 1981 and early 1982. In June 1982 Z's management was wondering what to do about its German subsidiary's dividends that were to be paid at the end of the year. They felt that the German currency was due for a rise, which would of course benefit them. However, the company's management was also aware that the West German political situation was shaky, which might spell troubled times in the currency markets.

In short, they viewed the Deutsche mark as strong but potentially highly variable. They were therefore unwilling to leave the DM cash flow unhedged. On the other hand they wished to take advantage of a possible upturn in the currency's fortunes, "to recoup the past years' losses," as they put it.

A put option to sell DM in December was the instrument best suited to this firm's needs and views. Management had a view both on the direction and the volatility of the German mark. But was it worth paying the option's price? And what would they give up compared to a pure forward hedge?

Graph 1 provides some clue to the answers to these questions. Had Corporation Z bought a put option on June 17, 1982, it would have paid $12,320 for each $1 million of DM (at June rates) deliverable on December 15, 1982 at an exercise price of $0.4215 per mark, which is equal to the forward rate on June 17. As it turned out, the mark did not rise; it wobbled around a bit for two or three months, and in September began a downhill slide to as low as about $0.38 in early November. This made the right to sell DM at $0.42 rather valuable, and the put option's value accordingly climbed, as the graph shows, and later fell as the DM rose once more to a rate approaching $0.42.

Thus, the option evidently *did* provide downside protection, and would have been exercised on December 15. The value of the option is thus a mea-

GRAPH 1

Estimate of Weekly Changes in the Price of Hypothetical Deutsche Mark Put Option as it Nears Maturity During the Last 6 Months of 1982.

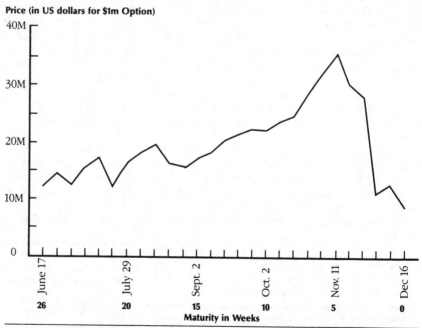

Price (in US dollars for $1m Option)

Maturity in Weeks

Note: Option prices computed based on Garman-Kohlhagen method for a "European" call option with an annualized Standard Deviation of the percentage change of the exchange rate of 11.171%, as calculated from monthly changes over the four years 1979-1982. Futures prices for the December 1982 contract were used in place of forward rates; these and the Eurodollar interest rates were obtained from the International Monetary Market's Weekly Bulletin. Exercise price equals the futures price as of June 17, 1982, which was $0.4215 per DM.

The options market opens up opportunities for betting on volatility not readily available in the forward or futures market.

sure of the downside protection it provides, as well as of the upside potential it allows. On the date of expiration, December 16, the option was worth precisely the difference between the exercise price, $0.4215, and the spot rate on that day, $0.4128, i.e., $8,700 for a $1 million contract. In the end, however, the firm would have paid over $12,000 compared to a forward contract which would have locked in the same rate at no up-front cost. Thus, if Corporation Z had felt strongly about the direction the currency was heading, without regard to volatility, it would have paid to retain an open position or to hedge in the forward market.

Applications of Currency Options in Corporate Exchange Risk Management

The previous section offered specific illustrations of corporate uses for currency options. To generalize from these cases, there are two basic conditions in which these instruments can be used effectively. Either is sufficient alone, but both are often present.

The first is whenever the firm already possesses a "natural option position," an uncertain foreign currency cash flow—that is, one where a third party has the right, but not the obligation, to buy or sell something in a foreign currency. The second is where the option buyer (or seller) has views about the direction and volatility of a currency's movements that differ from that of the market, i.e., where the option trader believes the option is under- or over-priced.

We have seen cases of companies that are willing to take a position on the direction and/or volatility of a currency. Suffice it to say that, for them, the options market opens up new opportunities for betting on expectations about volatility, bets that were not readily available in the forward or futures market.

Let us concentrate instead on the other situation—that is, on identifying the kinds of currency exposure for which options are particularly well-suited. We begin by stating the general rule:

A currency option is the appropriate hedging tool for any firm that has already granted an opposite currency option.

To put it differently, fight fire with fire, not with futures. Currency options can be employed to re-

duce exchange risk whenever a firm has given another party, such as a foreign customer, the right to buy or sell a product or service at a fixed foreign currency price. This brings us to the first application. . .

Fixing foreign currency prices? Buy a put on the foreign currency.

A firm that establishes a price list in, say, French francs as well as domestic currency (U.S. dollars) has in effect given away, for free, a put option on French francs.

Whenever any firm lists the price of the same good in two currencies, the firm has implicitly granted a currency put (or a currency call, depending on which currency you view it from—remember that a call option in one currency is a put option viewed from the other). What is the hedging implication? One cannot use a forward contract, for one never knows who's going to buy. Yet, because a foreign buyer will logically opt to purchase in the depreciated currency, the firm obviously faces a degree of exchange risk when its price lists are printed in two or more foreign currencies. If the customer opts to pay or buy in the weakened currency, the firm can protect itself by having the right to exchange the foreign currency for dollars at a prearranged rate. Buying an explicit call or put option in foreign currency thus offsets the exchange risk arising from the kind of international business that requires granting options in foreign currencies.

For example, an equipment firm may price a generator for European and Far Eastern customers in dollars, DM and yen. The firm then faces a combined "quantity" and "currency" risk: it faces uncertainty about both whether or not the equipment is bought, and the currency in which payment is made. Buying a put option to sell DM or yen will protect the firm against both risks.

Bidding on a contract in foreign currency? Buy a put on that currency!

This application of the foreign exchange option is commonly used by those advocating options as a hedging device. If your costing is done in one currency (such as dollars) and bidding must be done in another, you face the risk of the foreign currency having depreciated by the time your bid is accepted. As the opening example illustrated, such currency risk can make a deal far less attractive, and cannot easily be hedged by means of forward contracts.

The reader will observe, however, that this situation is but a variation of the previous application: one is simply setting a price for a single service in a foreign currency. What this example does emphasize is that in making a bid that stands over some time period, the firm is giving away something valuable; the price of the option necessary to hedge this risk provides a basis for estimating how valuable.

There is some debate as to whether the cost of the option should be incorporated into business costing when bidding on foreign contracts (see, in particular, "Currency Options Cope with Uncertainty" by Agmon and Eldor). In my view, the options cost should not go into the specific costs for each bid, but rather into the overhead costs—such as the cost of drawing up proposals—that firms in the contracting business face.

Making an offer to buy a foreign firm? Buy a call on the foreign currency!

A Californian producer of pollution-control equipment recently sought to purchase a controlling share in a German firm manufacturing atmospheric gas-measurement devices. The U.S. firm's management regarded their offered price of DM 42 million as a reasonable one, but only at the present depreciated rate for DM. The German company insisted on 90 days to consider the offer. The Californians agreed to this reluctantly. In past months, they recalled, the German mark's value had fluctuated as much as 5 percent in a single week. The treasurer voiced concern that they could end up paying several million dollars more than intended if the mark rose significantly during the next 3 months. Consequently, he suggested buying a call option to give the firm the right to buy Deutsche marks at a known rate.

The treasurer was able to find a bank to accommodate his firm's need. The price was two percent of the contract's dollar value, which he thought was reasonable. But was it? To obtain an idea of what a similar 3-month DM call option for $1 million would have cost at theoretical fair prices during 1980, 1981, and 1982, see the quarterly estimates I have presented in Graph 2. The "baseline" graph shows that the option's cost would have varied from about 0.7 percent to 1.4 percent of face value. Because the most difficult part of estimating option prices is gauging volatility, I have drawn bands showing how "high" and "low" estimates of the currency's variance would have altered the price. Only a volatility much greater than that found historically could justify the two percent charged the Californian firm for a three-month option.

To conclude this section, let me summarize what we have learned about the answer to the question: are currency options worth the up-front cost? The answer must be twofold. If the option is fairly priced in a competitive market, the option is always worth purchasing for a firm that wishes to avoid the *contingent exchange risk* that arises from having granted implicit options in foreign currencies. But if the option is overpriced, or if the market is so thin that a suitable option cannot be found or existing options unwound, the option may not be worth the protection it provides.

Yet all is not lost. Mispriced options, as with any mispriced goods or services, create opportunities to make some money. If options are overpriced, sell options; if they're underpriced, buy them. And if you can't find the currency option you need for hedging purposes, you have an alternative: create a do-it-yourself option!

The Do-It-Yourself Currency Option

The key feature of modern options pricing theory, as embodied most notably in the widely-used Black-Scholes model, is that the behavior of a call option's price is very similar to—and therefore can be mimicked by—a combination of holding the underlying security and investing (or borrowing) at the going risk-free interest rate.[2] The same is true of currency option pricing theory, except that instead of investing in securities and borrowing or lending, one simply holds long or short forward or futures contracts on the currency in some proportion to the amount to be hedged. This proportion, known as the "hedge ratio," changes continuously, and is a component of the option pricing model employed in this article: the Garman-Kohlhagen variation of the Black-Scholes model.

---

2. For a more thorough discussion of the intricacies of option pricing and the duplicating portfolio method, see the following article in this issue by Georges Courtadon and John Merrick, "The Option Pricing Model and the Valuation of Corporate Securities."

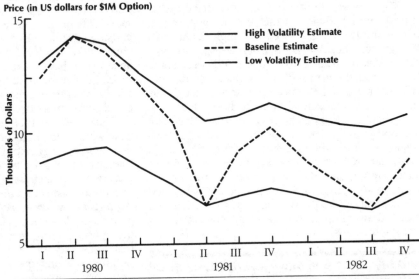

GRAPH 2
Estimate of Changes in the Price of Hypothetical Deutsche Mark 3 Month Call Options, 1980-1982

Price (in US dollars for $1M Option)

Thousands of Dollars

High Volatility Estimate
Baseline Estimate
Low Volatility Estimate

I   II   III   IV   I   II   III   IV   I   II   III   IV
1980   1981   1982

Note: Option prices computed using Garman-Kohlhagen method for a "European" call option of 3 months maturity and an annualized standard deviation of the percentage change of the exchange rate calculated from the immediately preceding 12 months' rates. Forward rates and the Eurodollar interest rates are Friday rates at the end of each quarter, as provided by the Harris Bank. The solid bands above and below the broken line represent hypothetical prices assuming "maximum" and "minimum" estimates of the DM's volatility, based on the highest and lowest estimates of volatility calculated over the entire period.

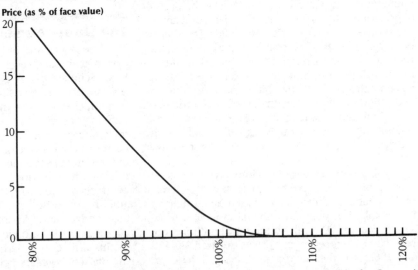

GRAPH 3
How the Price of a Currency Call Option Changes as the Exercise Price Changes in Relation to the Forward Rate

Price (as % of face value)

Exercise Price (as % of the Forward Rate, Expressed in the US Dollars per Unit of Foreign Currency)

Note: Option assumed to be a "European" call option with a Standard Deviation of the percentage change of the exchange rate of 10% and having three months to maturity. U.S. interest rate assumed to be 10%.

*One should speculate with options **only** if one's view of volatility differs from that implicit in the option's price.*

The do-it-yourself currency option replicating strategy relies on the fact that as the forward exchange rate for a currency changes, so does the price of an option to buy or sell that currency. Invariably, however, the option price changes by less than the change in the price of the forward exchange. Because the option price changes by less than the currency's value, in percentage terms, simulating an option by holding futures contracts implies holding less in futures than would be held in options. How much less depends on the sensitivity of the option price to the futures price.

This sensitivity, this hedge ratio, depends on a number of things: the time to maturity, the underlying currencies' volatility, the prevailing interest rate and, most of all, where the futures price is relative to the exercise price of the option. For example, when the futures price is *equal* to the exercise price (the option is "at the money"), a one percent change in the futures price produces about a ½ percent change in the call option price. Thus, to mimic a currency call option's hedging properties at this point, the hedger should hold about 50 percent (of the total amount being hedged) in futures contracts. But one cannot expect to construct a futures position to replicate a call or put option's behavior and then sit on one's ass. As the futures price and other conditions change, the proportion hedged must be revised.

There is not space here to go into more detail. Suffice it to say that if the technique described here can be used to *simulate* a currency option, it can also be used to hedge the risk incurred by anyone *selling* a currency option.

What Determines Currency Option Prices?

We have just seen that we can explain, and therefore mimic, the behavior of currency option prices using well-known instruments: futures or forward contracts. But if option price *behavior* can be explained in terms of the sensitivity of the option price to the forward or futures rate, can we not find the proper price *level* for an option in terms of the factors that influence this sensitivity?

Indeed we can, and this has been done in an elegant fashion in several recent papers (an incomplete selection of which is included at the back of this article). For our purposes it is important to know when a currency option is likely to be cheap, and when it is likely to be costly. The answers illustrated in 3, 4, and 5 turn out to be remarkably consistent with what common sense would tell us.

First and foremost, the value of a call option must always be positive (for no one would *pay* you to give you a right but not an obligation!). Further, it must at least equal the present value of the excess (if any) of the forward rate over the exercise price, in dollar terms. If it were less, you could buy the call option and sell the currency forward, and profit by eventually buying at the exercise price and selling at the higher forward price. The difference between the forward and the exercise price is thus called the *intrinsic value* of the call option.

But even if the forward rate is at or below the exercise price, a call option may still be valuable. The reason is that as long as the option has time before expiration there remains some chance that the forward will rise above the exercise price, and a profit can be locked in. This is shown in Graph 3. When the exercise price is equal to the forward rate, this hypothetical call option with a face value of $1.00 is worth about $0.02. When the exercise price is only 80¢ and the forward is $1.00, the option is worth only its intrinsic value: about 20¢. When the exercise price exceeds the forward by 20 percent, the call option's value is negligible because there is little chance of the currency rising by 20 percent in three months.

This brings us to the second major influence on option prices: time to maturity. The longer the time to expiration, the greater the chance of a favorable movement to the holder, and so the more the seller will charge for the option. As may be seen in Graph 4, however, the value of a longer horizon diminishes beyond about two years for a typical currency option.

Last but not least, the greater is the volatility of the currency, the greater the chance that the option can be exercised at a profit, and so the higher the option price. Graph 5 shows that for an option whose exercise price equals the forward rate, the option price rises linearly with the standard deviation of the currency's fluctuations. This serves as a reminder that the price of any option incorporates the market's expectations about the future volatility of the currency. Thus one should speculate with options *only* if one's view of volatility differs from that implicit in the option's price. From the corporate viewpoint, the implication is that when option prices begin to rise may be just the right time to use options—for higher options prices may spell troubled waters in the currency markets.

GRAPH 4

How the Price of a Currency Call Option Changes as Maturity Increases

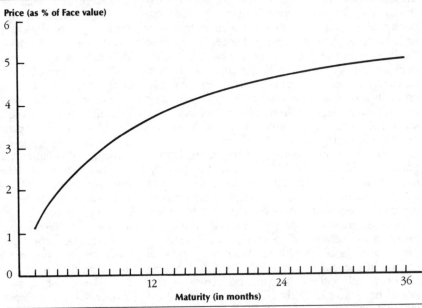

Price (as % of Face value)

Maturity (in months)

Note: Option assumed to be a "European" call option with a Standard Deviation of the percentage change of the exchange rate of 10% and an exercise price equal to the forward exchange rate. U.S. interest rate assumed to be 10%.

GRAPH 5

How the Price of a Currency Call Option Changes as Volatility Increases

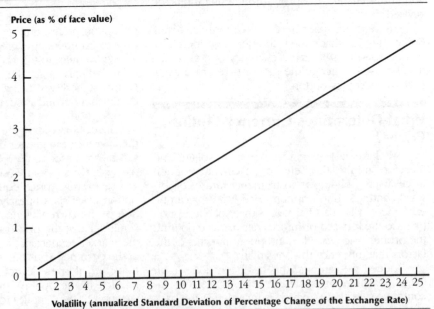

Price (as % of face value)

Volatility (annualized Standard Deviation of Percentage Change of the Exchange Rate)

Note: Option assumed to be a "European" call option with 3 months to maturity and an exercise price equal to the forward exchange rate. U.S. interest rate assumed to be 10%.

Concluding Remarks

Foreign [currency options are] une-
quivocally e[xcellent] tools
for managi[ng] provide
protecti[on] [abo]ut, a currency's vo[latility] [t]hey provide
the asymme[try] [necessa]ry for multinational firms tha[t] [a]t[ric] currency risk.
They are simple in [the sense tha]t their range of attributes and combinatio[n]s [i]s overwhelming. Consequently, many firms will hesitate to plunge in—and
this is no doubt as it should be. But the acceptance
currency options eventually gain will be a solid one.

Some firms will use options in inappropriate
ways, where forwards would do the trick better.
Those interested in the technique will therefore do
well to recall the two basic criteria for the use of
currency puts and calls:

- **When you have a view on *volatility* that differs from that of the market, buy or sell options; when you only have a view on *direction*, use futures or forwards.**

- **When your firm has *given* an implicit option in a foreign currency, hedge the risk by
buying the same kind of currency option.**

References

Agmon, Tamir and Rafael Eldor, (May 1983) "Currency Options Cope With Uncertainty," *Euromoney*, pp.
227-228.

Biger, Nahum and John Hull, (1982) "An Application
of Option Pricing Theory in Foreign Exchange Markets."
Unpublished working paper, York University, Canada.

Black, Fischer and Myron Scholes, (1973) "The Pricing of Options and Corporate Liabilities." *Journal of Political Economy*, Vol. 81, (May/June), pp. 637-659.

Eldor, Rafael, (1982) "On the Valuation of Currency Options, Exchange Rate Insurance Policies and Quota Li-
censes." Unpublished working paper, Harvard University.

Feiger, George and Bertrand Jacquillat, (1979) "Currency Option Bonds, Puts and Calls on Spot Exchange
and the Hedging of Contingent Foreign Earnings."
Journal of Finance, Vol. 33, No. 5, (December) pp.
1129-1139.

Giddy, Ian H., (1983) "Foreign Exchange Options."
Journal of Futures Markets, Vol. 3, No. 2,,pp. 143-166.

Gorman, Mark B. and Steven W. Kolhagen, (1982)
"Foreign Currency Option Values," Unpublished working
paper, University of California at Berkeley (December).

Grabbe, J. Orlin, (1983) "The Pricing of Call and Put
Options on Foreign Exchange." Unpublished working paper, Wharton School, University of Pennsylvania.

Smith, Clifford W., (1976) "Option Pricing: A Review."
Journal of Financial Economics, Vol. 3, (Jan/March) pp.
3-51.

Part III International Performance Measurement

FAS#52-Measuring the Performance of Foreign Operations

By Bryan Carsberg,
The London School of Economics

Introduction

During 1981, a British company purchased a business in the United States. The exchange rate was £1 = $2.50. The business made a low return during its first year—at least according to the dollar measurements. The value of the pound, however, fell to $2.00. Did the corresponding increase in the value of the dollar make the British company better off? Should the increase be reflected in the measurement of the income of the British company? How should the effect be measured and reported?

These questions seem to have been the most controversial considered in recent years by the bodies that set accounting standards in the United States and the United Kingdom. Other current issues such as accounting for the effects of changing prices, for leases, and for pension costs all present significant challenges. But none of them has provoked a level of concern in business comparable to that kindled by foreign currency translation.

No doubt this concern is attributable partly to the difficulty of the issues. Two methods of foreign currency translation have emerged as rivals, and neither has been acknowledged to have clear-cut superiority. A more important reason for corporate concern, however, is the magnitude of what is at stake. Many businesses now have large overseas operations; and exchange rates between different currencies can fluctuate with extreme volatility. Consequently, the choice of translation method can have a big impact on reported results.

Foreign currency translation also has an importance beyond its impact on financial statements published for shareholders and others. It is essential to the management functions of performance evaluation and control within the multinational company. Managers need to decide where changes should be made in their operations, where investment should be increased and where it should be cut back. And, in evaluating the success of such investment, multinationals need to be able to distinguish the performance of managers of overseas operations from the performance of the company as a whole.

The performance of overseas managers should be assessed mainly by comparing their performance with standards that reflect conditions in the local operating environment (i.e., local rates of interest and inflation). Finally, however, the success of a multinational's overseas investment policy must be evaluated according to the returns it generates for shareholders in the home country. Reported results should be consistent with investment policy in the sense that if the policy serves the interests of shareholders, and if actual results are as expected, then the reports should signal success.

Perhaps this aim of consistency is the most important consideration in formulating an approach to the translation of foreign currency. After translation, the reported results should reflect "economic reality"—insofar as this is possible, given the fallibility of accounting conventions — as perceived by everyone concerned. *The ultimate goal of overseas investment is to earn a satisfactory rate of return as translated into and measured in the home currency.* Many intermediate objectives like expanding market share, increasing profit margins, and minimizing political and economic risk will feature in management's decisions. But the translated rate of return is the "bottom line." Thus, earning a satisfactory rate of return in the overseas currency is neither necessary nor sufficient in itself. A return of 5 percent per year in a currency that is appreciating by 20 percent against the home currency will produce an effective return of over 25 percent per year, which may well be satisfactory. A return of 40 percent in a currency depreciating by 50 percent is not satisfactory.

The best way to assess whether an overseas investment has been satisfactory is to measure the net *cash flows* generated by the investment, translate them into terms of the home currency, and discount them at the appropriate cost of capital to obtain a net present value. This computation, however, can only be performed at the *end* of an investment's life. The challenge for accounting, of course, is to give good indications of the progress of the investment at *interim* stages — annually, or perhaps more frequently. In this routine accounting, future benefits have to be represented by asset measurements rather than estimates of cash flows. Because asset measurements often serve only as a rough indicator of future cash flows, accounting reports must inevitably remain an imperfect guide to the success of an investment. Nevertheless, as we shall see, some accounting methods are better than others.

Let us now consider a simple example which serves to illustrate the issues involved in choosing between the two main alternative methods of foreign currency translation. We shall consider again a company owned in Britain and operating in the United States, and we shall further assume that the exchange rate moved from exactly £1 = $2.50 at the start of the year to £1 = $2.00 at the end of the

year. This means that the dollar effectively gained 25 percent against the pound: $100 increased in value from £40 to £50. The income statement and balance sheet (in dollars) of this hypothetical American subsidiary are shown in Table 1 and the income computation is shown in Table 2.

Our company has earned $700 during the year, a return of 10 percent on the $7,000 of equity capital employed. When results are translated into pounds, and if the accounting measure is to be consistent with economic reality, the outcome should be a rate of return of about 35 percent — the dollar return of 10 percent combined with the effect of the appreciation of the dollar at 25 percent. (Strictly, the return should be 37.5 percent, the product of 1.10 times 1.25 less 1.00.)

The Temporal Method

The two most frequently advocated methods of foreign currency translation are known as the "temporal" method and the "current" method. The temporal method was the basis for FAS 8, the U.S. standard on foreign currency translation issued by the Financial Accounting Standards Board in 1975. The temporal method takes the view that each compo-

TABLE 1 **Illustrative Statement of Net Assets**		At Start	At End
	Fixed Assets		
	Cost	$20,000	$20,000
	Depreciation	8,000	9,000
		$12,000	$11,000
	Cash	—	1,700
		$12,000	$12,700
	Less Debt	5,000	5,000
	Equity	$ 7,000	$ 7,700

TABLE 2 **Income Statement**			
	Sales		$29,000
	Depreciation Expense	$1,000	
	Interest Expense	400	
	Other Expenses	26,900	28,300
	Income		$ 700

nent of the financial statements should be translated at the exchange rate that matches the timing of the accounting measurement of that component. For example, fixed assets and the related depreciation are measured at historical cost in conventional accounting. Under the temporal method, accordingly, they are translated at an historical exchange rate (the rate at the date of acquisition). Debt, however, is normally carried in the balance sheet at an amount that represents the current extent of the obligation. Consequently, under the temporal method, debt is translated at the current exchange rate.

To obtain the results of applying the temporal method to our numerical example, we need to know the exchange rate at the date of acquisition of the fixed assets. Let us truncate history and assume a historical rate of $4 to £1. The computations are set out in Tables 3 and 4.

The first step is to convert net assets at the start of the year into pounds. Fixed assets in dollars are divided by four to obtain the number in pounds; debt is divided by 2.5. Next, net assets at the end of the year are converted into pounds. We then can see that net assets (equity) increased from £1,000 to £1,100. Since no dividends were paid and no new equity capital was raised, income is equal to the increase in net assets, i.e., £100.

Direct translation of sales and expenses gives income of £600; this is reduced to £100 by the loss of £500 on translation. The loss arises because the translation rate for the loan is changed from 2.5 to 2, causing the amount of the loan in pounds to increase from £2,000 to £2,500. The computations are recognizing, in effect, that repayment of the loan will be more expensive if it is made in pounds.

The main shortcomings of the temporal method are appparent from our example. First, the method seems to produce a significant distortion in the ratio of debt to total capital employed. The ratio is 41.6 percent in the dollar report at the start of the year. In the corresponding statements in pounds, the ratio is 66.6 percent. This distortion results from the use of different rates for the translation of fixed

TABLE 3 Net Worth Converted Into £—Temporal Method		At Start			At End		
		$	$/£	£	$	$/£	£
	Fixed Assets						
	Cost	$20,000	4.00	£ 5,000	$20,000	4.00	£ 5,000
	Depreciation	8,000	4.00	2,000	9,000	4.00	2,250
		$12,000		£ 3,000	$11,000		£ 2,750
	Cash	—		—	1,700	2.00	850
		$12,000		£ 3,000	$12,700		£ 3,600
	Debt	5,000	2.50	2,000	5,000	2.00	2,500
	Equity	$ 7,000		£ 1,000	$ 7,700		£ 1,100

TABLE 4 Income Measured in £— Temporal Method		$	$	$/£	£	£
	Sales		$29,000	2.00		£14,500
	Depreciation Expense	1,000		4.00	250	
	Interest Expense	400		2.00	200	
	Other Expenses	26,900	28,300	2.00	13,450	13,900
	Operating Income		$ 700			£ 600
	Translation Adjustment					
	(Loss)		—			(500)
	Total Income		$ 700			£ 100

assets and debt. A similar problem afflicts the computation of income. A loss is recognized on the debt but no offsetting gain is claimed on the fixed assets as a result of the appreciation of the dollar. The rate of return on equity, far from being the 37.5 percent we expected, is shown as 10 percent (£100/£1,000).

The disparate treatment of fixed assets and debt has been the main reason for criticism of the temporal method. As businessmen have been quick to point out, loans are usually raised to finance purchase of the fixed assets, and such loans are likely to be repaid in the foreign currency rather than in home currency. Assets and loans effectively hedge each other, at least to some extent, and any translation method that treats the two items differently fails to reflect economic reality.[1]

The difficulties described are bad enough when currency exchange rates move steadily in the anticipated direction. When the rates fluctuate sharply around a trend, however, the effects on income can be dramatic. Indeed, the measurement of income can come to seem like the result of a lottery. Criticism directed at these arbitrary effects, and at the resulting distortions of real overseas operating performance, caused the Financial Accounting Standards Board to reconsider FAS 8 and the problem of foreign currency translation.

The Current Method

The idea that assets and loans should be translated at the same rate led naturally to the consideration of the current method. This method calls for translation of *all assets and liabilities at the exchange*

TABLE 5
Net worth converted into £—Current Method

	At Start			At End		
	$	$/£	£	$	$/£	£
Fixed Assets						
Cost	$20,000	2.50	£8,000	$20,000	2.00	£10,000
Depreciation	8,000	2.50	3,200	9,000	2.00	4,500
	$12,000		£4,800	$11,000		£ 5,500
Cash	—		—	1,700	2.00	850
	$12,000		£4,800	$12,700		£ 6,350
Less Debt	5,000	2.50	2,000	5,000	2.00	2,500
Equity	$ 7,000		£2,800	$ 7,700		£ 3,850

TABLE 6
Income Measured in £—Current Method

	$	$	$/£	£	£
Sales		$29,000	2.00		£14,500
Depreciation Expense	1,000		2.00	500	
Interest Expense	400		2.00	200	
Other Expenses	26,900	28,300	2.00	13,450	14,150
Operating Income		$ 700			£ 350
Translation Adjustment (Gain)		—			700
Total Income		$ 700			£ 1,050

1. If borrowing is at a fixed rate of interest while cash flows generated by fixed assets are variable, unexpected price changes can detract from the hedging to some extent. The best hope for dealing with such a situation is not in retaining the temporal method, but in using current measurements of both assets and liabilities.

rate prevailing at the balance sheet date. The results of applying this method to our example are shown in Tables 5 and 6. The computations follow the same process as before with one exception: net assets are translated at $2.50 at the start of the period, but at $2.00 at the end.

A comparison of net asset numbers shows that net income for the period is £1,050. The income statement shows this to be made up of operating income of £350 plus a translation *gain* of £700. In effect, the current rate method recognizes a gain on translation of the fixed assets. At the start of the year, the fixed assets are measured at £4,800, and £500 is deducted for depreciation during the year to leave £4,300; however, with the fall in the exchange rate, end-of-year assets are measured at £5,500 and a gain of £1,200 results. The gain of £1,200 less the loss (which still arises) of £500 on the loan gives net translation gain of £700.

The current rate method thus gives us a rate of return measured at 37.5 percent (£1,050/£2,800), which accords with the economic reality as identified above.

To the extent that we can generalize from this example, the current method is a major improvement over the temporal method. However, the users of accounts need to keep in mind that the usefulness of both methods is limited by the accounting convention of valuing assets at historical cost. Furthermore, if assets are measured at historical acquisition costs, translation of fixed assets at the current exchange rate will produce a number that is hard to interpret. Historical cost multiplied by the historical exchange rate produces a number that at least can be recognized as the sacrifice of funds of the "home currency" required to pay for the asset at the date of acquisition. Historical cost multiplied by the current exchange rate, however, produces a number that lacks any economic significance.

TABLE 7 Net worth converted into £; Revised Case—Current Method		At Start			At End		
		$	$/£	£	$	$/£	£
	Fixed Assets						
	Cost	$20,000	2.50	£8,000	$20,000	2.00	£10,000
	Depreciation	8,000	2.50	3,200	9,000	2.00	4,500
		$12,000		£4,800	$11,000		£ 5,500
	Cash	—		—	1,000	2.00	500
		$12,000		£4,800	$12,000		£ 6,000
	Less Debt	5,000	2.50	2,000	5,000	2.00	2,500
	Equity	$ 7,000		£2,800	$ 7,000		£ 3,500

TABLE 8 Income Measured in £; Revised Case—Current Method		$	$	$/£	£	£
	Sales		$28,300	2.00		£14,150
	Depreciation Expense	1,000		2.00	500	
	Interest Expense	400		2.00	200	
	Other Expenses	26,900	28,300	2.00	13,450	14,150
	Operating Income		$ 0			£ 0
	Translation Adjustment (Gain)		—			700
	Total Income		$ 0			£ 700

A preference for the current rate method rests on a belief in the desirability of eliminating one cause of the divergence of accounting reports from economic reality.

The implications of this situation can be illustrated by modifying slightly our above example. The result is a case that is less favourable to the current rate method. Suppose that the effective return in dollars remains at 10 percent but that, during the year under review, the return is earned partly in an increase in fixed asset values, reflecting an expected increase in future cash flows: the current cost of fixed assets (net of depreciation) is $11,700 compared to the historical cost of $11,000 in our previous illustration, but sales are only $28,300 and cash at the end of the year only $1,000 (a decrease of $700). The accounts based on historical cost measurements (see Tables 7 and 8) show income of zero in dollars, and £700 in sterling.

The return of 25 percent (£700/£2,800) now shown by the current method fails to match the "real" return of 37.5 percent; and the fixed asset measurement, still £5,500, now is simply historical cost times the current exchange rate and fails to represent any real economic magnitude.

In this same case, however, use of the temporal method of translation would actually show a loss (see Tables 9 and 10).

Thus, even though the current method is inadequate here, it still represents an improvement over the temporal alternative.

To strengthen further the correspondence between accounting and economic "reality," it would be necessary to use current cost measurements of all assets and liabilities. In that event, both the current and the temporal method would call for translation at the current exchange rate.

In practice, when accounting measurements reflect historic costs, we cannot generalise about the relationship between the choice of translation method and the usefulness of the accounting rate of return as an indicator of economic performance. In

TABLE 9 Net worth converted into £; Revised Case— Temporal Method		At Start			At End		
		$	$/£	£	$	$/£	£
Fixed Assets							
	Cost	$20,000	4.00	£5,000	$20,000	4.00	£5,000
	Depreciation	8,000	4.00	2,000	9,000	4.00	2,250
		$12,000		£3,000	$11,000		£2,750
Cash		—		—	1,000	2.00	500
		$12,000		£3,000	$12,000		£3,250
Less Debt		5,000	2.50	2,000	5,000	2.00	2,500
Equity		$ 7,000		£1,000	$ 7,000		£ 750

TABLE 10 Income Measured in £; Revised Case—Temporal Method		$	$	$/£	£	£
Sales			$28,300	2.00		£14,150
Depreciation Expense		1,000		4.00	250	
Interest Expense		400		2.00	200	
Other Expenses		26,900	28,300	2.00	13,450	13,900
Operating Income			$ 0			£ 250
Translation Adjustment (Gain)				—		(500)
Total Income			$ 0			£ (250)

Management's main responsibility should be to provide investors with the fullest possible disclosure of their international operations, and leave interpretation to the markets.

some cases, the temporal method may produce a better approximation of the actual return than the current rate method. For example, an unrecorded increase in the current cost of fixed assets may be offset by the failure, under the temporal method, to recognise the effect on the value of the assets of a fall in the value of the foreign currency. We do not know the average effect, based on empirical data. A preference for the current rate method rests on a belief in the desirability of eliminating one cause of the divergence of accounting reports from economic reality. Further improvement requires the adoption of current measurements for assets and liabilities.

It is difficult to say what effect the distortions caused by accounting currency translations have on the stock prices of multinationals. The stock market, under the guidance of sophisticated investment analysts, may see through most of these distortions. Investors, after all, use information about the company's past mainly as a basis for predictions of future performance. They may use a variety of disclosures to draw inferences about the real value of a multinational's foreign assets. If such is the case, the choice of method of currency translation would have little importance for investors — though use of a poor method may increase their costs of analysis. In a reasonably sophisticated market, however, management's main responsibility should be to provide investors with the fullest possible disclosure (of accounting methods as well as results) of their international operations, and leave interpretation to the markets.

Failure to use the best accounting methods may be more important for other uses, such as government economic policy decisions. For corporate purposes, however, greatest importance attaches to the application of these accounting methods to internal evaluation of overseas performance, which may in turn affect management compensation and capital investment decisions. Part of the problem of evaluating overseas managers can be dealt with by using local rates of interest and inflation as standards for assessing the adequacy of rates of return measured in the *local currency*. For the purpose of capital allocation, however, the home country financial management must attempt to estimate the effects of currency changes on the long-run profitability of proposed international investments; and control procedures will need to focus on a comparison of actual and estimated returns in the home currency. Management thus would benefit from knowing the current value of net assets employed, trans-

lated at the current exchange rate. This measures the amount in a way that gives a useful basis for assessing home currency rates of return.

Consequently, we find that the foreign currency translation problem cannot be resolved in a satisfactory manner until we have dealt with the logically prior deficiency of historical cost measurements. To the extent that fixed assets are valued at or near their current values on the balance sheet, translation at the current exchange rate will provide a useful picture of profitability. The fact that large multinationals like Phillips N.V., TRW, and GE have chosen to make current measurements, at least for internal purposes, suggests that recognition of their usefulness may be spreading. If such adjustments are not practicable, or cost too much to produce, then historical cost measurements may offer the most reliable, cost-effective estimate of the current worth of resources within the conventions of accounting (which place heavy store on the use of reliable measurements). Under these conditions, the translation of our best measurement of current worth in dollars at our best estimate of the value of the dollar — i.e., the current exchange rate — then seems quite reasonable.

Such, at any rate, was the thinking of the Financial Accounting Standards Board when they chose to adopt the current rate method in Statement No. 52, *Foreign Currency Translation,* issued in December 1981 as a revision to Statement No. 8. The U.K. Accounting Standards Committee has issued a statement in the last few months. It is the first U.K. standard on foreign currency translation and it also adopts the current rate method.

The Measurement of Income

Apart from the limitations of historical cost conventions, can we conclude that the difficult problem of foreign currency translation has now been solved in a satisfactory manner and that the issue can be allowed to rest? The answer, unfortunately, is "No." One small provision, included in both the US and the UK standard, means that the translated income statements still fail to capture the essence of overseas operations: "Translation adjustments shall not be included in determining net income but shall be reported separately and accumulated in a separate component of equity" (FASB Statement No. 52, paragraph 13). As a result of this provision, reported income in our basic numerical example would be determined under the cur-

The foreign currency translation problem cannot be resolved until we have dealt with the logically prior deficiency of historical cost measurements.

rent rate method to be only £350, a rate of return of 12.5 percent (See Tables 5 and 6).

The standard setters were probably led to exclude the translation adjustment from the income statement because of a wish to preserve, as far as possible in the translation process, all financial ratios at their levels in foreign currency statements. The observed distortion in the debt-to-equity ratio had helped to discredit the temporal method, and it was no doubt felt that distortion should be similarly avoided in the income statement. Also, the recognition of the gain on translating fixed assets may have been seen as akin to the recognition of an unrealized profit.

Both of these concerns, however, seem unrelated to the main purpose of financial reporting. Gains and losses on foreign currency are intrinsic parts of the reality of overseas investment, and that reality should be reflected in financial reports. This point may be illuminated by considering the likely cause of changes in exchange rates. A depreciation of the £ against the dollar is likely, over long periods of time, to reflect the existence of a higher rate of inflation in the U.K. than in the U.S. For example, a depreciation of 25 percent would be expected if the rate of inflation were zero in the U.S., but 25 percent in the U.K. This change in the exchange rate would keep the relative prices of goods in the two countries constant.

Suppose those circumstances actually held, and the rate of return net of inflation was 10 percent (as in our illustration) according to the dollar measurements. If the translation gain were excluded from income, the rate of return would be represented as 12.5 percent in sterling (as computed above), and the return net of inflation would appear to be negative. Inclusion of the translation adjustment in income would give a return of 37.5 percent in sterling, high enough to show that the investment overseas is worthwhile inspite of the high rate of inflation in the U.K.

From this perspective, the translation process can be seen in part as an adjustment of income numbers to reflect operating rates of return in the home country currency *gross of any adjustment for inflation.* Such a process effectively takes account of differences between the inflation rates of the countries concerned. Or so it would, if changes in exchange rates always perfectly reflected changes in relative rates of inflation.

Foreign currency exchange rates, however, do not perfectly reflect differences in rates of inflation, particularly over short periods of time. Short-term capital flows associated with differences in interest rates and other factors can cause significant changes in exchange rates independently of prices. Only over the long run can it be said that exchange rate changes are determined largely by differences in inflation rates.

Most importantly for our purposes, however, changes in exchange rates do make businesses better or worse off. They are prices that determine the ultimate worth, in the home country, of cash flows generated by the overseas business. An income computation should reflect, as far as possible, all factors that make a business more or less profitable.

The performance of an overseas manager may best be judged in terms of the results measured in overseas currency, and set against standards of performance in the country concerned. The performance of the whole business—that is, its contribution to the value of the parent company and stockholders' investment — must be measured in the home currency. For that purpose exchange gains and losses are a part of the performance. It may be reasonable to recognize the volatility of exchange rates by showing gains and losses on translation in a special section of the income statement, perhaps grouped with extraordinary items. If the intent is to measure real economic performance, however, it is not fitting to exclude them from income altogether.

A Proposal for Measuring International Performance

by G. Bennett Stewart,
Stern Stewart Putnam & Macklis, Ltd.

Introduction

In principle, there should be no difference between the evaluation of foreign and domestic operations. The central issues are the same: Has the operation added to the value of our shareholders' investment? To what extent is local operating management responsible for the unit's success or lack of it? Can additional capital be invested profitably?

Resolving these issues for foreign operations is more difficult, however, for several reasons. First, inflation rates overseas often are orders of magnitude higher than those in the United States. This renders conventional, historical-cost accounting statements nearly meaningless. When inflation is high, profits are overstated due to illusory holding gains, while assets, and thus the capital base, are carried at values well below current replacement cost.

Of course, this problem is not unique to foreign operations, just more pronounced. While the tendency has been for management to ignore the effects of inflation when evaluating performance in dollar terms (witness the general lack of interest in FAS #33 inflation-adjusted figures), this oversight becomes critical when evaluating foreign performance. For, differences in rates of inflation between countries are the primary reason — at least over the long run — why currencies change in value relative to each other. Currency translation and inflation accounting are thus inextricably linked. To measure performance properly, the effect of inflation must be built into local financial statements *before* it can be offset by currency translation.

The second problem is caused by exchange rate fluctuations that distort the income from, and thus the value of, foreign investments when translated into dollar terms. While local management may believe it is performing quite well, a sudden realignment of currency values can produce an entirely different impression for home country management. At other times, local performance may be exaggerated by translation gains that are unlikely to recur.

Corporate managers are understandably concerned that investors will penalize their company with a lower stock price because of the earnings volatility caused by currency fluctuations. The natural reaction is thus to hedge accounting exposure, and to shy away from foreign investments where there is a great likelihood of currency instability. Such a reaction, however, is clearly not always in the best economic interest of the firm, or its stockholders. In order to explain why this concern with accounting exposure is misplaced — whether under FAS #8 or the newly adopted FAS #52 — we need to begin with an understanding of (1) what causes exchange rates to fluctuate and (2) how influential investors really appraise the performance and value of foreign operations.

Exchange rates tend to fluctuate around an "intrinsic" value. They may be overvalued for a period of time, and then experience a dramatic devaluation that merely offsets the accumulation of past inflation. At other times exchange rates can move in *anticipation* of coming changes in economic conditions that will not affect the foreign unit's performance until some time in the future. Only some fluctuations in any given year will reflect changes in the intrinsic value of the currency. The majority of currency movements are temporary and likely to reverse themselves with the passage of time.

Investors consequently try not to place too much emphasis on any given year's exchange rate movements. Consider, for example, the following exchange between The Dexter Corporation's chairman, David Coffin, and the president of a leading investment advisory house:

David L. Coffin: [Foreign investment is] complex and frustrating. We have a number of successful foreign businesses that do well in local currencies but have suffered on a yearly comparison basis because of the stronger dollar of the past two years.

Edward M. Giles: It's frustrating for investors, too. It is difficult to make appropriate adjustments for currency-related change, whether positive or negative, and to determine whether the effects are transitory or fundamental.[1]

Sophisticated investors attempt to separate the fundamental from the transitory in order to pay for enduring value. This means, for one thing, that currently employed accounting methods of currency translation do not capture or simulate the process of valuation. If certain, but not all, exchange rate changes matter to price-setting investors, then accountants must inevitably fail to provide a measure of performance that reflects economic reality. They must choose between a technique like FAS #8, that places currency translation gains and losses on the income statement as if all exchange rate movements matter to investors; and one like FAS #52, that buries all adjustments in an equity reserve as if no currency fluctuations matter. Since the truth lies in between, reported results must be adjusted before meaningful measures of performance are possible.

The situation in Mexico over the past decade or so illustrates many of the problems encountered in measuring performance for international operations (and it will serve as the basis for the case study presented later in this article). Mexico experienced a much higher rate of inflation than the United States in the early 1970's, and yet the peso's value held steady at 12.5 to the dollar. This meant that, at some point, those economic forces that maintain

purchasing power parity throughout the world would inevitably bring about a correction in the value of the peso. In 1976, the peso suffered a devaluation (of over 60 percent) to 20 pesos to the dollar. Thus, instead of a gradual adjustment, most of the accumulated inflation differential between the U.S and Mexico was reflected in a single day's change in the rate of exchange. This drastic translation loss was not a real economic loss; it simply compensated for the overvaluation of the Mexican currency — and thus the overstatement of returns from Mexican operations — in prior years.

Much the same pattern was repeated over the period 1976-1982. The Mexican authorities pursued economic policies designed to keep the peso fundamentally overvalued in order to achieve the dual objectives of a favorable balance of trade and rapid expansion in economic growth. For some time they were able to sustain this policy by borrowing against future oil revenues. The day of reckoning came when the market lost confidence in Mexico's ability to further mortgage its oil wealth. While the precise date of the devaluation was not foreseeable, it was widely anticipated by investors and considered necessary to offset past inflation.

Those companies that made long-term investment decisions predicated on the continuation of the unrealistically high peso of recent years now find themselves in a difficult position. This problem might have been avoided by translating results from Mexico into dollars using a more realistic exchange rate, one that reflects the fundamental economic forces that eventually determine a currency's value. In this way home country management would have been made aware that the performance in Mexico was overstated, and that a large translation loss was inevitable.

In this article, I will propose an alternative accounting framework that combines adjustments for local inflation with a method of currency translation using "normalized" exchange rates. Such a framework should provide a much more realistic picture of the economic realities of international operations than either unadjusted FAS #8 or FAS #52 results. Although not likely to be adopted soon by the Accounting Standards Board, this framework has a number of important internal uses, serving potentially as the basis for corporate decisions affecting capital allocation, the hedging of currency risk, and management compensation.

---

1. The Dexter Corporation Annual Report, 1982.

Far from being an arcane economic supposition, PPP is simply the predictable outcome of more or less inevitable actions by businessmen.

The Determinants of Exchange Rates

Before approaching these questions, it is important to begin with at least a crude theory of exchange rates on which performance measures can be based.

Broadly speaking, exchange rate fluctuations can be attributed to one of three causes: (1) differences in rates of inflation, expected as well as actual; (2) relative economic competitiveness; and (3) government policy. Over any short interval of time, say, one-to-three years, changes in economic competitiveness and government policy may be the dominant factors affecting exchange rates. Hence, anticipating business cycles, fluctuations in interest rates, and election winners may be very useful in predicting short-term exchange rate movements. Over the longer term, however, these factors tend to cancel out, leaving inflation differentials the dominant force.

The impact of inflation on exchange rates is seen most clearly in those countries with consistently high or low rates of inflation. In Brazil and Argentina, for example, where inflation regularly runs in excess of 100 percent a year, their currencies suffer regular, indeed often programmed, devaluations. By contrast, the Swiss franc typically appreciates against other currencies due to the perennially low inflation enforced by conservative Swiss bankers. The same is generally true in Germany, where memory of the hyper-inflation of the 1920s is the dominant psychological force leading the country to low inflation and a strong currency.

In countries like the U.S., which have had inflation rates between these two extremes, or where the level of inflation is not as readily predictable, exchange rate movements are not as visibly linked to differences in inflation rates. From year to year, the influence of business cycles and changes in government policies will be a major determinant of currency appreciation or depreciation. Nevertheless, for almost all countries, the cumulative exchange rate movements over a, say, five-year time horizon can be explained largely by inflation differentials.

Purchasing Power Parity

The tendency of exchange rate changes to offset inflation differentials between any two currencies is known as Purchasing Power Parity (PPP). The theory of PPP relies on the simple notion that similar products will sell at roughly the same price at any given point in time throughout the world. This happens because astute international traders buy where goods are cheap and sell where expensive, thus ensuring that similar goods in geographically isolated markets do not differ in price when translated at current exchange rates. If prices of the same goods are identical at current exchange rates, and if they are to remain so in the future (when converted at future exchange rates), then the *change* in price levels over time must be offset by a corresponding equal and opposite *change* in exchange rates.

The theory of PPP maintains, for example, that if the rate of inflation is 20 percent in one country while only 10 percent in another, the country with the 20 percent inflation will see its currency depreciate by 10 percent against the other currency. Otherwise, the price of identical products would not be the same, and profit opportunities would abound. PPP, then, far from being an arcane, unrealistic economic supposition, is simply the predictable outcome of more or less inevitable actions by businessmen to exploit profit opportunities.

How, then, can exchange rates ever deviate from PPP? Why is it not possible for international traders to maintain the same price for the same product at all times, thus ensuring that exchange rates continuously conform to PPP? Deviations from PPP occur, for one thing, because certain "frictions" reduce the profitability and increase the risk of international trade. These frictions include the costs of transportation, taxes, and financing, restrictions such as import quotas, exchange and capital controls, and lack of good information about prices and profit opportunities.

The presence of these frictions means that exchange rates can fluctuate in a "band" around the level dictated by PPP without creating opportunities to profit through trade. If, for example, the cost of financing, taxes, and transportation came to 20 percent of the value of the trade, exchange rates could deviate as much as 20 percent from their intrinsic value without setting in motion corrective market forces.

International Competitiveness

Another cause of temporary deviations from PPP are changes in the underlying competitiveness of an economy in international markets. If the world operated strictly on a barter basis for trade, then the exchange rate would be the ratio at which exported goods were traded for imported goods. Any change in this ratio would lead to a revaluation in the fundamental value of the currency.

In the real world, changes in the supply and demand, and thus in the "relative prices," of certain goods can dominate exchange rate movements over considerable periods of time. One of the best examples of this in recent years was the British pound. For several years after 1976, the pound appreciated against the dollar even while Britain was experiencing a higher rate of inflation than the United States. This was partly attributable to the increasing value of North Sea oil as petroleum prices continued to rise. The pound, acting much like a share of stock in the British economy, rose in line with the general increase in British wealth. So closely did the pound's value seem to be tied to oil that the *Economist* of London dubbed the currency, "The Petro-Pound." Now that oil prices have weakened, the pound, along with other oil-driven currencies, has lost its premium value in exchange markets.

An increase in the pound's value due to oil, however, should not affect the value of other British investments. To remain competitive in international markets, businessmen in Britain would have to hold down their prices in pounds to maintain the same cost to foreigners. But by so doing, the price charged to pound consumers will be reduced, thus lowering reported profits in pounds. In this case the translation gain arising from the initial appreciation in the pound offsets a subsequent return shortfall, leaving foreign investors equally well off on net. Thus, the change in the value of the pound did not, in fact, represent an exchange risk.

It could be argued, then, that the ideal framework for evaluating foreign performance should include exchange gains or losses arising from changes in relative prices as part of the return earned from a foreign operation. My proposal for evaluating foreign operations does not, however, explicitly account for the effects of deviations from PPP caused by such changes in relative prices for several reasons. First, the initial gain recorded in the example above is potentially misleading to management. It does not reflect the difficulty local management subsequently will have to remain competitive in pound terms, and so could communicate a confusing signal to corporate management about the desirability of investing additional capital. Second, there is no practicable way to ascertain whether deviations from PPP are caused by changes

in relative prices, or by those changes in government policy which, as I shall argue, should be excluded from the evaluation of performance. Finally, and most important, evidence indicates that such changes in relative prices tend to average out over a period of 5 years or longer, leaving PPP as a valid long term predictor of exchange rate movements. Even a unified and dominant cartel like OPEC could not indefinitely maintain an artificially high price for oil against the economic forces of conservation, the development of substitutes, and the entry of new competitors. It is precisely these competitive forces that will drive exchange rates towards PPP over time.

Government Policy Affects Exchange Rates

Probably the most important reason why exchange rates fluctuate around their fundamental PPP value is government policy. Governments manipulate exchange rates to spur economic growth and employment, to cushion economic shocks, and, occasionally, to lead the country to painful, but necessary adjustments. Not surprisingly, the policies are frequently designed to help win elections. And while such policies can be successful for a short period of time (the benefits need last only through the next election), economic forces ultimately move the exchange rate back towards PPP.

By not allowing their currencies to depreciate to offset inflation differentials, governments preserve the prestige associated with stable currencies. More important, an overvalued exchange rate allows businessmen to import raw materials and consumers to import products at a lower cost than otherwise. But, while this may spur economic growth for a time, the free lunch cannot last forever.

The consequence of maintaining a currency artificially high is that payments due to foreigners for imports exceed payments received from foreigners for exports, and the government is thus forced to make up a balance of payments deficit. It will do so by using its own limited foreign exchange reserves to buy its currency in the forward exchange market. This provides its countrymen with the foreign currencies they collectively require to pay for the excess of imports over exports. At some point, however, the government will run out of money to subsidize the import spree, and the exchange rate will decline to the point where a balance will be achieved between desired imports and exports.

The day of reckoning can be further deferred by international borrowing, but only as long as the country has good credit in the capital markets. From 1976 to 1982, Mexico was able to maintain an over-valued peso by borrowing against its future oil revenues. In this way the country obtained the foreign reserves needed to subsidize its overvalued exchange rate. When the price of oil fell, the market's assessment of Mexico's creditworthiness was drastically reduced, the borrowing window closed, and the exchange rate plummeted.

Precisely the opposite economic policy is now being followed in Mexico. Mexico's recently elected government is forcing austerity by maintaining an exchange rate that is undervalued relative to its PPP value. In effect, the country is now being taxed through an undervalued exchange rate in order to pay for past excesses. The Mexican authorities used the exchange rate at first to subsidize and now to tax in a way that is not apparent to the ordinary citizen.

Management should not let itself be fooled by such manipulation of exchange rates. When the local currency is purposely overvalued, the results of local performance when translated into dollar terms will be *exaggerated* by the exchange rate subsidy. When the currency is undervalued, the results of foreign operations will be artificially *depressed* by the exchange rate tax. The result of government changes in policy transmitted through exchange rates is a potentially large and troublesome disparity in perception between corporate and local management.

Interest Rates Affect Exchange Rates

Through monetary policies implemented by their central banks, governments can affect interest rates and, thus indirectly, exchange rates. Exchange rates are tied even more directly to interest rates than to the prices of goods and services, so that when interest rates change, exchange rates follow — even though this may temporarily require a deviation from PPP.

Exchange rates are related to interest rates in an economic relationship known as Interest Rate Parity (IRP). IRP is based on the simple principle that identically risky investments must offer investors everywhere the same underlying real rate of return, or else financial traders will find a way to make a sure profit. For this reason, exchange rate movements over time will be expected to offset differences between interest rates on similarly risky bonds denominated in different currencies. The principle of IRP holds that, for example, a country with a 15 percent interest rate should expect a 5 percent annual devaluation in its exchange rate relative to another currency where the interest rate on similarly risky bonds is only 10 percent.

Like PPP, the condition of Interest Rate Parity is the inevitable result of the profit motive. But also like PPP, IRP is subject to frictions that limit its efficacy as a predictor of exchange rates. These frictions, however, are much smaller. Information about interest rates is much more readily available than information about goods and services. The transportation of funds to arbitrage interest rates requires just the cost of a telex. The existence of offshore markets circumvents regulations and taxes. For all these reasons financial market arbitrage (IRP) is more effective than goods market arbitrage (PPP) in determining exchange rate movements. Even casual observation confirms that interest rates respond immediately to the announcement of a change in the money supply, whereas businessmen adjust prices of goods and services only after the effect of money growth on demand is clear. This means deviations from PPP will arise when there are sudden changes in interest rates. These deviations will reverse themselves, however, as businessmen eventually adjust prices and exchange rates to PPP.

Governments, then, can dramatically change interest rates, thereby manipulating exchange rates, by unexpectedly easing or tightening monetary policy. When the money supply expands, for example, interest rates initially will fall due to the greater availability of credit. But because IRP must hold, capital will flow to seek higher returns available overseas, causing the local currency to depreciate in value.

But these are only the immediate consequences of a more rapid growth in the money supply. What happens next is even more important. Since yields on similarly risky bonds must be equilibrated by arbitrage in the financial markets, the currency will be expected to *appreciate* somewhat over time so that the total return from holding local debt is equivalent to that available overseas.

This is not to imply that the currency will appreciate to a higher value *on net* as a result of a shift to a more expansionary monetary policy. The appreciation I refer to merely corrects for the initial devaluation that itself is a reaction to the temporary lowering of interest rates. The final result of an expansive monetary policy is higher inflation, higher interest rates, and a lower currency value, all in conformity with PPP and IRP. But where the expected higher inflation and interest rates may take as long as 18 months to materialize, the exchange rate response is likely to be swift. Therefore, today's exchange rate depreciation often presages tomorrow's higher inflation. A devaluation now for inflation later means a temporary, but eventually self-correcting, deviation from PPP.

This poses a major problem for international performance measurement. The immediate devaluation of the currency will produce a translation loss in dollar-reported performance. But it is a loss that may have little economic significance. In following periods the foreign unit's return will be boosted by the additional inflation expected to follow. The higher (nominal) return in local currency combined with the subsequent currency appreciation will offset the already recorded translation loss so that, provided the company is able to raise prices sufficiently to match local inflation, there is no net economic loss. Such temporary deviations from PPP thus cause accounting statements to misrepresent true corporate performance.

This example illustrates another important aspect of exchange rates: namely, they are forward looking in much the same way that common stock prices are. As a dramatic example, the expectation alone of the socialist victory in France began driving down the exchange rate before the new (ultimately inflationary) policies had even been announced, much less put into effect. It would have been inappropriate for American or British multinationals to penalize their managers in France for the effect of an anticipated inflation that had not yet affected their reported results. But this, of course, is what the accounting system does.

To continue with our discussion of interest rates, let's consider what will happen when monetary policy is unexpectedly tightened. The effect of reduced credit availability is higher interest rates now, but lower interest rates later when inflation eventually subsides. As the real interest rate climbs, foreign capital is attracted, thus boosting the exchange value of the currency. Currency appreciation now presages lower inflation tommorrow.

This is precisely what has taken place in the U.S. as a result of "Reaganomics." With the tightening of Fed policy came the predictable increase in interest rates. Foreign investors, attracted by higher yields in the U.S., shifted their portfolios into dollars and away from other currencies; and the value of the dollar appreciated in anticipation of the actual decline in U.S. inflation. In fact, the dollar appreciated so much that a partial depreciation of the dollar can now be expected to restore parity between yields on German mark and U.S. dollar investments.

Accounting, as a result, is now distorting performance measures for American operations abroad. The tightening of U.S. credit has temporarily raised the dollar above PPP, thus producing artificial exchange losses. As the dollar subsides in exchange markets the value of foreign investments will be restored through exchange gains. The results of foreign operations also will compare favorably with the lower interest rates that will ensue in the U.S.

The message for management should be clear: exchange rates are more closely tied to interest rates *in the short run* than to the prices of goods and services that determine corporate profits. This means that any accounting technique that uses current exchange rates to measure translation gains or losses will either reward or penalize local managers for the effect of economic forces that have not yet affected reported profits. Translating past performance using current exchange rates thus has the effect of mixing expectations for the future with the reality of the past.

A more accurate measure of performance is obtained when results are translated using a "normalized" exchange rate that filters out the impact of temporary deviations from PPP — whether due to changes in monetary policy or to a shift to a more lenient or restrictive exchange rate policy. The "normalized" rate follows the path dictated by the fundamental economic forces experienced to date. The use of such a rate has the virtue of neither penalizing nor rewarding local management for exchange rate fluctuations beyond their control. It may also provide a more reliable basis for judging whether additional capital can be profitably invested.

The Enchilada Food Company: A Case Study

I will illustrate my proposal for evaluating international operations by considering the performance of a hypothetical Mexican subsidiary of an American multinational, The Enchilada Food Company.

Let us assume that the company was formed in Mexico at the beginning of 1977, and that we want to evaluate its operating performance through 1982. The major task facing home country management is to resolve the seeming paradox that the performance of Enchilada appeared to be quite attractive up until 1982, at which time a large peso devaluation appeared, virtually overnight, to substantially reduce the dollar value of the investment. The Enchilada case, an experience common to a number of American and European multinationals, raises issues like the following: Do such large devaluations, which are largely predictable, really represent a risk to U.S. corporations and their investors? Do translated results have any connection with economic reality when exchange rates fail to reflect past relative rates of inflation? If not, how can conventional accounting statements be made to reflect economic reality?

Before addressing these questions, let's go back a little farther into Mexico's economic history.

(Information concerning the actual and intrinsic value of the peso is presented in the table below.)

Over the period 1971-75, cumulative peso inflation exceeded dollar inflation by 44 percent, yet the peso's value was maintained, largely through Mexican central bank intervention, at 12.5 to the dollar. In 1976, the peso devalued from 12.5 pesos to 20 pesos to restore Purchasing Power Parity. The exchange rate adjusted in a single stroke to the cumulative excess of Mexican inflation over U.S. inflation.

This pattern repeated itself in the following period, 1976-1982. Over this period, cumulative Mexican inflation was some 285 percent higher than U.S. inflation, but the Mexican government insulated the currency through capital controls and borrowings, and only small devaluations in the peso

TABLE 1

	71-75	1976	1977	1978	1979	1980	1981	1982
Exchange Rates (peso/dollar)								
Actual Yr. End	12.5	20.0	22.7	22.7	22.8	23.3	26.2	100.5
"Normalized"	17.7	19.5	23.9	26.2	28.0	31.6	37.2	56.1
Peso Value								
Mexican Inflation	96.1%	15.8%	29.1%	17.3%	18.2%	26.4%	27.9%	57.0%
U.S. Inflation	38.7	5.8	6.5	7.5	11.3	13.5	10.4	6.0
Normlzd. Ex. Rte. Chng.	44.1%	10.0%	22.6%	9.8%	6.9%	12.9%	17.5%	51.0%
Actual Ex. Rte. Chng.	0.0	(60.0)	(13.5)	(0.0)	(0.4)	(2.2)	(12.4)	(283.6)
Deviations From PPP	44.1%	(50.0%)	9.1%	9.8%	6.5%	10.7%	5.1%	(232.6%)
Cumulative Deviations	44.1%	(5.9%)	3.2%	13.0%	19.5%	30.2%	35.3%	(197.3%)

EXHIBIT 1

Normalized and Actual Exchange Rate

Pesos Per U.S. Dollar

Normalized Exch. Rate ··············

Actual Exch. Rate ——————

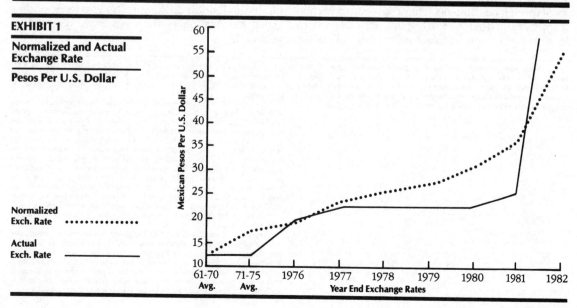

The procedure for evaluating foreign operations should closely parallel the approach sophisticated investors employ to evaluate the quality of foreign investments.

occurred. Then, in 1982, a dramatic peso devaluation caught up with and even overcompensated for the cumulative difference in inflation rates. (This pattern is portrayed in Exhibit 1.)

The characteristic, step-like movement of the peso is apparent as it suffers large devaluations after periods of relative stability. The "normalized" peso (plotted in the broken line) shows the exchange rate that would have resulted had devaluations been permitted to offset exactly the excess of Mexican inflation over U.S. inflation. By contrast, the "normalized" exchange rate depreciates each year in line with the excess of Mexican over American inflation. The actual peso value "plays leap-frog" with the normalized rate, falling behind when the government erects barriers to defend the peso, and then jumping ahead, even overshooting its mark, when the government surrenders to market forces.

The Standard Accounting Method

With this as a background, let's begin by showing how the current accounting technique, as prescribed in FAS #52, would translate the results of Enchilada into dollars.[2]

Before doing so, however, we should agree upon a basis for measuring and evaluating corporate performance. If performance is to be appraised in terms of contribution to share value, the procedure adopted should closely parallel the approach sophisticated investors employ to evaluate the quality of foreign investments. They take returns earned from both dividends and capital appreciation in local currency and translate them into dollars for

comparison with the performance of similarly risky investments. In similar fashion, management should evaluate international investments by measuring rates of return on invested capital in terms of local currency, and then translate those returns into dollar terms. The final stage of the evaluation process should then review the adequacy of the rate of return earned in dollars against the opportunity cost of that capital, also expressed in dollars. Those investments that earn more than their cost of capital, in relevant cash flow terms, will increase stock price; those that do not will detract from shareholders' wealth.

I also recommend that the rate of return be calculated on the *total* amount of debt and equity capital rather than on equity alone. The rate of return so calculated will be unaffected by fluctuations in interest rates and differences in capital structure between subsidiaries (which are generally determined by centralized financial management).

I calculated three different accounting Rates of Return (RORs) for the Enchilada Food Company over the years 1977-1982, in each case dividing Net Operating Profit before taxes (NOP) by Total Capital employed at the beginning of the year. The first is the rate of return *in pesos* using conventionally reported income statements and balance sheets. The second is the rate of return as reported in dollars using FAS #52, but excluding any translation gain or loss.[3] The third rate of return is calculated in dollars including any translation gain or loss.[4] These all are plotted in Exhibit 2, along with the corresponding actual devaluation in the peso from year-end-to-year-end.

2. The company's results over this entire period are translated into dollars using FAS #52, even though FAS #52 was adopted only last year and Mexico, because of its hyper-inflation, would be required to use FAS #8 conventions for translation into dollars. To further simplify our analysis, I assume that the company pays no taxes and that the company is financed using only equity capital.

3. Briefly, FAS #52 requires that the balance sheet, with the exception of the net worth account, be translated using year end exchange rates, and the income statement be translated using average exchange rates. See Bryan Carberg's article preceding.

4. Under FAS #52, a translation gain or loss is credited directly to net worth without passing through the income statement. A translation gain or loss is calculated in order to balance net worth with the difference between the translated value for assets and liabilities. Part of the justification offered for this is that currency gains and losses will tend to balance out over time, so there is no need to include on the income statement something that is expected to contribute nothing over time. In fact, this rationale is erroneous. Currencies that consistently appreciate over time due to conservative monetary policies will have a net translation gain even after ther passage of many years. Ignoring the gains passed to the translation reserve when evaluating performance means that an important and consistent part of the return available to U.S. investors is overlooked. Managers in these countries may be unfairly penalized, and potentially attractive investments may be rejected if management worries about potential future accounting returns.

In contrast, countries such as Mexico that are inclined towards inflationary policies will experience a consistent devaluation over time and a net translation loss. Without considering the effect of such losses, the return available to U.S shareholders may be overstated. Managers may be given bonuses where none is deserved, and investments may be accepted that are not attractive to investors. For this reason a rate of return was calculated using dollar reported results according to FAS #52, but including the translation gain or loss as part of the return.

The following observations are noteworthy:

- After a temporary decline in 1978, the peso rate of return steadily improved, even through 1982.
- Up to 1982, the dollar returns closely tracked the peso return. This occurred because the peso was relatively stable against the dollar over this period. In 1982, the dollar return *before* translation loss, although lower than prior years, was still in excess of 10 percent, in spite of the dramatic peso devaluation.

- In 1982, Enchilada's translation loss was equal to approximately *74 percent* of capital employed! The return in dollars *including* this loss was approximately -63 percent in 1982.

- The difference between peso returns and U.S. dollar returns each year roughly equals the actual percentage devaluation in the peso.

These results reveal several shortcomings of current accounting procedures. First, the reported

EXHIBIT 2

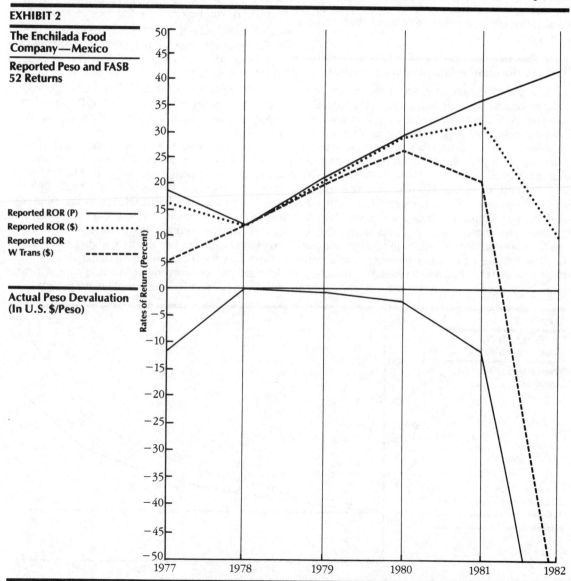

The Enchilada Food Company—Mexico

Reported Peso and FASB 52 Returns

Reported ROR (P) ——————
Reported ROR ($) ·············
Reported ROR W Trans ($) ― ― ― ―

Actual Peso Devaluation (In U.S. $/Peso)

peso results bear no relation to the real economic conditions in Mexico. Second, in those years in which the peso devalued only modestly, the returns reported in dollars are *overstated* because they reflect the higher rate of inflation experienced in Mexico without showing the offsetting effect of the inevitable, although deferred, devaluation. Finally, the return in dollars *including* translation loss is misleading because it concentrates the effect of the extreme devaluation in the peso into a single year. In reality, the devaluation is compensating for a cumulative overstatement of returns over the past five years.

Peso Performance Adjusted for Inflation

As stated earlier, the problems of currency translation and inflation accounting are inseparable. Consequently, before demonstrating how the use of "normalized" exchange rates would remedy this problem of currency translation, we must first deal with the prior problem of adjusting local currency numbers for inflation.

The results reported in pesos are severely distorted by inflation. Over the period 1976 to 1982, cumulative inflation in Mexico was more than 350 percent. This meant that a peso spent in 1982 had *less than one-fourth* the purchasing power of a peso in 1976. Yet the accounting statements mixed the two pesos as if they had equal value. When there is a large difference between the historic and current

cost of foreign assets, then translated accounting rates of return, whether using FAS #8 or FAS #52, will be all but meaningless.

In order to eliminate the distortions of inflation on reported earnings, standard financial statements can be adjusted as follows:

- No change is necessary for monetary assets (cash and receivables) because their face value represents their realizable value in current pesos.

- The FIFO value of inventory, provided it turns quickly, can be employed as a close approximation of their value in current pesos.

- The current value of plant can be estimated by writing up the accounting value at the rate of peso inflation each year.

The resulting estimate of capital employed at current peso prices (which I will call *Capital with Inflation*) and capital as reported are plotted in Exhibit 3.

By 1982, reported capital understates current value by about 30 percent. The dashed line portrays current value capital deflated by the Mexican price index to constant 1976 pesos. It reveals that the "real" amount of capital employed by Enchilada did not change over this period. Capital investment served only to replace depreciation and to meet working capital requirements at higher peso prices. The difference between capital deflated to constant 1976 pesos and current peso value capital represents the cumulative amount of inflation gains.

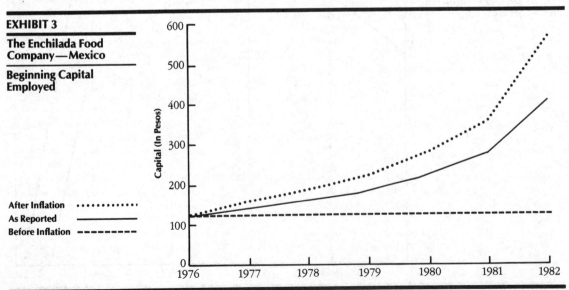

EXHIBIT 3

The Enchilada Food Company—Mexico

Beginning Capital Employed

After Inflation ···········
As Reported ————
Before Inflation – – – – – –

Capital (In Pesos)

The next step involves adjusting reported income for the effect of inflation. To do so, I computed Net Operating Profit (NOP) both before and after holding gains due to inflation. NOP *before Inflation* is calculated by subtracting operating costs at current peso prices from sales. Specifically, Cost of Goods Sold is computed on a LIFO basis and Depreciation Expense is based on the estimated current peso value of PPE. To calculate NOP *after Inflation, all* holding gains arising from inflation are added to NOP *before Inflation*. The inflation gain on inventories is estimated by the difference between LIFO and FIFO Cost of Goods Sold. The inflation gain on plant is estimated by multiplying the beginning of year value for net plant (at current prices) by the inflation rate over the year. There is no inflation gain on monetary assets. The NOPs so calculated are shown in the table below along with reported NOP (in millions of pesos):

TABLE 2	1977	1978	1979	1980	1981	1982
NOP Before Inf	10.9	5.8	19.3	28.0	43.3	25.0
NOP As Reported	23.6	15.5	35.0	55.0	82.2	118.6
NOP After Inf	40.0	28.2	47.0	75.2	106.5	190.0

The accounting profits consistently fall between profits *before* and *after Inflation* because *some, but not all,* of the holding gains arising from inflation are recorded. Inflation gains are realized on inventory sold and accounted for under FIFO accounting, but are expensed for LIFO inventories. Gains also are realized on plant insofar as depreciation charges based on historical acquisition costs understate true depreciation at current prices. The majority of holding gains on plant, however, are not recorded as long as plant is carried at a value well below its current peso cost.

Rates of Return can now be calculated by dividing NOP Before and After Inflation by the current value of capital employed at the beginning of the year. The Rate of Return *Before* Inflation is a "real" return. Subtracting costs at current prices means that enough funds have been set aside on the income statement to replace assets expended on the balance sheet at higher prices. Thus, the Real Return can be distributed to investors without impairing the company's ability to remain in business.

The Rate of Return *After* Inflation represents the "total" return available to investors in pesos

from a combination of "real" operating profits *and* appreciation in the value of assets over the course of the year. The Total Return cannot be distributed to investors because that portion of the return due to inflation gains must be reinvested to replace assets at higher prices. Thus, the Total Return is available to investors only through a liquidation of the business.

What, then, is the justification for including asset appreciation as a component of return? Is it that every asset appreciates with inflation? Obviously not. The important point is that all assets will be worth more with inflation than they would be worth in the absence of that inflation. Stated differently, holding gains arise not because assets appreciate in value, but because money depreciates in value, so that even assets of unchanged value are worth more in money terms after inflation. But even this is not wholly correct. All that is necessary is that the level of profits the assets generate is increased by inflation, so that if price-to-earnings ratios are constant, the capitalized value of profits, and hence the value of assets, will appreciate with inflation. Since investors realize inflation gains through higher stock prices, the corresponding holding gain on assets should be included in measures of corporate performance.

The Real and Total Rates of Return (ROR), along with the conventional accounting ROR, are reproduced in the table following (all RORs in pesos).

TABLE 3	1977	1978	1979	1980	1981	1982
Real ROR	8.7%	3.6%	10.2%	12.5%	15.3%	6.9%
Acctg. ROR	18.9%	12.1%	21.6%	29.8%	36.7%	42.6%
Total ROR	32.0%	17.4%	24.8%	33.6%	37.6%	52.5%
Mex. Grwth.	4.2%	3.4%	8.3%	9.2%	8.3%	2.0%
Inflation	29.1%	17.3%	18.2%	26.4%	27.9%	57.0%

As would be expected, Enchilada's Real RORs parallel economic growth rates in Mexico, while Total RORs mirror peso inflation. Reported accounting RORs fall between Total and Real RORs in each year. All three RORs followed the same pattern except in 1982, when both accounting and Total RORs increased while the Real ROR declined.

These results have several implications for performance measurement. It should again be apparent that the accounting ROR is meaningless as a performance measure. It will generally fall between the Real and the Total Return, but there is no guarantee even of this. Of the three RORs, the Real Return is

The best overall measure of performance in local currency is the Total Return deflated for local inflation.

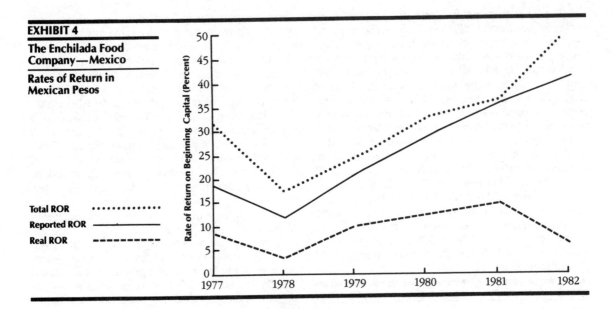

EXHIBIT 4

The Enchilada Food Company—Mexico

Rates of Return in Mexican Pesos

Total ROR · · · · · · · · · ·

Reported ROR ─────────

Real ROR ─ ─ ─ ─ ─ ─ ─

Rate of Return on Beginning Capital (Percent)

50 45 40 35 30 25 20 15 10 5 0

1977   1978   1979   1980   1981   1982

the best reflection of the true performance of the operation. It tracks most closely with those general economic conditions in Mexico that directly affect profitability.

The Real Return, however, does suffer from one important shortcoming. It fails to reflect the effect of "real" holding gains and losses that are important to investors. A real holding gain or loss arises when an asset appreciates by more or less than the general rate of inflation experienced across the entire economy. Normally it makes sense to exclude real holding gains or losses from performance measures because they arise from unpredictable changes in the value of assets that cannot be expected to continue. For example, a company that buys and sells gold jewelry will realize holding gains or losses on its inventory as the price of gold fluctuates. These price fluctuations cannot be expected to contribute consistently to profits. As a rule, holding gains and losses represent one-time adjustments to value rather than a continuing source of income that investors will capitalize at a multiple into the company's stock price. And, therefore, to the extent that stock prices reflect the capitalized value of an expected, normalized cash flow, real holding gains and losses should be excluded from internal performance measures.

One important exception to this rule are monetary assets like cash and receivables. The value of monetary assets is fixed in terms of the currency of

their denomination. Inflation in the currency diminishes the real value of net monetary assets and creates a holding loss for investors in direct proportion to the rate of inflation.

In 1982, for example, Enchilada's *Total Return* of 52.5 percent was less than the 57 percent rate of inflation in Mexico, indicating that the actual real return to investors was negative, even though the computed Real Return was *positive*. Investors suffered a real loss despite the fact that the business produced a real profit. This apparent contradiction is explained by recognizing that the company sustained a real holding loss on its net monetary assets — cash and receivables — that offsets the Real Return earned in the business. Therefore, *the best overall measure of performance in local currency is the Total Return deflated for local inflation*. This measure will incorporate both the real business performance and the real holding losses on monetary assets.

The same evaluation of performance and value also can be reached by comparing the Total Return with the cost of capital. Since both lenders and shareholders expect to be compensated in real purchasing power terms, the cost of obtaining debt and equity capital implicitly incorporates inflation. Consequently, a comparison of the Total Return with the "nominal" cost of capital will produce the same result as a comparison of the deflated return with the "real" cost of capital. In either case, when managers

By using the normalized exchange rate the company implicitly charges the operation each year for the translation loss that will eventually take place.

are evaluated according to these benchmarks, they will have an incentive to increase prices sufficiently to cover the loss incurred by holding monetary assets that lose value due to inflation.

Perhaps the most important advantage to using the Total Return, however, is that it produces the most meaningful result when translated into dollars. The holding gains included in the Total Return offset translation losses, leaving a net gain in dollars commensurate with the level of U.S. inflation.

Conversion To Dollars Using "Normalized" Exchange Rate

The next and final stage of the analysis, then, is to calculate Enchilada's rate of return translated into dollars. While it would be possible to appraise the performance of foreign operations in terms of the deflated Total Return measured in local currency, it is important that multinationals be able to review the results of all foreign operations expressed in the home currency.

In the case of Enchilada, the peso inflation-adjusted income statement (i.e., including holding gains) and balance sheet (at current peso prices) would be translated into dollar terms using FAS #52 conventions, *but substituting a "normalized" exchange rate for the actual rate.* As stated, the nor-malized exchange rate is that which would prevail if the peso conformed precisely to Purchasing Power Parity. Year-to-year changes in the normalized exchange rate would thus reflect only the differences in inflation between Mexico and the U.S.[5]

The translated statements can then be used to determine the Total ROR in dollars after Translation, which is calculated by dividing the dollar amount of total income, *including both peso holding gains and the translation loss,* by the translated value of Capital with Inflation. This return is shown in Exhibit 5, together with the Total ROR in pesos shown earlier in Exhibit 4.

As the graph makes clear, Enchilada's Total ROR in dollars including Translation Loss is *consistently* less than the Total ROR in pesos. Recall, by contrast, that in every year except 1982, the reported accounting RORs in dollars tracked the peso ROR because the peso did not depreciate against the dollar in accordance with inflation differentials.

By using the normalized exchange rate the company implicitly charges the operation each year for the translation loss that will eventually take place. It is like establishing a reserve against future translation losses that can be expected with a high degree of confidence. Then when the actual loss itself takes place, no great surprise is in store for management. Moreover, this encourages investment decisions to

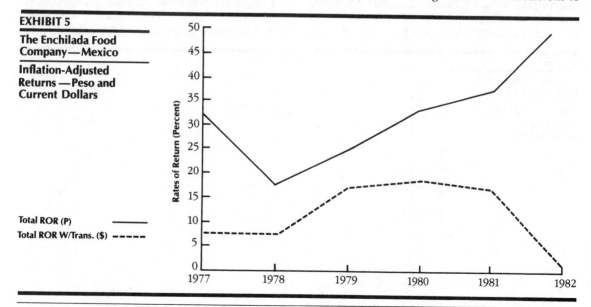

EXHIBIT 5

The Enchilada Food Company—Mexico

Inflation-Adjusted Returns — Peso and Current Dollars

Total ROR (P) ⸺
Total ROR W/Trans. ($) - - - - -

5. In the process, an exchange loss would be recognized to balance equity translated at the historical normalized rate with assets translated at the current normalized rate.

be made on the basis of the expected, rather than actual, currency values.

Another major advantage of this method is its consistent treatment of the dual consequences of Mexican inflation. The holding gains that arise from Mexican inflation are included in the peso Total Return, thus offsetting the translation loss that is also due to local inflation. The net effect is to record an inflation gain in dollars commensurate with the level of inflation experienced in the U.S.

One way to see this is to note (in the table below) that the Total Return in pesos, after subtracting the percentage devaluation in the "normalized" exchange rate, is approximately equal to the Total Return in dollars after Translation Loss.

TABLE 4	1977	1978	1979	1980	1981	1982
Total ROR (p)	32.0%	17.4%	24.8%	33.6%	37.6%	52.5%
Normalized Ex. Rte. Chng.	22.6%	9.8%	6.9%	12.9%	17.5%	51.0%
Difference	9.4%	7.6%	17.9%	20.7%	20.1%	1.5%
Total ROR Aft Trans ($)	7.6%	7.1%	16.8%	18.4%	16.7%	1.0%

This same relationship can be seen by noting that the percentage devaluation in the normalized exchange rate, plotted in Exhibit 6, explains the difference between the peso and dollar returns.

Currency translation thus takes out of the Mexican return the difference between Mexican and U.S. inflation, leaving behind gains to compensate dollar investors for dollar inflation.

An important implication is that historical cost accounting systems that do not recognize holding gains, but do record translation losses based on current exchange rates, will invariably report net losses where none in fact may exist. A more precise understanding of this can be gained by inspecting the table shown below.

TABLE 5	1977	1978	1979	1980	1981	1982
Infl Gain (p)	29.1	22.4	27.7	47.2	63.2	164.9
Infl Gain ($)	1.22	0.85	0.99	1.49	1.70	3.02
Tran Loss($)	−1.18	−0.59	−0.46	−0.91	−1.36	−3.29
Net Gain ($)	0.04	0.26	0.52	0.58	0.34	−0.27

The first line is the inflation gain in pesos arising from the appreciation in value of both inventories and net plant. In the second line, the peso inflation gain has been translated to dollars. In the third line, the foreign exchange loss arising from a change in the "normalized" exchange rate is subtracted to arrive at the Net Gain (Loss) appearing in the dollar statements. *In every year except 1982 the translation loss has been more than offset by inflation gains,* leaving investors unaffected by the devaluation. Without recording the holding gain, however, a potentially misleading loss would be recorded in each year.

In 1982, the inflation gain on assets was insufficient to cover the exchange loss. It would be a mis-

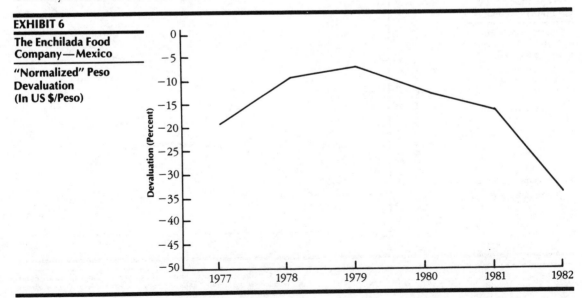

EXHIBIT 6

The Enchilada Food Company—Mexico

"Normalized" Peso Devaluation (In US $/Peso)

take, however, to interpret this as exchange risk. The net loss is attributable instead to the purchasing power loss sustained on monetary assets denominated in pesos in Mexico. The failure of these assets to appreciate along with inflation in Mexico means that their value translated to dollars has fallen. But this simply is saying that monetary assets have sustained a real holding loss due to Mexican inflation. What appears as an exchange loss, then, is no more than a inflation-induced holding loss. *The exchange loss has merely transmitted the inflation loss into its dollar equivalent.* The most effective way to hedge this loss is to pass on the costs of Mexican inflation to consumers through higher prices.

The contrast between the results reported under FAS #52 procedures and my inflation-adjusted, exchange-rate normalized method is illustrated by the plots appearing in Exhibit 7.

The translated ROR reported according to FAS #52 is represented by the dotted line. In each year it overstates the true economic performance of Enchilada because no adjustment is ever made for the higher rate of inflation in Mexico. (Of course the opposite would happen in a country that consistently had low inflation. Rates of return reported in dollars would miss the appreciation in translated value of capital invested overseas that is an important component of the return to investors in these countries.)

By including the FAS #52 translation loss in the calculation of ROR, one problem is solved, but two are created. The problem solved is that eventually, as PPP reasserts itself, the overstatement of returns is adjusted for by the translation loss. FAS #52 would thus accurately measure the return earned from a foreign investment, *but only on average and over time.* As a period-by-period measure of performance, it can be extremely misleading—especially, as in the Enchilada case, when a currency depreciates in one year to compensate for the excessive inflation of several prior years. The other problem introduced is that the translation loss is assessed without recognizing the offsetting holding gains. This means that losses will be recorded and accumulated on accounting statements where none may exist for investors.

The Total Return that includes both peso holding gains and currency translation losses (or gains), calculated using normalized exchange rates, avoids these shortcomings and thus provides the most meaningful measure of performance in dollar terms. *The use of the normalized exchange rate shifts the burden of adjustment from the year in which the currency revaluation actually takes place to those years in which the economic forces first arise that cause a change in the fundamental value of the currency.* Management therefore is charged or credited for exchange rate movements that correspond to

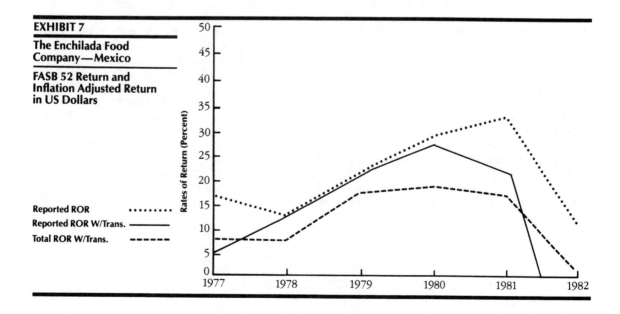

EXHIBIT 7

The Enchilada Food Company—Mexico

FASB 52 Return and Inflation Adjusted Return in US Dollars

Reported ROR ·········

Reported ROR W/Trans. ————

Total ROR W/Trans. – – – –

the actual conditions of the local operating environment. Furthermore, by including the holding gains due to local inflation as part of the return to be converted to dollars, the loss incurred through translation is properly accounted for as just another consequence of the inflation itself. The graphs in Exhibit 7 together show that this is the return in dollars that corresponds most closely to the real return experienced by the local operating manager. The internal adoption of this measure by multinationals will accordingly bring about greater agreement between local management and corporate headquarters about the performance and fundamental value of a foreign operation.

Summary

FAS #52 will provide a realistic measure of foreign operating performance only under the following conditions:

- Assets are carried on accounting balance sheets at values close to their current value.

- Exchange rates move in accordance with purchasing power parity.

- Translation gains and losses are included in the measure of profits.

In inflationary economies, of course, there will be a significant divergence between accounting values and current values. Furthermore, exchange rates deviate regularly, and often dramatically, from the course dictated by inflation differentials. This can be due to government intervention or changes in a country's competitiveness in international markets. Experience suggests that such deviations generally even out over time, leaving inflation differentials as the predominant force determining exchange rates over the long haul.

The real, economic performance of a foreign operating unit may be overstated or understated when the returns earned are translated at unrealistically high or low exchange rates. A more accurate appraisal of results is possible by using exchange rates that chart the fundamental course of currency values over time.

Specifically, the procedure I recommend involves first building inflation and inflation gains into the foreign unit's income statement and balance sheet. Without this, any currency translation procedure is likely to fail. Second, the results of the foreign operation can be translated to dollars using FAS #52 conventions, provided the translation gain or loss is included as part of the return. The exchange rate used for translation, however, should not be the actual exchange rate, which can be unduly influenced by government policy or temporary shifts in interest rates. Instead, a normalized rate — one that reflects inflation differentials and conforms to Purchasing Power Parity — should be substituted. The rate of return so calculated can then be compared with the cost of capital expressed in terms of dollar financing costs. In this way management has a common basis for comparing the performance of all foreign and domestic operations.

I contend that the Total Return in Dollars (adjusted for local inflation and including Translation Loss) using "normalized" exchange rates is the most appropriate measure of foreign operating performance for the following reasons: (1) it reflects the underlying real performance of the local economy and of local operating managers; (2) it reflects the cost of sustaining real holding losses on monetary assets that must be compensated for by a higher return in the business; (3) it includes holding gains which, after translation, would be commensurate with U.S. inflation, making it directly comparable to costs of capital expressed in dollars (which, of course, implicitly incorporate U.S. inflation); (4) it is equally applicable for countries that experience appreciating exchange values over time because the translation gain will be included as a systematic component of the return realized by investors; and, finally, (5) the use of normalized exchange rates forces management, both local and corporate, to see through distortions caused by the temporary suspension of fundamental economic forces, and to incorporate anticipated currency changes into forward planning.

Measuring the Performance of Operations Subject to Fluctuating Exchange Rates

Donald R. Lessard and David Sharp,
Massachusetts Institute of Technology

In the current era of varying rates of inflation and volatile, unpredictable exchange rates, traditional methods of international performance measurement no longer provide a reasonable indication of the contributions of local operating managers. As a result, they often distort managerial incentives. This is true not only for overseas activities, but often for domestic operations as well. With the recent increase in global competition, purely domestic firms are being subjected to the risk of exchange fluctuations to an extent far greater than ever before.

The problem of evaluating performance under such circumstances has deservedly attracted increasing attention. In 1977, Peter Lorange and one of the present writers proposed a simple means of defining managerial responsibility for exchange rate movements by choosing an appropriate exchange rate—in most cases, the beginning period forward rate—for converting local-currency income to dollars.[1] In the Summer 1983 issue of this journal, Bennett Stewart proposed measuring dollar returns using a "normalized" exchange rate—one that would have prevailed under conditions of purchasing-power-parity (PPP).[2] Both of these methods will work, but only under certain, somewhat restrictive circumstances: namely, when the underlying local currency operating profitability of the business is unaffected by exchange rate movements.

This means, for example, that Stewart's proposal will work well only for those multinationals with "balanced" foreign units: those businesses which source their inputs and sell their output locally, and face competition only from other firms with local operations. This was the norm for U.S. multinationals operating abroad in the 1960s and 70s. In the 1980s, such circumstances are becoming the exception rather than the rule. Recent years have seen the rise of *global* as opposed to *multi-domestic* competition.[3] Under global competition, a firm's costs and revenues are affected to a greater extent by movements in exchange rates; hence, the short-run profitability of any individual operating unit is likely to be more sensitive to exchange rates than under multi-domestic competition.

This introduces an additional layer of complexity into the measurement process. It is no longer enough that performance measures correctly convert foreign currency net worth into dollars (the accounting problem which Stewart's proposal solves). They must also incorporate the effects of

---

1. See Donald R. Lessard and Peter Lorange, "Currency Changes and Management Control: Resolving the Centralization/Decentralization Dilemma," *Accounting Review* (July 1977), pp. 628-637. In this article, we recommend use of the forward rate for budgeting purposes. For ex-post evaluation, we distinguish between those cases in which managers have significant opportunities to adjust to exchange rate changes and those in which they do not. In the latter case, we recommend that results be translated using the same forward rate which served as the basis for the budget. In the former case, we suggest using the realized spot rate at the end of the period in question.

2. G. Bennett Stewart, "A Proposal for Measuring International Performance," *Midland Corporate Finance Journal* (Summer 1983), pp. 56-71.

3. Global competition exists when a firm's competitive position in one national market is significantly affected by developments that transcend national boundaries. Multidomestic competition exists when firms compete in essentially isolated national markets, with global-scale activities limited to R&D and certain managerial functions. The "traditional" multinational corporation of the 1960s faced multidomestic competition. Contrast this with today's globally competitive environment, with centralized sourcing and large international, intracorporate flows of goods and services.

movements in *real* exchange rate changes on the *competitiveness* of operations. Indeed, to the extent that domestic operations are also affected by international competitive forces—of which the exchange rate is a critical component—this dependence must be addressed even though there is no foreign currency problem. In this article we propose a measure of performance that addresses the need both to translate foreign currency profits into dollars and to take account of the impact of exchange rates on underlying profitability.

In designing a performance measure for foreign operations, it is important to specify the purpose of the measure. In the Spring 1984 issue of this journal, Alan Shapiro made a distinction between measuring income in an absolute sense and measuring local managers' contribution to income.[4] As pointed out by Fischer Black and others, the appropriateness of an income measure depends on the use for which it is intended. One measure may be the best estimate of the change in the firm's value due to current operations; another may be the best estimate of sustainable profits as a basis for valuing the firm; still another may be a periodic measure of unit operating efficiency as a basis for management compensation.[5] But, clearly, no single measure can serve all purposes.

In fact, much of the current debate over dollar versus local currency accounting is really a debate among differing views of what an income measure should be. Some favor dollar-based accounting which attempts to measure the value of the firm to U.S. investors; others favor local currency accounting focusing on the performance of local operating managers. In this article, we develop measures of performance which explicitly separate the problems of measuring income and measuring managers' contribution to that income. Our income measure, grounded in GAAP (though adjusted for inflation), is conventional enough. For purposes of managerial evaluation, however, this measure is set against an adjusting budgeted standard—a flexible standard which reflects the anticipated effects of unexpected changes in exchange rates. Our proposed scheme also separates the impacts of exchange rate shifts into two groups—those associated with money-

fixed contractual items and those associated with non-contractual operating cash flows—and treats them differently in our calculation of income.

We address three key questions that arise in the context of volatile exchange rates and global competition:

1. Which currency and which exchange rate should be used to measure performance?

2. How can the performance of a foreign (or domestic) business or investment unit and its management be measured appropriately?

3. To what extent should operating management be held responsible for exchange rate fluctuations?

Our general conclusion is that effective measurement of managerial performance cannot be achieved by adopting a single, rigid standard of performance. Rather, the standard should be adjusted to reflect *unexpected* changes in crucial economic variables (in the case of international operations, changes in exchange rates) over which management has little or no control.

In the next section, we review the key issues to be resolved in designing a performance measurement system. Finally, we offer our proposal, which is presented in the form of a comprehensive example.

Issues

Defining Income

As noted earlier, income can be measured for a variety of purposes. It can be an estimate of the sustainable earnings of the firm, of the current period's contribution to the value of the firm, or of the managers' contribution to one or both of the above. The standard accounting definition, by matching revenues against costs, incorporating consumption of capital, and separately identifying extraordinary items, represents an attempt to estimate future sustainable earnings based on recent experience. The shortcomings of the accountant's measure of income as a guide to economic value are well known. For one thing, accounting income often reflects both "sustainable fundamentals" and chance ele-

---

4. Alan Shapiro, "The Evaluation and Control of Foreign Affiliates," *Midland Corporate Finance Journal* (Spring 1984), pp. 13-25.

5. Fischer Black, "The Magic in Earnings: Economic Earnings versus Accounting Earnings," *Financial Analysis Journal* 36 (November/December 1980), pp. 19-24.

ments that are unlikely to recur. More seriously, it is affected (typically biased upwards) by inflation of the currency "numeraire" in which it is measured.

But such problems notwithstanding, the accountant's measure of operating income (before interest and taxation) is still probably, for the majority of companies, the most useful, cost-effective measure of periodic operating results, and it accordingly provides the basis of our performance measure. Also, the last problem mentioned above can be easily remedied by incorporating inflation adjustments like those proposed by Stewart. And, as mentioned earlier, Stewart's use of exchange rates normalized to reflect purchasing power parity is one way to reduce or even eliminate the chance impact of exchange rate fluctuations on dollar income. But, again, it is important to recognize that when exchange rate changes have significant competitive impacts, this translation method provides a misleading measure of managers' contribution to performance.

Our objective in this paper is to measure the performance of operations subject to exchange risk, and also to attempt to identify the contribution of operating managers to that performance. For this purpose, we recommend comparison of a business unit's actual pretax net operating margin with a budgeted margin. The budgeted figure is a predetermined estimate, *given* the information available about the state of the world at the time the budget is prepared, of what is expected to be an acceptable level of profitability. Any deviation of actual performance from budgeted results is assumed to arise from two causes: (1) chance events over which management has no control (and which thus, for purposes of managerial evaluation, merely cloud the picture) and (2) above- or below-normal achievement by management, given the *actual* as opposed to the expected state of the world. Our proposal goes some way toward distinguishing between these two sources of variance.

The Exchange Rate Environment

While a great deal can be said about the behavior of exchange rates, two characteristics stand out: (1) the tendency for exchange rate movements to compensate for differences in rates of inflation over time and (2) the substantial volatility of exchange rates in the short run. The first tendency, known as "purchasing power parity," holds quite well over three- to five-year horizons. The short run, however,

is clearly marked by abrupt exchange rate changes and substantial deviations from PPP.

Figure 1 illustrates the extent to which various exchange rates match purchasing power parity on a cumulative basis over time. The vertical axis measures *nominal* appreciation or depreciation. The horizontal axis shows *real* appreciation or depreciation—that is, currency movements adjusted for relative rates of inflation. The open squares show the values as of December 1980 (which reflect the cumulative adjustment of those currency values since 1973, the beginning of the floating rate regime); the black squares show the values as of June 1982; and the "x"-d squares show the September 1983 values.

For example, from 1973 to 1980 the Swiss franc appreciated 85 percent relative to the dollar. This movement was fully accounted for by the accumulated difference in inflation rates between the two countries over that period; thus the real exchange rate was virtually unchanged at the end of 1980. From December 1980 to June 1982, however, the franc depreciated by roughly 15 percent even though Swiss inflation continued lower than U.S. inflation. Thus, the real exchange rate fell by more than 15 percent.

In 1980, as Figure 1 shows, the real values of the currencies *vis-a-vis* the dollar of all of the major industrialized countries (except the U.K.) fall within a 15 percent band around purchasing power parity (vertical axis). From 1980 to 1982, and from 1982 to 1983, however, the dollar shifts substantially within that band. In other words, from year to year, competitiveness can shift plus or minus 10 to 15 percent, but the differences tend not to compound over time. (This does not imply that the real exchange rates always remain within this range, but a situation like the current one, which reflects several successive real devaluations, is something of an anomaly.)

Why is the distinction between real and nominal exchange rate movements important? The reason is that nominal movements affect the value of companies' *paper* assets and liabilities, while real movements affect the value of their *real* operating assets. In the short run, nominal changes tend to be closely associated with real changes; but in the longer run, real movements are smaller and result from major structural or policy shocks. This contrasts with nominal changes, which cumulatively tend to fall in line with relative rates of inflation.

This brings us to the impact of exchange rate movements on a business's performance.

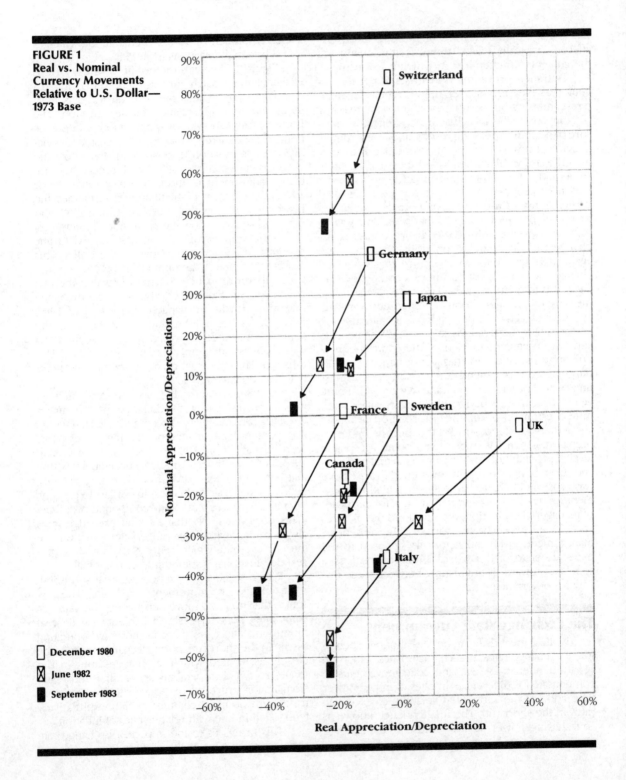

FIGURE 1
Real vs. Nominal
Currency Movements
Relative to U.S. Dollar—
1973 Base

Switzerland

Germany

Japan

France   Sweden

UK

Canada

Italy

☐ December 1980

☒ June 1982

■ September 1983

Nominal Appreciation/Depreciation

Real Appreciation/Depreciation

Foreign exchange exposure management is usually, though improperly, identified with contractual, treasury items rather than with exposures of operating cash flows.

Operating Impacts of Volatile Exchange Rate

Few would deny that floating exchange rates have a significant impact on the reported net income of a corporation. It is useful to separate this impact on measured performance into two components: a *translation* effect and a *dependence* effect.

The translation effect arises from the requirement that income be measured in the home currency and from the fact that, in the short run, exchange rate movements often diverge significantly from inflation differences[6]. For example, we typically measure operating income of a U.K. subsidiary first in pounds, and then translate into dollars. Unfortunately, while accounting conventions assume that accounting numeraires are stable, in fact they fluctuate daily relative to each other. This means, for instance, that a 10 percent nominal devaluation of the pound, even if it has *no* effect on (inflation-adjusted) net income measured in pounds, will reduce net income measured in dollars by 10 percent. This is a real reduction in profitability, not just an accounting illusion. (Whether or not we believe this reduction is temporary depends, however, on our beliefs about the long-run exchange rate and the corresponding "normal" level of operating profitability in dollars of the overseas unit.)

There is, though, an additional *dependence* effect when net income measured in local currency depends on the exchange rate. It arises because shifts in the exchange rate change the firm's competitive position and hence its underlying profitability.

The distinction between these two effects is often overlooked for two reasons. First, the translation effect is much more visible and measurable than the relatively subtle dependence effect. Second, foreign exchange exposure management is usually identified with contractual, treasury items rather than with exposures of operating cash flows. Because the value of contractual items remains constant in the currency of their denomination, there is an illusion that the problem of volatile exchange rates can be solved simply by choosing a numeraire to match the

firm's asset-liability characteristics. Consider, for example, a subsidiary operating in Italy with lire-denominated receivables, payables and short-term borrowings, and no significant cross-border competition (which would cause the underlying profitability to depend on the exchange rate). If it prepares accounts in lire, foreign exchange fluctuations will have a minimal impact on reported income. Once we recognize the existence of the dependence effect, however, it is clear that operating margins can in general be strongly affected by real exchange rates, no matter which currency unit is used for accounting.

The fact that real movements in exchange rates result in changes in the relative prices of local and imported goods, which in turn result in changes in operating margins—*whether measured in local or foreign currencies*—raises serious questions about the value of any performance measurement system that does not take into account the anticipated effect of real changes in exchange rates. This point is not restricted to those operations involved in international trade; it applies to any operation subject to international competition. Even if a business sources and sells a product only within the United States, *if it is also* subject to foreign competition, real changes in the exchange rate will affect its performance. For example, prior to the imposition of "voluntary" import quotas, the small-car segment of the U.S. auto industry had a substantial yen exposure. Prices of small cars were influenced, to a large extent, by the yen through competition.[7]

Let us illustrate the effect of exchange rates on profitability with a simple example. Consider the three different businesses shown in Table 1. All three have normal operating margins of 20 percent. The first, an exporter, buys LC80 of local inputs and sells its output in world markets for LC100. The second is a "balanced" operation—one that buys and sells locally. The third is an importer, which buys on world markets and sells locally.

Now, assume that exchange rates are initially at PPP, and that a 10 percent appreciation of the local currency (relative to the differential rates of infla-

6. In fact, the problem is more complex than this, since relative prices of the goods included in each price index will change, the weights of various goods in the indexes will differ, and the firm's specific input and output prices are unlikely to be perfectly correlated with any broad price index. For a discussion of these points, see Alan Shapiro, "What Does Purchasing Power Parity Mean?," *Journal of International Money and Finance* 2, pp. 295-318, and Michael Adler and Bernard Dumas, "International Portfolio Choice and Corporate Finance: A Survey," *Journal of Finance* 38, 925-84.

7. This analysis suggests that the auto industry should have hedged this exposure by borrowing yen or selling yen forward. Unfortunately, since this operating exposure is the sensitivity of cash flows to variations in real exchange rates, it is not possible to hedge it fully with traditional financial instruments. See Donald R. Lessard and John B. Lightstone, "The Impact of Exchange Rates on Operating Profits: New Business and Financial Responses," for a description of an alternative hedge which does offset this exposure.

If management is operating as effectively as before, and at the same level of activity, a "good" measure of managerial performance should be minimally affected by an unexpected change in the exchange rate.

TABLE 1
Impact of Exchange Rate Changes on Operating Margins

Panel A (in Local Currency LC)

Initial Situation		Net Exporter	Balanced Firm	Net Importer
100	Sales	90	100	100
80	Cost of Sales	80	80	72
20	Gross Margin	10	20	28
	Change in margin	−50%	0%	+40%

Panel B (In dollars at current exchange rate LC 1 = $1.10)

Initial Situation		Net Exporter	Balanced Firm	Net Importer
100	Sales	99	110	110
80	Cost of Sales	88	88	79
20	Gross Margin	11	22	31
	Change in margin	−45%	+10%	+55%

Panel C (In dollars at PPP rate of LC 1 = $1)

Initial Situation		Net Exporter	Balanced Firm	Net Importer
100	Sales	90	100	100
80	Cost of Sales	80	80	72
20	Gross Margin	10	20	28
	Change in margin	−50%	0%	+40%

tion) occurs—that is, a 10 percent increase in the price of local goods relative to world goods. (A 10 percent increase is well within the realm of possibility over one year as witnessed by the strengthening of the dollar in 1979-1980.) Since management is operating as effectively as before, and at the same level of activity, a "good" measure of managerial performance should be minimally affected by an unexpected change in the exchange rate, which is clearly beyond management's control. Let us examine what happens to the net income of each operation.

In practice a common solution to the problem of reducing the uncontrollable volatility of net income is to measure it in local currency. How does this work out in this case? The result is shown in Panel A of Table 1. The exporter loses since the foreign currency, and therefore revenues, have become worth less because the relative price of foreign goods against which it competes has fallen. Its contribution margin falls 50 percent from LC20 to LC10. Under the same circumstances, the balanced firm's contribution margin (assuming it does not compete with imports) remains unchanged from a local currency perspective. (The effect, of

course, is not restricted to importers and exporters. A purely "local" firm facing import competition, such as the American small car manufacturer above, is in the same position.) By contrast, the importer's contribution margin rises 40 percent from LC20 to LC28 because the prices at which it sells its product locally are unchanged, while the cost of its world-price inputs has fallen 10 percent.

Measuring income in *dollars* at the current exchange rate simply makes matters worse, as can be seen clearly in Panel B. The exporter's poor results are somewhat improved by the 10 percent rise in the value of the local currency (in which its income is *measured*), but that same exchange rate movement creates a windfall for the purely domestic firm and enhances the already super performance of the importer.

Furthermore, as can be seen in Panel C, Stewart's suggestion provides a net income measure that is unaffected by the exchange rate *only* in the case of the balanced operation.[8] The reason for this is clear: for the importer and exporter, the underlying performance itself *depends* on the real exchange rate.

So our conclusion is this: measuring income in

8. The PPP rate in our example remains LC 1 = $1 because we assume there has been no difference in inflation between the two countries.

Our goal in allocating responsibility for exchange rate movements is to ensure that those who are best able to manage exchange risks are held responsible for them.

FIGURE 2 Varieties of Exposure for Typical Transaction	non-contractual		quasi-contractual		contractual
	t–x acquire capacity, design product, etc.	t–4 publish price quote	t–2 obtain firm order	t ship/ invoice/ record sale	t+3 collect account receivable

dollars incorporates two effects. The first is the *translation* effect, which exists for any overseas operation whose results must be translated into the home currency. The second is the *dependence* effect, which is especially significant for an importer or exporter, or any firm subject to overseas competition, and which is a function of the real exchange rate. These two components are merged indiscriminately in conventionally translated financial statements; we later address the problem of designing a performance measure which separates these effects.

Responsibility for Floating Exchange Rates

Our goal in allocating responsibility for exchange rate movements is to ensure that those who are best able to manage exchange risks are held responsible for them. It is also to ensure that performance measures create incentives to maximize the value of the firm within defined limits of risk.

It is important to begin by clearly distinguishing between a firm's *financial* activities—which, unless the firm is a financial intermediary, are an incidental (though of course a necessary) part of operating the business—and those *real* activities, such as sourcing, manufacturing and marketing, which are its *raison d'être*. Real markets are characterized by "imperfections"—that is, abnormal profit opportunities. Since operating managers are presumed to have special expertise and sometimes even unique advantages in the real aspects of the business, they should be encouraged to use that expertise, and to take business risks whenever their judgment tells them it is advantageous to do so.

Financial markets, by contrast, are reasonably efficient, and transactions costs low, at least for the major currencies. Operating managers, it is wise to assume, have no special financial expertise. Performance measures, therefore, should not encourage speculation in financial markets.

In identifying the potential impacts of exchange rate changes on operating profits, it is useful to separate cash items and real items, to distinguish between what we call "contractual" and "non-contractual" exposures. Consider a single transaction as depicted in Figure 2. At some initial point a firm invests in real assets—a market franchise, product design, production capacity, etc. In so doing, the firm is counting on being able to quote an attractive price for the product at some point in the future. Once the firm quotes a price, there may or may not be a significant delay before it obtains a firm contract. Once the company has a firm contract, it then has a monetary asset and, hence, a contractual exposure.

Until the transaction results in a contractual commitment, whether in the form of a booked order or an account receivable, it represents in effect a series of non-contractual exposures. In fact, a company can be viewed as a portfolio of such transactions progressing from "real" to monetary positions.

The importance of this distinction between real/non-contractual and paper/contractual items arises from the difference in how their values are affected by real and nominal changes in exchange rates. Real items are exposed only to real changes in the exchange rate—changes that alter the relative prices of domestic and foreign goods. Monetary items, on the other hand, are exposed to the absolute or nominal movements of exchange rates. For example, a continuing devaluation of a currency such as the cruzeiro doesn't affect operating flows as long as it remains roughly in line with relative inflation in Brazil and the U.S. (and as long as prices are not controlled).[9] Cruzeiro monetary assets, though,

9. Laurent Jacque and Peter Lorange, "The International Control Conundrum: The Case of Hyperinflationary Subsidiaries", *Journal of International Business Studies*, forthcoming.

If the system doesn't take account of operating managers' expected response, it is likely to reward good luck combined with mediocre management.

will decline in dollar value along with the cruzeiro devaluation. On the other hand, if inflation in Italy outstrips inflation elsewhere in Europe, but the lira-DM exchange rate remains fixed, the international competitiveness of Italian production will suffer while the DM value of lira paper assets remains unchanged.

A second major difference between real and monetary items is that management can do nothing to change the exchange rate exposure of monetary items. An account receivable denominated in DM behaves just as DM-denominated commercial paper. It is a treasury asset, not an operating asset. There is no way to manage it. It can, however, be hedged very easily with offsetting forward contracts or short-term foreign currency borrowing. In contrast, non-contractual exposures—future cash flows such as those anticipated from speculative positions in plant, market, franchise, or product design—can be managed either to offset the effects of exchange rate changes or to take advantage of them. Managers often can shift the deployment of real assets in response to changes in relative prices.

Design of the Performance Measurement System

Design Criteria

Profitability is the result of a combination of good management— that is, the effective use of resources—and a large random component arising from surprise exchange rate movements. Although such movements are beyond management's control, the effect of such surprises on the profitability of foreign operations firm depends partly on management's ability to adjust to them. But this flexibility, of course, is at least partly limited by the firm's strategic position.

Measuring a business unit's total performance is complicated, but identifying the distinctive contribution of management is even more difficult. Conceptually, the use of such a measure requires that a standard level of performance be defined for a set of assumptions about the environment (including exchange rates, of course), and that actual performance be compared to the standard.

As mentioned, much of the variance between planned and actual results can be attributed to surprises in uncontrollable variables. To make a fair comparison, one has two choices. One approach is to explain deviations in actual performance in terms of key, uncontrollable factors (which is the approach of variance analysis in standard costing methods). The other is to revise the standard to reflect the impact of surprise events after they happen. The simplest form of this is known as "flexible" budgeting. We propose here a refinement of flexible budgeting which we call "contingent" budgeting.

Consider the typical multinational firm. Its businesses are likely to range from net-importing to net-exporting units. As such, they are subject to very different effects of exchange rate movements. Properly evaluating the performance of different units—even under the same set of economic conditions—may be quite difficult, in large part because management can and should react to changes in relative prices. Though there are clearly limits to what local operating managers can do in the short run to deal with relative price changes, an operating unit may be able to shift sources, to change its marketing and production mix, or to change its pricing and market share strategy.

In short, then, not only does each unit's measured performance differ, but so does the appropriate response by management; and a good performance measurement system should capture these differences. Whether this is done by adjusting the measure or by adjusting the benchmark makes little difference. What does matter is whether the measure or benchmark reflects foreseeable effects of surprise exchange rate impacts. (By "foreseeable" we don't mean exchange rate movements that can be forecast, but rather the *expected* impact on a business of a particular, though *unexpected*, exchange rate movement.) If the system doesn't take account of operating managers' expected response, it is likely to reward good luck combined with mediocre management.

What we propose is a set of performance measures, or standards, which reflect the "foreseeable" impact of exchange rate movements. To develop such standards, we first need to come up with an audit estimating the probable impacts of exchange rate changes on the profitability of different business units; and we need to decide who should bear these risks. The audit of expected impacts is important for several reasons. It provides an opportunity to think through and discuss in advance what will happen to a particular business when a currency appreciates or depreciates. If an understanding of

If an understanding of what is likely to happen is shared within the company, two-thirds of the problem of performance measurement is solved.

what is likely to happen is shared within the company, two-thirds of the problem of performance measurement is solved. To be useful, though, this discussion must clearly take place before, not after, the fact.

Whether we want to hold operating managers accountable for some, or all, of the effects of exchange rate fluctuations on operations depends on whether they have significant ways to respond. If they can alter key policies in response to exchange rate movements, then they should bear the responsibility. If operating management can do nothing, there's no benefit to imposing exchange gains and losses on them. Rewarding and penalizing local managers for the fortuitous effects of exchange rate changes will not result in any improvement in operating performance; it will only make the performance measure seem more arbitrary and perhaps distort managerial incentives by encouraging currency speculation. We should hold an operating manager accountable for a given risk only if this provides the manager with an appropriate incentive.

There is no reason why operating managers should be held responsible for the impact of exchange rates on financial items. But there are many reasons why management should bear some responsibility for the impact of the exchange rate on real, operating items.

Contractual Items: A fair standard of performance for the management of contractual financial items under the control of operating managers can easily be devised using an efficient currency-markets framework. It is necessary only to measure foreign currency working capital items, such as accounts receivable and payable, in dollars (or any other home currency) at the forward rate.[10] In computing operating contribution, we act as if the subsidiary is on a cash basis by booking all foreign currency receivables and payables at the forward rate. In accordance with our view that operating managers should not be responsible for managing contractual currency risk, we believe they should be *required* to sell receivables and payables at the forward rate, probably to the treasury department. Treasury's hedging (or speculative) performance could then be correctly evaluated relative to that forward rate.

Operating Margins: Setting standards for operating performance is more difficult, not just because the operating environment is uncertain, but because management decisions should be contingent on the state of the world at any given time. This suggests that budgets, too, should be made contingent on the state of the world. A single rigid standard of performance, even if based on the most sophisticated forecasts available, simply will not encourage operating management to think through alternative responses to exchange rate surprises. Instead, it will reward good forecasting.

Preparing a contingent budget requires three steps:

1. Prepare a budget based on a "most-likely" scenario. This is the traditional budget preparation process. It seems to be natural to prepare the budget in terms of local currency units, and this is how we do it in our illustration later.

2. Prepare an audit of the likely effect of a range of surprise deviations from existing exchange rate parities, in terms of impact on prices, costs and hence operating cash flows. The objective of this procedure is to develop, in advance, an expectation of the relationship between exchange rates, operating management's best efforts, and operating cash flows.

3. At the end of the year, when the exchange rates are *known*, use the results of the audit to compute a set of standards or benchmarks of performance, *given* the exchange rates that actually materialized. Actual results should then be compared with the contingent standards as the point of departure in discussing management performance.

The choice of currency to be used in the budget should depend on two considerations:

1. The currency of determination of the majority of the unit's revenues and costs; that is, the currency in which these revenues and costs are relatively independent of exchange rate movements.

2. The unit's position within the organization; that is, whether it is viewed as an autonomous operating unit, or part of the global organization.

---

10. To be complete, this requires the recognition of the time value of the remaining net monetary investment. However these considerations are incidental to our contingent budget, since our budget figure could be computed under any assumption underlying the calculation of income.

Rewarding and penalizing local managers for the fortuitous effects of exchange rate changes will not result in any improvement in operating performance.

An Illustration

We will now illustrate our proposal with the design of a performance measurement system for three very different subsidiaries of a U.S. multinational. For simplicity of exposition, they are all located in Mexico. The subsidiaries are:

- **Enchilada**—This is the example used by Stewart. It buys local inputs and sells in the local market.
- **Automex**—This is a car assembly operation. Approximately half of its costs are represented by components imported from the U.S.; the other half, by locally-sourced components and labor. Most of its output is sold in the local market, but the possibility of exporting to neighboring countries also exists. Currently, about 20 percent of its output is being exported, at prices comparable to those obtained in Mexico.
- **Digimex**—This is an electronics operation located just across the border for assembly of small computers for the U.S. market. Its dollar-priced components are sourced worldwide, and Mexican labor represents two-thirds of its costs.

For ease of comparison, we will assume that the 1984 budget operating margin of each subsidiary, based on the expected exchange rates, is the same. The budgets for each subsidiary, after adjusting for inflation, are shown in Table 2.

The January 1984 exchange rate is P207 = $1, which represents an undervaluation of about 20 percent by historical standards. The January 1984 PPP rate is therefore P173 = $1. The forecast average exchange rate for 1984 is P238 per dollar (a nominal 30 percent devaluation over the year). So, converted in the usual way, the budget dollar cash flow is $42,000 (P10M/238). Since Mexican inflation is also forecast at 30 percent, the expectation is that there will no *real* depreciation, and the peso will thus remain some 20 percent undervalued according to PPP.

We now review the contingent budget in each subsidiary. *Enchilada*'s peso operating profit is expected to be unaffected by exchange rate movements. True, there might be surprises in inflation, in which case operating management will need to adjust nominal prices to maintain them in real terms—but that is precisely management's responsibility. Note that this is an inflation, not an exchange-rate, effect, although the two are frequently confused. Inflation will also affect historic-cost accounting statements; but our proposal, as mentioned earlier, requires that all statements of performance be inflation-adjusted. Because all of *Enchilada*'s inputs are sourced and outputs are sold locally, *and because neither inputs nor outputs are subject to competition from overseas*, the only effect of exchange rate movements is the measurement effect; the change in value in dollar terms of a net income figure is unchanged when measured in local currency terms. (*Enchilada* is thus the simplest case, and the only one of the three for which Stewart's PPP-normalized exchange-rate proposal works.)

For the operations of *Automex*, the continuing expected undervaluation will cause imported component costs to be higher than otherwise. Since local costs and revenues are unaffected, margins on local sales will be squeezed. The position of *Automex* in export markets, however, will be strengthened. We assume that *Automex* management is anxious to increase its presence in these export markets, and will therefore attempt to maintain volume rather than seek higher margins. All of these expectations are incorporated into the *Automex* budget shown in Table 2.

If exchange rate surprises occur, *Automex* management will face a transfer price of imported components that is determined by the dollar, and it is accordingly expected to maintain its dollar export prices. In the event of a larger than expected peso devaluation, we assume they will hold peso prices constant and be able to increase export sales by 2

TABLE 2 Base Case Operating Budgets (in millions of Jan. 1984 pesos)			Enchilada	Automex	Digimex
Sales	(export)			20	110
	(local)		120	90	
Cost of	(locally sourced)		(80)	(20)	(30)
Sales	(imports)			(60)	(30)
Local expenses			(30)	(20)	(40)
Operating margin			10	10	10

A single rigid standard of performance, even if based on the most sophisticated forecasts available, simply will not encourage operating management to think through alternative responses to exchange rate surprises.

TABLE 3
Actual Operating Results (in millions of January 1984 pesos)

		Enchilada	Automex	Digimex
Sales	(export)		25	121
	(local)	120	90	
Cost of Sales	(locally sourced)	(80)	(20)	(34)
	(imports)		(66)	(33)
Local expenses		(30)	(20)	(42)
Operating margin		10	9	12

percent for every 1 percent of effective devaluation.

Digimex faces a different situation. Its sales volume is essentially fixed by the requirements of its U.S. parent. Its output prices are fixed in dollars, as is the price it pays for imported components. If the currency forecast is accurate, these prices are expected to remain high from a real peso perspective, and therefore peso profitability should continue at an above-normal level. This, too, has been incorporated into the budget in Table 2. If there are exchange rate surprises, they will directly affect the peso price obtained for exports, and the cost of imports.

To illustrate how a contingent budget works, we now suppose that the exchange rate does not follow expectations. Instead, the nominal rate depreciates by 35 percent (to an average rate of P250 per dollar), while inflation is brought down to 25 percent, resulting in a real devaluation of 10 percent. The actual operating results of each subsidiary, expressed in millions of January 1984 pesos and adjusted for local inflation, are shown in Table 3.

What are we to make of these? In peso terms, it appears that *Enchilada* has done exactly as planned, *Automex* has underperformed by 10 percent, and *Digimex* has done best of all with actual cash flow that is 20 percent over budget.

Our proposal calls for computing a revised standard based on actual exchange rates. For *Enchilada*, the audit shows that exchange rate changes were not expected to have any effect on real, local currency profits; therefore no adjustment needs to be made.

Automex's management, however, promised to deliver 2 percent extra volume, at the same peso price, for every 1 percent of the real peso devalua-

tion. Since there was an effective 10 percent real devaluation, their contingent export sales budget should have been 20 percent higher, at 24 million pesos. Domestic sales and local costs should have been unaffected, while import costs should have risen 10 percent to 66 million pesos.[11] The net effect is that, under the actual circumstances, the budgeted level of operating margin is 8 million pesos. Their achievement of 9 million was made through greater than expected exports.

By the same token, *Digimex* should have benefitted from the surprise devaluation because it is a net exporter. From a peso point of view, sales should have increased 10 percent from 110 to 121 million pesos. This sales increase should have been only partially offset by a corresponding 10 percent increase in imported costs, from 30 to 33 million pesos. The revised standard should thus be 18 million pesos of operating contribution. Their actual achievement of only 12 million pesos therefore represents a substantial underachievement.

Our revised standard now gives a very different picture of operating managers' performance: *Enchilada* is unchanged, but *Automex* is now *above* standard, while *Digimex* is well *below* standard. This is shown in the Table 4.

Ultimately, of course, corporate headquarters will want to evaluate the profitability of its foreign operations in terms of the home currency. So let's see what happens in the translation to dollars. Using the current (i.e., average) exchange rate, *Enchilada's* dollar profit is reduced from a budget of $42,000 (based on P238 to the dollar) to $40,000 (when converted at P250 to the dollar). This apparent loss in profit margin is purely a measurement effect—one which can easily be corrected by Stewart's proposal.

---

11. Of course, the increased sales volume should lead to increased variable costs. We ignore this for simplicity, however.

The long-term sustainable dollar earnings figure, the level of profitability in today's dollars which the company should be able to achieve if PPP held, is the income measure most relevant to investors' evaluation.

TABLE 4 Contingent Budget and Actual Performance (in millions of Jan. 1984 pesos)			Enchilada		Automex		Digimex	
			budget	actual	budget	actual	budget	actual
Sales	(export)				24	25	121	121
	(local)		120	120	90	90		
Cost of	(locally sourced)		(80)	(80)	(20)	(20)	(30)	(34)
Sales	(imports)				(66)	(66)	(33)	(33)
Local expenses			(30)	(30)	(20)	(20)	(40)	(42)
Operating Margin			10	10	8	9	18	12

TABLE 5 Expected Long-Term Performance Conditional on PPP			Automex	Digimex
Sales		(export)	16	88
		(local)	90	
Cost of		(locally sourced)	(20)	(30)
Sales		(imports)	(48)	(24)
Local expenses			(20)	(40)
Operating Cash Flow			18	(6)
In Dollars at PPP Rate			$104,000	$(34,700)

Using the PPP-normalized rate of 173 would result in a dollar profit of $57,800 (P10M/173). The proper interpretation of this number is that it represents the long-term sustainable earnings which would be achieved if the peso returned to parity. Along with Stewart, we believe that this long-term sustainable dollar earnings figure is the income measure most relevant to investors' evaluation of foreign income. By "long-term" and "sustainable" we mean the level of profitability in today's dollars which the company should be able to achieve if PPP held.

But, clearly, except in the *Enchilada* case, where profitability is independent of the real exchange rate, it is not enough just to translate actual year-to-year peso profitability at the PPP exchange rate. For *Automex* and *Digimex*, we must first calculate what the peso profit would have been if PPP had held, and *then* translate at the PPP rate. This would require that the budget be redrawn contingent on PPP.

Such a formulation is shown in Table 5 for Automex and Digimex. Note that a revaluation of 20 percent (to PPP) would certainly wipe out the profitability of *Automex*'s exports, and would raise serious questions about the long-term viability of that activity. At the same time, however, a revaluation would enhance the profitability of domestic operations. *Digimex*, as would be expected, would be ad-

versely affected; and at present levels of efficiency, it would not be profitable.

These results do not imply that *Digimex* should be closed down. They do show, however, the extent to which its current profitability depends on an (historically) undervalued real peso. If the peso were to strengthen, the firm would seriously want to consider alternatives to Mexican production. *Automex*, by contrast, because of its simultaneous orientation toward local and export markets, remains viable even assuming a return of the peso to PPP. In this case, the contingent budget should serve to underscore for operating management the importance of maintaining this operational flexibility.

Conclusions

While the need for an explicit treatment of real exchange rates is evident for less developed countries with highly volatile monetary situations, it is likely to be at least as important for industrial countries where the volatility of real exchange rates is perhaps less, but much larger relative to other contingencies.

We have shown that when a business is subject to cross-border competition, its performance, regardless of the currency in which it is measured, will depend on the real exchange rate. While exchange rates tend toward PPP in the long run, real exchange rates vary considerably in the short run. Thus, the effects of short-run movements must be taken into account in assessing managers' contribution to the performance of their units.

We believe that a performance measurement scheme can best accommodate deviations from PPP by adjusting the budget performance standard in light of realized exchange rates. Such standards should be based on a model of the linkage between operating performance and real exchange rates which has been agreed upon by both operating and corporate managers at the time the budget is prepared.

We have illustrated our proposal with a simple example of three Mexican subsidiaries. In the process, we have purposely avoided many of the complexities that would have to be dealt with. One of these is the effect on performance of transfer prices among affiliated business units. The contingent budget approach, however, could easily be extended to incorporate any arbitrary structure of transfer prices. It could also be extended to include other contingencies, such as relative prices of key commodities, or factors influencing demand. We are confident that our approach will go a long way toward solving the problem of distinguishing between the profitability of a business unit and operating management's contribution to that level of profitability.

References

Black, Fischer. "The Magic in Earnings: Economic Earnings versus Accounting Earnings," *Financial Analysis Journal* 36 (November/ December 1980), pp. 19-24.

Jacque, Laurent and Peter Lorange. "The International Control Conundrum: The Case of Hyperinflationary Subsidiaries", *Journal of International Business Studies*, forthcoming.

Lessard, Donald R. and Peter Lorange. "Currency Changes and Management Control: Resolving the Centralization/Decentralization Dilemma," *Accounting Review* (July 1977), pp. 628-637.

Shapiro, Alan. "The Evaluation and Control of Foreign Affiliates," *Midland Corporate Finance Journal* (Spring 1984), pp. 13-25.

Stewart, G. Bennett. "A Proposal for Measuring International Performance," *Midland Corporate Finance Journal* (Summer 1983), pp. 56-71.

The Evaluation and Control of Foreign Affiliates

Alan C. Shapiro,
University of Southern California

Financial managers of multinational corporations (MNCs) face the continuing responsibility of analyzing and comparing financial reports submitted to them by units under their surveillance. Managers of subsidiaries must, in turn, monitor their own units and report to the next highest level of management. The main objective of such activities is to track sales and control expenses so as to increase an MNC's income, its return on invested capital, and ultimately, of course, the returns to its stockholders. This process of analysis also yields the information necessary to evaluate performance and to decide on management promotions and resource allocation.

In the multinational firm, setting standards and measuring performance is complicated by wide variation in rates of inflation among countries, fluctuations in currency rates, and the effects of intracompany transactions on the allocation of costs and profits among the various units of the global MNC. This article deals with some of the special problems encountered in evaluating the profitability of foreign operations and the performance of their managers. The first section discusses the design and objectives of a management evaluation and control system for a multinational firm. Sections 2 through 4 develop general approaches for achieving the three main objectives of such a system: (1) the allocation of capital among foreign subsidiaries; (2) the evaluation of current performance of foreign operations from a home country or stockholder perspective; and (3) the evaluation of local management's operating profitability (and, thus, the creation of appropriate incentives for managers of foreign affiliates). The final section considers the important issue of how far to decentralize certain critical multinational financial decisions and responsibilities.

Unfortunately, the development of an evaluation and control system is still more of an art than a science, relying more on judgment than theory. No universal principles have yet appeared to use in designing such systems for domestic operations, much less for foreign operations. Nevertheless, finance theory can afford some useful insights in resolving questions of international performance evaluation and management compensation. This article, therefore, has the modest goal of suggesting a set of general guidelines for incorporating a variety of international elements into a framework for evaluating foreign operations.

Designing an Evaluation and Control System

The design of an evaluation system generally involves four stages:
1. **Specifying the system's purpose(s).**
2. **Determining the information requirements.**
3. **Designing the information collection system.**
4. **Conducting a cost/benefit analysis.**

The critical first stage of the design process is to specify the system's objectives. While this no doubt seems a trivial observation, many companies have gotten into trouble by failing to distinguish, for example, between the evaluation of subsidiary performance and managerial performance. In evaluating subsidiary performance, the focus should be on how well the subsidiary is doing as an economic entity. However, because of a number of factors that complicate the evaluation of foreign operations, a measure of the affiliate's value from the perspective of corporate headquarters may differ significantly from a fair measure of local management's operating efficiency. In such a case, it may be worthwhile to attempt to insulate affiliate management from the effects on reported results of changes in variables

The relevant investment base is the current market value of all incremental capital committed to the investment or operation.

beyond its control (e.g., local GNP growth rates, exchange rates and rates of inflation). Such a task, although a difficult one, may be necessary if the best possible promotion and investment decisions are to be made.

The second stage involves determining what decisions will be made on the basis of these evaluations and the information necessary to support such decisions. For example, when evaluating international managerial performance it may be helpful to separate, as suggested, the effects of uncontrollables like inflation or an unexpected devaluation from those factors management controls, such as credit extension or inventory accumulation. Furthermore, capital allocation decisions may require very different measures of subsidiary performance than does ensuring the smooth functioning of current operations.

The third stage is the design of a reporting or information system that can provide the necessary information, or at least a reasonable approximation. Many companies may find that their current reporting system is inadequate for such purposes, and that their data production and manipulation capability must be expanded. For example, an effective system for allocating capital and measuring performance may require the generation of inflation-adjusted numbers, as well as simulations of *operating* exposure to currency changes—estimates that are not routinely furnished or even attempted by many MNC's.

The final stage involves conducting a cost/benefit analysis of the evaluation system. This analysis does not have to be quantitative but it should be comprehensive. Potential benefits of the system are:

- **Greater control over current operations.**
- **More rigorous capital budgeting decisions.**
- **Greater awareness of managerial effectiveness.**
- **Improvement of local managers' incentives caused by a more sensible evaluation scheme.**
- **Better allocation of responsibility due to a more effective mix of decentralization and centralization.**

Against these benefits must be weighed the costs which might arise, including (1) the time and money involved in redesigning the information system, and (2) behavioral problems that might be associated with the new evaluation system. The latter cost might include reduced initiative on the part of local managers who feel they are being overly controlled. This need not occur since one of the goals

of an evaluation system should be to provide the information which is necessary to reward managers for their performance. An evaluation system which does not motivate managers to work in their company's best interest will not be an effective one, regardless of its other attributes.

It is all too evident that many multinational, as well as domestic, corporations have not fully thought through this design process. Subsidiary managers often complain that too much information is being demanded. At the same time, management at headquarters complains that too much data, but too little good information, is being supplied by the subsidiaries. The frequency of such complaints alone is strong evidence of dissonance between system design and goals.

The main objectives of the evaluation system that I shall discuss are to provide the following:

- **A rational basis for global resource allocation;**
- **An early warning system to detect if something is wrong with current operations;**
- **A means of evaluating the performance of individual managers, including a set of standards to create the desired incentives.**

The following sections explore each of these purposes in turn and comment on some of the methods currently used by MNCs in achieving these goals.

Resource Allocation

A key decision continually faced by multinationals is the allocation of capital among their various subsidiaries on a worldwide basis. One method widely employed in evaluating prospective investments is the expected return on investment (ROI). Although this measuring tool is potentially of great value, its usefulness in application depends on whether the relevant investment base and return are used.

Measuring Return on Investment

Using the return on existing investments as the relevant ROI figure for judging the profitability of future investments is appropriate to the extent that returns on past investments are indicative of future returns. But there will be problems if proposed investments are not comparable to existing ones, or if the returns on past investments have been measured incorrectly. These problems are most likely to

*Substantial differences can arise between subsidiary
cash flows and cash flows repatriated to the parent firm.*

exist when the firm uses historical subsidiary returns to allocate capital globally. Cross-country comparisons of historical returns will be useful *only* if these returns are good predictors of the relative returns on contemplated investments in other countries. Moreover, even if expected ROIs differ across countries, it is necessary to consider the element of risk as well. Certain low-risk, low-return investments may be preferable to high-risk, high-return investments. A policy that concentrates solely on achieving high returns is likely to generate a preponderance of high-risk projects.

Even where potential investments are comparable to past ones (e.g., replacement of depreciated assets), it is often difficult to decide on the *relevant* selection criteria. For example, a number of nonfinancial criteria such as market share, sales growth, and stability of production are often used in comparing investments. Ultimately, however, most firms —not to mention their shareholders—are interested in the return on corporate capital employed. A 1970 Conference Board study indicated that some version of return on investment is the most common means of measuring the long-run profit performance of foreign subsidiaries.[1]

But, as suggested, there are a number of measurement pitfalls involved in allowing return on past investments to guide this process. These problems fall into two areas: first, problems associated with measuring the correct investment base, and second, difficulties in determining the relevant returns.

There are a variety of definitions of capital used by corporations in evaluating performance. The investment base may include:

- **Parent's Equity**
- **Fixed Assets**
  a. Gross
  b. Net of depreciation
- **Working Capital**
  a. Total
  b. Net of supplier credits
  c. Net of intracompany accounts

Moreover, assets can be valued on an historical or current (replacement or market) cost basis.

Measuring the investment base. Fortunately, financial theory pinpoints the relevant investment base to use in evaluating the true economic return on investment for past as well as prospective investments. It equals the current market value of all incremental capital committed to the investment or operation. Thus, the investment should be measured on a *current or replacement cost* basis, rather than an historical cost basis, and should include gross fixed assets as well as total working capital requirements (net of external supplier credits). Using historical rather than replacement costs in a period of inflation will understate true capital requirements, thus overstating the projected return on investment. The working capital figure should include inventory valued on a current cost basis. Intracompany receivables should be excluded since these accounts cancel on a corporate-wide basis; increasing one subsidiary's intracompany receivables by one dollar will lead to a one dollar reduction in another unit's working capital requirements. Furthermore, these accounts are arbitrary and subject to corporate manipulation.

Measuring the returns. Measuring the *relevant returns* from foreign operations, whether actual or expected, is a more difficult task. Unfortunately, the conventional earnings figure provided by corporate accounting systems does not really measure true performance. What it really represents is taxable earnings. But this is a highly arbitrary figure that often has little to do with economic performance.

The ideal measure of returns would capture all incremental cash flows generated by the foreign operation. Substantial differences can arise, however, between subsidiary cash flows and cash flows repatriated to the parent firm due to, among other things, tax regulations and exchange controls.[2] In addition, adjustments in transfer prices and intersubsidiary credit arrangements can distort the true profitability of a given investment or subsidiary by shifting profits and liquidity from one unit to another. Furthermore, fees and royalties are costs to a subsidiary but benefits to the parent company.

Studies by the Conference Board and Business International have found considerable variation among firms in measuring returns.[3] Measured returns have included different combinations of for-

1. Irene W. Meister, *Managing the International Financial Function* (New York: The Conference Board, 1970).

2. See Alan C. Shapiro, "International Capital Budgeting", *Midland Corporate Finance Journal*, Spring 1983, pp. 26-45 for a discussion of this point, and for a much more detailed framework for evaluating international investments.

3. Op. cit. and Business International Corporation, "Evaluating Foreign Operations: The Appropriate Rates for Comparing Results with Budgets," *Business International Money Report*, May 20, 1977, p. 154.

eign earnings, royalties, fees, dividends, rentals, interest, commissions, and export profits. Some firms include only repatriated profits while others include most or all of these returns after foreign taxes. Still others take into account both U.S. and foreign taxes paid. One company, for instance, was using return on net book value of assets as its measure of return on investment. Since its foreign plant and equipment was much newer, and hence more expensive, than the corresponding domestic assets, management was operating under the premise that greater returns were available at home than abroad.

The correct approach to measuring returns again relies on economic theory. According to this theory, the value of an investment is determined by the net present value of all incremental cash flows back to the investor. The key concept here is *incremental*. Determining incremental cash flows for a multinational corporation involves taking the difference between worldwide cash flows *with* the investment and worldwide cash flows in the investment's absence. Thus, all interest charges, royalties, fees and overhead allocations paid by a subsidiary should be included in its profit calculation, as should all profits earned by other units owing to the subsidiary's existence. This calculation would include profits arising from the adjustment of transfer prices on goods bought from or sold to the subsidiary, as well as all profits on exports to the subsidiary which would not have occurred if the subsidiary did not exist. By the same token, any profits on sales or any licensing fees and royalties that would otherwise have been earned by another unit of the MNC are not economically attributable to the subsidiary. Further, affiliate cash flows affect corporate valuation only to the extent that they are capable, at some point, of being repatriated. Otherwise, shareholders derive no benefits in the form of dividends or future investment capital.

The cost of carrying intracompany receivables should be excluded from the subsidiary's profit and loss calculation since this cost is offset elsewhere in the corporation by a corresponding reduction in working capital requirements. By the same logic, the subsidiary should be charged for the cost of any intracorporate payables on its balance sheet.

To summarize, then, the basic problem with using the unadjusted historical return on investment as the basis for allocating resources in the future is that this figure may reflect neither the relevant cash flows nor the relevant investment base. Moreover,

returns and the investment base often vary greatly over the investment cycle. Thus, ROI comparisons may be misleading.

Also, for ROI analysis to be meaningful, accounting results must be brought into agreement with economic values. This would mean adjusting inventory to market value and adjusting depreciation to reflect the replacement cost of assets being consumed. In addition, profit figures should be revised to eliminate unusual or nonrecurring items. Although the results from such an analysis can only be considered tentative, they will generally provide a reasonable approximation to the investment's true economic performance, especially in light of the cost of conducting a thorough analysis.

Post-investment Audit

Once an investment has been made, it is largely a sunk cost and should not influence future decisions. Nevertheless, management wants to know when capital investment decisions have been made incorrectly for two reasons:

1. **Some action may be appropriate with respect to the managers responsible for the mistakes.**

2. **Some safeguard to prevent a recurrence may be appropriate.**

Thus, the most important comparison that can be made is likely to be between actual results and ex-ante budgeted figures. A post-investment audit can help a firm learn from its mistakes as well as from its successes. In the multinational corporation, where so many additional complexities enter into the capital budgeting decision, it is easier to make errors due to a lack of experience. Reviewing the record of past investments can help a firm determine whether there is any consistency in its estimation errors, such as generally under- or over-estimating the impact of inflation on costs or of devaluations on dollar revenues from foreign sales. Correction factors can then be included in future investment analyses. Even if estimation errors are random, a firm may be able to place bounds on the relative magnitudes of these errors and thereby supply useful inputs to an investment simulation model.

The most important benefit of flexible budgeting is that it may remove much of the effects of general economic events beyond management's control.

The Evaluation and Control of Current Operations

Frequent monitoring of operations in an uncertain environment is also useful to determine whether any tactical or strategic changes are warranted. This requires formal standards against which to judge performance. There are three types of standards used in control systems:

1. *Predetermined Standards or Budgets* – If carefully prepared, these are the best formal standards; they are the basis against which actual performance is evaluated.

2. *Historical Standards* – Based on past actual performance, this type of standard has two serious weaknesses: (a) conditions may have changed between the two periods and (b) the prior period's performance may not be acceptable to start with.

3. *External Standards* – Derived from other responsibility centers of other companies. The catch is that it is not easy to find two responsibility centers or companies that are sufficiently similar, or whose performance is affected by the same factors, to permit such comparisons on a regular basis.

Since profit is the corporate *raison d'etre*, most control systems are designed to measure profitability, but variations exist even in this basic measure. In addition to measuring profitability, the system highlights certain key variables, such as the ratio of working capital to sales, that have a significant effect on profitability. The appropriate measures to use in controlling foreign operations, however, will vary by company and subsidiary. For marketing-oriented companies, market share, sales growth, or cost/sales dollar may be the most relevant yardsticks. A manufacturing subsidiary may be most concerned about unit production costs, quality control, or the labor turnover rate. Others may find that return on assets, gross margin, or a working capital-to-sales ratio are better proxies for profitability. The important point is to use those measures which experience has determined are the key leading indicators of whether an operation is out of control.

In evaluating foreign operations, it may be necessary to employ different standards than those used in controlling the domestic business. *Inventory turnover*, for example, may be lower overseas because of the larger inventory stocks required to cope with longer lead times to delivery and more frequent delays in international shipments of goods. Where foreign production is taking place, it may be necessary to stockpile additional supplies of imported raw materials and components, given the possibility of dock strike, import controls, or some other supply disruption.[4]

Receivables may also be greater abroad, particularly in countries experiencing rapid rates of inflation. During times of inflation, consumers normally prefer to purchase on longer credit terms, expecting to repay their debt with less valuable future money. Furthermore, local credit standards are often more relaxed than in the home market, especially in countries lacking alternative credit arrangements. To remain competitive, MNCs may feel compelled to loosen their own credit standards. This is not always the best policy, though. The MNC should weigh the profits on incremental credit sales against the additional carrying costs, including devaluation losses and bad debts, associated with an easier credit policy.[5]

Different cost standards are usually necessary for foreign operations due to local value-added requirements (which mandate the use of more expensive local goods and services), import tariffs, and government limitations on laying off or firing workers. In the latter case, labor becomes a fixed rather than a variable cost.

Flexible Budgeting

Furthermore, most firms find it helpful to draw up budgets based on explicit assumptions about the internal and external environment. In a foreign environment, with its greater uncertainties, *flexible budgeting* might be even more useful than it is domestically. Flexible budgeting involves drawing up alternative budgets based on different projections of future rates of inflation, exchange rate changes, relative price changes, wage settlements, and so on. Perhaps the most important potential benefit of flexible budgeting is that it may remove much of the effects of general economic events beyond management's control from performance measures, thereby providing a measure which better identifies management's contribution to subsidiary results.

4. See Chapter 10 of Alan C. Shapiro, *Multinational Financial Management* (Boston: Allyn and Bacon, 1982).

5. Ibid.

For example, given a particular scenario, such as a 3 percent rise in real GNP along with 15 percent inflation, the subsidiary would project its expected profit, along with any working capital and fixed asset requirements. The profit forecast, in turn, would be based on the company's estimate of the responsiveness of sales volume, sales price, and costs to inflation and real GNP growth. And if this scenario in fact comes to pass, then this profit forecast becomes the standard of performance for that period.

Inasmuch as it is impossible to develop a different budget for each potential future scenario, a limited number of the most likely scenarios should be selected for further study. By carefully selecting these scenarios, but concentrating also on those that would most strongly affect the business, the firm should have an advantage in coping with foreseeable changes in its operating environments. Moreover, these alternative budgets will provide a more reasonable and reliable basis for evaluating the performance of its overseas managers.

Return on Investment Comparisons

Although ROI may have severe limitations as a measure of divisional performance for capital budgeting purposes, it is useful for diagnosing areas of profit deficiency and thus directing management's attention to potential areas of improvement. The object is to find some standard of potential performance against which to judge the subsidiary's actual performance. In practice, this usually means comparing the subsidiary's ROI with the ROI's of similar business—of which there are several likely candidates. These include local competitors, the firm's other subsidiaries and/or competitors on a regional or global basis, and parent company operations. In addition, comparisons can be made with the firm's original investment plans, or with the subsidiary's own past operating profitability.

Caution must be exercised, however, in making such comparisons. Comparisons with local or regional competitors can be misleading because of different accounting and disclosure requirements which lead to different depreciation and earnings reports under similar operating circumstances. Some foreign firms, for example, do not separate non-recurring income arising out of the sale of assets from operating income. Even if comparisons were limited to home country competitors, it is usually impossible to determine the actual profitability of local operations because of the high degree of integration and the less-than-arm's length dealings between units of a multinational corporation.

Cross-country comparisons with other affiliates of the multinational corporation are possible, but to what purpose? After the fact, of course, some investments will always turn out to have been more profitable than others. It is necessary to go beyond the numbers to determine the extent to which the operating environments are similar. Otherwise, different ROIs could just indicate that the subsidiaries are facing different economic circumstances.

The same caveat holds when comparing the current ROI with the subsidiary's historical performance. Specifically, a changing ROI over time may be due to changes in the subsidiary's operating environment. The key issue is, how much of the change in performance is caused by management actions and how much is due to uncontrollable factors?

Furthermore, multinationals have strategic reasons for going abroad which are not necessarily expressed in ROI calculations. For example, a firm may willingly forgo economies of scale in production in order to achieve greater security of supply by having multiple and redundant production facilities. In addition, operating in several nations may give a firm greater bargaining leverage in dealing with local governments or labor unions. Being multinational may also lower the firm's risk profile by reducing its dependence on the state of just one nation's economy.

In analyzing actual results, therefore, it is necessary to bear in mind those non-financial strategic rationales that may have prompted the original investment. Any evaluative criteria that are ultimately devised should accurately reflect the affiliate's performance as measured against its strategic purposes. Otherwise, an investment undertaken for one reason may be judged on the basis of different criteria, resulting in a misleading comparison.

Evaluating Managerial Performance

The standards used to evaluate managers will presumably serve to motivate them. A key goal, therefore, in designing a management evaluation system is to ensure that the resulting managerial incentives are consistent with overall corporate objectives. A good strategy that managers are not motivated to

*The most logical approach appears to be to hold local managers responsible for net operating income expressed in dollars, but **using a projected rather than the actual exchange rate**.*

follow will be of little value. Thus, it is necessary to think through the likely response of a rational manager to a particular set of evaluation criteria.

For example, managers evaluated on the basis of current earnings will likely emphasize short-run profits to the detriment of longer-term profitability. This is especially true if executives are frequently transferred, enabling them to escape the longer-run consequences of their actions. These myopic actions might include reducing advertising and maintenance, cutting back on R & D expenditures, and investing less in employee training.

Managers judged solely according to the current year's ROI may also concentrate on short-run profits. They may be slower to replace used equipment, particularly during a period of rapid inflation, even when the investment is economically sound. This is both because new investments will increase the investment base and because ROI measured on an historical cost basis will be greater than ROI on a replacement cost basis. Furthermore, if return on equity is used as the measure of performance, managers will have an incentive to substitute local debt for retained earnings and parent company equity. This will increase the MNC's worldwide debt ratio, perhaps causing a deterioration in the parent company's credit rating and a possible reduction in its share price.

Consistent with the goal of properly motivating employees is the principle that a manager's performance should be judged on the basis of results in those areas over which he or she has control. It is crucial to recognize that achievement in a given circumstance is a function not only of the manager's inherent skills and hard work, but also of the operating environment. Furthermore, it is unreasonable, as well as counter-productive, to reward or penalize a manager for the impact of economic events beyond his or her control.

Consequently, to whatever extent possible, corporate headquarters should attempt to distinguish between managerial performance and subsidiary performance. A subsidiary can be doing quite well despite the performance of its management, and the reverse is probably equally prevalent. For example, during a time of rapid local inflation but no currency change, a foreign subsidiary selling to local customers will show a proportional increase in its

dollar profitability. Even with poor management, profits should rise, although less than they would otherwise. After the inevitable devaluation, however, dollar profitability will invariably decline, even with good management in control.[6] Furthermore, a consistently poor profit performance by a manager may just be evidence of a past mistake in approving the original investment.

Instead of evaluating managerial performance on the basis of a subsidiary's profitability or ROI, both of which are subject to uncontrollable events, it might often be more useful to compare actual results with budgeted figures. Revenue and cost variances can then be examined to determine whether these were likely to have been caused by external economic factors (such as inflation or devaluation), by corporate policy shifts (such as transfer price adjustments), or by managerial decisions (a new product strategy). The key to this analysis is the set of explicit assumptions incorporated into the budget and the knowledge of how changes in these assumptions are likely to affect the budgeted numbers.

For example, if a strategic decision was made to switch some production to Spain, even if it was not the lowest-cost source, then the French manager who must now buy from the Spanish affiliate should not be held responsible for the resulting decline in the profitability of French operations. In fact, it is not clear that an affiliate without control over either its costs or its revenues should be a profit center. If the Spanish affiliate is only a manufacturing operation selling to other affiliates, it should probably be treated as a cost center because it does not control its sales. Similarly, the French affiliate should be evaluated on the basis of its sales and selling expenses, rather than on profit, because it has no control over its cost of goods sold.

The crucial issue in terms of management evaluation is where one draws the line for local responsibility. Should local managers be held responsible for net operating income only, or should they be held responsible for the final net income figure? And should these figures for which local managers are held responsible be expressed in dollars or the local currency?

As discussed later in this article, the most logical approach appears to be to hold local managers

6. See Bennett Stewart, "A Proposal for Measuring International Performance," *Midland Corporate Finance Journal*, Summer 1983, pp. 56-71 for further discussion of this point.

Even if a manager wanted to act in the best interests of the corporation, his or her perspective would be too limited.

responsible for net operating income expressed in dollars, but *using a projected rather than the actual exchange rate*. The treasurer, in turn, should be held responsible for *unanticipated* exchange gains and losses and interest expense. Such a system would give local managers an incentive to make those operational moves that are necessary to counterbalance the effects on operations of any *expected* change in exchange rates or other shocks.[7]

An unavoidable problem when relying on a budget to judge performance is that it is based on circular reasoning: good performance is what management earlier thought it to be. Whether the budget really incorporates reasonable objectives is always questionable. The combination of accurate prediction and poor management might result in higher rewards for managers than good management combined with a poor prediction.

The budget must also allow for long-term profit-maximizing behavior. Or, at least it must constrain the use of those short-run oriented policies that may provide immediate benefits for the local manager while hurting the company's long-run interests. For example, including allowances for training programs, R&D, and other vital functions in the budget will help counteract the natural tendency to neglect these areas. It is also necessary to consider other, less tangible factors when evaluating performance. For example, a profit-oriented manager may allow relations with the host country to deteriorate. A study by Negandhi and Baliga indicates that, in contrast to the typical American MNC's concentration on profits, European and Japanese multinationals emphasize the cultivation of harmonious relations with host government officials and others in the local environment.[8] Given the difficulties facing multinationals abroad, qualitative determinants of long-run profitability are likely to be more important in the future and should be included in any performance evaluation. The inability to measure objectively the state of host-country relations is not a reason to ignore them. Ultimately, any performance measure is subjective, even if it is quantitative, because the choice of which measures to stress is itself inevitably a matter of subjective judgment.

The Effects of Interaffiliate Transfers

Frequently, it is desirable in the multinational firm to create relationships between subsidiaries that would not be willingly assumed if the subsidiaries were independent entities, but which benefit the overall corporation. The problem for the MNC is to adjust performance standards so as to encourage such beneficial behavior. Three such areas of current concern in performance evaluation are transfer pricing, adjusting intracorporate fund flows, and the choice of appropriate exchange rates for internal use.

Transfer pricing. In a decentralized profit center, transfer prices on goods and services (fees and royalties) can be a significant determinant of a manager's performance. A manager who is held accountable for the influence of changes in transfer prices on his or her reported profits is likely to react in ways which are counterproductive to the organization as a whole. Cases have arisen, for example, where managers selling to subsidiaries which are forced to buy from them behaved as monopolists and attempted to gouge their captive customers. On the other hand, purchasers of goods and services from other units of the MNC may try to act as monopsonists and underpay their suppliers.

Even if a manager wanted to act in the best interests of the corporation, his or her perspective would be too limited. Thus, individual managers are likely to ignore, or be ignorant of, the broader legal, tax, and liquidity considerations involved in setting a corporate-wide transfer pricing policy. For these reasons, transfer pricing is too important to be left to subsidiaries.[9] However, budgeted profit requirements for individual subsidiaries should recognize, and adjust for, the distorting influence of less-than-arm's length transfer prices. In other words, managerial evaluations should be separated or *decoupled* from the particular transfer prices being used. This can be done by charging managers who are buying goods the marginal cost of production and shipping while crediting sellers with a reasonable profit on their sales. Managers of subsidiaries producing only for sale to other units of the corporation should be

7. Some of these operational moves are discussed in Bradford Cornell and Alan C. Shapiro, "Managing Foreign Exchange Risks," *Midland Corporate Finance Journal*, Fall 1983, pp. 16-31.

8. Anant R. Negandhi and B.R. Baliga, "Quest for Survival and Growth: A Study of American, European, and Japanese Multinational Corporations" (Working paper, International Institute of Management, 1976).

9. See, for example, Edgar M. Barrett, "Case of the Tangled Transfer Price," *Harvard Business Review*, May-June, 1977, pp. 20-36; and David P. Rutenberg, "Maneuvering Liquid Assets in a Multinational Corporation," *Management Science*, June 1970, pp. 671-684.

evaluated on the basis of their costs of production, rather than their profits, because they have no control over their revenues.

As an example of the harmful effects of one transfer pricing scheme, a manufacturing firm set transfer prices on the basis of cost plus an allocation for overhead, and then used these prices for evaluation purposes. It found that its sales managers were pushing its low-margin instead of its high-margin products. Due to their high overhead costs and consequently high transfer prices, the high-margin products were less profitable to the sales managers than to the company. Further investigation showed that the demand for these high-margin products was quite elastic and that significant potential profits were being lost due to this transfer pricing strategy.

Decoupling may present problems at times, though. For example, the transfer prices of multinational drug companies are closely monitored worldwide and this information is shared by a number of governments, necessitating uniform transfer prices worldwide. Given the low elasticity of demand for many branded pharmaceuticals, these prices are normally set quite high. However, due to competitive circumstances, some individual subsidiaries may be hurt by the necessity to market these drugs at high prices. But to sell to these subsidiaries at lower prices would jeopardize the firm's worldwide

The combined effects of transfer price and interaffiliate credit adjustments are illustrated in Table 1. In this example, a change in the transfer price, from $100 to $95 per unit, results in an after-tax profit decline of $125,000 for the selling affiliate and a reduction in its net margin on sales from 5 percent to 2.6 percent. Similarly, a change in interaffiliate credit terms will increase total assets employed by $500,000. Depending on which of the four transfer price/credit terms combinations is selected, the affiliate's calculated return on investment can vary from 7 percent to 20 percent, even though the underlying operations and assets on which each figure is based are identical.

TABLE 1
Effects of Transfer Price and Interaffiliate Credit Adjustments

Profits	A		B	
Price	100		95	
Quantity	50,000		50,000	
Total revenue		5,000,000		4,750,000
Operating cost	3,000,000		3,000,000	
Overhead	1,200,000		1,200,000	
Depreciation	300,000		300,000	
Total cost		4,500,000		4,500,000
Net profit before tax		500,000		250,000
Income tax @ 50%		250,000		125,000
Net profit after tax		$ 250,000		$ 125,000
Return on sales	$\frac{250,000}{5,000,000} = 5\%$		$\frac{125,000}{4,750,000} = 2.6\%$	
Assets	C		D	
Interaffiliate receiveables	250,000		750,000	
Other assets	1,000,000		1,000,000	
Total assets		1,250,000		1,750,000

Return on Investment

		Profits	
		A(250,000)	B(125,000)
Assets	C(1,250,000)	20%	10%
	D(1,750,000)	4%	7%

The use of forecast rates at both the budgeting and evaluation stages appears to be the most desirable combination because it excludes unanticipated currency fluctuations but recognizes expected changes at the outset.

pricing strategy because other countries would protest against paying higher prices. These effects must be considered to evaluate management performance fairly, particularly when making comparisons across subsidiaries.

Adjusting intracorporate fund flows. The ability to adjust intracorporate fund flows by speeding or slowing payments on intracorporate accounts is of potentially great benefit in the management of cash, exchange risk and blocked funds. However, use of this tool, known as *leading* and *lagging*, is also likely to distort the various working capital ratios of subsidiaries. For example, a subsidiary ordered to extend longer credit terms to another unit will show an increase in its receivables-to-sales ratio. Furthermore, its interest expense will increase while its customer's working capital costs will decline. Since leading and lagging is a corporate policy, its effects should be removed when evaluating subsidiary management. This can be done by eliminating the cost of carrying intracompany receivables from a subsidiary's profits and adding these costs to those subsidiaries with intracompany payables. Similarly, each profit center's investment base should reflect only those corporate assets required for its business. Unless these adjustments are made, suppliers of credit are likely to resist further liberalization of credit terms. It would be advisable, of course, to consider the real cash flow effects of fund flow adjustments when evaluating the financial staff at headquarters.

Exchange rates for evaluation purposes. The exchange rates used by MNCs in setting budgets and evaluating performance can have a major effect on the performance measure.[10] When setting the operating budget, for example, there are two exchange rates that can be used: the actual spot rate at the time or a forecast rate. In addition, if the budget is revised when exchange rate changes occur, an updated spot rate can be used. In evaluating performance relative to the budget, there are three alternative rates that can be used: the actual rate at the time the budget is set, the projected end-of-period rate, or the actual end-of-period rate. Thus, there are six exchange rate combinations possible.

A study of 200 MNCs showed that in fact only three budget evaluation combinations were actually

used.[11] Half of the firms surveyed used a projected rate for budgeting but measured performance with the actual end-of-period rate; 30 percent used a projected rate both for budgeting and performance evaluation; and the remaining 20 percent used the spot rate for budgeting and the end-of-period rate for tracking performance.

When choosing the appropriate combination of budgeting and evaluation rates to use, it is necessary to consider the behavioral consequences involved. If, at the one extreme, the budget and evaluation rates assume no exchange rate change (by using the actual beginning-of-period rate for both purposes), then managers will have no incentive to consider any exchange rate changes—whether anticipated or not—in their decisions. For example, a marketing manager rewarded on the basis of the spot rate prevailing at the date of sale, rather than the anticipated rate upon collection of the receivables generated, will likely engage in an uneconomical expansion of credit sales. At the other extreme, if exchange rate changes are ignored in the budget, but the end-of-period rate is used for evaluation, the manager will probably behave in an overly risk adverse manner since he or she will bear the full consequences of any exchange rate fluctuations. The harmful effects of such a system will likely include "padding" of budgets as well as decentralized hedging by managers to reduce their perceived risks.

The use of forecast rates at both the budgeting and evaluation stages appears to be the most desirable combination because it excludes unanticipated currency fluctuations but recognizes expected changes at the budgeting stage. This combination will be superior to all other combinations that hold managers responsible for unforeseen exchange fluctuations but do not force them to consider likely currency changes at the budgeting stage. This standard seems the fairest since the local decision-maker receives no blame or credit for unanticipated currency fluctuations. It is also the most realistic since it serves to make decentralized decision-making consistent with corporate-wide goals and information.

Inasmuch as these projected rates (which Donald Lessard and Peter Lorange have called *internal forward rates*) are going to influence the affiliate's management of exchange risk, they should reflect

10. Donald R. Lessard and Peter Lorange, "Currency Changes and Management Control: Resolving the Centralization/Decentralization Dilemma," *Accounting Review*, July 1977, pp. 628-637.

11. Business International Corporation. "Evaluating Foreign Operations," p. 154.

By holding managers responsible for their performance based on internal forward rates, corporate headquarters can make full use of local knowledge while ensuring that managers act in the company's best interest.

the value or cost of the MNC's exposure.[12] As such, they may differ significantly from the actual forward rates because of a firm's particular tax situation, the costs of its alternative hedging options, and its attitude toward risk. In an efficient market, however, if the subsidiary has no special tax circumstances, and headquarters feels it has no special information about the future exchange rate, the *current forward rate* should be used as the internal forward rate for budgeting and performance evaluation.

By holding managers responsible for their performance based on such internal forward rates, corporate headquarters can make full use of local knowledge while ensuring that managers act in the company's best interest. Headquarters, in effect, is offering to sell insurance to local managers to cover their exposure. If a manager decides it is cheaper to hedge locally, fine. At least he or she has taken into consideration the cost to the corporation of hedging.

One firm that appears to follow this mixture of strong headquarters controls with decentralization is Transamerica. According to Business International, Transamerica's exposure management is run by a committee that acts as an insurance firm for its foreign affiliates.[13] The committee is made up of a small group at headquarters, including the financial vice president and treasurer, and one or two subsidiary executives. The committee "evaluates the probabilities of gains or losses in specific currencies, determines the likely impact on the overall corporate exposure, examines the relation between the probabilities by currency and the cost or gain of forward cover, and determines the size of exposure risk that Transamerica may be willing to take if its calculations are wrong, i.e., how much self-insurance to assume and at what cost."[14]

The committee decides on an appropriate currency position to take and then makes exposure management recommendations to its affiliates, but they are not required to obey its suggestions. Presumably, the affiliate is allowed to make its own hedging arrangements (e.g., local currency borrowing or tightening credit) as opposed to relying on forward contracts. Otherwise, some of the advantages of decentralization are lost. It is not clear what happens if a subsidiary decides to hedge an exposure that the committee prefers to leave uncovered.

If forward contracts are available, however, it would be simple enough for Transamerica's management to achieve its desired level of exposure.

If the exchange rate changes dramatically, it may be necessary to adjust the projected rate during the operating cycle. The need for adjustment will depend on the magnitude of these changes as well as the amount of exposed assets and local currency earnings. Most importantly, it will depend on the extent to which operating decisions can be changed in response to a new exchange rate. As Lessard and Lorange have argued, if decisions are irreversible then the evaluation rate should not be adjusted.[15] Such a change would violate the principle of insulating operating managers from random currency changes whose effects are uncontrollable. If decisions are reversible, albeit at a cost (which is the more typical situation), new plans should be drawn up with updated rates. However, any change in budget and evaluation rates should apply only for the remainder of the period, the time during which new operating decisions can be made. In all cases, it appears that updating the projected rates when appropriate is preferable to holding operating managers responsible for any actual exchange rate changes, whether anticipated or not. Furthermore, adjusting these rates would permit a sharing between headquarters and local management of the responsibility for results caused by unforeseen developments. And this is clearly preferable to imposing the entire burden on operating units.

Centralization vs. Decentralization

A key concept in the design of a reporting and control system is *responsibility reporting*. This involves the flow of information from each decision area to the manager accountable for the results of these decisions. A general rule of thumb in organizational design appears to be to decentralize responsibility as much as possible. The fewer the linkages between activity areas, the better decentralization will function. Some firms have partly decentralized operations by establishing regional headquarters for different geographical areas. This shortens the lines of communication.

In the multinational corporation, however, the

12. Lessard and Lorange, "Currency Changes and Management Control."

13. Business International Corporation, "Firm's Exposure Management Mixes Strong HQ Controls with Decentralization," *Business International Money Report*, December 23, 1977, pp. 401-402.

14. Ibid, p. 402.

15. Lessard and Lorange, "Currency Changes and Management Control," pp.628-637.

interactions among various units are often so great —because of tax factors or currency controls, for example—that complete decentralization will not be optimal. Also working against centralization is the complexity and size of the multinational corporation. This makes it difficult, if not impossible, for any headquarters group to completely coordinate financial activities worldwide. And companies with a dearth of experienced international financial managers have an added incentive to centralize decisions. The talents of a limited number of experienced managers might best be used at headquarters, where fullest advantage can be taken of their knowledge.

A Conference Board study of the level of corporate involvement in certain key multinational financial decision areas indicated that the wider the perspective required, the more likely it was that a particular decision would be controlled by headquarters.[16] The following are some of the results of the Conference Board study:

Repatriation of funds–Of the companies surveyed, 85 percent indicated that decisions involving repatriation of funds were made at the corporate level. However, respondents appeared to have little control of the repatriation decision in joint ventures where they were minority partners.

Intersubsidiary financing–In most companies, either the chief financial executive of the parent company or the treasurer, with the advice of tax counsel, decided on which intracorporate fund flows should take place.

Acquisition of funds–Of the firms studied, 85 percent indicated that all medium and long-term financing was approved at corporate headquarters. But many firms allowed their subsidiaries much more leeway with regard to short-term financing.

Protection of assets–Many of the firms questioned did not have any formal plans for asset protection although a number indicated that they were beginning to change towards greater centralization. The advent of FAS #8 and now FAS #52 has speeded up the centralization of exposure management.

Planning and control–The responses here were quite varied. The more financially-oriented (as opposed to marketing-oriented, for example) the firm, the more likely it was to have a centralized planning and control function.

Another study, by Stobaugh, indicated significant differences in attitudes toward centralization among small (average annual foreign sales of $50 million), medium-sized (average annual foreign sales of $200 million), and large (average annual foreign sales of $1 billion) multinationals.[17] Small MNCs generally allowed subsidiaries a great deal of leeway in financial management, perhaps due to the lack of sophistication in international financial management at headquarters. The tendency among medium-sized firm was to try to optimize worldwide results, treating each subsidiary as just one unit in a global system. These firms required very sophisticated control and reporting systems. Large MNCs appear to reverse the centralization trend somewhat, providing subsidiaries with formal guidelines but allowing them considerable initiative within those guidelines. This apparently reflects a recognized inability to optimize in such a complex system.

Summary and Conclusions

The advantages of an effective multinational control and evaluation system include:

- **Greater control over current operations;**
- **A more rigorous and objective capital budgeting process;**
- **Greater awareness of managers' operating effectiveness and, consequently, improved managerial incentives.**

As stated at the beginning of this article, there is no set of scientific principles that can guarantee the development of a successful reporting, control, and evaluation system. Nevertheless, it is possible to suggest some guidelines that should aid in the design of such a system. Here, in brief, are some of the suggestions I offer.

First, return on investment, when used properly, is a powerful tool for allocating resources and evaluating current performance. The ROI figures used in practice, however, frequently rely on accounting data which measure neither the relevant investment base nor the relevant cash flows. The investment base should include the current market value of all capital committed to an investment or operation. The return should include all incremental after-tax cash flows generated. Some suggestions

---

16. Meister, *Managing the International Financial Function.*

17. Robert B. Stobaugh, "Financing Foreign Subsidiaries of U.S.-Controlled Multinational Enterprises," *Journal of International Business Studies*, Summer 1979, pp. 43-64.

for modifying conventional accounting statements are offered.

Second, in order to counteract the incentives created by ROI to maximize short-term earnings at the expense of longer-run profitability, the budget should provide for necessary capital investment, R&D, marketing expenditures, and the like.

Third, the most logical approach appears to be to hold local managers responsible for net operating income expressed in dollars, but *using a projected rather than the actual exchange rate*. The treasurer, in turn, should be held responsible for *unanticipated* exchange gains and losses and interest expense. Such a system would give local managers an incentive to make those operational moves that are necessary to counterbalance the effects on operations of any *expected* change in exchange rates or other shocks.

Fourth, flexible budgeting—the use of a flexible standard which varies with certain key economic factors, e.g., local GNP, inflation, and the exchange rate—is a potentially effective means of isolating management's contribution to value from complicating environmental factors beyond its control.

Fifth, and finally, affiliate performance measures should be adjusted for the distorting effects of transfer pricing and interaffiliate credit variations.

Beyond these quantitative suggestions, a truly globally-oriented system should encourage a free flow of ideas and information worldwide. Headquarters must avoid the temptation of trying to over-control field operations or else run the risk of stifling local initiative. Local managers should have the opportunity to explain their operating results and seek help for their problems. The lack of such communication between headquarters and subsidiaries will cause the kind of problems associated with a too rigid adherence to strictly numerical criteria.

Managers who feel they are not rewarded on a sensible basis for their job performances may put less effort into their work. But the real damage is likely to be the loss of the entrepreneurial spirit that appears to be necessary to cope with a rapidly changing environment. The incentive to take risks is encouraged by the existence of significant rewards for success. Without such rewards, a manager's initiative may be severely diminished. He or she might work as hard as before, but only in more traditional areas, shunning new ventures that offer greater potential but greater risks.

References

Barrett, M. Edgar. "Case of the Tangled Transfer Price." *Harvard Business Review*, (May-June 1977), pp. 20-36.

Business International Corporation. "Evaluating Foreign Operations: The Appropriate Rates for Comparing Results with Budgets." *Business International Money Report*, (May 20, 1977), pp. 16-31.

Cornell, Bradford and Shapiro, Alan C., "Managing Foreign Exchange Risks," *Midland Corporate Finance Journal*, (Fall 1983), pp. 16-31.

Lessard, Donald R., and Lorange, Peter. "Currency Changes and Management Control: Resolving the Centralization/Decentralization Dilemma." *Accounting Review*, (July 1977), pp. 628-637.

Meister, Irene W. *Managing the International Financial Function*. New York: The Conference Board, (1970).

Robbins, Sidney M., and Stobaugh, Robert B. "The Bent Measuring Stick for Foreign Subsidiaries," *Harvard Business Review*, (September-October, 1973), pp. 80-88.

Shapiro, Alan C., *Multinational Financial Management*, Boston: Allyn and Bacon, (1982).

Shapiro, Alan C., "International Capital Budgeting." *Midland Corporate Finance Journal*, (Spring 1983), pp. 26-45.

Stewart, Bennett, "A Proposal for Measuring International Performance" *Midland Corporate Finance Journal*, (Summer 1983), pp. 56-71.

Stobaugh, Robert B. "Financing Foreign Subsidiaries of U.S.-Controlled Multinational Enterprises." *Journal of International Business Studies*, (Summer, 1970), pp. 43-64.

Treasury Performance Measurement

Ian Cooper and Julian Franks,
The London Business School *

The decisions made by corporate treasurers have a potential impact on corporate profits which is often as large as the earnings from operations. In recent years, the sophistication of analytical tools and financial instruments used by corporate treasuries has increased dramatically. The evaluation of treasury performance, however, continues to remain in a primitive state. As a rule, treasury performance evaluation is part of the accounting system of the firm; in fact it is probably no exaggeration to say that the major criterion (whether implicit or otherwise) by which corporate treasurers are judged by headquarters is the measurable effect of their decisions on reported earnings.

By contrast, sophisticated, *market-based* measurement techniques have long been available for monitoring the performance of investment fund managers. The measures provided by such techniques offer an assessment of a fund manager's performance relative to some benchmark, and relative to the risks taken to achieve that performance. Moreover, it seems logical that similar performance analysis can (and will someday) be applied to at least some aspects of treasury management. The purpose of this paper is to outline the techniques available for performance measurement and to discuss their application to specific areas of treasury management.

An Introduction to Treasury Performance Appraisal

A corporation has operating assets and liabilities which produce a stream of current and future cash flows. The value of these cash flows, which may be denominated in a variety of currencies, responds to many economic factors such as inflation, interest rates, exchange rates, and commodity prices. The economic value of these cash flows is reflected in the market value of the liabilities used by the corporation to finance its operations.

While no two treasury departments would agree on precisely the objectives that are being pursued, most behave as though they are seeking to accomplish a combination of the following:
• Raise funds as cheaply as possible;
• Invest liquid balances to earn as high a return as possible; and
• Control the risk exposure of the company's earnings (or equity).

Any particular transaction can have an influence on two or, in some cases, all three of these objectives. Decisions to borrow fixed or floating, for instance, are motivated by both the interest-rate differential between the two types of debt and the relative impact of each on the risk of the company's equity.

The most difficult aspect of treasury management is the determination of the precise effect of a transaction on the risk of the company's equity. For instance, is there less risk in borrowing floating or borrowing fixed? Floating-rate borrowing adds less risk to the company if its cash flows, and thus its equity value, tend to be positively related to movements in interest rates. On the whole, this means that a company which believes that its cash flows and equity value will respond positively to unexpected changes in inflation has less equity risk if its borrowing is floating rate.

The goal of a treasury management and performance appraisal system is to produce that set of treasury

*We are grateful to the First National Bank of Chicago for sponsoring the work contained herein. This work is part of a larger study of Treasury Performance Measurement sponsored by the Bank. The opinions expressed in this paper, as well as any errors it contains, are the responsibility of the authors and do not necessarily represent the views of the Bank.

decisions which, given the operating assets and liabilities of the corporation, produces the "best" balance of cost and risk characteristics. If an opportunity to save on borrowing costs is missed, the loss is as costly to the corporation as paying an excessively high interest rate. If the treasury takes a "view" on exchange rates and proves to be correct, the decision will have exposed the corporation to risk. Thus, systems of treasury decision-making and performance appraisal which aim to take advantage of the increasing choices available to reduce borrowing costs and manage risk must be able to focus on opportunity costs and risk measurement. It is these aspects that are lacking in most existing systems.

As suggested above, the overwhelming proportion of treasury management is concerned with the following three functions: (1) borrowing; (2) investment of liquid funds; and (3) foreign exchange exposure. Given that these functions all involve choices among various capital market instruments, a treasury management appraisal system should be governed by the following principles:

Market Value Measurement. Prices for most transactions are available in the capital markets. If a particular transaction has no observable market price, a price can be imputed from similar transactions where observed prices are available. Therefore, quantitative performance appraisal should almost always be possible.

Economic Returns. The change in value of a capital market instrument is part of the gain or loss to the corporation. Profit and loss systems which do not recognise this fact give an inaccurate picture of the true profitability of the treasury function. An economic accounting system in which changes in the market values of assets and liabilities are included in the measured return is the only consistent basis for performance appraisal.

Opportunity Gains and Losses. If interest is earned on liquid balances, not all the income is attributable to the specific choice of investments made by the treasurer. Even a completely passive investment policy would earn interest. The "economic" gain made by the treasury decisions is the extra income relative to that earned by an alternative. This concept of opportunity gain or loss applies to all three areas of treasury management.

The Benchmark. A benchmark is required when the firm has two or more mutually exclusive transactions and when the direct and indirect costs of those transactions varies. For example, a benchmark transaction may be based on internal hedging or self-insurance if external insurance markets are more costly than those available internally. But if the company were indifferent between those transactions, then there would be little purpose to choosing one as a benchmark over another. (Indeed, there would be little point to measuring performance at all.)

Risk Assessment. Each treasury decision involves a change in the risk to the corporation. Assessment of this risk should be an integral part of the decision. Opportunity gains and losses must be weighed against these risks to provide an accurate picture of treasury performance.

EXAMPLE: Fixed Income Transactions: A Single Trade

A corporate treasurer borrows 7-year funds at 12 percent fixed. As an alternative he could have borrowed 7-year floating-rate funds at LIBOR + 75 basis points. (There are several justifications for a corporation choosing a variable rate as a benchmark; one is when variable rates provide the company with a natural hedge against unanticipated inflation.)

At the time of the decision, LIBOR was 10 percent. LIBOR is now (one year later) 11 percent and the 6-year fixed borrowing rate for this corporation is 12.5 percent.

Quantification of Market Values: The value of the fixed-rate liability at the end of the year is the present value of a 12 percent coupon 6-year bond at a yield of 12.5 percent. By discounting the cash flows on the bond at the current 6-year rate for such a bond (observed from current market yields), we come up with a value of 98.

Economic Return from Actual Strategy: The cost of the bond issue over the year can be calculated as follows:

$$\text{Cost} = \frac{\text{Coupon rate} + \text{change in value}}{100}$$

$$= \frac{12 + (98\text{-}100)}{100} = 10\%$$

Note that the increase in interest rates and the reduction in value of the liability lowers the cost of borrowing.

Opportunity Cost or Gain: One alternative for this company would have been to issue a 7-year floating-rate note. Assuming that the price of this note would not have changed over the year, its cost for the year would have been 10.75 percent. The opportunity gain can be calculated as follows:

[Arbitrage] transactions offer opportunity gains with little or no risk. As such, they represent the most unambiguous contribution of the treasury function to the profitability of the corporation.

Opportunity gain $=$ Cost of issued bond
$\quad\quad\quad\quad\quad\quad -$ Cost of alternative
$\quad\quad\quad\quad\quad\quad = 10\% - 10.75\% = -0.75\%$

In this case the issuance of the fixed-rate bond resulted in an opportunity gain of 75 basis points on the issue over the year.

Risk Assessment: In this case, rates moved favourably for the fixed-rate issuer and a gain was made. Even if the issuer forecast this move, there was a chance that the forecast would turn out to be wrong. The transaction therefore involved risk. The risk of a financial asset or liability is commonly measured by the uncertainty about its value. This is most often quoted as a volatility in percent per annum. Based on observation over a 55-year period, the average volatility of a 7-year fixed-rate bond has been estimated to be about 6 percent. This means that such bonds typically experience unexpected value changes of about 6 percent per annum. By borrowing long, as in this case, the treasurer exposed the corporation to the risk that the value of its liability would rise by 6 percent over the year.

Overall Performance Appraisal: As we have seen, the transaction resulted in an opportunity gain of 0.75 percent; and the expected variation of this return, based on historical experience, was roughly 6 percent. The final step in such an analysis is to determine whether the potential gains were adequate to justify the risks taken. We shall return to this question later.

Identifying the Sources of Gains and Losses

The gains and losses resulting from treasury decisions must be weighed against the risks taken to achieve them. In some cases these risks are small, as in a swap transaction designed to lower a borrowing rate. In other cases, such as leaving a foreign exchange risk uncovered, the risks are much larger.

Apart from the size of the risk involved, there is also an important distinction between those risks that are reflected (and thus compensated for) in rates offered in the market place, and those that are not. If liquid balances, for instance, are moved into lower-grade paper, there is an increase in risk and an increase in promised return. If, however, the treasurer chooses to leave a foreign exchange exposure uncovered, there is no explicit risk premium offered in the market place to compensate for the risk involved.

To highlight the relationship between the gains and losses made and the risks taken, we shall categorise all transactions as one of four types.

1. "Arbitrage" Transactions. These transactions offer opportunity gains with little or no risk. As such, they represent the most unambiguous contribution of the treasury function to the profitability of the corporation.

Some examples are financial leasing rather than borrowing, currency swaps, and tax-arbitrage in bond markets. In each case, the expertise of the treasurer results in an opportunity gain relative to a particular alternative transaction with little or no increase in risk. Choosing a vehicle for foreign exchange cover that minimises transaction costs (in the form of the bankers' spread) is also an "arbitrage" transaction in the sense that it does not involve risk.

2. Spread-motivated Transactions. Other transactions are motivated, at least in part, by differences in rates offered on similar but not identical instruments. In fixed-income markets these spreads may reflect differences in the maturity, default risk, liquidity, and currency denomination of the securities. For instance, a shift of liquid assets into lower-quality paper gives a yield gain. This yield gain, however, is simply the market's compensation for the extra risk involved.

In evaluating the opportunity gain from such transactions, it must be recognised that the price of this gain was the extra risk which made the yield spread necessary. This comparison can be achieved by first identifying the source of the yield spread (that is, whether liquidity, maturity, quality, or currency) and then measuring the extent of the risk involved. Examples of transactions which fall into this category are buying illiquid or low-quality money market instruments and borrowing long rather than short.

3. Hedging Transactions. A large proportion of treasury transactions, particularly in corporations with a relatively passive treasury function, are directed at reducing the risk facing the corporation. While performance measurement of such transactions might seem redundant, this is frequently not the case. Whenever a risk is hedged, it may be necessary to take a relatively unfavourable rate or to pay a spread to the intermediary providing the hedging instrument. If the hedge is, for instance, a long-term forward contract, the rate obtained will include a substantial bid/ask spread.

In such a case, the relevant question is this: Is

Because a decision not to hedge a known exposure is tantamount to speculation, speculative decisions need not involve an actual transaction. Indeed, all treasury decisions, with the possible exception of those motivated by arbitrage, involve some element of speculation.

the size of the risk being hedged sufficiently large to warrant paying the spread? For example, we may believe the risk has simply been mispriced in the market (and there is convincing evidence, for example, that *non-traded* options on equities were severely overpriced before the establishment of a traded options market). Alternatively, if the spread contains a component for transactions costs, it may be that the company has lower transaction costs than the market-makers (perhaps because the company has more information about its own risks). Risk analysis in such cases therefore involves measuring the size of the risk and assessing it against the effective cost of the hedging instrument. This analysis again involves the quantification of the two elements of any final decision: opportunity cost and risk.

In this case, however, there is a problem in deciding how to measure the effective cost of the transaction. In the case of the long-term forward rate, the effective cost to the corporation is equivalent to half of the bid/ask spread charged by the bank. Our reasoning is simply that because the opening and closing of a long-term forward position will incur the full spread, each half of the transaction can be viewed as having an effective cost equal to half of the spread.

Apart from forward cover, other treasury decisions motivated by hedging are foreign currency borrowing, matching the maturity of borrowings to asset maturity, and hedging commitments with interest rate futures.

4. Speculative Transactions. The final category of treasury decisions involves speculation based on a particular forecast of interest rates or exchange rates. Because a decision *not* to hedge a known exposure is tantamount to speculation, speculative decisions need not involve an actual transaction. Indeed, all treasury decisions, with the possible exception of those motivated by arbitrage, involve some element of speculation. For example, spread-motivated transactions will expose the corporation to a speculative risk if there is a possibility that rates can move unfavourably and wipe out the gain being sought through the spread. If the returns on spread-motivated transactions are uncorrelated, however, then a sufficiently large number will reduce these speculative (or specific) risks.

The natural way to classify speculative transactions is by the underlying source of the speculation. Transactions depending upon the movement of a particular interest rate form one group, those depending upon a particular exchange rate form an-

other, and so on. The most typical kinds of speculative transactions in treasury management are, therefore, decisions not to hedge exchange exposures and decisions to lengthen maturities of borrowings or investments.

EXAMPLE: Sources of Opportunity Gain: Liquidity Management
Transaction: Purchase of $500,000 6-month commercial paper
Benchmark: 3-month high-grade Certificates of Deposit (CD's)
Rates at date of transaction:
   3-month CD 10%
   6-month CD 11%
   6-month commercial paper 11.5%
Rate after 3 months
   3-month CD 9%
   3-month commercial paper 9.5%

Economic Return over Six Months on Actual Policy: $((1.115)^{1/2} - 1) = 5.59\%$

Economic Return on Benchmark: 4.64%
$$-500 + \frac{(1.10)^{1/4} \times (1.09)^{1/4} \times 500}{(1 + R)} = 0$$
$$R = 0.0464$$
Opportunity Gain:
$(5.59\% - 4.64\%) = 0.95\% \times \$500,000 = \$4750$
Components of Gain:
Maturity spread = 11% 6mo. CD − 10% 3mo. CD
                $(1.11/1.10)^{1/2} - 1 = 0.45\%$
Liquidity spread = 11.5% 6mo. commercial paper
         − 11% 6mo. CD
               $(1.115/1.11)^{1/2} - 1 = 0.22\%$
Speculative gain = 0.95% − 0.45% − 0.22%
                = 0.28%

Discussion: The three components of the gain should be viewed differently. The maturity spread was gained from the market-determined difference between the three-month and six-month rates. This is a combination of the market's expectation concerning the movement in interest rates over the next three months, and a maturity premium. To achieve this gain, the treasurer took a risk amounting to a speculation on interest rates. On the other hand, the liquidity spread is the market's price for not being able to trade the asset easily. If the treasurer was certain that the funds would not be needed at short notice, he would not value liquidity as much as the mar-

TABLE 1
Treasury Transactions:
Classification

	Transactions	Opportunity Gain (Cost)	Risk
Arbitrage	—Lease vs Borrow —Swaps —Round Tripping	Yield Spread	Low
Spreads	—Hold Liquid Balances in Lower Grade Paper	Yield Spread	Default Risk
	—Hold Liquid Balances in Less Liquid Paper	Yield Spread	Illiquidity
	—Borrow Long/Lend Long	Term Premium	Interest Rate Volatility
Hedging	—Currency Forward Hedge	Bid/Ask Spread (Cost)	Currency Volatility (Reduction in Exposure)
Speculation	—Borrow Long/Lend Long	Actual Rate Gained Relative to Short Rate	Interest Rate Volatility
	—Leave Exposure Uncovered	Actual Rate Gained Relative to Forward Rate	Currency Volatility

ketplace, and this could be viewed as an "arbitrage" gain relative to the benchmark.

In Table I we have classified treasury transactions with an estimate of their respective opportunity costs and risks.

Measurement of Asset/Liability Values

Before the economic return from a treasury decision can be measured, the values of assets and liabilities extant at the beginning and end of the performance appraisal period must be estimated. In the areas of treasury involvement this requires the valuation of currency forward, futures, and spot contracts, as well as the valuation of various debt instruments in various currencies issued and held by the corporation.

When these assets and liabilities are traded in liquid markets, the valuation problem involves simply revaluing the asset or liability at the current market rate at the end of the performance appraisal period. In the case where the assets and liabilities are illiquid or non-standard, the valuation must be performed by reference to the most similar securities traded in relatively liquid markets.

EXAMPLE: Valuation of a Forward Contract Prior to Maturity

On 1 December, three-month forward cover at $1.35/£ was taken on £300,000. The two-month forward rate on 31 December is $1.38/£. The dollar interest rate is 10 percent.

The company is short forward sterling at $1.35. It could liquidate this position at $1.38, resulting in a gain of $9,000 on 1 March of the next year. The present value of this strategy on 31 December is $9,000 discounted for two months at an annual rate of 10 percent. This gives an economic value of $8,858.30 on 31 December.

Economic Returns

In almost all areas where financial performance measurement is applied, there is a controversy over whether returns should be measured by accounting profits, economic returns, or some other standard. In some cases, such as short-term foreign exchange hedging, this controversy is empty because both accounting profit and economic profit will be the same for transactions that are opened and closed within the performance measurement period.

In other cases, such as long-term debt instruments, the difference can be substantial and centers on the valuation of long-term assets and liabilities at the end of the performance measurement period. Quite simply, the difference is that economic return measurement revalues assets and liabilities at current market rates whereas accounting profit meas-

A belief that accrued accounting values represent the fundamental value of a security more closely than market values would imply a staggeringly powerful ability to speculate against the market.

urement revalues them according to a particular set of accounting accrual rules which may or (more likely) may not be similar to market values.

One common argument for using accounting accrual rules is that market values are not available. This is clearly not the case for the capital market transactions involved in treasury management. In most cases, market values that can be used for revaluation are readily available. When they are not, benchmark rates on similar securities can be used as the basis of the revaluation.

A second argument cited against using economic returns and market values is that market values are subject to random, transitory fluctuation and, therefore, provide a distorted picture of "true" value changes. This view flies in the face of all the evidence on the behaviour of security market prices. In fact, a belief that accrued accounting values represent the fundamental value of a security more closely than market values would imply a staggeringly powerful ability to speculate against the market. Few people believe this is the case.

The other arguments in favour of using accounting profit as a performance measure tend to be pragmatic. Existing controls systems, reporting systems, and tax systems tend to incorporate a large element of accrual accounting rather than market-value measurement. Therefore, it is argued, performance measurement systems should be based on the same conventions. However, there are other sectors, such as fund management, where performance appraisal is based entirely upon economic returns despite the necessity of providing reports based upon accounting rules for other purposes.

In general, therefore, treasury management satisfies the principal necessary condition for using a measurement system based on economic returns: the availability of market prices to revalue assets and liabilities at the beginning and end of the performance appraisal period.

EXAMPLE: Economic Return vs. Accounting Profit

At the beginning of the year the corporation issued a five year straight Eurodollar bond of $50 million at a coupon rate of 12.5 percent. Rates on four-year comparable Euros at the end of the year are now 11 percent. (Once again, we shall defer discussion of whether fixed or floating rates provide the appropriate benchmark here, and focus solely on the issue of economic versus accounting profit.)

Accounting cost: The annual accounting cost of the bond is the 12.5 percent coupon payment, or $6.25 million.

Economic Cost: The liability extant at the end of the year has a market value per $100 face value equal to the present value at 11 percent of the remaining coupon and principal payments. This value can be calculated as follows:

$(12.5 \times 11\%$ 4-year Annuity Factor$)$
$+ (100 \times$ Discount Rate for year 4 at $11\%)$
$= (12.5 \times 3.102) + (100 \times 0.6588) = 104.66$

The total cost of the issue over the year has been:
(Coupon rate + Value change)/Starting value
$= 12.5\% + 4.66\% = 17.16\%$

Discussion: The economic cost recognises that the decision to issue the bond has already resulted in a substantial loss to the corporation. The payments promised to the holders of the bond could now, at the end of the year, be used to service a bond issue of $52.33 million.

Opportunity Gains and Losses

The economic returns from treasury decisions must be compared with a benchmark alternative to show the "net" return of the decisions. This net return is the opportunity gain or loss.

The general notion of evaluating the gain or loss relative to a benchmark is widely accepted in performance measurement. The choice of a specific benchmark is sometimes problematic, however, and thus a source of controversy. In foreign exchange hedging, for instance, a policy of full forward cover provides a useful benchmark—one which would be achieved by a passive treasury department. In the case of evaluating debt policy, on the other hand, there appears to be no such obvious passive benchmark. The appropriate, non-speculative maturity structure for borrowing will depend upon the particular funding requirements of the corporation. The benchmark will also depend critically on the sensitivity of operating cash flows to movements in interest rates; for example, an interest-rate sensitive firm would be better off with a fixed-rate benchmark whereas an interest insensitive firm would be best served with a floating-rate benchmark.

The fact that we observe large-scale hedging of risks by corporations should suggest that some hedging is desirable (although it is an interesting, and as yet unanswered, question as to what is the optimal amount of hedging).

Some possible benchmarks are the following:
• **Foreign exchange**: Full forward cover
• **Liquidity**: Short-term, high-grade liquid paper
• **Debt**: Floating-rate borrowing
These benchmarks have the common characteristic that they minimise the exposure of the corporation to the sources of treasury risk: exchange rate risk, default and liquidity risk, and, in the case of interest-insensitive firms, long-term interest rate variation. In so doing, they minimise the risk exposure of the holders of the equity of the company.

The measurement of the opportunity gain or loss for a particular transaction is then quite straightforward:

Opportunity gain = Economic return earned on transaction − Economic return on benchmark
Similarly, the risk of the transaction is measured as the extra risk resulting from the actual transaction compared with the benchmark.

EXAMPLE: Opportunity gain: Liquidity Management
Transaction: Purchase of 6-month commercial paper.
Benchmark: 3-month high grade CD's.
Rates at date of transaction:
    3-month CD 10%
    6-month commercial paper 11.5%
Rate after 3 months
    3-month CD 9%

Economic Return: Return on commercial paper over 6 months:
    $(1.115)^{1/2} = 1.0559$
    Return = 5.59%
Benchmark Return:
    Return on 3-month CD rolled over
    $(1.10)^{1/4} \times (1.09)^{1/4} = 1.0464$
    Return = 4.64%

Opportunity gain: Return on actual transaction − Return on benchmark
    = 5.59% − 4.64% = 0.95%

Discussion: The opportunity gain has been generated partly by the spread of low-grade commercial paper over high-grade CD's and partly by a speculative gain resulting from lengthening the maturity and experiencing a favourable move in interest rates.

Choosing the Proper Benchmark

The first question is, why do we need a benchmark at all? The simple answer is that we can only evaluate a transaction if we know the opportunity cost; and that opportunity cost implies an alternative transaction. For example, a benchmark transaction may be chosen because it has lower transaction costs than other transactions. Or the best benchmark might be the transaction that has least risk.

However, if those risks are properly priced by the market and the transaction costs of hedging are zero or insignificant, then the firm should be indifferent between taking one risk position and another. A belief in this proposition would suggest that all forms of hedging are unnecessary. After all, shareholders are diversified and can always hedge corporate risks by changing the risk of their own investment portfolios. Nonetheless, the fact that we observe large-scale hedging of risks by corporations should suggest that some hedging is desirable (although it is an interesting, and as yet unanswered question as to what is the optimal amount of hedging for a corporation).

Why, then, should firms choose to hedge at all? Put another way, why do firms choose low- or minimum-risk positions as benchmarks? One answer is that high-risk positions increase the probability of financial distress or insolvency. If such distress creates costs by diverting management time, postponing profitable projects, or forcing the unprofitable sale of assets in illiquid markets, then there can be a strong incentive to hedge.

A second motive for hedging may be tax. The U.S. tax system, like most others, is asymmetrical. That is, if the corporation makes taxable profits it pays taxes; but if taxable losses arise, tax benefits can be obtained only by carrying losses forward and offsetting them against future taxable profits. As a result the present value benefits of a dollar of tax losses is less than the tax cost of a dollar of taxable profits.

A third reason for hedging may be that it provides an efficient mechanism for having risks monitored and processed by outside experts. Indeed, some creditors may demand that some risks be hedged which the corporation has little control over or no skills in estimating or monitoring.

In sum, then, the case for corporate hedging of financial risks may come down to this: Corporations may not wish to bear certain risks (a) which are not part of its business activities, (b) for which it is not fully compensated by capital markets for bearing, and (c) which may impose significant tax disadvantages.

The Criteria

To return to our search for the appropriate benchmark, the following represents a tentative set of criteria for choosing such a benchmark:

1. Does the benchmark represent a policy that could actually have been followed?

2. Could the benchmark have been specified at the beginning of the performance period?

3. Does the benchmark provide a lower-cost strategy than some of the alternative transactions?

A traditional view of treasury management is that all significant risks should be hedged using the lowest-cost instrument. This view ignores the possibility that shareholders, by holding a diversified portfolio of securities, avoid exposure to many of these risks. It also presupposes that the cost of the hedging is outweighed by the benefits of risk-reduction. Furthermore, it ignores the possibility of self-insurance. Self-insurance involves leaving risks open which, in aggregate and when combined with the entire activity of the company, are effectively diversified.

An alternative view is that because financial risks are properly priced in financial markets from the point of view of diversified shareholders, all risks should be left open. In such circumstances any transaction costs incurred to hedge such risks would represent a net loss to shareholders.

An intermediate view is that the risk and cost of treasury transactions should be measured. One purpose of this measurement is to determine whether the cheapest available instrument is being used to hedge risk. The other is to measure the ratio of the cost being paid for hedging to the risk reduction achieved. An emphasis on the former would suggest a benchmark which is the lowest-cost form of hedging. The benchmark in the second case is not undertaking hedging transactions—that is, self-insurance.

Some Examples of Possible Benchmarks

Transaction: Purchase of fixed-interest rate bonds
Benchmark: Long-term fixed-rate bonds
Alternative transactions: Short- or medium-term bonds

Motive for the benchmark: Long-term interest rates contain a term premium and the company has little or no need for liquidity. Also, the firm's operating cashflows are negatively affected by unexpected increases in interest rate movements (and vice versa), thus making fixed rates a natural hedge.

Transaction: Hedging foreign exchange risks
Benchmark: Costs of hedging foreign exchange risks internally
Alternative transactions: Hedging foreign exchange risk in the financial markets
Motive for the benchmark: Buy-sell spreads in the financial market reflect larger transaction costs than internal hedging.

Transaction: Insuring fixed assets against fire, accident risks, etc.
Benchmark: Costs of self-insurance
Alternative transactions: Purchase of insurance in external markets
Motive for the benchmark: Lower costs of processing information on risks internally compared with external insurers.

We shall now review some of these examples in more detail.

A Benchmark for Cash Management

The manager of the liquid balances of a corporation faces the following problem. On any date he knows the amount of liquid balances on hand, and he has forecasts of how these will be increased or depleted in the future. The accuracy of these forecasts diminishes with their horizon. He knows what the balances are currently invested in, and he knows the current rates on all relevant securities that provide alternative investment opportunities.

His goal is to earn the highest rate of return possible, while retaining the balances in a sufficiently liquid form to be available when needed. There will also be a tax consequence of the decisions (which we will ignore here, though the reader is referred to the Appendix). The three dimensions of the cash management decisions are as follows: (1) rate of return; (2) risk; and (3) liquidity (or ease of realisation).

One possible benchmark against which to measure his performance could be the policy of holding all the balances in very short-term deposits or short-term government paper. This will be the strategy with the lowest risk and the highest liquidity since the markets for these securities are the most heavily traded. This benchmark will also offer considerable opportunities for superior performance. To the extent that the treasurer can forecast that part of the balances which will not be needed for longer periods of time, he will be able to pick up a term premium without increasing risk or reducing liquidity in any way that matters.

If the manager knew precisely the future inflows and outflows to the liquidity pool, he could pursue a policy of matching precisely the maturity of the instruments held with the cash requirements of the corporation. The benchmark strategy would then consist of holding government securities with maturities matching the maturity profile of the cash requirements.

The treasurer will deviate from these benchmark policies if he feels that the extra return he can earn on some alternative investment is sufficient compensation for the increased risk and reduced liquidity. Some of these switches will be unambiguous gains, such as switching to overnight deposits when the overnight rate is sufficiently high. Some will be speculative, such as moving to longer-term instruments when he expects rates to fall. Others will be increases in return offset by higher risk or lower liquidity, such as moving into lower-quality paper when he feels that the yield gain is high enough.

The details of the performance measurement will then require the following:

• **Agreement on the benchmark**
  -short-term government paper
  -government paper matched to the maturity profile of cash requirements
• **Rates on the benchmark investment.**
• **Actual investments held.**
• **Rates earned on actual investments.**
• **Market revaluations of benchmark investments and actual investments at the end of performance evaluation period.**

The performance measure would then be the return on the actual policy relative to the rate of return on the benchmark. If extra risk or lower liquidity had been taken to achieve a higher rate of return, it would be reflected in the average yield spread between securities held and the benchmark securities. The performance measure could be adjusted for this yield spread to give a risk- and liquidity-adjusted performance measure.

A Benchmark for Debt

The problems of choosing a benchmark for borrowing are very similar to those of choosing the liquidity management benchmark. The treasurer is faced with a forecast of the cash needs of the corporation and rates on various instruments. To measure whether his actual borrowing strategy is successful we need a benchmark. Here again, one natural benchmark is a policy of always using floating-rate or short-maturity instruments. If he chooses to borrow fixed rate for a particular maturity, this would be considered a speculation that interest rates will rise. The net borrowing cost could then be compared with the all-in cost of a floating-rate note of the same maturity. The information required would be as follows:
• **The rate and characteristics of any actual borrowing.**
• **The all-in rate on floating-rate notes matched to any actual borrowing; and**
• **A valuation at current market interest rates of all debt outstanding at the beginning and at the end of the performance measurement period.**

The performance measure would then be the difference between the economic return on the actual debt issued and the economic return on the benchmark floating-rate note policy.

A Benchmark for Managing Currency Exposure

The sequence of events for foreign exchange hedging by corporate treasurers is this:
• Exposure is identified
• Exposure arises
• Exposure is liquidated
For instance, an exposure on receivables is identified when a potential sale in a foreign currency is identified. When the sale is made, the exposure is taken into the books; and when the receivable matures, the exposure is liquidated.

The natural strategy for some commercial and industrial corporations is to fully hedge all foreign exchange exposure, using either the forward market or foreign currency borrowing. This is the benchmark strategy against which the management of foreign exchange risk by the corporate treasurer could be measured.[1]

When the identified exposure is certain to arise, the benchmark strategy would consist of fully hedging forward as soon as the exposure is identified. A treasurer who chose not to do this would be viewed as speculating on the currency movement relative to the forward rate at the time the exposure is identified.

To measure performance in this case, we would require the following information:
• **Forward rate for cover at the time the exposure is identified.**
• **Whether or not the exposure was covered at that time.**
• **If the exposure was left open, the rate at which it was subsequently covered. If it was not covered, the rate at which it was liquidated.**
• **Rates for valuation of forward contracts and uncovered|exposures at the beginning and end of the performance appraisal period.**

If the identified exposure will not arise with certainty, the benchmark strategy must be carefully defined. Suppose that a UK company identifies a potential sale in dollars, on which it fixes a dollar price. It is still not certain, however, that the sale will actually be made. There is now no perfect hedging strategy available. In such a case, we would have to let the corporate treasurer specify his own normal benchmark strategy, and then measure him relative to that strategy. Although this might appear to give too much discretion to the treasurer whose performance is being measured, as long as the general benchmark policy to be pursued on such occasions is specified *before the fact*, the treasurer will be less able to manipulate the benchmarks in the light of actual market movements.

Risk and Treasury Performance

Each treasury transaction involves a change in the risk facing the corporation. Frequently, the transaction will reduce the overall risk, as in the case of foreign exchange hedging transactions. In some cases the transaction will result in an increase in risk as, for instance, when liquid assets are shifted into low-quality paper or when borrowing maturities are lengthened to take advantage of a forecast rise in interest rates. Thus, there are two components to risk measurement when appraising decisions: (1) measuring the size of the risk involved and (2) deciding whether the transaction reduced or increased the level of risk. In many cases, the first of these tasks can be performed more easily than the second.

There are now well-developed techniques for measuring risk in financial markets. Risk is typically measured as the level of price volatility of an asset where price reflects the risk involved. So if, for instance, the risk involved is that of dollar/sterling exchange rate fluctuations, such risk would be measured by the variability of the dollar/pound spot exchange rate.

It has even become a convention to quote these risk measures in terms of annual equivalent standard deviations or "volatilities." (Using a single measure of volatility is possible because most financial markets exhibit two common features: variation of prices is almost random and the distribution of price changes is approximately normal.) Typical figures for the volatilities of particular instruments are as follows:
• **Typical common stock: 30% annual standard deviation**
• **Typical exchange rate: 10% annual standard deviation**
• **Typical long-term bond: 10% annual standard deviation**
It is also possible to give fairly precise interpretations of these measures. A volatility of 10 percent annual standard deviation means that the price of the asset in question has about a two-thirds chance of being within 10 percent of its current value after one year. Thus, if the dollar/pound starts the year at $1.40/£, there is a two-thirds chance that it will be between $1.26 and $1.54 at the end of the year.

It is also possible to convert the annual volatility to an equivalent volatility over a shorter or longer period of time. This conversion is complicated slightly because volatility does not increase one for one with the length of time involved. For example, volatility over six months is not half the volatility over a year. In fact, the correct conversion is to multiply the volatility by the square root of the amount of time

1. In this section, we focus only on transaction exposures. In fact, economic operating exposures may well be just as important. For a discussion of foreign exchange exposure, see the articles by Donald Lessard, "Finance and Global Competition: Exploiting Financial Scope and Coping with Volatile Exchange Rates," Midland Corporate Finance Journal, Vol. 4, No. 3, Fall 1986; and Bradford Cornell and Alan Shapiro, "The Managing of Foreign Exchange Risks", Midland Corporate Finance Journal, Vol. 1, No. 3, Fall 1983.

involved. So the six-month volatility of an asset with an annual volatility of 10 percent can be calculated as follows:

Annual volatility x square root of time
$$= 10\% \times \sqrt{0.5} = 7.1\%$$

This means that in the case of an asset with an annual volatility of 10 percent, there is a two-thirds chance that the price at the end of the six months will be within about 7 percent of the starting price.

For an individual treasury transaction, we can divide the process of assigning a risk measure into four steps:

1. Identify the source of the risk.
2. Measure the annual volatility for that risk.
3. Convert the annual volatility to a risk measure appropriate to the duration of the exposure.
4. Decide whether the transaction was a hedge (i.e., it reduced risk) or a speculation (it increased risk).

The most common sources of risk for treasury transactions are the fluctuations of exchange rates and interest rates. A treasury risk-monitoring system could simply monitor the volatility of the relevant exchange rates and interest rates (or bond prices) to provide the basis of a risk score for each potential or actual treasury transaction.

The basic information for measuring volatility comes from two sources: (1) actual price movements and (2) the volatility forecasts implicit in option prices. These two measures of volatility will be different because they use different information. If, for instance, a foreign exchange exposure was left uncovered for the first two months of 1985, the risk of this decision could be measured by calculating (from the daily exchange rate moves over that period) the volatility of the relevant exchange rate during the time that the exposure was left uncovered. Such a procedure, however, although it correctly measures the actual risk that resulted, may be unfair in that it uses information that would not have been available to the decision-maker at the time of the decision.

An alternative that avoids this problem is to use as a measure of risk the volatility forecast that was being employed by the options market at the beginning of the two-month period. This number is known to option specialists as the "implied standard deviation" (ISD), and it represents the market consensus volatility forecast that has been traded into the option price. In this case, the appropriate option to use to compute the implied volatility would be an option on the particular currency in question, trading at the beginning of January 1985, when the hedging decision was made.

EXAMPLE: Risk Assessment of Foreign Exchange Hedging Transaction

An exposure is identified long $500,000 in three months. The company is sterling-based. At the time the exposure is identified, the spot rate is $1.40/£ and the three-month forward is $1.38/£.

The exposure is left uncovered for one month and then closed at $1.36/£ two-month forward.

Opportunity Gain:
- Actual value − Value of alternative
- $500,000/1.36 − $500,000/1.38
- $5,328

Risk Measures (Annual Volatilities):
Implied annual standard deviation at beginning of month of exposure = 12%
Actual annual volatility over month of exposure = 16%

Risk of Transaction (% Standard Deviation over Life of Exposure):
Equivalent one-month standard deviations:
Actual volatility: $16\% \times \sqrt{1/12} = 4.6\%$
Implied volatility: $12\% \times \sqrt{1/12} = 3.5\%$

Size of Exposure (Money Amounts):
£362,319 × 4.6% = 16,667
£362,319 × 3.5% = 12,681

5. Discussion: As a benchmark in judging whether a particular risk-return tradeoff is acceptable, a commonly used reference is the equity market. This has historically provided an annual return of about 8% in excess of the interest rate, in exchange for an annual volatility of about 20%. Thus a ratio of gain to risk of about 0.4 might be viewed as "normal" in this context.

Analysing the Components of Aggregate Opportunity Gains and Risks

As we have suggested, the gains resulting from treasury transactions can be classified according to

TABLE 2
Components of
Aggregate Performance

Risk Source	Arbitrage	Yield Spread	Hedging		Speculation	
Foreign Exchange:						
$/£			−$0.4*	(−$8.3)*	$1.4	($3.7)
$/SF			XX	(YY)	XX	(YY)
$/YEN			XX	(YY)	XX	(YY)
$/DM			XX	(YY)	XX	(YY)
Liquidity:						
Maturity shift		XX			XX	(YY)
Quality shift		XX			XX	(YY)
Liquidity shift		XX			XX	(YY)
Debt:						
Maturity shift		XX			XX	(YY)
None (arbitrage)	XX					

* First number represents opportunity gain/loss to that transaction. Second number represents the risk of the transaction group.

whether they are gains from arbitrage, spreads, hedging, or speculation. They can also be split into the separate components of the risks involved—that is, those associated with movements in a particular exchange rate or interest rate.

All transactions that depend upon the same source of risk (movements in the yen/sterling, for example) can first be aggregated to give an overall picture of performance with respect to that component of risk. The total opportunity gain on this group of transactions can then be measured and split into components according to whether they result from one of the four categories mentioned above: arbitrage, spreads, hedging, or speculation. The risks resulting from the hedging and speculation can also be measured.

To aggregate all transactions that depend upon a common interest rate or exchange rate, the performance of each transaction must be measured in dollar (or other currency) amounts rather than percentages. If measured in this way, the opportunity gains and losses can simply be added to give an overall opportunity gain from that particular kind of transaction.

Fortunately, the risks, as measured by the standard deviation or volatility expressed in dollars, can also be added to give the overall volatility figure. This is the case when the risks being aggregated all depend on a common source, such as the dollar/DM exchange rate. If performance is aggregated across different sources of risk, then constructing the ap-propriate risk depends on the level of intercorrelation between the different sources of risk.

Table 2 gives a possible framework for the presentation of overall performance. Performance from foreign exchange transactions involving the dollar/sterling exchange rate resulted in two types of gain—with two associated risks. Hedging transactions had an opportunity cost of $0.4 million, but reduced risk to the corporation by an amount equivalent to a standard deviation of $8.3 million. Speculative transactions, on the other hand, resulted in an opportunity gain of $1.4 million, with an associated increase of risk equivalent to a standard deviation of $3.7 million.

Figure 1 gives a diagrammatic presentation of the same information. On the vertical axis we plot opportunity costs or gains of a transaction in dollars. On the horizontal axis we plot the risk of the transaction. Notice that transactions in the lower left-hand quadrant reduce the risk of the company, but there is an opportunity cost to that risk reduction. At this point, management is in a position to weigh the returns against the risks associated with each transaction.

How Might We Measure Abnormal Performance

We have explained in some detail how opportunity gains and losses from Treasury transactions can be measured, with consequent changes in risks. In

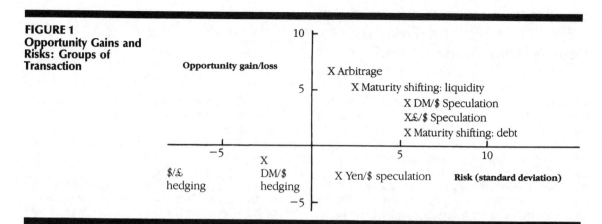

FIGURE 1
Opportunity Gains and Risks: Groups of Transaction

Figure 1 we sketched out how those incremental returns and risks might be presented. But we have left it for management to trade off those risks and returns in order to decide if the transaction was worth undertaking. In other words, management must calculate the "abnormal" or economic returns on the transaction.

Of course if the transaction is riskless (for example, an arbitrage), then the abnormal return is simply the opportunity gain since there is no risk to consider. For risky transactions, however, we require a model of risk and return. One obvious one is the Capital Asset Pricing Model (CAPM). In this case, estimates from past data suggest that the equity market has provided an annual return of about 8 percent in excess of the interest rate in exchange for an annual volatility of about 20 percent. Thus, a ratio of gain to risk of about 0.4 may be a useful way of determining if a transaction's opportunity gain is worth accepting or not. A word of warning, however: the CAPM assumes that certain risks can be diversified away by shareholders and, therefore, that corporate diversification is unnecessary to achieve such risk reduction. But, if some risks are better diversified away or hedged by corporations rather than by shareholders, then following the prescriptions suggested by the CAPM may not be the best policy.

Summary

The overwhelming proportion of treasury management is concerned with foreign exchange, debt, and liquidity decisions. These decisions are choices among various capital market alternatives. They all involve hedging risks or taking risks.

Performance measurement of treasury decisions should be based upon measurement of opportunity gains and losses together with consideration of the risks involved. Opportunity gains and losses should be measured as economic returns on the actual policy pursued, relative to the return on a viable benchmark. Economic return measurement should be based upon market values of treasury assets and liabilities.

The benchmark policy used to measure the opportunity gain should represent a policy that could be specified *a priori* and actually followed. Likely benchmarks include full forward cover for evaluating exchange risk management, floating-rate debt for evaluating corporate borrowing, and short-term government paper for evaluating cash management. Different circumstances may dictate other choices.

Risk can be measured in two ways. Measurement of the actual variability of exchange rates and interest rates gives an indication of the actual risks taken. Measurement of implied volatility from option markets gives an indication of the risk forecast available at the time of the decision.

The opportunity gain or loss and risk of each transaction should be measured in dollars (or other base currency) and classified in two ways. Classification by type of transaction (that is, whether as arbitrage, yield spreads, hedging, or speculation) gives an indication of the activeness of the treasury policy. Classification by source of risk gives an indication of the major sources of exposure in the decisions taken. Both classifications aid in diagnosing the causes of treasury performance and in controlling future activity.

APPENDIX: Tax and Treasury Performance Management

The impact of tax on treasury behavior is very complex. Complexities arise because of differential actual or effective tax rates over time, differential treatment of gains and losses, of income and capital, of domestic and foreign income, and particular detailed tax laws such as those on zero coupon bonds, and holdings of government debt. To fully incorporate all these details into a decision model is practically impossible, since the comparisons to be made are so heavily dependent upon specific tax laws. Each decision, such as the choice between issuing a low-coupon bond and a high-coupon bond requires analysis based upon the particular tax rules that apply to that choice.

A general concept that can be applied to treasury decisions affected by tax is as follows: given two transactions with the same maturity, liquidity, and risk, choose the one with the most favourable after-tax rate of return. Thus a lease will be desirable if it has a lower all-in, after-tax cost than the all-in, after-tax cost of an equivalent secured term loan. Even this simple rule may, however, be misleading in certain cases where the difference in after-tax rates of return is not directly equivalent to a difference in present values.

Where tax rates are different over future years, the problem of after-tax benchmarks for comparison becomes even more complex. Consider the situation in the UK. In 1984 it was known that the corporate tax rate would fall in the subsequent two years.

Year	84/85	85/86	86/87
Rate	45%	40%	35%

For a corporation whose tax year ends at a date other than April 15, the rate in each year is a weighted average.

The corporation is confronted by different pre-tax borrowing rates for different maturities. The after-tax borrowing cost for a particular maturity depends on the pre-tax borrowing rate and the tax deductions resulting from the borrowing. These deductions depend upon the tax year in which the interest is paid or accrued, and so the after-tax borrowing cost for a particular maturity will vary during the year.

If the corporation is currently not paying taxes, it faces a series of "effective" tax rates that depend upon the date at which it expects to resume paying corporation tax. For instance, if the corporation expects to resume paying tax in 86/87, its "effective" tax rates are roughly:

Year	84/85	85/86	86/87
Effective Rate	28%	31%	35%

The tax rates in the early years are equivalent to the tax rate at the resumption date discounted back to the date in question. Interest payments in 85/86, for instance, will result in a tax saving in 86/87 at a rate of 35 percent so their present value benefit in 85/86 is 35 percent discounted by one year.

More subtle questions of tax timing arise, in most circumstances, because tax accrued in a particular tax year is paid with a delay. Sophisticated lease evaluation systems, for instance, keep a daily calendar of tax accruals and payments, so that the optimal lease rental pattern can be chosen for a company with a particular tax position.

This might make it seem hopeless even to try to build a general after-tax performance measurement system. In fact, it would not be intellectually demanding, just extremely tedious, to put in the correct tax rules and make sure that every actual decision was compared with an appropriate alternative.

For instance, consider a corporation that uses a benchmark of the all-in, after-tax cost of floating-rate debt. When it enters into a fixed-rate leasing transaction, we know that the lease should be compared with fixed-rate secured borrowing of the same maturity as the lease. The performance of the leasing transaction, therefore, consists of two parts:

Lease spread =
    After-tax cost of fixed rate borrowing −
    after-tax cost of lease

Fixed/floating spread =
    After-tax cost of floating-rate term borrowing −
    after-tax cost of fixed-rate borrowing

In this case, the lease is causing the corporation to deviate from its normal passive borrowing strategy to pick up the spread available in the fixed-rate leasing market.

How should one analyse this transaction in terms of its performance? One might argue that the deviation from the FRN strategy is unavoidable, and therefore should be ignored in measuring the performance of the transaction. Then one would just use the spread between the lease and fixed-rate borrowing. But what if a floating rate lease is available, as is probably the case? Other comparisons are then possible:

The equity market has historically provided an annual return of about 8 percent in excess of the interest rate in exchange for an annual volatility of about 20 percent.

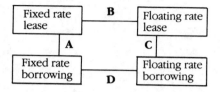

An alternative view would be that the decision consists of two parts: the decision to lease, as measured by spread C, and the decision to use fixed-rate borrowing, as measured by spread B.

This seems to be a more natural way of thinking about the problem, in that it views the decision to deviate from the floating-rate policy as an explicit rather than an implicit decision. The only problem is that the market for floating-rate leases may be relatively thin, so that the only way to pick up the full benefits of leasing may be to use fixed-rate leases.

Part IV The International Investment and Financing Decisions

International Capital Budgeting

by Alan C. Shapiro,
University of Southern California

Multinational corporations evaluating foreign investments are forced to confront several capital budgeting issues that are rarely, if ever, encountered by wholly domestic firms. Here are just a few: How do foreign tax regulations affect the expected profitability of international investments? Should management evaluate projected cash flows from the standpoint of a foreign subsidiary, and in terms of local currencies, or from the home currency perspective? How can the use of foreign sources of financing be reflected in investment analysis? Should the required rate of return on international investments be raised to reflect risks like expropriation, currency controls, and exchange rate fluctuations? Are there significant benefits to investors from international portfolio diversification? and if so, how does this affect the value of foreign investment by multinationals?

My purpose in this article is to address these issues in the context of modern finance theory, and to present a practical framework that incorporates the special complications of international investment into the standard discounted cash flow (DCF) capital budgeting method. By reducing to a common denominator the effects of these complex factors on the expected profitability of contemplated foreign investments, the framework enables management to evaluate international projects on a uniform basis and, thus, to compare them directly with all other investment opportunities. The principle aim of the framework is to make the greatest possible use of available information about the expected risks and returns of foreign investment. At the same time, it eliminates some of the arbitrary adjustments of cost of capital and cash flow that are now common practice in multinational capital budgeting.

Before turning to the subject of international investment, I want to review the standard DCF method that most companies use to evaluate their capital investment alternatives. Then I will discuss the modifications of the standard DCF framework necessary to accommodate the special features of foreign project appraisal. This is followed by a discussion of the required rate of return, or cost of capital, for foreign investments. Finally, having proposed a financial framework for quantifying the value of investments, I offer a theoretical rationale for direct foreign investment that attempts to identify the characteristics most likely to distinguish— *prior* to any detailed, systematic financial analysis— profitable from unprofitable foreign projects. Such a rationale should serve as a basic guide for multinational strategic thinking; it can also be used to furnish the criteria for the first screening of foreign investment opportunities.

The Discounted Cash Flow Framework

The standard capital budgeting analysis has two steps. The first, and ordinarily the most time-consuming, is the estimation of expected after-tax cash flows associated with a prospective investment. The second is the discounting of those cash flows back to the present using the company's weighted average cost of capital. If the resulting number, known as the net present value (NPV) of those cash flows, is positive the investment should be undertaken; if negative, it should be rejected.

The weighted average cost of capital (WACC) is conceptually simple and easy to apply. Recall that the calculation of WACC involves weighting the after-tax cost of each component of capital by its proportional representation in the company's (target) capital structure. For a company with only debt and equity in its capital base, its overall cost of capital and, hence, its required rate of return on normal investments, would be expressed as follows:

WACC = (Cost of Debt × Debt/Total Capital) + (Cost of Equity × Equity/Total Capital)

The use of the weighted cost of capital is thus predicated on the assumption of a specific financing structure, or debt-equity ratio, *for each individual project*. Consequently, the indiscriminate, corporate-wide use of a single rate is appropriate only when the financial structures and commercial risks are similar for all investments considered. The costs of debt and equity will vary with different project risks. Furthermore, because projects with different risks are likely to have different debt capacities, their required rates of returns should be calculated using not the company's capital structure, but rather the financial structure supported by the project standing apart from the company.

Another objection to the use of a single corporate-wide discount rate—one especially pertinent to foreign investments—is its failure to reflect the availability of project-specific loans at concessionary rates. There also may be cases where the multinational (MNC) may choose to use foreign source funds having a higher cost due to home country exchange controls. The benefits or costs of these unusual sources of financing should be reflected in the analysis.

An Adjusted Present Value Approach

One way to reflect these deviations from the company's typical investment and financing policy is to adjust the company's weighted average cost of capital. But, for some companies, such as those in extractive industries, there is no norm. Project risks and financial structure vary by country, raw material, production stage, and position in the life cycle of the project. Such problems can be dealt with by using an alternative procedure, known as the "adjusted present value" (APV) approach. Developed by Stewart Myers[1] in the early 1970s, the APV approach involves discounting cash flows at a rate that, by removing the effects of financing, reflects only the business risks of the project. This rate, called the *all-equity* rate (also known as the "cost of capital for business risk"), represents the required rate of return on a project financed entirely with equity.

The all-equity rate, c, can be used in capital budgeting by viewing the value of a project as the sum of the following components: (1) the present value of project cash flows after taxes but before financing costs, discounted at c; (2) the present value of the tax savings on debt financing, discounted at the company's normal domestic borrowing rate, b; and (3) the present value of any savings on (or penalties from) interest costs associated with project-specific financing, discounted also at b.[2] This latter differential would generally be due to government regulations and/or subsidies that caused interest rates on restricted funds to diverge from domestic interest payable on unsubsidized, arm's-length borrowings.

In equation form, the APV of a project can be expressed as follows:

$$APV = -I + \underbrace{\frac{X}{c}}_{(1)} + \underbrace{\frac{(b \times D) \times t}{b}}_{(2)} + \underbrace{\frac{(b - b') \times D'}{b}}_{(3)}$$

where:

I   is the initial investment, assuming a one-time initial outlay

X   is the expected annual operating after-tax cash flow, assuming the project is financed with all equity (and has an infinite life)

c   is the risk-adjusted required rate of return on the specific project, assuming the project is financed solely with equity

b   is the company's normal domestic borrowing rate

D   is the amount of debt financing supported by the project (assumed to be constant throughout the project's life)

t   is the company's marginal tax rate

b'   is the rate of interest (translated into its domestic equivalent) on special foreign source financing

D'   is the amount of special foreign source debt financing used (also assumed to be constant throughout)

It should be emphasized that the all-equity cost of capital equals the required rate of return on a *specific* project; this in turn can be broken down into the riskless rate of interest plus an appropriate risk premium based on the project's particular risk.

---

1. Myers, Stewart C. (1974), "Interactions of Corporate Financing and Investment Decisions," *Journal of Finance*, March, pp. 1–26.

2. In a paper published in 1979, Donald Lessard discusses these issues in his extension of the APV approach to foreign project appraisals. See Donald R.

Lessard, "Evaluating Foreign Projects: An Adjusted Present Value Approach," in Donald R. Lessard, ed. *International Financial Management*, Boston: Warren, Gorham & Lamont.

The interaction of a project's returns with the returns of the company's other investments is largely irrelevant.

Thus c varies according to the risk of the specific project.

Recall also that, in accordance with the capital asset pricing model (CAPM), the risk reflected in c is only "systematic risk." As measured by "beta," systematic risk reflects not the total variability of a company or project's expected returns, but rather its co-variability with market-wide (e.g., S&P 500) average returns. It is a measure of investors' exposure to "non-diversifiable" or market risk and, as such, reflects the sensitivity of an investment's return to general economic conditions which affect all stock prices.

For project analysis, this means that a project's risk and, thus, its minimum required rate of return should reflect its correlation only with overall market returns. The interaction of the project's returns with the returns of the company's other investments is largely irrelevant, and thus should be ignored, in the valuation and capital budgeting process. The message of modern finance is that, in well-functioning capital markets, *corporate* diversification does not add value. Why, after all, should investors pay premiums for diversified companies when they can privately and cheaply accomplish the same end by buying a mutual fund? Casual observation, combined with what evidence we have on this question, says that the market doesn't reward companies for diversification it can easily duplicate at the same or lower cost.

In short, each individual project should be viewed as having its own required return; and this risk-adjusted minimum return, or "cost of capital," is completely unaffected by the composition of the company's portfolio of present and prospective investments.

Issues in Foreign Investment Analysis

With this review of the principles of valuation as background, let's turn to two troublesome issues confronting foreign project analysts:

1. Should expected cash flows be measured from the standpoint of the project (or the foreign subsidiary's managers) or from that of the parent company?
2. Should the uniquely foreign economic and political risks be reflected by raising the required rate of return (or the discount rate) or by adjusting expected cash flows?

Parent Versus Project Cash Flows

Because of tax regulations and exchange controls, a substantial difference can exist between the cash flow of a project and the amount that can be remitted to the parent multinational corporation. Also, many project expenses, such as management fees and royalties, are actually returns to the parent company. And, yet another source of this discrepancy, the *incremental* revenue contributed to the parent MNC by a project can differ from total project revenues if, for example, the project involves substituting local production for parent company exports, or if transfer price adjustments shift profits elsewhere in the system. (It is only incremental revenues, of course, that should be credited to the project.)

Given the appreciable differences between parent and project cash flows likely to exist, what, then, are the relevant cash flows to use in evaluating a foreign project? The managers of a foreign subsidiary can be expected to focus only, of course, on those project cash flows accruing locally. Unless compensated for doing otherwise, they will tend to ignore the consequences of their investment policies on the economic situation of the rest of the MNC.

Partly because of the impracticability of expecting local management to take a global view, and partly out of a desire to decentralize decision-making and offer foreign managers greater autonomy, some have suggested that the effect of restrictions on repatriation be ignored. According to economic theory, however, the value of a project is determined by the net present value of future cash flows *back to the investor*. Thus, the parent MNC should value only those cash flows (net of any transfer costs such as taxes) that are—or, more precisely, *can be*—repatriated. Only remittable funds can be used to pay dividends and interest, to amortize the firm's debt, and to reinvest.[3]

To overcome the problem caused by the difference between project and parent cash flows, I recommend that the financial analysis of foreign investments proceed in three stages. In the first stage, project cash flows are computed solely from the subsidiary's standpoint, as if it were a separate national corporation. In the second stage, the perspective shifts to that of the parent company. This step

---

3. This principle also holds, of course, for a domestic firm. For example, dividends received by a parent firm from an unconsolidated domestic subsidiary (less than 80% ownership) are taxed at a 15% rate and, hence, should be valued at only 0.85 of the original dividend paid.

The parent MNC should value only those cash flows that can be repatriated.

requires specific forecasts of the amounts, forms, and timing of transfers (assuming all repatriable cash is actually remitted) to headquarters. It also involves gathering information about taxes and other expenses incurred in the transfer process. Third and last, the parent company should take into account the indirect benefits and costs this investment confers or imposes on the rest of the system, such as an increase or decrease in export sales by another affiliate. This, of course, may not be easy to do. In some cases, management may be able to estimate incremental cash flows to the parent only by subtracting worldwide parent company cash flows (without the investment) from post-investment parent company cash flows.

While the principle of adjusting and valuing incremental cash flows is conceptually simple, it can become quite complicated in its actual application. Let's look at how this recommended procedure might be applied, with special attention to the tax question.

Incorporating Tax Factors: Because only after-tax cash flows are relevant, it is necessary to determine when and what taxes must be paid on foreign-source profits. On the basis of existing tax laws, taxes paid are a function of the time of remittance (are profits remitted immediately or are they reinvested?), the form of remittance (whether as dividends, loan repayments, or transfer price adjustments), the foreign income tax rate, the existence of withholding taxes, the treaties between home and host countries, and the existence and usability of foreign tax credits.

Because of these complexities in estimating actual after-tax cash flows back to the parent, I propose a simpler approach for calculating the tax lia-

bilities on the foreign investment. This approach makes two conservative assumptions: first, the maximum amount of funds available for remittance in each year is actually remitted; second, the tax rate applied to these cash flows is the higher of the home or host country rate. This means that a project is evaluated as if the maximum allowable amount of dividends were repatriated each year.

The fact that there are substantial tax savings from reinvesting locally instead of repatriating can be ignored at this initial stage of the investment analysis. The recognition of excess foreign tax credits and alternative, lower-cost remittance channels should also be deferred. Finally, in order to avoid understating the parent's tax liability (by understating remitted cash flow), all funds expected to be transferred back to the parent in the form of management fees, royalties, and licensing fees are included in this initial stage of the analysis.

The reasoning behind this division of the investment analysis procedure into these stages is straightforward: if the investment is acceptable under conservative assumptions, then it will be acceptable under a more liberal set of circumstances, and it will not be necessary to calculate all the additional tax savings possible. If the initial net present value is negative under these conservative assumptions, then the additional tax savings can be estimated and added back.

Political and Economic Risk Analysis

All else being equal, multinational companies prefer to invest in countries with stable currencies, healthy economies, and minimal political risks. But because all else is usually not equal, management

A simple calculation of an MNC's marginal tax rate on remitted foreign-source earnings illustrates the procedure. Suppose after-tax earnings of $120,000 will be remitted by an affiliate to its U.S. parent in the form of a dividend. Assume the foreign tax rate is 40%, the withholding tax on dividends is 4%, and excess foreign tax credits are unavailable. The marginal rate of additional taxation is found by adding the local withholding tax to the U.S. tax owed on the dividend. Withholding tax in this case would equal $4,800 ($120,000 × .04), while U.S. tax owed would be $7,200. (The U.S. tax is calculated as *follows. With a before-tax local income of $200,000 ($200,000 × (1 − .4) = $120,000), the U.S. tax owed before foreign tax credits would equal $200,000 × .46, or $92,000. The firm would receive foreign tax credits equal to $84,800, for the $80,000 in local tax paid and the $4,800 dividend withholding tax. This leaves a net of $7,200 owed the IRS.) The incremental taxes on the MNC's remitted foreign-source earnings would thus equal $12,000 ($4,800 + $7,200) and the marginal tax rate would be 10% ($12,000/$120,000).*

*Using a higher discount rate to reflect expropriation
risks only serves to distort the meaning of the
present value of a project.*

must carefully evaluate the consequences of various political and economic risks for the viability of potential investments.

There are presently, to my knowledge, four practical (though not necessarily correct) methods of incorporating international political and economic risks, such as the risks of currency fluctuations and expropriation, into foreign investment analysis. They are:

1. Shortening the minimum payback period.
2. Raising the required rate of return of the investment.
3. Adjusting cash flows for the costs of risk reduction; e.g., charging a premium for overseas political risk insurance.
4. Adjusting cash flows to reflect the specific impact of a given risk.

Adjusting the Discount Rate or Payback Period

The additional risks confronted abroad are usually discussed in general terms rather than in direct relation to specific investments. This rather vague view of risk probably explains the popularity of two questionable approaches to account for the added political and economic risks of overseas operations. One is to use a higher discount rate for foreign operations, the other to require a shorter payback period. For example, if exchange restrictions are anticipated, a normal required return of 15% might be raised to 20%, or, alternatively, a five-year payback standard may be shortened to three years.

Neither of these approaches lends itself to careful evaluation of the actual impact of a particular risk on expected investment returns. Thorough risk analysis requires an assessment of the magnitude and timing of such risks, and their implications for the projection of cash flows. For example, an expropriation expected five years hence is likely to be much less threatening than one anticipated next year, even though there is a higher probability associated with the former. Using a uniformly higher discount rate to reflect these quite different expropriation risks only serves to distort the meaning of the *present value* of a project by penalizing future cash flows relatively more heavily than current

ones. It is not a good substitute for careful risk evaluation.

Furthermore, the choice of a risk premium (or risk premiums, if the discount rate is allowed to vary over time), whether 2% or 10%, is an arbitrary one. Adjusting cash flows instead of assigning some more or less arbitrary risk premium makes it possible to make fuller, more specific use of the information available about the effects of a specific risk on the future returns from an investment.

The two principal methods for adjusting cash flow estimates to reflect international risks are: (1) uncertainty absorption and (2) adjustment of expected values of future cash flows.

Uncertainty Absorption

Uncertainty absorption is used to quantify the effect of international risk by charging against each year's flows a premium for political and economic risk insurance, whether or not such insurance is actually purchased.[4] Political risks like currency inconvertibility or expropriation can be covered by insurance bought through the Overseas Private Investment Corporation, a U.S. government agency. Economic risks like currency fluctuations can be hedged in the forward exchange market. In the latter case, the uncertainty absorption approach involves adjusting each period's dollar cash flow by the cost of a hedging program (again, regardless of whether the program is put in place).

There is, however, a problem with the uncertainty absorption method: it does not accurately measure the effect of a given political or economic risk on the present value of a project. In the case of expropriation, political risk insurance normally covers only the book value, not the economic value, of expropriated assets. The relationship between the book value of a project's assets and the economic value of a project, as measured by its future cash flows, is at best tenuous. It is worthwhile, of course, to compare the cost of political risk insurance with its expected benefits. But insurance is no substitute for a careful evaluation of the impact of political risk on the expected profitability of a specific project.

As a method for dealing with exchange risk, the uncertainty absorption technique is fine if local currency cash flows are fixed, as in the case of interest

---

4. This is the approach recommended by Arthur Stonehill and Leonard Nathanson in "Capital Budgeting and the Multinational Corporation," *California Management Review*, Summer 1968, pp. 39–54.

Political risk insurance normally covers only the book value, not the economic value, of expropriated assets.

on a foreign currency-denominated bond. But, where income is generated by an ongoing business operation, the operating cash flow in local currency will itself be affected by changes in the exchange rate.[5] This effect is entirely ignored by the uncertainty absorption technique.

Adjusting Expected Values

In 1978, I published a paper recommending that the expected cash flows, not the discount rate, of a project be adjusted to reflect the *specific* impact of each perceived risk. The argument was based largely on my firsthand observation that management typically has more and better information about the effect of a given risk on a project's cash flows, than about its effect on shareholders' required return. Such cash flow adjustments, by assigning probabilities to various economic and political events, will generate an *expected* value for the project; that is, the value resulting from this adjustment will reflect the expected "mean" or average outcome of a number of possible effects on cash flow caused by specific international risks.

In adjusting expected cash flow downward and allowing the discount rate to remain unchanged, this procedure does not assume that shareholders have a neutral attitude toward risk. What it does assume, however, is that either (1) risks such as expropriation, currency controls, inflation, and exchange rate changes are unsystematic or (2) the diversification provided by foreign investment may actually *lower* a firm's systematic risk. If the latter is true (and, as I will argue later, there is some persuasive evidence to support this belief), adjusting only the expected values of future cash flows will yield a *lower bound* on the value of the investment to the firm.

According to modern capital asset pricing theory, adjusting expected cash flows, instead of the discount rate, to reflect incremental risks is justified so long as the systematic risk of a proposed invest-

ment remains unchanged. To the extent that these international political and economic risks are unsystematic, there is no theoretical reason to adjust the cost of capital of a project to reflect those risks. The possibility that foreign investments may actually reduce a firm's systematic risk by providing international diversification means that this approach, if anything, underestimates the present value of a project to the parent corporation.[6]

The Impact of Political Risk

In recent years, there has been a significant increase, in developing and developed countries alike, in the kinds and magnitude of political risks that multinational companies have historically faced. Currency controls, expropriation, changes in tax laws, requirements for additional local production or expensive pollution control equipment—these are just some of the more visible forms political risk can take. The common denominator of such risks, however, is not hard to identify: government intervention into the workings of the economy that affects, for good or ill, the value of the firm. While the consequences are usually adverse, changes in the political environment can provide opportunities. The imposition of quotas on autos from Japan, for example, was undoubtedly beneficial to U.S. auto manufacturers.

Measuring Political Risks

A number of commercial and academic political risk forecasting models are available today. These models typically supply country indices that attempt to quantify the level of political risk in each nation. Most of these indices rely on some measure(s) of the stability of the local political regime. Such measures may include the frequency of changes of government, the level of violence in a country (for example, violent deaths per 100,000 population), number of armed insurrections, con-

---

5. As pointed out by Ian Giddy (1976) and a number of others, there is a set of equilibrium conditions in an efficient foreign exchange market that generally cause exchange rate changes and inflation to have only a minimal impact—at least over the long run—on real cash flows. To be more specific, the relative version of purchasing power parity states that changes in the ratio of domestic and foreign prices will equal changes in the equilibrium exchange rate. This means, for example, that the effect on cash flows of a foreign currency depreciation should be largely offset by a higher rate of foreign inflation.

6. Although the suggestion that cash flows from politically risky areas be discounted at a rate that ignores those risks is contrary to current corporate practice, the difference may be more apparent than real. In 1979, Donald Lessard observed that most firms evaluating foreign investments discount most

likely ("modal") rather than expected ("mean") cash flows at a risk-adjusted rate. If an expropriation or currency blockage is anticipated (though with a probability well under .50), then the mean value of the probability distribution of future cash flows will be significantly below its mode. Thus, the negative effect of the widespread practice of raising the discount rate may, in the typical case, be offset by the perhaps equally popular practice of using most likely rather than average cash flows. From a theoretical standpoint, of course, cash flows should always be adjusted to reflect the change in the mean or expected values caused by a particular risk. But such flows, to repeat, should be further discounted only in cases where the attending international risks can be shown to be systematic.

flicts with other states, and so on. The basic function of these stability indicators is to determine how long the current regime will be in power and, equally important, whether that regime will also be willing and able to enforce its foreign investment guarantees.

Other popular indicators of political risk include various economic factors such as inflation, balance of payments deficits or surpluses, and the level and growth rate of per capita GNP. The intention behind these measures is to determine whether the economy is in good shape or requires a "quick fix." Foreign governments with sagging economies often resort to expropriations to increase government revenues, or to measures blocking currency conversions to improve their balance of payments.

Despite the increased sophistication of these models, there is little evidence of their success in forecasting political risk. For one thing, political instability by itself does not necessarily contribute to political risk. Changes of government in Latin America, for example, are quite frequent; yet, most multinationals continue to go about their business undisturbed.

The most important weakness of these indices, however, is their implicit assumption that each firm in a country faces the same degree of political risk. As indicated by the empirical evidence on the post-World War II experiences of U.S. and British MNCs, this assumption is manifestly untrue. The data clearly show that, except in those countries that went Communist, companies differ in their susceptibilities to political risk according to their industry, size, composition of ownership, level of technology, and degree of vertical integration with other affiliates.[7] For example, expropriation—or, its more prevalent form, creeping expropriation—is more likely to occur in the extractive, utility, and financial service sectors of an economy than in the manufacturing sector.[8] Also, the expected effect of currency controls will probably not be the same over the life of an investment. It is only when a project is throwing off excess cash that restrictions on profit repatri-

ation generally become a problem.

Because political risk has a different meaning for, and effect on, each firm, it is doubtful that any index of generalized political risk will be of much value to a company selected at random. The specific operating and financial characteristics of a company will largely determine its susceptibility to political risk and, hence, the effects of that risk on the present value of its foreign investment.

Managing Political Risk

Once a firm has assessed the political environment of a country, it must then decide whether to invest, and if so, how to structure its investment to minimize political risk. The important point to keep in mind, once again, is that political risk is not independent of the firm's activities. The substance and form of the firm's investments will, in large measure, determine their susceptibility to changing government policies. For example, a multinational can reduce the risk of expropriation by keeping the project dependent on affiliated companies for markets, supplies, transportation, and technology. Another defensive ploy is to offer local foreign investors or government agencies a stake in the venture's success.[9] Similarly, a firm can reduce the impact of currency controls by investing in the form of debt rather than equity (because governments are more hesitant to restrict loan repayments than dividends), borrowing locally, and setting high transfer prices on goods sold to the subsidiary while buying goods produced by the subsidiary at lower prices where legally possible.[10] Obviously, it is important to incorporate these methods into a capital budgeting and planning procedure that is completed *before* the initial commitment of funds.

One other point: the automatic inclusion of depreciation in computing cash flows from domestic operations is questionable when evaluating a foreign project. Dividend payments in excess of reported profits will decapitalize the enterprise, thereby inviting closer host government scrutiny.

---

7. See. for example, Truitt, J. Frederick (1970), "Expropriation of Private Foreign Investment: Summary of the Post-World II Experience of American and British Investors in the Less Developed Countries," *Journal of International Business Studies*, Fall, pp. 21–34. Also Hawkins, Robert G.; Mintz, Norman; and Provissiero, Michael (1976), "Government Takeovers of U.S. Foreign Affiliates," *Journal of International Business Studies*, Spring. pp. 3–15.

8. See David Bradley (1977), "Managing Against Expropriation," *Harvard Business Review*, July–August, pp. 75–83. Bradley argues that companies whose inputs and services are more easily replaced are more likely to be subject to expropriation.

9. In a paper published in 1981, I provided a framework for the assessment and management of political risk, concentrating on the methods available to reduce the risk of expropriation. See Alan C. Shapiro (1981), "Managing Political Risk: A Policy Approach," *Columbia Journal of World Business*, Fall, pp. 63–70.

10. Numerous other mechanisms available for accessing or otherwise using blocked funds are described in my own paper, "Managing Blocked Currency Funds," University of Southern California Working Paper (1980). They include swap, parallel, and back-to-back loans, leading and lagging, purchase of commodities and local services for use abroad, conducting research and development locally, and hosting corporate conventions and business meetings locally.

Using depreciation cash flows to service parent company debt, however, is generally more acceptable. Thus, while parent company funds—whether called debt or equity—require the same return, the cash flow from foreign projects could very well be affected by the form of the investment.

Cash Flow Adjustments for Political Risks

To make the greatest possible use of available information, political risks should be incorporated into foreign investment analysis by adjusting the expected cash flows of a project, not its required rate of return. In this section, I want to demonstrate the application of my proposed cash-flow adjustment method using the extreme case of political risk: an expropriation. The aim of this exercise is to illustrate how a multinational investment analyst could quantify the effect of an expropriation (or any other form of political risk) on the present value of a contemplated foreign investment.

Let's assume that, in the absence of expropriation, the expected cash flow of a given project over a specified period is $1 million. Assume also that if expropriation occurs prior to that time, the expected cash flow is zero. If we can assign a probability of expropriation of .25, the expected cash flow during that period would be $750,000 $((.75 \times \$1,000,000) + (.25 \times 0))$.[11]

Calculating the probability of expropriation with any level of confidence is of course difficult, if not impossible. In cases of extreme uncertainty about the timing of a possible expropriation, an alternative to assigning probabilities is to use a form of break-even analysis. Suppose, for instance, that management is reasonably certain that expropriation will occur either in the third year of the project, or not at all. If no expropriation occurs, the project's net present value (NPV) is estimated to be $3 million. If an expropriation does occur, however, the

expected NPV is $−$2 million. In this case, the expected NPV (in millions) equals $-2p + 3(1-p)$, where p is the unknown probability of expropriation. The value of p at which the project breaks even can be found by solving for p^* where $-2p^* + 3(1-p^*) = 0$, or $p^* = .6$. Thus, if the probability of expropriation is less than .6, the project will have a positive expected net present value. This probability break-even analysis is often more easily applied because it is normally easier, and certainly requires less information, to ascertain whether p is less or greater than .6, than to decide on the absolute level of p.[12]

Cash Flow Adjustments for Changes and Inflation

Projected cash flows can be stated in any combination of nominal (current) or real (constant) domestic or foreign currency terms. To ensure comparability among the various cash flows and with today's home currency outlays, however, all cash flows must finally be expressed in real terms; i.e., in units of constant purchasing power. Nominal cash flows can be converted to real cash flows by adjusting either the cash flows or the discount rate. That is, nominal cash flows can be discounted at the nominal discount rate or real cash flows can be discounted at the real discount rate. Both methods yield the same results.[13]

In order to assess the effect of exchange rate changes on expected cash flows, it is first necessary to remove the effect of offsetting changes in inflation and exchange rates. Over the long run, purchasing power parity (or the "law of one price") is a reasonably good approximation of economic reality; and thus, these changes tend to be almost completely offsetting.

But because there is often a lag between a

---

11. In the event of an expropriation, the expected return is not likely to be zero. Thus, it is also necessary to estimate the expected value of the net compensation provided in such a case. While difficult to foresee with any precision, such post-expropriation compensation can be expected to come from several sources:

• Direct compensation paid to the firm by the local government. (This compensation can be delayed, as in Chile, for example, where many MNCs were expropriated by the Allende government with little or no compensation. When Allende was overthrown, however, his successors began returning property and otherwise compensating these MNCs.)

• Indirect compensation, such as the management contracts received by oil companies whose properties were nationalized by the Venezuelan government.

• Payment received from political risk insurance. (Insurance payments may lag expropriation by several years as well.)

• Tax deductions in the home country associated with such an extraordinary loss.

• A reduction in the amount of capital that must be repaid by the project equal to the unamortized portion of any local borrowing. It is inconceivable that a firm which has had a foreign operation expropriated would pay back any local borrowing except as part of a total compensation package worked out with the government. Suppliers of capital from outside the host country would normally be repaid by the parent company (whether or not loans were guaranteed) in order to preserve the parent's credit reputation.

12. In 1978, I published a paper developing a variety of analytical formulas to deal with the impact of expropriation and currency controls on a project's expected NPV. See Alan C. Shapiro (1978), "Capital Budgeting for the Multinational Corporation," *Financial Management*, Spring, pp. 7–16. In this article, I provide a more complex and less artificial illustration of how such cash flow adjustments for expropriation could be made.

13. See Lessard, Donald R. (1979), "Evaluating Foreign Projects: An Adjusted Present Value Approach." In Donald R. Lessard, ed. *International Financial Management*, Boston: Warren, Gorham & Lamont; or Shapiro, Alan C. (1982), *Multinational Financial Management*, Boston: Allyn and Bacon.

given change in relative rates of inflation and the exchange rate change necessary to maintain international equilibrium, it is worthwhile to analyze each effect separately. This is particularly true when government intervention occurs, such as in a fixed-rate system or a managed float. Furthermore, local price controls may not allow the normal adjustment of internal prices to take place. This will result in relative price changes, leading to deviations from purchasing power parity.

The possibility of relative price changes within a foreign economy can be incorporated easily by altering projected nominal local currency project cash flows. To capture the effect of exchange rate fluctuations, the MNC should list for each period the various possible exchange rates along with the anticipated local currency (LC) cash flow associated with each particular currency scenario. By assigning probabilities to these different exchange rates, management can then calculate for each period an expected home currency cash flow. This can be done by first converting each LC cash flow into its home currency equivalent, and then multiplying by the probability assigned to that scenario.[14]

Thus, the present value of future cash flows from a foreign project can be calculated in a two-stage procedure: (1) convert nominal foreign currency cash flows into nominal home currency terms; and (2) discount those nominal flows at the nominal expected domestic required rate of return. This procedure, to reiterate, will yield the same results as first converting nominal foreign currency cash flows into *real* home currency terms, and then discounting them at the *real* domestic required rate of return.

The Cost of Capital for Foreign Investments

A central question that must be addressed by the multinational corporation is whether the required rate of return on foreign projects should be higher, lower, or the same as that for comparable domestic projects. To answer this question, it is necessary to examine one of the most complex issues in international financial management: the cost of capital for multinational firms.

Recall that the opportunity cost of capital for a given investment is the minimum risk-adjusted return required by shareholders of the firm for undertaking that investment. As such, it is the basic standard of corporate performance. Unless the investment generates sufficient funds to provide suppliers of capital with their expected returns, the firm's value will suffer. This return requirement is met only if the net present value of future project cash flows, using the project's cost of capital as the discount rate, is positive. An alternative, and generally equivalent, investment criterion is to use the cost of capital as a cut-off rate for the internal rates of return on proposed investments.

The development of appropriate cost-of-capital measures for multinational firms is tied to how those measures will be used. When used as discount rates to aid in the global resource allocation process, they should reflect the value to firms of engaging in specific activities. Thus, the emphasis here is on the cost of capital for specific foreign projects rather than for the firm as a whole. As pointed out earlier, unless the financial structures and commercial risks are similar for all projects considered, the indiscriminate use of an overall cost of capital for project evaluation is inappropriate. Different discount rates should be used to value prospective investments that are expected to change the risk complexion of the firm.

My approach to determining the project-specific required return on equity is based on modern capital market theory.[15] According to this theory, an equilibrium relationship exists between an asset's required return and its associated risk. This relationship is formulated by the Capital Asset Pricing Model. As mentioned earlier, the CAPM is based on the notion that intelligent risk-averse shareholders will seek to diversify their risks and, as a consequence, the only risk that will be rewarded with a risk premium is systematic or "non-diversifiable" risk. Systematic risk, as measured by beta, is the sensitivity of an investment's value to changes in general economic conditions. Statistically, it is the covariance of a security's (or any investment's) returns with broad, market-wide average returns.

Discount Rates for Foreign Investments

The importance of the CAPM for the international company is that the relevant component of

14. It is impossible to do justice to the complex question of exchange risk management in the allotted space. In the third issue of this journal, Brad Cornell and I will present an extended treatment of this issue alone.

15. For a good review of this theory, see William F. Sharpe (1978), *Investments*, Englewood Cliffs, NJ: Prentice-Hall.

The total risk associated with variations in cash flows appears to be reduced by international investment.

risk in pricing a firm's stock is its systematic risk; in other words, that portion of return variability that cannot be eliminated through diversification, whether by investors or corporations. Much of the systematic or general market risk affecting a company, at least as measured using a domestic stock index such as the S&P 500 or the NYSE index, is caused by the cyclical nature of the national economy in which the company is operating. For this reason, it is highly possible that multinationals, by having operations in a number of countries whose economic cycles are not perfectly in phase, may be reducing the variability of their earnings through international diversification.

A number of studies suggest this, in fact, is the case.[16] Such studies suggest that there is little correlation among the earnings of the various national components of MNCs. Thus, to the extent that foreign cash flows are not perfectly correlated with those of domestic investments, the total risk (systematic and unsystematic) associated with variations in cash flows appears to be *reduced*, not increased, by international investment. Furthermore, most of the economic and political risks faced by the multinational corporation appear to be unsystematic and can, therefore, be eliminated through stockholders' diversification.

Rather surprisingly, it is the less-developed countries (LDCs), where political risks are greatest, which are likely to provide the greatest diversification benefits. This is because the economies of LDCs are less closely tied to the U.S., or to any other Western, industrialized, economy. By contrast, the correlation among the economic cycles of developed countries is considerably stronger; and the diversification benefits from investing in industrialized countries, from the standpoint of an American or Western European MNC, are proportionately less.

It should be noted, however, that the systematic risk of projects even in relatively isolated LDCs is unlikely to be far below the average for all projects, because these countries are still tied into the world economy. The important point about LDCs, then, is that their ratio of systematic to total risk is generally quite low; their systematic risk, while perhaps slightly lower, is probably not significantly less than that of industrialized countries.[17]

Even if a nation's economy is not closely linked to the world economy, the systematic risk of a project located in that country might still be rather large. For example, a foreign copper-mining venture will probably face systematic risk very similar to that faced by an identical extractive project in the United States, regardless of whether the foreign project is located in Canada, Chile, or Zaire. The reason is that the major element of systematic risk in any extractive project is related to variations in the price of the mineral being extracted, which is set in a world market. The world market price is in turn a function of world-wide demand, which itself is systematically related to the state of the world economy. By contrast, a market-oriented project in an LDC, whose risk depends largely on the evolution of the domestic market in that country, is likely to have a systematic risk that is small both in relative and absolute terms.

One of the major issues in selecting a discount rate for foreign investments is choosing the relevant market portfolio for evaluating a project's systematic risk, or its beta coefficient. Is the relevant base portfolio against which covariances are measured the domestic portfolio of the investor or the world market portfolio? Selecting the appropriate portfolio is important because a risk that is systematic in the context of the home country market portfolio may well be diversifiable in the context of the world portfolio. If this is the case, then using the domestic market portfolio to calculate beta will result in a higher required return than if risk were measured using the world market portfolio. On the other hand, a risk that is unsystematic in a domestic context may be systematic in a global context, with corresponding implications for the measurement of beta. Thus, the choice of a base portfolio could well affect the present value of a project and, hence, its acceptability.

Which market, then, domestic or global, is the relevant context for measuring the risks of international investment? The appropriate market portfolio to use in measuring beta depends largely on one's view of world capital markets. More precisely, it depends on whether world markets are integrated or not. If they are, then the world portfolio is the correct choice. If they are not, the correct choice is

16. See, for example, Benjamin I. Cohen, *Multinational Firms and Asian Exports*, New Haven, Conn.: Yale University Press, 1975; and Alan Rugman, "Risk Reduction by International Diversification," *Journal of International Business Studies*, Fall 1976, pp. 75–80.

17. This point was made by Fischer Black.

Due to various government regulations and other market imperfections, the integration of world capital markets is not complete.

the domestic portfolio. The test of capital markets' integration is whether international assets are priced in a common context; that is, world capital markets are integrated to the extent that security prices offer all investors worldwide the same trade-off between systematic risk and real expected return. In a perfectly integrated market, the risk premium expected by investors for holding a foreign stock would reflect that stock's risk relative only to a globally-diversified portfolio.

The truth probably lies somewhere in between.[18] Capital markets are now integrated to a great extent, and can be expected to become ever more so with time. But, due to various government regulations and other market imperfections, that integration is not complete.

Accordingly, my present recommendation to American managers is to measure the betas of international projects against the U.S. market portfolio. My reasons for this are three:
1. It ensures comparability of foreign with domestic projects which are evaluated using betas calculated relative to a U.S. market index.
2. There is as yet no readily accessible global market index.
3. The relatively minor amount of international diversification attempted (as yet) by U.S. investors suggests that the relevant portfolio from their standpoint is the U.S. market portfolio.

International Capital Market Integration and Corporate International Diversification

To the extent that international investments actually reduce the systematic risk of the firm, management is justified in using proportionately lower hurdle rates in evaluating such investments. If, in addition to this condition, capital markets are not fully integrated internationally (so that, say, an American investor seeking to invest in the Brazilian economy could do so only by buying the shares of an American multinational with Brazilian operations), then international diversification by multinationals could be providing investors with benefits they can not achieve simply by buying foreign securities. This means that where there are barriers to international portfolio investments, MNCs could accept lower rates of return than firms operating only locally because of their ability to diversify investment risks internationally.

The net effect of such financial market imperfections, then, may be to enable MNCs to undertake overseas projects that would otherwise be unattractive. But if international portfolio diversification can be accomplished as easily and as cheaply by individual investors, then although the required rates of return on MNC securities would be lower to reflect the reduced co-variability of MNC earnings caused by international diversification, there would no further reduction of the discount rate to reflect investors' willingness to pay a premium for the indirect diversification provided by the shares of MNCs.

The fact is, though, very little foreign portfolio investment is actually undertaken by U.S. investors. This lack of investment in foreign securities is normally explained by various legal, informational, and economic barriers that serve to segment national capital markets, deterring investors seeking to invest abroad.[19] These barriers include currency controls, specific tax regulations, relatively less efficient and less developed capital markets abroad, exchange risk, and the lack of readily accessible and comparable information on foreign securities. The lack of adequate information can significantly increase the perceived riskiness of foreign securities, giving investors an added incentive to keep their money at home.

Furthermore, no other country in the world has the breadth or depth of industry that the United States has. Hence, to diversify adequately within foreign economies, it will usually be necessary to acquire shares of multinational firms in industries where indigenous firms do not exist. Diversifying into the computer industry in Venezuela, for example, means buying the shares of IBM or some other multinational computer manufacturer with Venezuelan operations. To the extent that their international investment opportunities are so restricted, U.S. investors may be able to achieve low-cost international diversification only by purchasing the shares of U.S.-based MNCs. Moreover, investors in countries like France and Sweden that restrict overseas portfolio investment would appear to benefit even more by being able to purchase shares in domestically-based multinationals. All these conditions would lead investors to pay a premium for the

18. Michael Adler and Bernard Dumas discuss this and related issues at great length in "International Portfolio Choice and Corporation Finance: A Survey," a CESA working paper soon to be published in *The Journal of Finance*.

19. For a good description of the various barriers to international portfolio diversification, see Gunter Dufey's "Institutional Constraints and Incentives on International Portfolio Investment," *International Portfolio Investment*, U.S. Department of the Treasury OASIA, 1976.

Very little foreign portfolio investment is actually undertaken by U.S. investors.

international diversification provided by the shares of multinational corporations.

Because the world's economies are not perfectly synchronized, and also because of these imperfections in world capital markets, the value of international diversification to investors appears to be significant. Donald Lessard[20] and Bruno Solnik,[21] among others, have presented evidence that national factors have a stronger impact on security returns than any common world factor. In addition, they find that returns from the different national

equity markets have relatively low correlations with each other. (See Exhibit 1)

In short, Lessard and Solnik's results suggest that international diversification significantly reduces the risk of portfolio returns. In fact, the variance of an internationally diversified portfolio appears to be as little as 33 percent of the variance of individual securities (as compared to 50 percent for a diversified portfolio of U.S. securities alone). In other words, the risk of an internationally-diversified portfolio is about one third less than the risk of

a domestically-diversified portfolio. (See Exhibit 2)

Thus, the ability of multinationals to provide an indirect means of international diversification should be an important advantage to international investors. As noted earlier, however, such corporate diversification will prove beneficial to MNC shareholders only if there are barriers to direct international portfolio diversification by individual investors.

Nevertheless, regardless of whether investors are internationally diversified or not, the apparently lower degree of systematic risk of foreign investments means that the required returns on such projects will still probably be lower, not higher, than required returns on comparable domestic projects.

EXHIBIT 1

Risk Measures for Foreign Market Portfolios[a]

Country	Annualized Standard Deviation of Returns (%)[b]	Correlation with U.S. Market[c]	Market Risk (beta) from U.S. Perspective
France	26.4	.50	.71
West Germany	20.4	.43	.47
Japan	20.1	.40	.43
The Netherlands	21.9	.61	.72
Switzerland	22.7	.63	.77
Great Britain	41.0	.51	1.13
United States	18.5	1.00	1.00

[a] All figures estimated form data for 1973–1977 period
[b] Measured in U.S. dollars
[c] The S&P 500 Stock Index is used to represent the U.S. market

Source: Donald R. Lessard, "An Update on Gains from International Diversification," 1977. This table appeared in Donald R. Lessard, "Evaluating Foreign Projects: An Adjusted Present Value Approach," in Donald R. Lessard, ed., *International Financial Management* (Boston: Warren, Gorham & Lamont, 1979), p. 590. Reprinted by permission of the author.

EXHIBIT 2

The Potential Gains from International Diversification

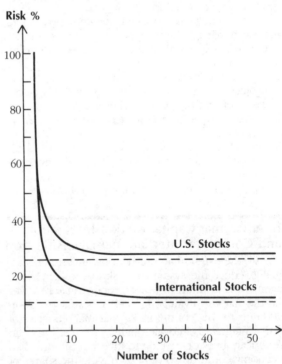

Source: Bruno Solnik, "Why Not Diversify Internationally Rather Than Domestically?," *Financial Analysts' Journal*, July–August 1974, p. 51. Reprinted by permission of publisher.

20. Lessard, Donald R. (1974), "World, National, and Industry Factors in Equity Returns," *Journal of Finance*, May, pp. 379–391.

21. Solnik, Bruno H. (1974), "Why Not Diversify Internationally?" *Financial Analysts Journal*, July–August, pp. 48–54.

At the very least, therefore, when evaluating prospective foreign investments, executives of multinational firms should seriously question the use of a risk *premium* to account for the added political and economic risks of overseas operations.

International Capital Budgeting and Corporate Strategy

The capital budgeting process typically involves calculation of the net present values of the various investment opportunities, domestic and foreign, facing the firm. Those projects with positive net present values (excess returns) are accepted; those that fail this test are rejected. The emphasis is on estimating future cash flows and required rates of return.

Only rarely, however, is the issue raised as to the origin of investments yielding excess returns. It is taken for granted that they do exist and can be found using fairly straightforward capital budgeting techniques. Yet, it should be recognized that identifying positive net present value projects in this way is very similar to (and as unreliable as) selecting under-valued securities on the basis of fundamental analysis. The latter can only be done with confidence if financial market imperfections exist which prevent asset prices from reflecting their equilibrium values. Similarly, the existence of economic rents—excess returns that lead to positive net present values—results largely from imperfections in real markets. Such imperfections take the form of monopolistic control over product or factor supplies. In less technical terms, companies can have a distinctive superiority in knowledge of specific markets, technological expertise, trademarks, patents—all of which exist in the real as distinguished from the financial sector of the business.

The imperfections that presently characterize world capital markets are not likely to be around for long. But, unlike the financial sector, where prices are continuously and rapidly adjusting to reflect new information, and where all companies can expect to get a fair deal based on their expected risks and returns, imperfections in the real markets may last for some time. Technological edges, production cost efficiencies, superior management capability,

vertical integration—all these factors can enable companies to earn consistently abnormal returns. In the long run, though, even such differences can be expected to be neutralized by the inevitable forces of competition.

But, over the short- to intermediate-term, the availability of positive NPV projects depends largely on a company's ability to exploit imperfections in real markets. The essential focus of the corporate planner should thus be on identifying, strengthening, and then capitalizing on those comparative advantages which distinguish it from its competitors, both actual and potential. A thorough understanding of such imperfections, and the company's ability to exploit them, should provide the qualitative basis for determining—prior to any systematic financial analysis—which foreign investments are likely to have positive net present values.

Various studies of the phenomenon of direct foreign investment[22] have helped to identify those market imperfections that have allowed, or encouraged, firms to become multinational. Among those market imperfections contributing to the rise of the multinational are government regulations and controls, such as tariffs and capital controls, that impose barriers to free trade and private portfolio investment.

Real market imperfections, however, in the areas of firm-specific skills and information are probably the most important single reason for the rise of multinationals. This is the explanation provided by Richard Caves (1971),[23] who sought to understand not only why firms engage in direct foreign investment, but also why they choose that option over licensing or exporting. Caves's work on multinationals, which relies on the theory of industrial organization, points to certain general circumstances under which each approach—exporting, licensing, or local production—will be the preferred alternative for exploiting foreign markets.

According to Caves, multinationals have intangible capital in the form of trademarks, patents, general marketing skills, and other organizational abilities. If this intangible capital can be embodied in the form of products without much adaptation, then exporting will generally be the preferred method of market penetration. Where the firm's knowledge takes the form of specific product or process tech-

22. Direct foreign investment, or DFI, is defined as the acquisition abroad of physical assets such as plant and equipment.

23. Caves, Richard E. (1971), "International Corporations: The Industrial Economics of Foreign Investment," *Economica*, February, pp. 1–27.

nologies that can be written down and transmitted objectively, then foreign expansion will usually take the licensing route.

Often, however, this intangible capital takes the form of organizational skills. Among these specialized skills are knowledge about how best to service a market (including new product development and adaptation), quality control, advertising, distribution, after-sales service, and the general ability to read changing market desires and translate them into saleable products. Because it is difficult, if not impossible, to separate these services and sell them apart from the firm, we expect this form of market imperfection to lead to corporate attempts to exert control directly through the establishment of foreign affiliates. There will also, of course, be added costs in establishing and administering an operation overseas. Consequently, as Ian Giddy has pointed out, "The market in an intermediate good (product, factor, service or knowledge) will be internalized if and only if the benefits from circumventing imperfections outweigh the administrative and other costs of central control."[24]

Because local firms have an inherent cost advantage over foreign investors (who must bear the costs of operating in an unfamiliar environment together with the stigma of being foreign), multinationals can succeed abroad only if their monopolistic advantages cannot be purchased or duplicated by local competitors. Eventually, however, all barriers to entry erode, and the multinational firm must find new sources of competitive advantage to defend itself against the inevitable increase in competition both at home and abroad.

My approach to international strategic planning can be reduced to the following four interrelated propositions:

1. Effective corporate planning should be directed toward identifying those investments likely to provide the most profitable returns. (Without suggesting that the firm adopt a myopically short-run view, profitability should be regarded as the prerequisite, not merely a by-product, of multinational survival and expansion.) The strategic response of a firm to a competitive threat, which includes the decision to invest in operations overseas, should be designed to exploit its distinctive advantages. Such advantages will stem, in large part, from imperfections in international product or factor markets. Effective corporate planning, accordingly, should be grounded in a thorough understanding of the company's competitive advantages, and on the associated barriers to entry that would prevent competitors from eroding those advantages.

2. The global approach to investment planning requires a systematic evaluation of individual entry strategies in foreign markets, a comparison of the options, and selection of the best method of entry. Many multinationals seem to disregard the fact that a market's sales potential, and thus its profitability, is at least partly a function of the entry strategy.[25]

3. Investment planning requires a continuous audit of the effectiveness of current entry methods. As knowledge about a foreign market increases, or sales potential grows, the optimal market penetration strategy will likely change.

4. A systematic investment analysis requires the use of appropriate evaluation criteria. Despite the added complexities of overseas investment evaluation (and perhaps *because* of the difficulties they present), most multinationals continue to use simple rules of thumb in making international investment decisions. Analytical techniques are used only as a rough screening device or as a final checkoff before project approval. While simple rules of thumb are obviously easier and cheaper to use, there is a danger of obsolescence and misuse as the fundamental assumptions underlying their applicability change.

The use of the theoretically sound and recommended present value analysis is anything but straightforward. The strategic rationale underlying many investment proposals can be translated into traditional capital budgeting criteria, but it is often necessary to look beyond the returns associated with the project itself to determine its true impact on the overall, worldwide risk and return of the multinational. For example, an investment made to save a market threatened by competition or trade barriers must be judged on the basis of the sales that

24. Giddy, Ian H. (1978), "The Demise of the Product Cycle Model in International Business Theory," *Columbia Journal of World Business*, Sp., p. 93.

25. For example, a study by the Conference Board in 1966 (*U.S. Production Abroad and the Balance of Payments*, New York: The Conference Board) showed that 62 percent of firms surveyed made no attempt to determine the net profits from their existing foreign licensing agreements. Instead, they simply treated these agreements as a free good, ignoring the opportunity costs that would have been revealed by a comparison of alternatives. Similarly, a survey by David Rutenberg ("Shunning the Risks of Eastern Europe," Queens University Working Paper (1978)) of 120 companies disclosed that, on average, these companies accepted only about 11% of the joint venture proposals they received, rejecting 83% out of hand without evaluating them. Also, only one-third had a policy of actively searching for joint venture opportunities.

would otherwise have been lost. As another example, export creation and direct investment often go hand in hand. ICI, the British chemical company, found that its exports to Europe were enhanced by its strong market position there in other product lines—a position due mainly to ICI's local manufacturing facilities. Such cash flow synergies should be reflected in the capital budgeting analysis.

Summary and Conclusions

Because of the length of this article, I want to review a few of the major issues in multinational capital budgeting it examines, and to offer an outline of the solutions it proposes.

The first major complication of international investment addressed is accounting for the significant differences that can arise between project (or foreign subsidiary) and parent cash flows. To deal with this problem, I offered a three-stage procedure for incorporating such differences into the traditional discounted cash flow framework. The first involves the projection of expected after-tax cash flows strictly from the perspective of the local project or subsidiary managers. The second step was to estimate the timing and magnitude of both actual and allowable repatriations (which also gives the multinational's management a means of estimating their marginal tax rate on foreign-source earnings). The final phase attempts to project any effect that the given investment would have on worldwide corporate cash flows.

Next, I offered a rationale for adjusting project cash flows instead of the discount rate to reflect the key political and economic risks that MNCs face abroad. Cash flow adjustments are preferred on theoretical grounds: most distinctively foreign risks are unsystematic or diversifiable, and thus do not raise investors' required rates of return. Adjustments of cash flows are also preferred because management generally has access to more and better information about the specific effect of such risks on cash flow projections. The popular practice of adjusting a foreign project's required rate of return to reflect incremental risk does not usually allow for adequate consideration of the time pattern and magnitude of the risk being evaluated. Using a uniformly higher discount rate to reflect additional risk indiscriminately penalizes future cash flows relative to less distant ones.

Some investments, however, do entail more systematic risk than others, and such risks should be reflected in project discount rates. The key question, therefore, in setting discount rates for foreign projects is whether the incremental risks are systematic. The use of an international risk premium ignores the fact that the risk of an overseas investment (which should be viewed in the context of all other investments of the firm's shareholders, domestic as well as foreign) may be considerably lower than the total risk of the project. For this reason, the automatic inclusion of a premium for risk when evaluating foreign projects is not a necessary element of conservatism. It is instead a management shortcut that may penalize the firm's shareholders by causing management to reject positive net present value foreign investments.

Unlike the diversification sought by wholly domestic conglomerates (especially in the 60s), there may be significant benefits to multinationals from international diversification. The theoretical justification for such benefits depends on the extent to which international capital markets are imperfectly integrated, thus preventing investors from achieving such diversification on their own. On the assumption that world capital markets are not fully integrated, multinational managers may be justified in actually *lowering* the required rates of return on foreign projects that offer significant additional diversification.

Finally, the article offers a theoretical rationale for the multinational firm, one which should serve as the basis for international strategic planning. Such a rationale should provide the qualitative criteria for the initial screening of foreign investment opportunities. The existence and success of multinationals is attributed largely to their success in defending and exploiting barriers to entry created by product and factor market imperfections. Multinational corporate planning, accordingly, should be based on identifying and preserving those competitive advantages that distinguish it from its competitors. Given the inevitability of competition, and of the eventual lowering of barriers of entry, corporate planners must continually reassess both their competitive vulnerabilities and strengths.

References

Adler, Michael and Bernard Dumas, "International Portfolio Choice and Corporation Finance: A Survey," CESA Working Paper (1981), forthcoming *Journal of Finance.*

Caves, Richard E., "International Corporations: The Industrial Economics of Foreign Investment," *Economica,* (February 1971), 1–27.

Cohen, Benjamin I., *Multinational Firms and Asian Exports,* New Haven, Conn.: Yale University Press (1975).

Dufey, Gunter, "Institutional Constraints and Incentives on International Portfolio Investment," *International Portfolio Investment,* U.S. Department of the Treasury OASIA (1975).

Giddy, Ian H., "An Integrated Theory of Exchange Rate Equilibrium," *Journal of Financial and Quantitative Analysis* (December 1976), 883–892.

Giddy, Ian H., "The Demise of the Product Cycle Model in International Business Theory," *Columbia Journal of World Business,* (Spring 1978), 90–97.

Hawkins, Robert G., Norman Mintz, and Michael Provissiero, "Government Takeovers of U.S. Foreign Affiliates," *Journal of International Business Studies,* (Spring 1976), 3–15.

Lessard, Donald R., "World, National, and Industry Factors in Equity Returns," *Journal of Finance,* (May 1974), 379–391.

Lessard, Donald R., "Evaluating Foreign Projects: An Adjusted Present Value Approach," in Donald R. Lessard (ed.) *International Financial Management,* Boston: Warren, Gorham & Lamont (1979).

Rugman, Alan, "Risk Reduction by International Diversification," *Journal of International Business Studies,* (Fall 1976), 75–80.

Rutenberg, David P., "Shunning the Risks of Eastern Europe," Queens University Working Paper (1978).

Shapiro, Alan C., "Capital Budgeting for the Multinational Corporation," *Financial Management,* (Spring 1978), 7–16.

Shapiro, Alan C., "Managing Blocked Currency Funds," University of Southern California Working Paper (1980).

Shapiro, Alan C., "Managing Political Risk: A Policy Approach," *Columbia Journal of World Business,* (Fall 1981), 63–70.

Shapiro, Alan C., *Multinational Financial Management,* Boston: Allyn and Bacon (1982).

Solnik, Bruno H. "Why Not Diversify Internationally?" *Financial Analysts Journal,* (July–August 1974), 48–54.

Truitt, J. Frederick, "Expropriation of Private Foreign Investment: Summary of the Post-World War II Experience of American and British Investors in the Less Developed Countries," *Journal of International Business Studies,* (Fall 1970) 21–34.

Guidelines for Global Financing Choices

Donald R. Lessard,
Massachusetts Institute of Technology

Alan C. Shapiro,
University of Southern California

Introduction

The financing choices of a firm operating within a single country are typically limited to the type of instruments it issues and the timing of those issues. Multinational corporations (MNCs) are faced with other financing choices as well. They must decide on the currency of issue, the jurisdiction of issue, and the corporate legal vehicle through which the issue is made. Also, if funds are raised by a legal unit other than the one where they are needed, the MNC must select the form of inter-affiliate transfer of the funds. In making these choices, management must consider the availability of funds, their relative costs, and the extent to which such financing either increases or offsets the firm's operating risks.

Besides choosing the best financing vehicles, financial executives of multinationals must address a number of other important financing issues. One concerns the firm's global financial structure. Should each affiliate have a capital structure based on local norms, or instead attempt to mirror the firm's worldwide debt-equity target? And to what extent should this decision be influenced by the tax deductibility of interest payments and also by considerations of "agency costs"—those potential problems associated with the incentives and the accountability of local subsidiary management that can be affected by the firm's method of financing its subsidiaries?

Another issue concerns the cost and risk associated with debt denominated in different currencies. For example, should Volkswagen finance its U.S. operations with deutschemark debt at 8 percent or dollar debt at 12 percent? This choice will be influenced by expectations about future movements in the deutschemark/dollar exchange rate relative to the 4 percent interest differential, and also by the nature and degree of exchange risk facing Volkswagen.

The possibility of credit and exchange controls and other forms of political risk will also influence the firm's choice of how to finance its overseas operations. For example, political risk considerations will determine, in part, whether firms investing in Mexico will do so with parent equity or debt, or by borrowing from Mexican banks. Such considerations will also affect the extent to which the parent's investment will be guaranteed by an agency of the MNC's home government.

As a general rule, the corporate financing decision reduces to a trade-off between two objectives: minimizing the expected after-tax cost of financing and keeping risks within acceptable levels. Evaluating this trade-off may be a much more complicated exercise for multinationals than for purely domestic companies. For not only do tax laws vary from country to country, but the risks can also be of a kind and magnitude not encountered at home. Finance theory, to be sure, has contended that stockholders can benefit only from the firm's reduction of so-called "systematic" or market risk (the risk of the firm as part of the market portfolio of stocks). In the case of multinationals especially, however, we argue that financial executives must take account of the potential effects of idiosyncratic or "unsystematic" risks— those associated specifically with the industry, the country of operations, and with the firm itself—in determining how to fund its activities.

Establishing a worldwide financial policy is thus an extraordinarily complex undertaking. It is made more so by the lack of an explicit analytical framework for quantifying these trade-offs. International finance scholars have proposed partial solutions to the problem,[1] but few comprehensive solutions have even been attempted. Further, those

Finance theory maintains that reducing corporate risks which are diversifiable at the portfolio level does not benefit stockholders.

"total system" mathematical programming approaches that have been proposed are far too complex for practical application. They also typically omit important aspects of the problem.[2]

Unfortunately, it is not currently within our power (if indeed it will ever be) to quantify the impact on shareholder wealth of the various factors involved in designing such a plan. And how these factors interact with each other seems even less amenable to measurement. Thus, our objective in this article is necessarily modest. We seek to develop a set of reasonable guidelines for multinationals in evaluating their financing options. Such guidelines are "reasonable" in the sense that they are based on our understanding of how financial markets function.

Our proposed approach for evaluating global financing choices breaks down the overall problem into three largely separable objectives:

1. minimizing taxes,
2. managing currency and political risks, and
3. exploiting financial market distortions.[3]

These three objectives can be pursued through financing strategies that can be classified either as "passive" or "active." Passive financing strategies are those based on the assumption that management has no special information or forecasting skills; active strategies are based on an assumed ability to systematically "beat the market" in forecasting prices or exchange rate movements. In this sense, both arbitrage and hedging are passive strategies, while speculation is active.

The remainder of this article is organized in six parts. We begin by discussing the basic considerations inherent in all financing choices. In the next three sections, we explore the three major considerations of multinational financing: minimizing taxes, managing risks, and exploiting market distortions. In the fifth section we discuss how these three objectives relate to the firm's overall capital structure. Finally, we identify the conditions under which each of these three financing considerations are truly separable.

Basic Considerations in International Financing Choices

In line with mainstream financial theory, we assume that the goal of the firm is to maximize the market value of its shares. The market value of the shares, in turn, is said to reflect the present value of the firm's expected future after-tax cash flows, discounted at a rate which reflects the market's assessment of the firm's systematic or non-diversifiable risk—that is, the risk of the firm from the perspective of a well-diversified stockholder.[4]

What evidence do we have that the market "prices" risk in this way? Research on capital markets demonstrates that, on average and over time, stockholders expect and receive returns on their investment commensurate with the risks they bear. The higher the risks the higher the average returns. And as the bulk of the evidence also suggests, average returns on investment correlate most strongly (as predicted by the Capital Asset Pricing Model (CAPM)) with measures of systematic or non-diversifiable risk. This systematic or "market" risk, generally measured by "beta," is the sensitivity of a firm's stock price to market-wide and general economic developments. The CAPM thus implies that stock market investors are concerned, for the most part, *not* with the total variability (i.e., "total risk") of the firm's cash flows, but only with the "co-variability" of those flows with the performance of the economy as a whole.

Finance theory thus maintains that, in general, reducing corporate risks which are diversifiable at the portfolio level does not benefit stockholders. Most company specific risks, provided they do not significantly raise the possibility of bankruptcy, can be managed more efficiently by stockholders.

In this article, however, we are going to depart somewhat from the implications of the CAPM for risk management to argue that the total risk of the firm's equity (that is, diversifiable as well as non-diversifiable risks) must be taken into account in

1. For a review of early studies in this area see Naumann-Etienne (1974). More recently, Shapiro (1975) has examined the impact of taxes on financial choices, Remmers (1980) has extended Shapiro's work to include uncertainty, Dufey and Giddy (1978) have emphasized the implications of efficient international financial markets for financing choices.

2. These include Ness (1972) who incorporates various financial constraints in a cost-minimizing linear program, Schydlowsky (in Robbins and Stobaugh (1973)) who develops a similar model, Lietaer (1971) who incorporates uncertainty in a quadratic programming model but does not address taxes, and most recently Kornbluth and Vinso (1981) who stress system versus local country capital structures but whose treatment of currency expectations is highly simplified. Several commercial models have been developed, but most have fallen into disuse.

3. This breakdown of the problem follows Lessard (1979b), pp. 349–351.

4. In this paper we ignore the more complex issues of valuation in a multicurrency, multicountry environment where different investors may display different currency preferences. We believe that this is not a serious problem since investors can readily offset the currency component of a firm's equity returns in their own portfolios as long as they know what that component is. This view outlined in Lessard and Stulz (1983) contradicts the position taken by Wihlborg (1980).

The uncertainty created by volatile earnings and cash flows may hinder management's ability to take a long view of the firm's prospects.

multinational financial decision-making. We are not arguing that the presence of firm- and country-specific risks raises the market's discount rate, but rather that such diversifiable risks, if unmanaged, may have significant effects on the expected *level* of the firm's cash flow. Excessive earnings variability, for example, may affect a firm's access to credit and, hence, its ability to benefit from interest tax shields. It may also restrict its ability to raise money for attractive projects (especially if the alternative of an equity issue requires the firm to disseminate information of value to its competitors). Also, it may influence the willingness of suppliers, customers, and employees to commit themselves to relationships with the firm. Finally, and perhaps most important, the uncertainty created by volatile earnings and cash flows may hinder management's ability to take a long view of the firm's prospects and make the most of opportunities.

With these considerations in mind, we have "rewritten" the objective function of the firm as follows:

Maximize $V_F = \sum V_i - P(\sigma)$ $\qquad$ **(1)**

where V_i is the present value of each of the firm's activities (divisions, business units, or projects) and $P(\sigma)$ is a penalty factor that reflects the impact on expected after-tax cash flows of the total risk of the firm's equity. According to this formulation, the value of the firm *is reduced* by an increase in the expected variability of cash flow.[5]

The crucial implication of this inclusion of a penalty factor for total risk is that the multinational might want to "lay off" those "unsystematic" risks which, by contributing substantially to the expected variability of its cash flow, may endanger the financing and operating flexibility of the company. For example, it may want to purchase insurance against major casualties, provided the insurance is fairly priced to reflect the expected probability and size of the loss. It also may want to hedge major risks associated with changes in commodity prices and foreign exchange—again, provided the relevant contracts are fairly priced according to the CAPM. Although such hedging transactions will have a zero present value in their own right, they will reduce this penalty factor associated with total risk at the level of the corporation.

A further rationale for hedging at the level of the corporation is that limited information and incomplete markets can prevent investors from replicating the firm's hedging activities at an equivalent cost. This is especially likely in the case of political risks, which the firm can sometimes reduce or shift through appropriate financing decisions.

In the case of very large, well-capitalized multinationals like IBM, with operations spread throughout the world, the probability of such idiosyncratic risks causing financial distress is small. Under these conditions, this penalty factor should probably be valued at zero. For, at any given time, such multinationals are taking many small, partly offsetting bets on exchange rates, inflation rates, political stability, etc. And when viewed relative to the capitalization of the company, such risks may add up to a very low risk profile.

In such cases, the multinational's financing choices would depend only on the additive present values of each transaction. The only choices which would matter under such circumstances are those that reduce taxes or those that are "bargains"—that is, financing options priced at below market rates. Bargains can be the result of concessional financing policies, distortions due to restrictions imposed on transactions, or information not yet reflected in market prices.

Passive Versus Active Policies

Financing choices often involve taking advantage of perceived bargains as well as reducing taxes or risks. Using an analogy from investment management, we can draw a distinction between "passive" and "active" financing decisions. Passive financing decisions or strategies are those that don't involve any special information; they are based on the assumption that all financing options are fairly priced—that is, there are no bargains because markets work well. Active financing strategies depend on the ability to spot bargains and to exploit them by taking positions.

Passive strategies include tax arbitrage, riskless financial market arbitrage, and hedging. In contrast, active considerations assume market inefficiency or distortion, and they lead to speculation.[6] This cate-

---

5. Adler and Dumas (1977) employ a similar objective function.

6. Although it is impossible to differentiate between the hedging and speculative motives either in theory or practice, we assume for purposes of this paper that hedging involves the desire for pure risk reduction whereas speculation involves the willingness to trade off risk and return.

Holding risk constant, the difference in interest rates between countries should equal the expected change in the exchange rate during the term of the loan.

gory includes those risky financing opportunities that depend on government-induced market distortions. But, as we shall argue later, exploiting such opportunities may not necessarily depend on special information or forecasting skill possessed by the firm.

Passive choices logically precede active choices. Thus, in any situation a firm should first determine what choices it would make if it had no special information. Only then should it consider altering its financing choices to exploit a perceived bargain. This would mean weighing the present value of the bargain, taking into account its systematic risk, against its impact on the total risk of the firm. For example, a firm may decide that, all other things equal, it should finance its affiliate with yen debt in order to reduce its yen exposure. Suppose, however, that the firm has access to French francs at a below market rate. Its choice, then, would depend on the trade-off between lower expected financing costs and the higher penalty associated with increased exchange risk. Arbitrage opportunities are the exception to the rule here, since they have positive net present values without having any impact on corporate risk.

Minimizing Taxes

The asymmetrical tax treatment of various components of financial cost, such as the treatment of dividend payments versus interest expense and of exchange losses versus exchange gains, often means that equality of before-tax costs will lead to inequality of after-tax costs. Moreover, the U.S. and many European countries impose withholding taxes on dividends and interest paid to foreign investors by domestic corporations. And this has led inevitably to a proliferation of foreign finance subsidiaries designed to avoid this additional tax burden.

Financing choices aimed at reducing taxes typically have two components: 1) selecting the tax-minimizing investment, currency, jurisdiction, and vehicle for external issues, and 2) selecting the tax-favored vehicle and currency for *internal* (inter-affiliate) financial transfers that minimize transfer taxes and position profits or losses in the jurisdiction which minimizes overall income taxes.

Structure of External Claims

Choice of Investment. Because interest payments on debt are tax-deductible and dividends are not, there is an incentive to increase the firm's financial leverage. In addition, because interaffiliate dividend payments may lead to different tax consequences than interest and principal payments, parent company financing of its affiliates in the form of debt rather than equity has tax advantages under certain circumstances. (These and other factors are discussed later.)

Choice of Currency. International covered interest arbitrage normally ensures that the annualized forward exchange premium or discount equals the nominal yield differential between debt denominated in different currencies. For example, if the one-year U.S. dollar interest rate is 12 percent while the equivalent pound sterling interest rate is 17 percent, the pound should be selling at a one-year forward discount relative to the dollar equal to 5 percent. Otherwise, an arbitrage opportunity would present itself. Moreover, a rational expectations approach to exchange rates implies that the forward premium or discount equals the expected rate of change in the exchange rate adjusted by an appropriate risk premium.[7] This means that, holding risk constant, the difference in interest rates should equal the expected change in the exchange rate during the term of the loan. Thus, in the example cited above, the pound is predicted to devalue by about 5 (17-12) percent during the coming year. To the extent that these theories hold, as a good deal of empirical evidence suggests, a firm unconcerned with the total risk of its cash flows would be indifferent between issuing debt in one currency or another.

The presence of taxes, however, may distort the interest arbitrage relationship from the perspective of the firm because its tax situation may differ from that of the marginal transactors in the market. For example, Shapiro [1982a] has shown that if arbitrage and speculation equilibrate real yields before tax, then the classic corporate prescription to issue weak-currency debt will minimize expected after-tax financing costs. There are exceptions, of course. For example, a firm operating under the laws of a country like Sweden is permitted to recognize unre-

7. Major contributions to the evolving discussion of currency risk premiums include Solnik (1978), Frankel (1979), and Stulz (1982).

If arbitrage and speculation equilibrate real yields before tax, then the classic corporate prescription to issue weak-currency debt will minimize expected after-tax financing costs.

alized exchange losses on foreign currency immediately for tax purposes, while taxes on exchange gains are deferred until realized.[8] Although this doesn't mean that it is always cheaper for firms based in Sweden to issue hard-currency debt, the fact that Swedish tax law accelerates tax credits for foreign exchange losses shifts the balance towards borrowing in currencies likely to appreciate relative to the krona. By contrast, England is a special case where government regulations reinforce the rule to borrow in the local currency when it is weak. This is because England's Inland Revenue will not permit the deduction for tax purposes of exchange losses on the principal amount of foreign currency loans—while the higher interest rate on pound debt, which reflects the expected pound devaluation, is fully tax deductible.

In general, where there is asymmetrical tax treatment of foreign exchange gains and losses or where interest expenses are subject to one tax rate and exchange gains and losses are subject to a different rate, the expected after-tax cost of borrowing will differ across currencies even if their expected before-tax costs are the same.

Choice of Jurisdiction. To the extent that the choice of currency to be borrowed can be separated from the choice of the country in which the borrowing takes place or in which the borrowing firm is domiciled, the firm will want to borrow so as to maximize its tax deductions. As long as national tax systems are not indexed for inflation, a firm typically will benefit most by borrowing in the country with the highest inflation and nominal interest rates. In so doing, the firm maximizes its interest deductions, provided interest charges and gains or losses on currency movements are treated equivalently.[9] To take full advantage of these tax deductions, the firm should use internal financial transfer mechanisms to shift funds throughout the system.

Choice of Vehicle. In the U.S. the withholding tax rate on dividend and interest payments to foreign investors varies between zero and 30 percent, depending on the bilateral tax treaty with the foreign country to which these payments are made. Even though this tax is nominally paid by the for-

eign recipient, foreign investors demand a higher before-tax rate of return as compensation, thus shifting the incidence of the tax to the security issuer.[10]

The approach taken by many American multinationals to avoid these taxes is to establish offshore finance subsidiaries. An offshore finance subsidiary is a wholly-owned affiliate incorporated overseas, usually in a tax haven country, whose function is to issue securities abroad for use in either the parent's domestic or foreign business.[11]

Structure of Internal Transfers

To the extent that tax minimization requires that the firm issue claims in countries other than where the funds are required, it must transfer the funds internally. The way this is done has important tax implications. If internal financial transfers are at "arm's length," reflecting external financing costs, then the potential advantages outlined in the previous section are largely negated. However, by choosing the appropriate instrument—and in the case of debt claims, the appropriate currency and interest rate—withholding taxes on transfers within the firm can be reduced or avoided, and revenues or costs can be shifted to jurisdictions where they have the most favorable tax consequence.[12]

Managing Risks

In principle, firms should not try to minimize risks. Rather, they should take risks whenever they expect to be rewarded for doing so. This risk-return trade-off is captured in the investment rule derived from the capital asset pricing model: namely, invest in all projects where the expected returns exceed the required return (which is a function of interest rates and the projects' *systematic* risks only). Recall, however, that earlier we added to the firm's objective function (eq. (1)) a penalty factor associated with *total* risk or variability. And, as suggested, this has very different implications for corporate risk management. To the extent that a particular element of risk contributes materially to the firm's total risk, management will want to lay off that risk as long as

---

8. See Levi (1977) for a discussion of the simultaneous arbitrage opportunities for investors of two countries that arise when interest and currency movements receive differential tax treatment in each country.

9. This prescription assumes that international Fisher parity holds before tax.

10. This assumes that the supply of funds facing a firm is much more elastic than its demand for those funds.

11. The Netherlands Antilles (N.A.) is a particularly attractive location for

such a venture since the bilateral tax treaty between the U.S. and N.A. specifically exempts interest payments by the finance subsidiary to foreign bondholders from U.S. withholding tax, even where 100 percent of the finance subsidiary's gross income is derived from U.S. sources (because proceeds were lent to the parent).

12. See Lessard (1979a) and Shapiro (1982b) for overviews of the role of internal financial transactions. Horst (1977) and Adler (1979) provide more in-depth analyses on the impact of inter-affiliate financial structures on taxes.

the expected excess return associated with bearing that risk is not large. Or, putting it the other way around, it will want to lay off such risks unless the cost of doing so is too great.

This implies that the firm will want to lay off those risks that contribute materially to its total risk but are priced fairly in relation to the CAPM. Those risks which are most likely to be fairly priced are those for which substantial, specialized markets have developed. Such markets exist for risks that are faced by large numbers of firms, especially when many of them hold offsetting positions. Examples of such risks include interest rate risks, currency risks, commodity price risks, certain political risks and funding risks.

Foreign Exchange Risks

If financing opportunities in various currencies are fairly priced, firms can structure their liabilities so as to reduce their exposure to foreign exchange risk at no cost to the value of the firm. In the case of contractual items, i.e., those fixed in nominal terms, this simply involves matching net positive positions in each currency with borrowings of similar maturity. The goal is to offset unanticipated changes in the home currency value of operating cash flows with identical changes in the home currency cost of servicing its liabilities. With non-contractual operating cash flows the same principle applies. But perfect hedging is more difficult due to the great uncertainty in estimating the expected effects of currency changes on operating flows. Further, special contracts are required exactly to offset currency risk because changes in relative prices across countries measured by the real exchange rate are associated, but not perfectly correlated, with variations in the nominal exchange rate.[13]

Quite often, however, simple rules of thumb will suffice. For example, a firm that has developed a sizable export market should hold a portion of its liabilities in the currency of determination of the export revenues—often, but not always, the currency of that country. This would allow any reduction in operating cash inflows due to an exchange rate change to be offset by a reduction in the debt service cash outflows. To illustrate this principle, a company such as Volkswagen, which exported almost half its output to the U.S. prior to 1971, should have financed about half its assets with dollar debt.

The failure to do so almost bankrupted Volkswagen following the sharp appreciation of the deutschemark beginning in August of 1981. In 1974 alone, Volkswagen lost over $310 million by lowering its deutschemark price in an attempt to maintain its market share.

Political Risk

In the hedging of exchange risks, the firm should seek financing that will offset risks inherent in the business. The use of financing to reduce political risks typically involves mechanisms to avoid or at least reduce the impact of certain risks, such as those of exchange convertibility. It may also involve financing mechanisms that actually change the risk itself, as in the case of expropriation or other direct political acts.

Firms can sometimes reduce the risk of currency inconvertibility by appropriate inter-affiliate financing. Methods for dealing with such risks include investing parent funds as debt rather than equity, arranging back-to-back and parallel loans which interpose a bank between the parent and the subsidiary, and using local financing to the extent possible. Of course, such arrangements will be most valuable when the banks or local investors face significantly fewer restrictions or smaller risks— especially if the risk in question involves possible discrimination against direct foreign investors. While local investors may often have an advantage in this regard, it cannot be taken as a general rule. Even if a particular political risk cannot be modified by shifting it from one firm or investor to another, a firm with substantial exposure will benefit by laying off such risks to firms or investors with less exposure. This is the economic basis for commercial political risk insurance.

Another approach used by MNCs to reduce their political risk exposures is as follows: instead of supplying subsidiaries with direct or guaranteed capital, the parent company may want to raise capital for a foreign investment from the host and other governments, international development agencies, overseas banks, or even from customers. Because repayment is tied to the project's success, the firm(s) sponsoring the project can create an international network of banks, government agencies, and customers with a vested interest in the fulfilment of the host government's contract with the sponsoring

---

13. See Lessard, Lightstone, and Hodgeson (1983) for further discussion.

MNCs can arrange their financing so as to shift certain key business risks to well-diversified investors concerned only with the systematic component of these risks.

firm(s). In such a case, any expropriation threat is likely to upset relations with customers, banks and governments worldwide.[14]

Again, this type of financing arrangement is beneficial to the extent that the expected gain from shifting these political risks exceeds the risk premium charged by lenders. This will be the case if the political risks facing external lenders are lower than those facing the firm. International banks, for example, to the extent that they maintain close relationships with the countries in which they do business, are likely to possess substantially more leverage with local governments than MNCs.[15]

Product Market Risk

In a well-functioning market a firm can lay off currency risks at no cost and thus reduce the penalty term in the objective function (Eq. 1). It also can arrange its financing so as to shift certain key business risks to well-diversified investors concerned only with the systematic component of these risks. A firm engaged in the extraction and processing of minerals, for example, is overwhelmingly exposed to product price fluctuations. And though these risks may be largely diversifiable for investors, the company will clearly want to protect against such risks. Examples of instruments used to shift product market risks, besides the relatively short-term commodity futures contracts, are the silver-linked bonds issued by the Sunshine Mining Corporation and the oil-linked bonds issued by Mexico. Financing linked to advance sales contracts (known as "take-or-pay" contracts) or to production shares (common in the oil industry) also plays a similar role. In all these instances, payments to investors rise and fall with the fortunes of the company, thus stabilizing the company's earnings and cash flow.

Securing Access to Funds

A continuing concern of firms, both domestic and multinational, is to secure a stable source of funds. Two elements of this strategy include diversification of fund sources and buying insurance through excess borrowing.

Diversification of Fund Sources. A key element of any MNC's global financial strategy should be to gain access to a broad range of fund sources to lessen its dependence on any one financial market. A further benefit is that the firm broadens its sources of economic and financial information, providing a useful supplement to its domestic information sources and aiding in its financial decision-making process.

An interesting example of this strategy is provided by Natomas, the San Francisco-based oil producer. In 1977, Natomas sold a $30 million, seven-year Eurobond issue even though it could have obtained funds at a lower cost by drawing on its existing revolving credit lines or by selling commercial paper. According to Natomas, the key purpose of this Euroissue was to introduce the company's name to international investors as part of its global financial strategy.[16] By floating a Eurobond, the firm was able to make the acquaintance of some of the largest non-U.S. financial institutions in the world, including Swiss Bank Corporation, the issue's lead manager. Each lead underwriter was handpicked by the company, with an eye to its overall financing needs. For example, a Swiss bank was selected as manager because Natomas felt that European banks, and Swiss banks in particular, have greater placing power with long-term investors than do U.S. underwriters operating in Europe. In addition, these European institutions were expected to serve Natomas as a source of market and economic information to counterbalance the input it already was receiving from U.S. banks.

For similar reasons, a number of Japanese firms have recently begun to sell equity shares in the United States. In 1976, for example, Pioneer raised over $27 million in the United States through the sale of 4 million shares of Pioneer common stock. This was in keeping with its multilateral financing strategy, designed to familiarize U.S. investors with its name.[17] In conjunction with this sale, Pioneer had previously applied for listing of its stock on the New York Stock Exchange.

Excess Borrowing. Most firms have lines of credit with a number of banks which give them the right to borrow up to an agreed upon credit limit.

---

14. Moran (1973) shows how this strategy was used successfully by Kennecott to finance a major copper mine expansion in Chile. Despite the subsequent rise to power of Salvador Allende, who promised to expropriate all foreign holdings in Chile with "ni un centavo" in compensation, Allende was forced to honor prior government commitments to Kennecott.

15. See, for example, Lax and Sebenius (1981).

16. "Diversifying Sources of Financing," *Business International Money Report*, September 23, 1977, pp. 297-298.

17. "Why Japanese Firms Float Equity Abroad, *Business International Money Report*, February 11, 1977, pp. 44-45.

Arbitrage opportunities are most likely to be available between controlled or subsidized domestic rates and freely determined offshore rates.

Unused balances carry a commitment fee, normally on the order of .5 percent per annum. In order not to tie up funds unnecessarily, most banks periodically review each credit limit to see whether the customer's account activity level justifies that credit line. Some firms are willing to borrow funds that they do not require (and then place them on deposit) in order to maintain their credit limit in the event of a tight money situation. In effect, they are buying insurance against the possibility of being squeezed out of the money market. One measure of the cost of this policy is the difference between the borrowing rate and the deposit rate, multiplied by the average amount of borrowed funds placed on deposit. Another cost may be considerable banker ill will if a corporation borrows when money is tight (i.e., when the firm is worried about financial sources) and does not use the money productively.

Exploiting Capital Market Distortions

Government credit and capital controls can lead to deviations from the equilibrium tendencies of interest rate parity, forward parity, and international Fisher parity. As a result, the firm may encounter financing choices that are not fairly priced. Some of these can be exploited through riskless arbitrage, which requires no special forecasting skills. Others may require speculation on uncertain future outcomes. Further, even in the absence of government intervention, firms may be able to identify instances where there are opportunities for arbitrage or speculation. In fact, opportunistic financing by firms is a key factor in assuring that the various equilibrium conditions hold. The most consistent opportunities, though, will result either from credit and exchange controls or explicit financial subsidies.

The condition for covered interest arbitrage is

$$1 + R \neq (1 + R^*) * F/S \qquad (2)$$

where R and R* are the nominal interest rates in the home and foreign currencies respectively, and F and S are the forward and spot rates in terms of direct quotes (home currency price of foreign currency).[18] Arbitrage opportunities are most likely to be available between controlled or subsidized domestic rates and freely determined offshore rates, in which case a comparison of the two rates in a single currency is all that is necessary.

The condition for speculation is

$$1 + R \neq (1 + R^*) * E(S)/S \qquad (3)$$

where E(S) is the expected value of the future spot rate.[19] In 1981, for example, Pacific Southwest Airlines borrowed yen rather than dollars on the speculation that the dollar would not fall enough relative to the yen to offset the percent interest differential between borrowing rates in the two currencies.[20] As of the end of 1983, they had gained substantially from this position. However, because PSA's revenues had little to do with movements in the yen/dollar rate, this choice did increase the firm's overall risk and undoubtedly weakened the position of its creditors. Had the dollar dropped sharply relative to the yen, as it did for example in 1978–79, the firm would have faced a large loss due to its financing choice with no corresponding business gain.

Government Credit and Capital Controls

Governments often intervene in domestic financial markets to achieve goals other than economic efficiency. For example, a government might limit corporate borrowing to hold down interest rates, thereby providing its finance ministry with a lower-cost source of funds to meet a budget deficit. Or overseas investment flows may be restricted, as they were in the United States from 1968 to 1974 under the Overseas Foreign Direct Investment (OFDI) regulations.

Where governments restrict access to local credit markets, local interest rates are usually at a lower-than-equilibrium level on a risk-adjusted basis. If there is an effective offshore market for the currency, the controls will result in a difference between domestic and offshore rates and thus give rise to an arbitrage opportunity. The firm can borrow in the domestic market and, to the extent that the short position exceeds its desired passive position in that currency, the firm can lend the same currency in offshore markets. Or, equivalently, it can transform

---

18. Forward parity need not hold in the presence of political risk (see Aliber (1973)) or forward contract default risk (see Adler and Dumas (1977)) so that deviations thereof need not indicate bargains.

19. Strictly speaking, E(S) should be replaced with CE(S), the certainty equivalent of the future spot rate. The certainty equivalent will differ from the expected spot rate if S has non-zero systematic risk (beta) or if the currency in question is that of a country which is a significant net borrower. See references in note 7 above.

20. "Turning to Japan for Cut-rate Loans," *Business Week*, November 23, 1981.

the short position to a position in another currency through forward or swap transactions linked to the offshore rate. As a result, the firm should borrow as much as possible in the credit-rationed market. In many instances, the MNC with its multiple citizenship has greater access to these lower-cost funds. Moreover, it has a greater ability to shift these funds through its internal financial transfer system.

If there is no offshore market, the mispriced credit can be exploited only by taking a risk. As a result, the firm will have to trade off the positive net present value against the effect on its total risk. As a result, the firm will not necessarily borrow as much as possible.

Government Subsidies

Many governments offer incentives to MNCs to influence their production and export sourcing decisions. Direct investment incentives include interest rate subsidies, very long loan maturities, loan guarantees, official repatriation guarantees, direct grants related to project size, favorable prices for land and favorable terms for the building of plants. The Canadian government, for example, provides firms with grants of up to $30,000 for each job created in areas characterized by high unemployment and slow economic growth—and also with direct loans and loan guarantees. Similarly, new investments located in the Mezzogiorno region of Italy can qualify for cash grants which cover up to 40 percent of the cost of plant and equipment, as well as low interest rate loans, cheaper electricity, and reduced rail charges. Governments will also often agree to build transportation, communications and other links to those factories. Some indirect incentives include corporate income tax holidays, accelerated depreciation, and a reduction or elimination of the payment of other business taxes and import duties on capital equipment and raw materials.[21] Perhaps the best-known example of such tax relief is the case of the Republic of Ireland, which does not tax profits on exports of locally-manufactured goods during the first fifteen years of operation. In addition, Ireland permits firms to write off 100 percent of the cost of new plant and equipment in the first year, without deducting state grants toward the cost of the equipment.

Strictly speaking, most of the above are examples of subsidies which affect *investment* rather than *financing* decisions. But, in many cases, the value of the subsidy will depend on how the investment is financed. For example, in the case of investment in countries granting tax holidays, a multinational might wish to shift the financing of that investment to a different jurisdiction in order to benefit from the tax shield provided by interest payments.

In addition, governments of developed nations have export financing agencies whose purpose is to boost local exports by providing long repayment periods, low interest rates, and low-cost political and economic risk insurance. These export credit programs can often be used to advantage by multinationals. The form of use will depend on whether the firm is looking to export or import goods or services. But the basic strategy remains the same: shop around among the various export credit agencies for the best possible financing arrangement.

Firms engaged in projects that have sizable import requirements may be able to finance these purchases on attractive terms from various export financing agencies. To do this, the firm must compile a list of goods and services required for the project and relate them to potential sources by country. Where there is overlap among the potential suppliers, the purchasing firm (or country) may be able to extract more favorable financing terms from the export credit agencies involved. Perhaps the clearest application of this strategy in recent years was the financing of the Soviet gas pipeline to Western Europe. The Soviet Union played off various European and Japanese suppliers and their export financing agencies against each other and managed to get extraordinarily favorable credit and pricing terms.

Interactions with the Firm's Overall Financial Structure

In our discussion of specific financing choices, we have implicitly assumed that the firm has somehow determined its overall mix of debt and equity and is merely deciding where, in which currencies, and through which legal vehicle it should borrow or lay off specific risks. These individual financing choices can be treated as independent of the firm's

---

21. For a discussion of how these financial incentives should be incorporated in project analyses see Lessard (1981).

*Any accounting rendition of a separate capital structure for subsidiaries is illusory **unless** the parent is willing to allow its affiliate to default on its debt.*

overall debt-equity determination as long as two conditions hold: 1) financial distress and agency factors which enter into this determination depend only on the firm's consolidated debt-equity structure, and 2) the firm can, at zero cost, offset over- or underborrowing in one jurisdiction elsewhere in the system. Clearly, these conditions do not hold exactly but it appears that, in many cases, they hold closely enough to allow separation of the issues of the overall debt-equity mix and the selection of specific financing sources. In this section, we explore some of the constraints on subsidiary financial structure. We do not deal with the determination of the overall mix because it is discussed amply, though inconclusively, in the literature.[22]

A problem that has long perplexed financial executives of multinational corporations is how to arrange the capital structures of their foreign affiliates and what factors are relevant in making this decision. Specifically, the problem is whether subsidiary financial structures should

a. conform to parent company norms;
b. conform to the capitalization norms established in each country; or
c. vary so as to take advantage of opportunities to minimize taxes, offset risks, or exploit distortions in financial markets.

What is often overlooked, however, when deciding on a wholly-owned subsidiary's funding is that any accounting rendition of a separate capital structure for the subsidiary is illusory *unless* the parent is willing to allow its affiliate to default on its debt or unless external factors such as credit controls limit the enforceability of cross-border controls. As long as the rest of the MNC group has a legal or moral obligation to prevent the affiliate from defaulting, the individual unit has no independent capital structure.[23] In such a case, its true debt/equity ratio is equal to that of the consolidated group.

Some evidence on parent willingness to guarantee (implicitly if not explicitly) their affiliates' debts is provided by two surveys, one by Stobaugh (1970) and the other by Business International (1979). In the survey by Stobaugh, not one of a sample of twenty medium and large multinationals (average annual foreign sales of $200 million and $1 billion, respectively) said it would allow its subsidi-

aries to default on debt which did not have a parent company guarantee. Of the small multinationals interviewed (average annual sales of $450 million), only one out of seventeen indicated it would allow a subsidiary to default on its obligations under some circumstances. The 1979 survey by Business International of eight U.S.-based MNCs had similar findings.[24] The majority of firms interviewed said they would make good the non-guaranteed debt of a subsidiary that defaulted on its borrowings.

It is likely that the market has already incorporated this practical commitment in its estimate of the parent's worldwide debt capacity. An overseas creditor, on the other hand, may not be as certain regarding the firm's intentions. The fact that the parent doesn't guarantee its subsidiaries' debt may convey the information that under certain circumstances the parent will choose to walk away from its subsidiary.

Many multinationals view subsidiary financial structures as having little relevance. In the 1979 survey by Business International, for example, most of the firms expressed little concern with the debt-equity mixes of their foreign affiliates. One possible reason for this lack of concern is the fact that, for most of the firms interviewed, their affiliate debt ratios had not significantly raised their consolidated debt ratios. Again, however, they focused on their worldwide rather than individual subsidiary's capital structures.

The third option, therefore, to vary affiliate financial structures so as to take advantage of local financing opportunities, appears to be the best choice. There are, however, several constraints to such an approach. These constraints arise from the fact that a firm's operations in different jurisdictions have different groups of noncorporate stakeholders—governments, managements, workers, lenders, joint venture partners, suppliers, customers—whose interests are affected by subsidiary capital structures.

Capital Structure Requirements

Many jurisdictions require that locally incorporated firms maintain particular levels of equity capitalization or equity ratios. In some cases, these are simply holdovers of national incorporation laws

---

22. See, for example, Stewart C. Myers, "The Search for Optimal Capital Structure," *Midland Corporate Finance Journal*, Vol.1 No.1.
23. This point is made by Adler (1974) and Shapiro (1978).

24. "Policies of MNCs on Debt/Equity Mix," *Business International Money Report*, September 21, 1979, pp. 319–320.

While financial autonomy may be a useful control device, its costs in the form of constraints on global financing and operation should be carefully monitored.

which apply imperfectly to multinationals. In others, they are express attempts to require potentially footloose multinationals in effect to "post bond" against future actions considered undesirable by local authorities. However, as long as a nation does not simultaneously apply capital controls, the firm still has substantial freedom of choice regarding the currency and tax consequences of its financing, given the array of potential offshore and interaffiliate financing options.

Management Control

Despite the logic of the argument that a subsidiary's capital structure is relevant only insofar as it affects the parent's consolidated worldwide debt ratio, some companies still follow a policy of not providing parent financing beyond the initial investment. Their rationale for this policy, which is to avoid "giving local management a crutch," can best be understood in the context of agency theory. By forcing foreign affiliates to stand on their own feet, the parent firm is tacitly admitting that its powers of surveillance over foreign affiliates are limited, due to physical and/or cultural distance. In effect, the parent is turning over some of its monitoring responsibilities to local financial institutions. At the same time, affiliate managers will presumably be working harder to improve local operations, thereby generating the internal cash flow that will help replace parent financing.

The existence of agency costs can also affect corporate policy regarding parent guarantees. As Robbins and Stobaugh have commented, when a firm provides an affiliate with a loan guarantee, it "lose[s] the bank as your [its] partner in controls."[25] Because the bank will be repaid regardless of the affiliate's profitability, it will have less incentive to monitor the affiliate's activities.

While financial autonomy may be a useful control device, its costs in the form of constraints on global financing and operation should be carefully monitored. For example, in the absence of a guarantee, the local bank will probably insist on inserting various complicating covenants in its loan agreement with the subsidiary. These restrictive covenants could result in a significant loss in operational and financial flexibility. If the costs imposed by these constraints are high, alternatives should be sought—for example, a more effective system for controlling local operating management.

One possibility is to allocate only certain financing decisions and responsibilities to local management, and retain the rest under central corporate control. For example, local management might be held responsible for financing its local currency working capital requirements, while home country management would make all other financing decisions. Such differentiation, of course, requires a considerable degree of sophistication in performance measurement and control. The costs of such a control system must be traded off against the gains in financial flexibility.

Jurisdictional Matching

Even if legal requirements and control considerations do not cause the financial structures of an MNC's subsidiaries to differ significantly from one another, a firm may wish to limit cross-border commitments, including direct parent financing or parent guarantees, because of the difficulty of enforcing its cross-border claims. The threat of currency controls or outright expropriation in one jurisdiction, for example, may expose the parent to financial distress if it borrows against these anticipated revenues in another jurisdiction. Even if local lenders face the same political risks and incorporate them in their lending rates, local borrowing without a parent guarantee may reduce the "financial distress penalty." To protect lenders from the risk of subsidiary bankruptcy, however, the parent usually will provide a conditional guarantee in the form of a comfort letter obligating the parent to make good on its subsidiary's debts except in the event of expropriation.[26]

These considerations do not apply equally to all countries. In the case of relatively stable jurisdictions with open capital and currency markets, firms are likely to be willing to issue guarantees and engage in other necessary cross-border transactions to minimize taxes or risks or exploit distortions. In countries more apt to impose limits on cross-border transactions, though, firms will have to weigh carefully the benefits of financial flexibility against the costs of cross-border exposure.

---

25. Robbins and Stobaugh (1973), p. 67.

26. Hodder (1982) discusses the relationship between political risk and financing choices at greater length.

There are likely to be some significant agency problems associated with joint ventures.

Joint Ventures

Because many MNCs participate in joint ventures, either by choice or necessity, establishing an appropriate financing mix for this form of investment is an important consideration. Our previous assumption that affiliate debt is equivalent to parent debt in terms of its effect on perceived default risk may no longer be valid. This assumption was based on the increased risk of financial distress associated with more highly leveraged firms. In countries such as Japan and Germany, however, increased leverage does not necessarily lead to increased financial risks because of the close relationship between the local banks and local corporations. Thus, debt raised by a joint venture in Japan, for example, may not be equivalent to parent-raised debt with respect to its impact on default risk. The assessment of the effects of leverage in a joint venture is a judgmental factor which requires an analysis of the partner's ties with the local financial community, particularly with the local banks.

Unless the joint venture can be isolated from its partners' operations, however, there are likely to be some significant agency problems associated with this form of ownership. Transfer pricing, establishment of royalty and licensing fees, and allocation of production and markets among plants are just some of the areas where each owner has an incentive to engage in activities that will harm its partners. This probably explains why bringing in outside equity participants is generally such an unstable form of external financing. In recognition of their lack of complete control over a joint venture's decisions and its profits, most MNCs will, at most, guarantee joint venture loans in proportion to their share of ownership.

Summary and Conclusions

In this article, we have attempted to provide a framework for multinational firms to use in arranging their global financing. We have broken down the international aspects of the problem into three largely separable objectives: minimizing taxes, managing risks, and exploiting market distortions. The first two of these rely on passive considerations in that they do not rely on any superior forecasting skills, whereas the third may or may not have an active component. In either case, these functions are largely separate. Tax minimization typically can be pursued without altering the currency risk position of the firm. Overall risk management can be carried out without any special information about capital market opportunities. Once the firm has established its desired passive position, it then can decide by how much it is willing to alter its risk exposures to exploit perceived bargains. Arbitrage opportunities, of course, are simple to deal with because they have no overall risk implications.

Following this discussion, we described how each of these three financing considerations influences the firm's choice of overall financial structure. Clearly, parent and affiliate structures must be allowed to differ if the firm is to exploit the special opportunities of being multinational. However, it may wish to constrain the extent to which it distorts the financing of a particular subsidiary because of undesired behavioral effects on local managers, or in the case of joint ventures, conflicts with local shareholders.

Although there are many areas in which our recommendations are qualitative rather than quantitative, our approach to developing a financing strategy should be useful in a domestic as well as international context.

References

Adler, M., (1974), "The Cost of Capital and Valuation of a Two-Country Firm," *Journal of Finance* (March).

——— (1979), "U.S. Taxation of U.S. Multinational Corporations," in M. Sarnat and G. Szego (eds.), *International Trade and Finance* Vol. IV. Ballinger.

——— **and B. Dumas** (1977), "The Microeconomics of the Firm in an Open Economy," *American Economic Review* (February).

——— **and** ——— (1977), "Default Risk and the Demand for Forward Exchange," in H. Levy and M. Sarnat, (eds.), *Financial Decision Making Under Uncertainty*. Academic Press.

Aliber, R. Z. (1973), "The Interest Rate Parity Theorem: A Reinterpretation," *Journal of Political Economy* (November/December).

Barnea, A., R. Haugen, and L. Senbet (1981), "Market Imperfections, Agency Problems, and Capital Structure: A Review," *Financial Management* (Summer).

Cohen, B. (1972), "Foreign Investment by U.S. Corporations as a Way of Reducing Risk," Yale University Economic Growth Center Discussion Paper No. 151, September.

Dufey, G. and I. Giddy (1978), "International Financial Planning," *California Management Review* (Fall).

Fama, E. (1980), "Agency Problems and the Theory of the Firm," *Journal of Political Economy* (April).

Frankel, J. (1979), "The Diversifiability of Exchange Risk," *Journal of International Economics* (August)

Hodder, J. (1982), "Hedging International Exposure Capital Structure Under Flexible Exchange Rates and Expropriation Risk," Stanford University Working Paper.

Horst, T. (1977), "American Taxation of Multinational Firms," *American Economic Review* (June)

Jensen, M. and W. Meckling (1976), "Theory of the Firm: Managerial Behavior, Agency Cost, and Ownership Structure," *Journal of Financial Economics* 3.

Kornbluth, J. and J. Vinso (1981), "Financial Planning for the Multinational Corporations: A Fractional, Multiobjective Approach," *Journal of Financial and Quantitative Analysis* (December).

Lax, D. and J. Sebenius (1981), "Insecure Contracts and Resource Development," *Public Policy*, (Fall).

Lessard, D. (1979a), "Transfer Prices, Taxes and Financial Markets Implications of Internal Financial Transfers within the Multinational Firms," in R. B. Hawkins (ed.), *Economic Issues of Multinational Firms*. JAI Press.

———— (1979b), "Financial Management of International Operations," in D. Lessard (ed.), *International Financial Management*. Boston Warren, Gorham, and Lamont.

———— (1981), "Evaluating International Projects: An Adjusted Present Value Approach," in R. Krum and F. Derkindiren (eds.), *Capital Budgeting under Conditions of Uncertainty*, Hingham, MA Martinus Nijhoff.

———— **and R. Stulz** (1982), "Currency Considerations in International Equity Investment," unpublished manuscript, M.I.T. May.

————, **J. Lightstone, and R. Hodgeson** (1983), "The Impact of Exchange Rates on Operating Profits New Business and Financial Responses," unpublished MS.

Levi, M. (1977), "Taxation and 'Abnormal' International Cash Flows," *Journal of Political Economy* (June).

Lietaer, B. (1971), *Financial Management of Foreign Exchange*, Cambridge, MA: M.I.T. Press.

Modigliani, F. and M. Miller (1958), "The Cost of Capital, Corporation Finance, and the Theory of Investment," *American Economic Review* (June)

Moran, T. (1974), *The Politics of Dependence: Copper in Chile*, Princeton, N.J. Princeton University Press

Nauman-Etienne, R. (1974), "A Framework for Financial Decisions in Multinational Corporations — A Summary of Recent Research," *Journal of Financial and Quantitative Analysis* (November).

Ness, W. (1972), "A Linear Programming Approach to Financing the Multinational Corporations," *Financial Management* (Winter).

Remmers, L. (1980), "A Note on Foreign Borrowing Costs," *Journal of International Business Studies* (Fall).

Robbins, S. and R. Stobaugh (1972), *Money in the Multinational Corporation*. New York Basic Books.

Rugman, A. (1979), *International Diversification and the Multinational Enterprise*. Heath Lexington.

Shapiro, A. (1975), "Evaluating Financing Costs for Multinational Subsidiaries," *Journal of International Business Studies* (Fall).

———— (1978), "Financial Structure and Cost of Capital in the Multinational Corporation," *Journal of Financial and Quantitative Analysis* (June).

———— (1982a), "The Impact of Taxation on the Currency-of-Denomination Decision for Long-Term Foreign Borrowing and Lending," *Journal of International Business Studies*, forthcoming.

———— (1982b) *Multinational Financial Management*. Boston Allyn & Bacon.

Solnik, B. (1978), "International Parity Conditions and Exchange Risk," *Journal of Banking and Finance* 2.

Stobaugh, R. (1970), "Financing Foreign Subsidiaries," *Journal of International Business Studies* (Summer).

Stonehill, A. and T. Stitzel (1969), "The Financial Structure of Multinational Corporations," *California Management Review* (Fall).

Stulz, R. (1982), "The Forward Exchange Rate and Macroeconomics," *Journal of International Economics*, 12.

Wihlborg, C. (1980), "Exposure Management of Foreign Subsidiaries," *Journal of International Business Studies* (Winter).

An International Perspective on the Capital Structure Puzzle

by Janette Rutterford, *The London School of Economics**

The debate over corporate capital structure has raged for nearly 30 years. Since the early work of Modigliani and Miller and others in the 1950s, the basic question, "Does the firm's debt-equity ratio matter?," has continued to dominate academic discussions of the issue. The logical next question, "If the firm's debt-equity ratio does matter, what ought it to be?," is as yet far from being answered.

The basis of the many models of the capital structure decision is the M&M 1958 paper which demonstrated that, in the presence of perfect, frictionless capital markets, the debt-equity ratio decision is irrelevant to the value of the firm. In this artificial world, the benefit of cheap fixed interest debt in the capital structure is exactly offset by a consequently higher cost of equity from the associated increase in financial risk. The subsequent introduction into the model of corporate tax, against which debt interest is deductible, swings the pendulum decidedly in favour of debt. However, once both corporate and personal taxes are introduced, the choice of debt-equity ratio may or may not matter at the level of the firm (depending on the particular tax assumptions), though differential taxes on debt and equity income will certainly affect the aggregate amount of debt in the corporate sector. More recent models introducing the agency costs of debt financing (such as bankruptcy costs) and non-interest tax shields generally have the effect of reducing the optimal amount of debt in corporate capital structures—although some

of the new information asymmetry models, as represented by Stewart Myers in the first article in this issue, imply a preference for debt over new equity.

The complexity and lack of unanimity in this literature can in part be explained by the failure of empirical tests to provide overriding support either for the irrelevance of capital structure to firm value or for any major factor, such as tax, which may affect it. Cross-sectional tests are precluded if the explanatory variables, for example nominal corporate tax rates, do not vary across firms. Time series tests have been hampered by disagreement over the choice of surrogate for target corporate leverage ratios. Some authors, Zwick and Corcoran,[1] for example, have argued that U.S. corporate debt-equity ratios have increased sharply over the past 20 or 30 years. Others, such as Miller,[2] have asserted that corporate leverage ratios have remained remarkably stable over time. Tests of more recent agency cost models have been hampered by difficulties in quantifying agency costs.

Although these issues are of critical importance in an international context, the longstanding debate on capital structure—perhaps the most popular of all corporate finance issues—has concentrated almost exclusively on U.S. corporations, U.S. taxes and U.S. agency costs. There is general agreement that there are substantial differences between countries in observed leverage ratios; this is highlighted in the OECD statistics shown in Table 1. Indeed, in the U.K., these documented differences in leverage ratios

*The author is grateful for the financial support of the Bank of England Houblon-Norman Fund for this research project.

1. See B. Zwick, "The Market for Corporate Bonds," *Federal Reserve Bank of New York Quarterly Review* (Autumn 1977), pp.27-36 and P. J. Corcoran, "Inflation, Taxes, and Corporate Investment Incentives," pp.1-10 of the same issue of the *Federal Reserve Bank of New York Quarterly Review*.

2. See M. Miller, "Debt and Taxes", *Journal of Finance*, 32 (December 1977), page 271.

TABLE 1
Aggregate Debt-Equity Ratios in the U.S., U.K., France, Germany and Japan

		Total Debt to Total Assets						Total Debt to Stockholders Funds			
		Stonehill et al. 1965[1]	Toy et al. 1966–72[2]	OECD[3]				Samuels[4] et al. 1967	Wilson[5] Report		
				1970	1975	1980	1982		1970	1972	1976
U.S.		39	42	44	37	37	37	25	57	60	53
U.K.		46	n/a	52	51	49	50	28	56	55	53
France		37	58	65	70	70	73	33	111	126	152
Germany		59	n/a	63	63	64	63	45	n/a	97	89
Japan		70	67	84	85	84	83	98	299	325	359

[1] Equally weighted debt-to-asset ratios for samples of companies from the same nine industries in each country.

[2] Equally weighted debt-to-asset ratios for the major companies in each country in the electronics, paper, food and chemical industries.

[3] Non-financial companies from each country:

U.S.	Estimated total for all non-financial corporations; consolidated accounts.
U.K.	All large(capital employed > £4 million) non-financial companies; consolidated accounts.
France	577 industrial and 112 commercial firms from a variety of industries with a minimum turnover of FF 25 million in 1977; unconsolidated accounts.
Germany	A large random sample of 74,000 corporations, sole proprietorships and partnerships; unconsolidated accounts.
Japan	Privately owned non-financial corporations; a random sample from each sector of economic activity; unconsolidated accounts.

[4] Based on National Accounts data for each country.

[5] Based on OECD statistics and Sonderdrucke der Deutschen Bundesbank Nr. 5.

have been used to support pressure for a change in the government's attitude towards corporation debt finance. It has been argued that one of the reasons for British industry's failure to grow as fast as industry in France, Germany and especially Japan is the greater relative reliance on debt finance by firms in these countries[3].

This argument presumes that debt dominates equity as a source of finance equally in both the U.K. and Japan. An equally plausible explanation for differences in countries' corporate debt-equity ratios, however, could be that tax systems, tax rates or agency costs differ across countries. For example, the tax advantage to corporate debt may be greater for Japanese firms than for their British counterparts. A model of optimal capital structure incorporating these factors may be sufficient to explain differences in choice of debt-equity ratio across countries. Alternatively, the observed differences, although generally agreed to exist, may be more apparent than real; the differences may be attributable simply to variations in accounting or reporting procedures rather than to variations in the tax advantages of debt finance.

The purpose of this article is to extend the optimal capital structure puzzle to an international context. We concentrate on the U.K., France, Germany and Japan, as well as on the U.S.; these five countries afford us a complete range of tax systems,[4] as well as a wide variety of potential agency costs. We try to explain the apparent differences in leverage ratios using these models, bearing in mind the difficulties inherent in comparing ratios from different sources and subject to different reporting systems. The remainder of the article is structured as follows: the first section considers the available data on different countries' corporate debt-equity ratios, the second attempts to appraise the likely importance of measurement differences, the third extends the major tax models of optimal capital structure to all tax systems, the fourth considers differences in agency costs, and the final section presents our conclusions.

3. The U.K. discussion over the adequacy of the amount of debt available to industry dates from as far back as the 1931 Macmillan Committee on Finance and Industry Report, Cmnd. 3897, which first mentioned a possible financing gap. More recent arguments have been summarized in an article entitled "More Ingenuity from Mr. Grylls" in *The Guardian*, January 26, 1982.

4. The extension to other tax systems is timely given the likely departure of the U.S., in the light of the U.S. Treasury's proposals, from the long-established classical tax system.

Japanese firms appear to rely most heavily on debt finance, with the U.S. and U.K. showing greatest use of equity financing. French and German firms have leverage ratios somewhere between the U.S./U.K. and Japanese extremes.

Comparison of Debt-Equity Ratios

Table 1 provides available data on book value debt-equity ratios over a number of years for the corporate sectors of the U.S., U.K., France, Germany and Japan. All the ratios shown in Table 1 are book value surrogates for the market value ratios implicit in the majority of tax and agency cost models of optimal capital structure. As Stewart Myers remarks: "At first glance, some of the oddest practical rules of thumb for judging debt policy are those which depend on ratios of debt to the book value of equity or to total book capitalization. Anyone familiar with modern finance theory considers ratios based on market values much more pertinent."[5] As Myers goes on to suggest, however, the expression of capital structure targets in terms of book values rather than market values may reflect the fact that tangible assets ("assets-in-place," as he calls them) provide better collateral than the intangible assets, often capitalizing nothing more solid than "growth opportunities," reflected in market values.

The use of book values can also be supported on the basis that such ratios represent clearer measures of target leverage ratios adopted by corporate finance managers. In a questionnaire survey carried out by Stonehill and others of financial executives of firms from the U.S., France, Japan, the Netherlands and Norway, the authors found that only seven out of 87 respondents used market values in determining their desired debt-equity ratio.[6] Market values of debt and equity are less subject to the control of management, being sensitive to market price changes. Also, market values of equity will reflect any benefits to debt financing accruing to stockholders, thus reducing the impact of any debt issue on firms' market debt-equity ratios and hence their role as target debt ratios.

The ratios shown in Table 1 are of two types, debt to total assets and debt to stockholders' funds. There is support for the use of both these measures of corporate leverage. In the questionnaire survey cited above, 45 respondents, primarily from Japan

and Norway, preferred the debt to total assets measure with another 34—mainly from France, the Netherlands and the U.S.—preferring the debt to equity measure. Despite these cultural preferences, both measures are equivalent estimates of corporate leverage provided there are no items on the liabilities side of the balance sheet not defined as either debt or equity. However, the division between debt and equity can be blurred by such items as provisions (as we shall see in the next section), so that the use of debt to total assets measure may contain fewer sources of measurement error. This seems to be confirmed in Table 1, where there is greater variation in the debt-equity ratios from different sources if stockholders' equity is used in the denominator.

Whichever measure of corporate leverage is used, and whichever year is considered, Table 1 shows there to be substantial differences between countries in the proportion of debt used to finance investment in the corporate sector. In all years, Japanese firms appear to rely most heavily on debt finance, with U.S. and U.K. corporations showing greatest use of equity financing. French and German firms have leverage ratios somewhere between the U.S./U.K. and Japanese extremes. In general, these rankings appear to have changed very little over the last twenty years, as have levels of debt-equity ratios—except for French and Japanese ratios, which appear to have risen over the period.

Measurement Differences

Comparison of corporate financial statistics across national boundaries is subject to many difficulties. These include not only variations in choice of sample of firms to represent the corporate sector, but also variations in accounting standards and legal requirements imposed on corporations (as well as the extent to which any such requirements are adhered to). An example of sample differences is the inclusion or not of small firms and their importance to the corporate sector in each country. For example, the sample used to calculate the OECD German

5. S. Myers, "Determinants of Corporate Borrowing," *Journal of Financial Economics*, 5 (1977), pp.149-50.

6. See A. Stonehill, T. Beekhuisen, R. Wright, L. Remmers, N. Toy, A. Pares, A. Shapiro, D. Egan, T. Bates, "Financial Goals and Debt Ratio Determinants: A ~ey of Practice in Five Countries," *Financial Management* (Autumn 1977), ~1.

debt-equity ratios shown in Table 1 includes partnerships and sole proprietorships as well as corporations, whereas the U.K. and French samples specifically exclude small corporations. This will bias the comparison if small firms have different debt-equity ratios from those of their big brothers. In the U.K. small firms (defined as having capital employed of less than £100,000) have higher proportions of debt financing with an average debt to total assets ratio approaching 75 percent in 1980.[7] The quality of the data also varies across countries. Compare the controls imposed on the reporting of U.S. corporations with listed Japanese firms whose stockholders' reports were only required to be subject to an independent audit after 1974. However, since we are unable to quantify the impact of these differences, we concentrate here, faute de mieux, on the accounting and legal factors which may substantially affect the debt-equity ratios shown in Table 1.

Consolidation

The first major accounting difference in the five countries' debt-equity ratios is the use or not by corporations of consolidated accounts. U.K. and U.S. ratios shown in Table 1 are based on consolidated accounts, whereas this is not the case for France, Germany and Japan. Indeed, Japanese quoted corporations have only been required to publish consolidated accounts since 1977. Thus, the leverage ratios for France, Germany and Japan could be overstated by the extent of inter-firm indebtedness. This is likely to be particularly important in the case of Japan, given the strong financial links between firms in the same group, especially those groups based on the old pre-war "zaibatsu" system.[8]

Historic Cost

As mentioned above, we rely for our statistics on book rather than market values. These book values are based on balance sheet measures of items such as stockholders funds and total assets. When comparing book values across countries, we must bear in mind that accounting systems vary from country to country in the extent to which balance sheet entries represent historic cost, an arbitrary written-down value or an estimate of current value. The amount of rapid change experienced, the flexibility of accounting standards and the intended readership for the accounting data are all factors which will determine the balance sheet values attributed to assets and liabilities. Items on which differences can be wide include assets such as trade investments, property, and plant and equipment. The relative importance of these items in each country will also influence debt-equity ratio comparisons.

Although in the five countries under consideration, trade investments are usually accounted for at the lower of cost or market value, the importance of any undervaluation will vary according to the size of this item in the balance sheet. This potential undervaluation is most acute in Japan, where Japanese firms owned 26 percent of listed Japanese corporations' equity in 1980 when this item only accounted for around 2 percent of total assets in their balance sheets. Since many of these stockholdings were acquired in the immediate post-war period, both total assets and owner's equity are likely to be understated and hence leverage ratios overstated.

If we consider property, it has been standard practice for French and U.K. corporations to revalue their property portfolios every few years, either using professional advisers or directors' valuations. In contrast, U.S., German and Japanese firms include property in the balance sheet at historic cost. This can lead to balance sheet asset values substantially below current market values if, as is the case in Japan, property prices have risen sharply over time. (For example, the Japanese industrial land price index rose from 100 to 3288 between 1955 and 1981.)

Again, contrasting the U.K. and Japanese methods of accounting for plant and equipment, U.K. corporations depreciate plant and equipment in their accounts according to the expected life of the assets (although major tax concessions have been available on this type of investment). Japanese corporations show plant and equipment in the accounts net of their similarly generous tax allowances.

---

7. See HMSO *Business Monitor* MA3 (Fifteenth Issue 1984), Table 6.

8. The "zaibatsu" were family concerns under the control of a family-owned holding corporation dating back to the nineteenth century. Although officially abolished after World War II, the zaibatsu concept still exists in such groups as Mitsui, Sumitomo, and Mitsubishi.

Provisions

Tax allowances can also affect another balance sheet entry—that of provisions. This term can cover a variety of notional accounting reserves, whether for tax, development costs, doubtful debts, inventory price fluctuations or pensions. Each country permits the use of different amounts and types of provisions, some of which are genuine long-term liabilities which will eventually have to be paid out (for example, pensions), whilst others are simply the result of generous tax concessions and effectively form part of stockholders' equity (as is the case with many of the French and Japanese provisions). The importance of these provisions will also vary over time. For example, in the U.K., deferred tax provisions became important in the 1970s with generous depreciation allowances on physical investment, but practically disappeared after the introduction of an accounting standard which required a deferred tax provision only if it was felt that the tax would be paid "with reasonable certainty."[9]

Since it is difficult to distinguish the extent of the true liability, if any, behind balance sheet provisions, the OECD ratios in Table 1 have uniformly included provisions as part of stockholders' equity. However, the need to allocate provisions can to a great extent be avoided if the debt to total assets ratio is used as a measure of corporate leverage (except, again, in the case where a provision could be viewed as part of debt or in the case of pensions, to which we now turn).

Pensions

A significant proportion of provisions made by German corporations (14 percent of total liabilities in 1981) are for future pension liabilities. There are no such provisions in U.K. or U.S. balance sheets, where corporate pensions are legally separate funded entities, none in France where pension payments are made directly to industry-wide central bodies, but a small element in Japan where provision for pensions is made both within the firm and out-side it. In the U.K. and U.S., pension funds are invested in corporate bonds, government bonds and equities. In France, as pension arrangements are generally on a "pay as you go" basis, large funds do not accumulate. Such funds as do exist are reinvested in the corporate sector, usually through the medium of loans. In Germany, and to a lesser extent Japan, pension fund provisions in the balance sheet represent funds retained and invested in physical assets by the corporations concerned. For firms in these countries, the effect of pension fund provisions is to inflate both total assets and total liabilities.

For example, suppose we compare $100 of assets in the U.S. and Germany, financed by $40 of equity, $10 of debt and $50 of pension liabilities. In the U.S., the $50 assets and liabilities associated with the (fully funded) pension fund would be off-balance sheet, giving a debt-to-assets ratio of 20 percent and a debt-to-stockholders' equity ratio of 25 percent. In Germany, the full $100 of assets would be in the balance sheet, giving a debt-to-assets ratio of 10 percent and a debt-to-stockholders' equity ratio of either 11 percent or 25 percent, depending on whether the pension fund provision is included in owners' equity. So, for strict comparability, debt-equity ratios should be calculated on the basis of "augmented" balance sheets,[10] or with both provisions for pensions and their associated assets ignored. The effect of the OECD treatment of pension provisions is therefore to understate German and Japanese leverage ratios.

Pensions can affect debt-equity ratio comparisons in another way. With externally funded schemes, any unfunded liabilities can be expected to reduce stockholders' equity. This may be reflected in the market value of equity if the unfunded liability is disclosed, but will only affect book value if the unfunded liability is a balance sheet item. For example, the U.S. requires only a note to the accounts quantifying the amount of underfunding and the U.K. as yet requires no disclosure at all on this point. Such underfunding, itself subject to measurement difficulties, can be significant. For example, Lasman and Weil, in a survey of five U.S. corporations (admittedly

---

9. Statement of Standard Accounting Practice 15 introduced in October 1978.

10. An augmented balance sheet comprises both the corporate and pension fund assets and liabilities. This concept was first proposed by W. Bagehot in "Risk and Reward in Corporate Pension Funds" in the January-February 1972 issue of the *Financial Analysts Journal*. For an argument in favour of treating pension fund liabilities as debt rather than equity, See J. Treynor's article "The Principles of Corporate Pension Finance" in the *Journal of Finance*, 32 (May 1977), pp.627-638.

In 1980, the U.S. corporate sector financed 17.1 percent of its gross capital formation through leasing, followed by the U.K. with 8.7 percent, Japan 4.0 percent, France 3.2 percent and Germany 1.0 percent.

chosen for the particular difficulties the analysts had in determining comparable measures of leverage for them) found unfunded pension liabilities of 2.3 times their long-term debt.[11] If General Motors were excluded, however, the ratio dropped to 0.3! The inadequacy of pension provisions in unfunded schemes is less evident.

Debt

We now consider the measurement of debt itself. In the early U.S. capital structure literature, it was implicitly assumed that debt was entirely fixed interest bonds and equity entirely composed of ordinary stock. Short-term bank debt was ignored because of its relative insignificance and because of its role as working capital finance rather than as part of long-term capital prior to the 1970s. However, the split between short-term and long-term debt and between bank debt and debt securities cannot strictly be applied when making international comparisons. For example, the U.K. corporate sector depended substantially on bank overdrafts recallable on demand as a source of permanent debt finance during the 1970s, whereas medium- and long-term loans account for over half the total bank loans to industrial corporations in the U.S., France, Germany and Japan. Similarly, U.K. firms prior to 1974 and U.S. firms throughout the period shown in Table 1 raised from 5 to 15 percent of their net external finance in the form of corporate bonds, whereas the proportion never exceeded 3.5 percent for France, Germany and Japan.

The OECD statistics in Table 1 therefore include all definitions of debt in the numerator of their ratios. As well as debt provided by the financial markets and institutions, they also incorporate trade debt, which creates difficulties when comparing Japan with other countries; in Japan it is common practice, to a greater extent than any other country in the survey, for the larger listed corporations to extend trade finance to smaller subcontracting firms. This increases the apparent leverage ratio for Japanese firms, which would not be the case if creditors were also taken into account.

A further difficulty in the definition of debt is the role of liquid assets. In both the U.S. and Japan, banks extending loans to corporations often require compensating balances to be made which, in the case of Japan, can be as high as 20-30 percent of the loan extended (although they have been less popular in the U.S. in recent years). This practice inflates the apparent debt-equity ratios of these countries.

Leases represent an item relevant to corporate leverage which remains off-balance sheet, except in the U.S., reflecting the delays other countries have experienced in changing accounting disclosure to keep up with changes in methods of corporate financing. The relevance of leases to debt-equity ratios stems from the fact that they can be viewed as an alternative form of corporate debt, so that any debt-equity ratio measure which excludes leases from the definition of debt may underestimate corporate leverage.[12] The extent to which leasing has been used to supplement traditional debt finance has varied across countries—one fact affecting the use of leasing being corporate tax exhaustion.[13] In 1980, the U.S. corporate sector financed 17.1 percent of its gross capital formation through leasing, followed by the U.K. with 8.7 percent, Japan 4.0 percent, France 3.2 percent and Germany 1.0 percent. If leases are to be included in the definition of debt, the U.K. would appear to have the most understated debt-equity ratios in Table 1.

Size of Measurement Error

From our discussion above, it would seem that many of the factors—fixed assets at historical cost, non-consolidation and substantial use of trade debt—tend to lead to overstatement of corporate leverage, particularly for Japan and to a lesser extent for Germany and France. Leases are likely to understate the leverage ratios, particularly of the U.K. and possibly of the U.S., and pensions may have a mixed effect on these countries' ratios since funded pensions can overstate leverage relative to a "pay as you go" and provisions system; but the inclusion of unfunded pension liabilities will increase leverage.

Estimates of the effects of possible accounting biases in debt-equity ratios have been mainly restricted to two countries, Japan and the U.S. For ex-

11. See D. Lasman and R. Weil, "Adjusting the Debt-Equity Ratio," *Financial Analysts Journal* (September-October 1978), pp.49-58. Recent studies would be more likely to find *over*funding.

12. See, for example, R. Brealey and S. Myers, *Principles of Corporate Finance*, Second Edition, McGraw-Hill (1984), Chapter 24.

13. For further discussion of this point see, for example, H. DeAngelo and R. W. Masulis, "Optimal Capital Structure under Corporate and Personal Taxation," *Journal of Financial Economics*, 8 (March 1980), pp.2-30.

Adjusting for accounting differences across countries is probably to narrow the gap between countries, with Japanese leverage approaching the levels of German and French firms, and with the U.K. and U.S. at significantly lower levels.

ample, two studies have confirmed the reduction of Japanese leverage ratios if market values are used. The first, by Kuroda and Oritani, using 1977 data on 559 quoted Japanese manufacturing firms, reduced the average debt to total assets ratio from 78 percent to 67 percent by using market values for the equity element of the balance sheet.[14] A 1974 study by the Yamaichi Securities Company of 594 Japanese corporations adjusted assets to current market values and thereby reduced the average debt-to-total assets ratio from 84 percent to 52 percent. Two thirds of the decrease was due to the use of current values for land.

Kuroda and Oritani performed a similar exercise (applying market values of equity) on 559 U.S. manufacturing firms and found that the average debt-to-assets ratio fell from 50 percent to 40 percent. Gordon and Malkiel, using a sample of 2000 non-financial U.S. firms, found that market value ratios reduced leverage from 36 percent to 32 percent in 1977.[15] For the U.K., the use of replacement costs for fixed assets in a Bank of England survey led to a reduction in the debt-to-assets ratio for the industrial and commercial sector of from 22 percent to 12 percent.[16] The effect of adjusting for unfunded pension liabilities and non-capitalized leases has been quantified by Gordon and Malkiel on the same sample. They found an increase in the average debt-to-assets ratio of from 36 percent to 47 percent. It is likely that the impact of these items would be as least as great in the U.K., where no leases are capitalised in the balance sheet.

The above adjustments reduce leverage ratios for Japan and, to a lesser extent, for France and Germany. The impact of using market values in U.K. and U.S. debt ratios may be more or less counterbalanced by the impact of pension and leases. Thus, the overall effect of attempting to adjust for accounting differences across countries is probably to narrow the gap between countries, with Japanese corporate leverage approaching the levels of German and French firms, and with the U.K. and U.S. at significantly lower levels. Unfortunately, no

comprehensive survey can reassure us that this conjecture is correct.

The Impact of Taxes

We now turn to taxes as a possible explanatory factor for the remaining differences in leverage ratios between countries. In Europe, the U.S. and Japan, we can currently identify three main tax systems in use: the classical, imputation and hybrid systems (where the hybrid system is a combination of dual corporate tax rates and an imputation tax system). Table 2 briefly provides details of the tax systems of the U.S., U.K., France, Germany and Japan. It can be seen from the table that only the U.K. and France use pure imputation systems, with Germany and Japan employing hybrid systems.

It is not within the scope of this article to discuss the merits and disadvantages of each type of tax system. We merely note that, in the classical system, corporations and investors are separately and independently taxable on corporate income flowing to investors. By contrast, dual rate and imputation systems both attempt, at least in part, to mitigate this effective double taxation of income. Dual rate systems do this by imposing a lower corporate tax rate on distributed profits when compared with undistributed profits, and imputation systems by giving stockholders relief for corporate taxes already paid on distributed income. In all four countries other than the U.S., tax systems have been altered since World War II to provide or increase relief from double taxation: France introduced imputation in 1965; the U.K. in 1973; Japan added a dual rate element to its imputation tax system in 1957; and Germany an imputation element to its pure dual rate system in 1977.[17]

Thus, the major impetus for tax reform in all countries has been governments' desire to influence the dividend decisions of firms. Although interest payments on corporate debt are tax deductible in all five countries, only in the Japanese change to a hy-

---

14. See I. Kuroda and Y. Oritani, "A Reexamination of the Unique Features of Japan's Corporate Financial Structure," Japanese Economic Studies, 8 (Summer 1980).

15. See R. H. Gordon ad B. G. Malkiel, "Corporation Finance," in H. Aaron and J. Pechman, eds., How Taxes Affect Economic Behavior, Brookings Institution (1981), pp.131-98.

16. The figures are lower since liquid assets have been deducted from debt ⸳ᵈᵉ debt has been excluded. See the *Report of the Committee to Review the ⸳ⁱⁿg of Financial Instititutions* (the "Wilson Report") (1980), Cmnd. ⸳0³.

17. The preference, particularly in Europe, for imputation rather than dual rate systems (i.e. relief at stockholder rather than corporate level) was to prevent overseas investors from automatically obtaining relief from double taxation.

Dual rate and imputation systems both attempt to mitigate the effective double taxation of income.

TABLE 2
Tax Systems in the U.S., U.K., France, Germany and Japan[1]

	U.S.	U.K.	France	Germany	Japan
Tax System	Classical	Imputation	Imputation	Hybrid	Hybrid
Corporate Tax Rate	46%	52%	50%	36%[2] Distributed 56% Undistributed	32%[2] Distributed 42% Undistributed
Imputation Rate (on gross dividend)	n/a	30%	33.3%	36%	9.1%
Personal Tax Rates					
On Dividend Income (t_{pd})					
Standard Rate	n/a	30%	n/a	n/a	n/a
Range	18%–50%	30%–75%	5%–60%	22%–56%	10%–75%
On Investment Income (t_{pb})					
Standard Rate	n/a	30%	n/a	n/a	n/a
Range	18%–50%	30%–75%	5%–25%[5]	22%–56%	10%–35%
Capital Gains Tax (tg)	12%[3]	30%[4]	15%[6]	0%	0%

[1] Based on 1982 to relate to the debt-equity ratios shown in Table 1. More recent changes include the reduction of German corporate tax on distributed profit to zero and reduction of U.K. corporate tax to 35% by 1987.
[2] We ignore local taxes in Germany and Japan. These can increase the corporate tax rate in Germany on distributed profit to a maximum of 47% and 64% on undistributed profit.
[3] Assuming 60% of gains are tax deductible for income tax purposes and an income tax rate of 30%. We consider only nominal rates on long term gains.
[4] U.K. capital gains tax is now only payable on *real* gains.
[5] The maximum rate varies according to the type of interest income from 25% for bond interest to 38% for bank deposit interest.
[6] Payable only on gains of over approximately $18,000.

brid system and in the current U.S. tax reform proposals do we see any explicit desire to influence the relative merits of corporate debt relative to equity.

The extent of any tax advantage to corporate debt depends not only on the type of tax system, but also of course on the tax rates applied to corporations and investors. If we consider the simplest tax model of optimal capital structure, in which investor taxes are assumed constant across all corporations, we can compare the relative tax advantages of debt to equity for each of these countries' tax systems in the following manner.

We define t_{ps} to be the tax rate on investor income from equity investment (which can be in the form of dividends or capital gains), t_{pb} the investor tax rate on debt income, and T_c the corporate tax rate. Under the classical tax system, the income stream accruing to stockholders and debt holders from a levered corporation can be written:

$$(\widetilde{X} - R)(1 - T_c)(1 - t_{ps}) + R(1 - t_{ps}) \qquad (1)$$

where X is the uncertain pre-interest and tax income of the firm and R the periodic interest payment on its

debt. The income to investors in an unlevered firm with identical operating cash flows can be written as

$$\widetilde{X}(1 - T_c)(1 - t_{ps}) \qquad (2)$$

Subtracting (2) from (1), we obtain the difference between otherwise identical levered and unlevered firms.

$$R\left((1 - t_{pb}) - (1 - T_c)(1 - t_{ps})\right) \qquad (3)$$

Capitalising these periodic debt cash flows at the after-tax cost of debt, we obtain the excess value of the levered as compared with the unlevered firm:

$$B\left(1 - \frac{(1 - T_c)(1 - t_{ps})}{(1 - t_{pb})}\right) \qquad (4)$$

where B is the amount of debt in the levered firm. The expression in (4) represents the change in value of a firm through raising an additional amount B of debt.

Where $t_{ps} = t_{pb}$, the familiar Modigliani and Miller T_cB result is obtained from equation (4) for the classical tax system. However, this equality of tax rates is unlikely to hold in practice since t_{ps} represents one or other or a combination of income tax on dividends and of capital gains tax; and taxes on capital gains are in all countries different from taxes on dividend income. For example, under an imputation tax system, the tax advantage of debt expression becomes

$$B \left(1 - \frac{(1 - T_c)(1 - t_{pd})}{(1 - t_{pb})(1 - t_i)} \right) \qquad (5)$$

if all profits are paid out as dividends and

$$B \left(1 - \frac{(1 - T_c)(1 - t_g)}{(1 - t_{pb})} \right) \qquad (6)$$

if profits are paid out as gains (through share repurchase, for example). Only if all investor taxes are zero will expressions (5) and (6) give the same answer. Also, under a hybrid tax system, T_c in (5) will be the rate on undistributed profits, T_{cd}, and T_c in (6) will be the rate on undistributed profits, T_{cu}.

Some assumption must therefore be made about how stockholders receive their income in order to quantify the expressions (5) and (6). So, in Table 3, which shows the tax advantages of debt for each of the five countries using the tax rates shown in Table 2, the tax advantage has been calculated assuming that stockholders receive entirely gains or dividends, the two extreme cases. We also make two alternative assumptions concerning investor taxes on equity income. We first assume, as is the case for nominal tax rates in all five countries, that income taxes on dividends are paid at the same rate as on debt income, and we use a notional 30 percent for all countries.[18] The second scenario allows for dividend laundering of some kind, as in the Miller and the Miller and Scholes models,[19] with the laundering not extending to debt income. Thus, we have $t_{pd} = t_g = 0$ and $t_{pb} = 30\%$. Table 3 shows the results.

The first point to note from Table 3 is that the tax advantage will appear higher when a non-optimal distribution policy is assumed. For example, in the U.S., with taxes of 30 percent on dividends and an assumed 60 percent of gains nontaxable for capital gains purposes at income tax rates, dividends should never be paid. Replacing equity with debt will therefore increase the value of the firm more if dividends rather than gains are replaced, giving an increase in the value of the firm for an additional unit of debt of 42 percent for a dividend-paying firm and 36 percent for a non-dividend-paying firm. Second, we can see from the Table that, if zero taxes on dividends and gains are assumed, there may be no tax advantage to debt at all.

If we compare the tax advantages of debt to firms in each country shown in Table 3 with the debt-equity ratios of Table 1, the relative rankings bear little relation to each other. Under the more realistic assumptions A of Table 3, the tax advantage of debt is greatest for U.S. corporations and least for German and Japanese firms, exactly the opposite of what might be expected from a comparison of leverage ratios. Also, despite the reductions in the tax advantage of debt as Japan, France, Germany and the U.K. moved towards an imputation tax system during the 1960s and 1970s, we can see from Table 1 that leverage ratios appear in most cases to have increased over time.

If we relax the assumption of constant tax rates across investors, a Miller-style equilibrium condition can be obtained, provided suitable assumptions are made concerning t_{ps} and t_{pb}. For example under the classical tax system, Miller assumed $t_{ps} = 0$ and t_{pb} varies across investors. Under such a scenario, with a sufficient spread of investor tax rates, there will be no optimal capital structure at firm level, but there will be an optimal aggregate debt-equity ratio for the corporate sector as a whole. This optimum will be determined by the relative size of the investor clientele preferring debt to the size of the clientele preferring equity. If we make the same assumptions as Miller for t_{ps} and t_{pb}, we can use expressions (4) and (5) to calculate the breakeven t_{pb} rate and to determine whether debt irrelevance can hold in each of the five countries. These data are shown in Table 4.

We can see from Table 4 that, under these as-

---

18. Except in the case of France, which has a maximum rate on bond income of 25 percent. We cannot use a "standard" rate for each country since this is only ʾplicable in the U.K. The use of the minimum personal tax rate in each country ʾot substantially alter the results.

ʾ. Miller, op. cit., and M. Miller and M. Scholes, "Dividends and Taxes", ʾnancial Economics, 6 (December 1978), pp.333-64.

From consideration of tax factors alone, we would expect the highest aggregate demand for debt in France, followed by the U.S., U.K. and Japan, with German investors having least demand for debt.

TABLE 3
Tax Advantage of Debt Under Modigliani-Miller Assumptions with Personal Taxes

Increase in Firm Value for an Additional Unit of Debt	A Equal Tax Rates on Dividend and Debt Income of 30%*		B Zero Taxes on Dividend Income and Capital Gains 30% on Debt Income	
	Profits distributed as: Dividends	Gains	Profits distributed as: Dividends	Gains
U.S.	0.46	0.32	0.22	0.22
U.K.	0.31	0.52	0.02	0.31
France	0.25	0.43	−0.06	0.33
Germany	0.00	0.37	−0.42	0.37
Japan	0.25	0.17	−0.07	0.17

*Except in the case of France with a maximum tax rate on debt income of 25%.

TABLE 4
Possible Debt Irrelevance Under the Miller Assumptions
Zero taxes on dividend income and capital gains for all investors j.
Non-zero taxes on debt income for some investors j.

	Breakeven $t_{pb}j$ condition $1 - t_{pb} = \dfrac{(1 - T_c)}{(1 - t_i)}$	Actual Range of $t_{pb}j$	Possible Debt-Equity Irrelevance
U.S.	$t_{pb}j = 46\%$	0–50%	Possible Irrelevance
U.K.	$t_{pb}j = 31\%$	0–75%	Possible Irrelevance
France	$t_{pb}j = 25\%$	0–25%	Debt Dominates
Germany	$t_{pb}j = 0$	0–56%	Equity Dominates
Japan	$t_{pb}j = 23\%$	0–35%	Possible Irrelevance

sumptions, debt irrelevance can hold in the U.S., U.K. and Japan. Debt dominates in France due to the low maximum rate for t_{pb} of 25 percent and equity dominates in Germany because of the high rate of imputation. Estimates of clientele sizes on either side of the equilibrium t_{pb} rate, to determine the aggregate expected debt-equity ratio, are hindered by lack of data. Nevertheless, from a comparison of breakeven $t_{pb}j$ with the actual range of t_{pb} in each country, we would expect the highest aggregate demand for debt in France, followed by the U.S., U.K. and Japan, with German investors having the least demand for debt. Again, we find the implications of the Miller model for corporate leverage in different countries bear no obvious relationship to observed debt-equity ratios adopted by the firms concerned.

A more recent tax model by DeAngelo and Masulis[20] allows for non-interest tax shields which reduce the effective rate of corporate tax below the nominal rate T_c. Under this model, the debt-equity decision becomes relevant at the individual corporation level as well as the aggregate level. The greater the amount of non-interest tax shields (such as depreciation or inflation allowances) deductible from taxable profits, the lower the expected leverage ratio.

To estimate the importance of this factor in each of the five countries, we turn to a survey by Kay and Sen which estimates effective average rates of corporation tax on undistributed profits for a variety of countries.[21] Table 5 shows the nominal rates and average effective rates for each of the U.S., U.K., France, Germany and Japan for 1980, the latest year covered by the survey. From the table, Germany and the U.K. have the lowest effective corporate tax rates relative to their high nominal rates. However, the typical nominal corporate tax rate of around 50 percent is substantially higher than the average effective rates in all five countries. This is hardly surprising given the generosity of allowances. For example, in the U.K., 100 percent depreciation in the first year was allowable in 1980 for all plant and equipment, as well as 100 percent for increases in inventory values attributable to inflation. It has been estimated that, by 1982, U.K. firms had 30 billion of unused tax allowances. Thus the tax advantage of debt values shown in Table 3 appear overstated across all countries, in particular for the U.K.

20. See H. DeAngelo and R. W. Masulis, op. cit.

21. See J. Kay and J. Sen "The Comparative Burden of Business Taxation," *Institute for Fiscal Studies* working paper No. 45 (July 1983).

In Japan, France and Germany, the banking sectors also provide the bulk of debt finance to the corporate sector, but they are closely linked to their clients in a variety of ways.

TABLE 5
Nominal and Effective Average Rates of Corporation Tax (1980)

	Nominal Rate[1]	Effective Average Rate[1]
U.S.	46.0%	17.8%
U.K.	52.0%	9.2%
France	50.0%	10.5%
Germany	56.0%	9.7%
Japan	42.0%	17.8%

[1] On undistributed profits.
Source: J. Kay and J. Sen, the Comparative Burden of Business Taxation, Institute of Fiscal Studies Working Paper No. 45, July 1983.

Agency Costs

The failure of tax factors to explain satisfactorily differences in observed debt-equity ratios between firms in different countries leads us to consider non-tax factors, in particular agency costs, as possible explanatory variables for these differences. The conflicts of interest between agent and principal inherent in a situation where an agent's actions cannot be costlessly observed by the principal can be applied to the theory of optimal capital structure in two main ways.

First, there is the risk that the managers, acting as agents for the owners of the firm, will not act in the interest of stockholders or debtholders. In the case of stockholders, owner-managers not owning 100 percent of equity will be tempted to take part of the firm's profits in the form of perquisites. On the other hand, providers of debt to the firm run the risk that owner-managers can take actions which may make them worse off in certain situations. For example, there is an incentive for owner-managers to take on high risk projects which will involve a transfer of wealth from debtholders to stockholders. Also, the use of debt finance means that the firm may default on its loan obligations; and the costs associated with the consequent bankruptcy, reorganisation, takeover or liquidation of assets may be substantial. Lenders of debt will charge more to take account of these expected agency costs, which cannot be avoided through explicit contracts. For example, even if debtholders are given precisely defined rights in the context of reorganisation, a bankruptcy court judge may well alter these rights in order to allow the firm to continue trading. Thus, the relative agency costs of debt and equity will determine the type of external finance and hence the capital structure chosen by owner-managers.

There are several ways, however, in which such agency costs can be lessened. Agency costs of equity can be reduced through stockholders meetings, the auditing of accounts, and so on, provided sufficient outside equity is raised. These costs are likely to be lower in the U.S. than in the U.K., and lower in the U.K. than in Europe and Japan. For example, U.S. corporations produce quarterly reports and pay quarterly dividends;[22] U.K. quoted firms do so semi-annually and French firms only annually. Also, the quality of an audit can vary. The auditor's statement in a Japanese firm's report and accounts does not always have the weight of a U.S. accounting firm's statement.

Similarly, agency costs of debt can be reduced by allowing debtholders as well as stockholders to have an influence on project investment decisions, either through stockholdings or seats on the Board. Debtholders can also use informal reorganisations in the face of financial distress, where they negotiate directly with the stockholders, with lower costs than formal bankruptcy proceedings and a greater likelihood of enforcing their rights.

To ascertain the likely importance of the agency costs of debt in each country, we can compare the relationships established in each country between firms and their creditors. The use of publicly-issued bonds requires a formal system for protection of creditors in the event of default, whereas dependence on bank loans allows flexibility. In the U.S., formal re-organisations involving a number of types of corporate bonds can involve substantial costs.[23] In

---

[22]. Of course, some of this information may be superfluous and produced to ~ith regulation. Such information also aids debtholders, in particular ~bt securities.

23. Although Jerry Warner's study of railroad bankruptcies ("Bankrupcty Costs: Some Evidence," *Journal of Finance*, 32 (May 1977), pp.337-47 found these costs to be fairly small.

The close, stable relationships developed between banks and their client firms in France, Germany and Japan mean that the quality of information held by banks is high and is obtained at low cost.

the U.K. a major source of external finance is secured bank debt; banks with a floating charge on debt can put in a receiver to realise their claim and run the firm as they think fit. This is a relatively public and hence costly method of coping with default. In Japan, France and Germany, the banking sectors also provide the bulk of debt finance to the corporate sector, but they are closely linked to their clients in a variety of ways.

For example, in Germany, banks hold equity (currently 9 percent of the German corporate sector), often vote on behalf of individual stockholders who deposit their (bearer) shares with the banks, and bank directors sit on supervisory boards to which German boards of directors are answerable. In France (where equity participation is through the banques d'affaires on a lower level than in Germany) and in Germany, banks employ industry specialists who both require information from and give advice to client firms. In Japan, the ties can be even closer, with financial institutions holding 37 percent of listed Japanese corporations' stock in 1980, and Japanese corporations holding a further 26 percent.[24] It is common for the bank and corporate stockholders of large corporations to belong to the same holding group and for banks and corporations to exchange personnel. Given these close relationships, it is likely that in these countries creditors will be involved in capital investment decisions and will be accommodating in the event of financial distress. This analysis would lead one to expect lower debt-equity ratios in the U.K. and U.S. than in France, Germany and Japan.

The second type of agency cost which may affect the debt-equity decision is due to information asymmetry. An example is the case where management seeks outside finance to fund project investment and have information on the project outcome which they are unable to transmit unambiguously to market investors. As a result, investors are unable to correctly value the impact of the project. In this context, the agency cost is the difference between the value the securities would have if the information were known to them and the price for which they can be sold without the benefit of the information.

Stewart Myers, in the article printed at the head of this issue, argues that these information asymme-

try costs explain the types of finance employed by corporations: predominantly retained earnings with no such agency costs, followed by those securities whose value will change least when the information is finally disclosed to the market. The "safest" of these securities is debt, then preference stock, and the least "safe" is equity. Campbell has adopted a similar framework to argue that firms will choose to finance with bank debt rather than debt securities for the same reason: namely, that inside information can be unambiguously and cheaply given to a few banks (provided they do not exploit it by trading in equity) in a way not possible for financial securities.[25] So, the "pecking" order for outside finance will be as follows: bank debt, then debt securities, followed by preferred stock and, finally, ordinary common stock.

If we consider the impact of information asymmetry costs across countries, various factors will affect the relative use of retained earnings, bank debt and market securities. First, the faster growing firms will more quickly use up retained earnings and be forced to resort to external finance. Second, the closer the relationship to the banking community, and the less developed the stock market, the greater the difference between the agency costs of bank debt and the agency costs of market securities. Thus, the close, stable relationships developed between banks and their client firms in France, Germany and Japan mean that the quality of information held by banks is high and is obtained at low cost. Third, the use of bond and equity markets requires the development of an adequate accounting system for the dissemination of information to investors and an efficient primary and secondary stock market. Only as other, cheaper sources of finance dry up will the fixed costs inherent in developing accounting systems and standards or stock markets be incurred. The increase in the use of consolidated accounts by Japanese firms in the late 1970s and early 1980s, as they sought to raise capital in the international equity markets, is one example. A move by the Commission des Operations de Bourse towards requiring French firms to provide more detailed disclosure in annual reports and towards more rapid presentation of accounts, as new equity issue activity increased in the early 1980s, is another.

---

24. Since 1977, Japanese banks have been allowed to hold no more than 5 percent of the equity of any one client firm.

25. See T. S. Campbell, "Optimal Investment Financing Decisions and the Value of Confidentiality," *Journal of Financial and Quantitative Analysis*, 14 (1979), pp.913-24.

The use of bond and equity markets requires the development of an adequate accounting system for the dissemination of information to investors as well as an efficient primary and secondary stock market.

Finally, another relative difference between bank debt, debt securities and equity depending on the relative efficiency of the banking system and the stock market is issue costs. Relatively inactive securities markets are also likely to have higher new issues costs for both debt and equity. For example, studies of German capital markets found that stock issue costs amounted to between 6.5 percent and 9 percent of the amount raised and to between 3.3 percent and 4.3 percent for bond and long-term loan issues.[26] Similarly, the Japanese system of issuing new stock at par to a pre-determined bloc of investors was both cumbersome and expensive and is only now being phased out.

Concluding Remarks

This article has attempted a whistle-stop tour of the factors which may explain why corporate debt-equity ratios apparently differ so much across countries, with Japanese firms depending heavily on debt, European firms less highly levered and U.S. and U.K. firms seeming to prefer equity finance. In this much discussed area of corporate finance, we make the following tentative conclusions:

● *Accounting variations across countries appear to exaggerate the differences in debt-equity ratios between countries but, if these variations are allowed for, the essential differences still remain.*

● *Tax factors, whether assuming a Modigliani and Miller model or an investor clientele model such as that proposed by Miller, do not appear to be able to explain cross-sectional differences. A relatively high tax advantage to debt or likely demand for debt in a particular country is not related to a high aggregate leverage ratio.*

● *Agency costs of debt, on the other hand, do seem to be able to explain why Japanese, French and German corporations continue to rely heavily on debt finance, a dependence which dates in most cases from post-World War II reorganisation and central government encouragement. The close relationships established between the banks and their client firms reduce both moral hazard risk and the costs associated with information asymmetry. Firms in these countries have therefore not needed to rely heavily on the more expensive (in agency cost terms) external finance.*

● *U.S and U.K. corporations have had lower agency costs of equity relative to those for debt, since banks, at least in the U.K., appear to have restricted their lending and the agency costs of debt securities are higher than for bank finance. As a result, both countries have well-developed equity markets, with efficient information dissemination, stringent auditing and monitoring procedures and low issue costs which keep the agency costs of equity to a minimum.*

26. See B. T. Bayliss and A. A. S. Butt Philip, *Capital Markets and Industrial Investment in Germany and France*, Saxon House (1980), page 29 and the OECD *Capital Market Survey* (1966).

References

Bagehot, W., "Risk and Reward in Corporate Pension Funds," *Financial Analysts Journal* (January-February 1972).

Bayliss, B. T., and A. A. S. Butt Philip, *Capital Markets and Industrial Investment in Germany and France*, Saxon House (1980).

Brealey, R. A., and S. Myers, *Principles of Corporate Finance,* Second Edition, McGraw-Hill (1984).

Campbell, T. S., "Optimal Investment Financing Decisions and the Value of Confidentiality," *Journal of Financial and Quantitative Analysis*, 14 (1979), pp.913 - 924.

Corcoran, P. J., "Inflation Taxes and Corporate Investment Incentives," *Federal Reserve Bank of New York Quarterly Review* (Autumn 1977), pp.1 - 10.

DeAngelo, H., and R. W. Masulis, "Optimal Capital Structure under Corporate and Personal Taxation," *Journal of Financial Economics*, 8 (Mar.1980), pp.2 - 30.

Gordon, R. H., and B. G. Malkiel, "Corporate Finance" in Aaron, H., and J. Pechman, eds., *How Taxes Affect Economic Behaviour*, Brookings Institution (1981), pp.131 - 198.

Kay, J., and J. Sen, "The Comparative Burden of Business Taxation" Institute for Fiscal Studies Working Paper No. 45 (July 1983).

Kuroda, I., and Y. Oritani, "A Re-examination of the Unique Features of Japan's Corporate Financial Structure," *Japanese Economic Studies*, 8 (Summer 1980).

Lasman, D., and R. Weil, "Adjusting the Debt-Equity Ratio," *Financial Analysts Journal* (September - October 1978) pp.49 - 58.

Miller, M., "Debt and Taxes," *Journal of Finance*, 32 (December 1977), p. 271.

Miller, M., and M. Scholes, "Dividends and Taxes," *Journal of Financial Economics*, 6 (December 1978), pp.333 - 364.

Myers, S., "Determinants of Corporate Borrowing," *Journal of Financial Economics*, 5 (1977), pp.149 - 150.

Myers, S., " The Capital Structure Puzzle," *Journal of Finance*, 39 (July 1984), pp.575 - 592.

Samuels, J. M., R. E. Groves and C. S. Goddard, "Company Finance in Europe," The Institute of Chartered Accountants in England and Wales (1975).

Stonehill, A., T. Beekhuisen, R., Wright, L. Remmers, N. Toy, A. Pares, A. Shapiro, D. Egan and T. Bates, "Financial Goals and Debt Ratio Determinants: A Survey of Practice in Five Countries," *Financial Management* (Autumn 1977) pp.27 - 41.

Treynor, J., "The Principles of Corporate Pension Finance," *Journal of Finance*, 32 (May 1977), pp.627 - 638.

Toy, N., A. Stonehill, L. Remmers, R. Wright and T. Bates, "A Comparative International Study of Growth, Profitability and Risk as Determinants of Corporate Debt Ratios in the Manufacturing Sector," *Journal of Financial and Quantitative Analysis*, 9 (November 1974) pp.875 - 876.

Warner, J. B., "Bankruptcy Costs: Some Evidence," *Journal of Finance*, 32 (May 1977) pp.337-347.

Zwick, B., "The Market for Corporate Bonds," *Federal Reserve Bank of New York Quarterly Review* (Autumn 1977) pp.27-36.

Part V International Banking

International Banking and Country Risk Analysis

Alan C. Shapiro,
University of Southern California

During the 1970s, the big money-center banks, as well as many regional banks, rechanneled billions of petrodollars to less-developed countries. Major banks earned fat fees for arranging loans to Mexico, Brazil, Argentina and other such borrowers. The regional banks earned the spreads between their cost of borrowing Eurodollars and the rates at which these loans were syndicated. These spreads were minimal, usually on the order of 0.5 to 0.75 percent.

All this made sense, however, only as long as banks and their depositors were willing to suspend their disbelief about the risks of international lending. By now, the risks are big and obvious. The purpose of this paper is to gain some perspective on the origins of risk in international lending.[1]

The focus here is on "country risk," the possibility that a nation will be unable to service or repay its debts to foreign lenders in a timely manner. The essence of country risk analysis at commercial banks, therefore, is an assessment of factors that affect the ability of a country such as Mexico to generate sufficient dollars to repay foreign debts as they come due. These factors are the quality and effectiveness of a country's economic and financial management policies, the country's resource base, and its external financial position. Political factors include the degree of political stability of a country and the extent to which a foreign entity, such as the United States, is willing implicitly to stand behind the country's external obligations. Lending to a foreign private sector borrower also exposes a bank to commercial risks as well as to country risk. But because these commercial risks are generally similar to those encountered in domestic lending, they are not treated separately here.

In analyzing country risk, it is impossible to avoid discussing currency risk. As used here, the term "currency risk" refers to the possibility that exchange rate changes will alter the expected dollar amount of interest and principal the bank will collect on the loan. Specifically, there is the risk that exchange rate changes will so increase the loan's real cost to the borrower that it will default. To the extent that exchange rate changes systematically affect the ability of a nation to repay its foreign loans, currency risk begets country risk.

The paper divides into three parts. The first examines the links between country risk and currency risk, the second discusses the analysis of country risk, and the third offers some insights into indicators of country risk.

Country Risk and Currency Risk in International Lending

Banks typically try to cope with currency risk when lending to foreign firms and governments either by both denominating and funding their loans in the foreign currency or, failing that, by denominating their foreign loans in dollars. The latter practice appears to protect the banks by shifting any risk associated with exchange rate fluctuations to the borrowers. Yet to the extent that changes in currency values affect the ability or willingness of foreign borrowers to repay their dollar loans, the currency risk on these loans doesn't disappear; rather, it manifests itself as credit risk.

1. Much of this paper is based on my article, "Currency Risk and Country Risk in International Banking," *Journal of Finance* (July 1986), pp. 881-891.

Currency risk is most likely to occur when a government attempts to fix its exchange rate at an artificially high level.

Currency risk is most likely to occur when a government attempts to fix its exchange rate at an artificially high level. Given the prevalence and, indeed, the universality of controlled rate systems among countries facing international debt problems, it is worth exploring the currency risks associated with such a system. For purposes of our analysis, the most relevant feature of a controlled exchange rate system (one in which the government maintains a fixed rate through mandatory currency controls) is that the local currency is likely to be overvalued. This means that there will be a substantial deviation from purchasing power parity (PPP). (PPP holds when changes in the purchasing power of a nation's currency relative to the purchasing powers of other currencies are reflected in offsetting exchange rate movements.)[2]

The further out of alignment the currency is (that is, the greater the deviation from purchasing power parity), the more stringent must be the controls on flows of physical goods and capital. These restrictions can prove a costly proposition for local industries that depend on imports for spare parts, raw materials, and the like, reducing their ability to repay their dollar loans. Moreover, even if the dollar value (at the official exchange rate) of the firm's local currency cash flows is sufficient to service its dollar debts, the firm may be unable to acquire those dollars.

There is also the possibility of government-imposed price controls in a fixed rate system. These price controls are especially likely following devaluation of the local currency in an attempt by the government to moderate the resulting inevitable rise in prices. This will have the effect of removing one more degree of freedom from the firm's ability to respond to a changing economic environment.

The consequences of deviations from purchasing power parity on the credit risk associated with a loan can best be understood by introducing the concept of the real exchange rate.

The Real Exchange Rate

The *real* exchange rate is defined as the *nominal*, or actual, exchange rate adjusted for changes in the relative purchasing power of each currency since some base period. Specifically,

$$e'_t = e_t \times \frac{(1 + i_f)}{(1 + i_h)}$$

where e'_t = the real exchange rate (home currency per one unit of foreign currency) at time t; e_t = the nominal exchange rate (home currency per one unit of foreign currency) at time t; i_f = the amount of foreign inflation between time 0 and t; and i_h = the amount of domestic inflation between time 0 and t.

Importance of the Real Exchange Rate. If nominal exchange rate changes just cancel out changes in the foreign price level relative to the domestic price level, exchange rate movements should have no effects on the relative competitive positions of domestic firms and their foreign competitors. Thus, changes in nominal exchange rates may be of little significance in determining the true effects of currency changes on a firm and a nation. Therefore, in terms of currency changes affecting relative competitiveness, the focus must be not on nominal exchange rate 'changes but instead on changes in the real purchasing power of one currency relative to another.[3] This is what the *real* exchange rate attempts to measure.

Illustration. The unfortunate example of Chile provides a particularly dramatic illustration of the effects of a rise in the real value of a currency. As part of its plan to bring down the rate of Chilean inflation, the government fixed the exchange rate at 39 pesos to the U.S. dollar in the middle of 1979. Over the next two-and-a-half years, the Chilean price level rose 60 percent, while U.S. prices rose by only about 30 percent. Thus, by early 1982 the Chilean peso had undergone a real revaluation of approximately 23 percent against the U.S. dollar. (These calculations are shown in Table 1.) Moreover, during this same time period the dollar itself strengthened in real terms by about 20 percent against other currencies.

An 18 percent corrective devaluation was enacted in June 1982. But it was too late. The artificially high peso had already done its double damage to the Chilean economy: It made Chile's manufactured products more expensive abroad, pricing many of them out of international trade; and it made imports cheaper, undercutting Chilean domestic industries. The effects of the overvalued peso were

---

2. For a review of the issues surrounding purchasing power parity, see my "What Does Purchasing Power Parity Mean?," *Journal of International Finance* (December 1983), pp. 295-318.

3. For an extended discussion of the nature of exchange risk and the consequences of real versus nominal exchange rate changes, see Brad Cornell and Alan C. Shapiro, "Managing Foreign Exchange Risks," *Midland Corporate Finance Journal* (Fall 1983), pp. 16-31.

212

As the example of Chile demonstrated, a firm may face more exchange risk if nominal exchange rates do not change than if they do.

TABLE 1 The Real Exchange Rate Change for the Chilean Peso: 1979–1982		Price Level		Exchange Rate	
		Chile	U.S.	Nominal	Real
	1979	100	100	P1 = $.0256	P1 = $.0256
	1982	160	130	P1 = $.0256	P1 = $.0256 × $\dfrac{1.60}{1.30}$ = $.0315

Real value of the Chilean peso rose by $\dfrac{.0315 - .0256}{.0256} = 23\%$.

devastating. Banks became insolvent, factories and copper smelters were thrown into bankruptcy, copper mines were closed, construction projects were shut down, and farms were put on the auction block. Unemployment approached 25 percent and some areas of Chile resembled industrial graveyards.

Currency Risk Identification and Real Exchange Rate Changes

Banks have frequently failed to distinguish adequately between nominal and real exchange rate changes and the consequences of this distinction for credit risk analysis. As the example of Chile demonstrated, a firm may face more exchange risk if nominal exchange rates do not change than if they do. The combination of relatively high Chilean inflation and a fixed nominal exchange rate pushed up the real value of the peso and devastated Chilean firms that either exported or competed domestically against imports.

The implications for credit risk analysis of real exchange rate changes are especially important in the case of local firms selling domestically and facing little or no import competition—mainly because they are less obvious. Such firms will find their local currency (and, hence, their dollar cash flows when converted at the fixed exchange rate) rising along with local inflation. Based on their rapidly rising profits, it is tempting to rate these firms good credit risks and provide them with substantial loans. And many banks did just that. But comes the inevitable devaluation, the dollar value of their local currency flows will decline approximately in line with the exchange rate change and so will their ability to repay these loans. Banks must constantly be wary of such false prosperity.

For example, some major American banks lent a great deal of money to one of the largest Chilean brewers in the late 1970s. This brewer faced essentially no competition and so was highly profitable in both peso and dollar terms prior to devaluation of the peso. Although its credit looked impeccable, this brewer's loans are now in default. The bankers forgot to assess the conditions that led to the brewer's high profits and the likelihood that these conditions would persist.

Fixed exchange rates in such countries are rather like the surface before an earthquake. Although the ground usually seems stable enough, underground stresses are building up and gathering force for the inevitable upheaval. Similarly, in a fixed exchange rate system, while the nominal exchange rate remains constant, the real value of the currency running the higher rate of inflation is rising, causing pressures that will ultimately be released through devaluation. Thus, in assessing credit risk for foreign borrowers operating in a controlled rate system, it is necessary to assess their creditworthiness both before and after the inevitable devaluation.

Country Risk Analysis

Turning to a government borrower, its ability to repay a dollar loan is determined by its capacity to extract the necessary quantity of foreign exchange from the public. The government can, of course, outbid any private economic unit for dollars because it can print unlimited quantities of its own currency at close to a zero marginal cost. But there are costs to doing this. It is these costs that help determine whether a nation will honor its obligations.

Country Risk and the Terms of Trade

What ultimately determines a nation's ability to repay foreign loans is its ability to generate U.S. dollars and other hard currencies. This, in turn, is based on the nation's terms of trade—the weighted

Fixed exchange rates in such countries are rather like the surface before an earthquake. Although the ground usually seems stable enough, underground stresses are building up and gathering force for the inevitable upheaval.

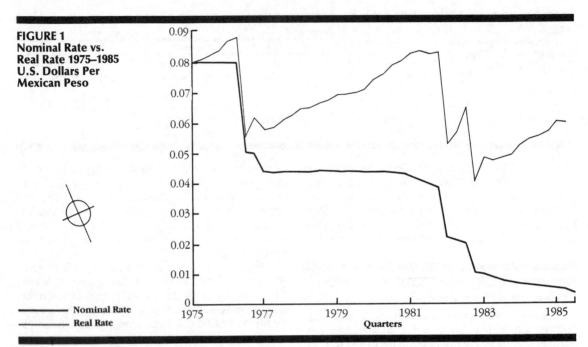

FIGURE 1
Nominal Rate vs. Real Rate 1975–1985
U.S. Dollars Per Mexican Peso

——— Nominal Rate
——— Real Rate

Quarters

average of the nation's export prices relative to its import prices; that is, the exchange rate between exports and imports. Most economists would agree that these terms of trade are largely independent of the nominal exchange rate, unless the observed rate has been affected by government intervention in the foreign exchange market.

In general, if the nation's terms of trade improve, it will be a better credit risk. Alternatively, if the nation's terms of trade decrease, it will be a poorer credit risk. This terms-of-trade risk, however, can be exacerbated by political decisions. When a nation's terms of trade improve, foreign goods become relatively less expensive, the nation's standard of living rises, and consumers and businesses become more dependent on imports. But because there is a large element of unpredictability to relative price changes, shifts in the terms of trade will also be unpredictable. When the nation's terms of trade decline, as must inevitably happen when prices fluctuate randomly, the government will likely face political pressure to maintain the nation's standard of living.

A typical response is for the government to fix the exchange rate at its former (and now overvalued) level—that is, to subsidize the price of dollars ̶ nce, foreign goods and services. Loans made terms of trade improved are now doubly

risky: first, because the terms of trade have declined and, second, because the government, in maintaining an overvalued currency, is further reducing the net inflow of dollars. The usual result is added government borrowing.

Illustration. When Mexican oil revenues jumped in the late 1970s, the Mexican government thought it saw the answer to the future: Use these revenues to build a strong industrial economy so the nation wouldn't wind up dependent on oil alone. International bankers eagerly endorsed that plan. Convinced that growing oil revenues would allow Mexico to meet growing debt payments, they rushed to make loans. But the nation never managed to pump oil at the pace that it borrowed. As fast as it borrowed money from abroad, the Mexican government spent money even more rapidly. To meet the growing government deficit, Mexico printed more pesos, leading to rapid inflation.

The resulting rise in the real value of the peso, depicted in Figure 1, choked off exports outside the oil sector. Mexican goods and services (such as tourism) were too expensive to compete. At the same time, Mexicans used their overvalued pesos to import luxury goods, travel abroad, and buy billions of dollars worth of U.S. real estate and other assets. This situation might have continued beyond 1982 if oil

The cost of austerity is primarily determined by the nation's external debts relative to its wealth, as measured by its GNP. The lower this ratio, the lower the relative amount of consumption that must be sacrificed to meet its foreign debts.

TABLE 2
External Debt: National Income Ratios for Various Countries

Country	External Debt* (in billions)	% of Gross Domestic Product
Brazil	$85.2	59%
Mexico	$87.0	52%
Canada	$99.5	34%
Argentina	$36.5	30%
France	$106.1	20%
Italy	$66.0	19%
W. Germany	$119.4	18%
U.S.A.	$200.0**	5%**

* Source: Estimates by U.S. banks as reported in *Fortune,* April 30, 1984, p. 166.
** Estimate of US foreign debt as percentage of GNP as reported in *Fortune,* Dec. 3, 1985.

prices had continued to rise. But such was not to be. When oil prices dropped in mid-1981, the government refused to cut back spending or realign the peso. The foreign debt used to prop up the peso grew so fast that the government couldn't keep track of it. Even as the strains became evident, bankers continued lending money to Mexico at preferential rates. Mexican citizens were smarter; worried by the excesses of their government, they exported an estimated $20 billion in capital from 1980 through 1982, draining Mexican reserves. By August 1982, the party was over: Mexico ran out of dollars and bankers refused to lend more.

To summarize, a terms-of-trade risk can be exacerbated if the government maintains the old exchange rate so as to avoid the drop in the nation's standard of living that would otherwise occur when the terms of trade decline. In reality, of course, this element of country risk is a political risk. The government is attempting by political means to hold off the necessary economic adjustments to the country's changed wealth position.

A key issue, therefore, in assessing country risk is the speed with which a country adjusts to its new wealth position. In other words, how fast will the necessary austerity policy be implemented? The answer depends in part on what the government perceives to be the costs and benefits associated with austerity versus default.

The Government's Cost/Benefit Calculus

The cost of austerity is primarily determined by the nation's external debts relative to its wealth, as measured by its GNP. The lower this ratio, the lower the relative amount of consumption that must be sacrificed to meet its foreign debts. The relative magnitudes of this ratio for a sample of developed and developing countries is provided by Table 2.

The cost of default is the likelihood of being cut off from international credit. This possibility brings its own form of austerity. Most nations will follow this path only as a last resort, preferring to stall for time in the hope that something will happen in the interim. That something could be a bailout by the IMF, the Bank for International Settlements, or the Fed (or some other major central bank). The bailout decision is largely a political decision. It depends on the willingness of citizens of another nation, usually the U.S., to tax themselves on behalf of the debtor nation.[4] This is a function of two factors: 1) the nation's geopolitical importance to the U.S., and 2) the probability that the necessary economic adjustments will result in unacceptable political and social turmoil.

The more a nation's terms of trade fluctuate, and the less stable its political system, the greater the odds the government will face a situation that will tempt it to hold off on the necessary adjustments. Terms-of-trade variability is negatively correlated with the degree of product diversification in the nation's trade flows. With limited diversification in the nation's trade flows (for example, in cases of dependence on the export of one or two primary products or imports heavily weighted towards a few commodities), the nation's terms of trade are likely to be highly variable. This characterizes the situation facing many Third World countries. It also describes, in part, the situation of those OECD nations heavily dependent on oil imports.

---

4. For a discussion of this point, see Tamir Agmon and J. Kimball Dietrich, "International Lending and Income Redistribution: An Alternative View of Country Risk," *Journal of International Banking and Finance* (December 1983), pp. 483-495.

A controlled rate system goes hand in hand with an overvalued local currency leaves the economy little flexibility to respond to changing relative prices and wealth positions. This will exacerbate any unfavorable trend in the nation's terms of trade.

TABLE 3
Debt Burden Ratios
as of Year-End 1982*

Country	Debt Service/Exports	Debt Service/GNP
Mexico	.70	.080
Brazil	.56	.063
Argentina	.41	.024
Chile	.54	.099
Venezuela	.32	.090
Spain	.28	—
Philippines	.25	.040
South Korea	.17	.063
Non-OPEC LDCs	.24	.056
OPEC countries	.11	.054

* Source: Robert E. Weintraub, *International Debt: Crisis and Challenge,* George Mason University, Department of Economics monograph, April 1983, pp. 17 and 19.

The current account structure of the United States reveals that American exports are much more broadly based than even the exports of Germany and Japan. The U.S. receives much more service and investment income, exports many more agricultural products, and is a major exporter of primary products. In 1982, for example, only 44 percent of U.S. export receipts came from manufactures, as opposed to 69 percent and 76 percent, respectively, for Germany and Japan. Similarly, U.S. imports are more diversified than the imports of most other countries. Consequently, the terms of trade for the United States tend to fluctuate less than the terms of trade for other countries.

Country Risk Indicators

Fiscal irresponsibility is one sign of a problem debtor. Thus, one country risk indicator is the government deficit as a percentage of GDP. The higher the relative deficit, the more the government is promising to its citizens relative to the resources it is extracting in payment. This lowers the possibility that the government can meet its promises without foreign borrowing.

The correlation between having a controlled rate system and having foreign debt-servicing problems, pointed out earlier, is not coincidental. A controlled rate system goes hand in hand with an overvalued local currency, which is the equivalent of taxing imports and subsidizing imports. The risk of tighter currency controls and the ever-present threat of a devaluation provide strong incentives for residents to move their funds abroad. Similarly, multinational firms will try to repatriate rather than reinvest their local affiliates' profits. Most importantly perhaps, a controlled exchange rate system leaves the economy little flexibility to respond to changing relative prices and wealth positions. This will exacerbate any unfavorable trend in the nation's terms of trade.

Another indicator of potential debt-servicing problems is the degree of waste inherent in the economy. To the extent that capital from abroad is used to subsidize consumption or is wasted on showcase projects, there will be less wealth to draw on and the country will have more difficulty repaying its debts. Additionally, funds diverted to the purchase of assets abroad (capital flight) will not add to the economy's dollar-generating capacity unless investors feel safe in repatriating their overseas earnings.

One standard measure of the risk associated with a nation's debt burden is its coverage ratio, the ratio of exports to debt service.[5] For example, Table 3 contains 1982 year-end statistics on two debt-service measures for both individual countries and groupings of OPEC and non-OPEC developing countries. To put these figures in perspective, most bankers consider a debt-service:export ratio of .25 or higher to be dangerous; that is, a coverage ratio of less than 4:1.

5. Ex ante, however, what matters is not just the coverage ratio but also the ~bility of the difference between export revenues (X) and import costs (M) to the nation's debt service requirements; that is, expressed in equation $(X - M)/D]$, where c.v. is the coefficient of variation and D is the debt ~ement. When calculating this measure of risk, one must recognize ~me is likely to be positively correlated, and import volume negatively correlated, with price. These correlations exist because a high price for exports usually reflects strong demand, and vice versa, while a low price of imports usually stimulates domestic demand for foreign products. In addition, import expenditures are usually positively related to export revenues. These correlations add to the variability of trade flows.

Resource Base

The resource base of a country consists of its natural, human, and financial resources. Other things being equal, a nation with substantial natural resources, such as oil or copper, is a better economic risk than one without those resources. But typically, all is not equal. Hence, resource-poor nations such as South Korea or Taiwan turn out to be better risks than resource-rich Mexico or Argentina. The reason has to do with the quality of human resources and whether these resources are allowed to be put to their most efficient use.

A nation with highly-skilled and productive workers, a large pool of scientists and engineers, and ample management talent will have many of the essential ingredients to pursue a course of steady growth and development. Two further factors are necessary: (1) a stable political system that encourages hard work and risk-taking by allowing entrepreneurs to reap the rewards (both positive and negative) from their activities, and (2) a free market system which ensures that the prices people respond to correctly signal the relative desirability of engaging in different activities. In this way, the nation's human and natural resources will be put to their most efficient uses.

A Portfolio Perspective

Clearly, an exchange rate change that harms one nation can often be beneficial to others. For example, an overvalued South Korean won will hurt Korean industry and make South Korea a poorer credit risk. At the same time, it will help Brazil by making its manufacturing industries that compete against South Korean industry, such as shoe manufacturing, shipbuilding, and steel, more competitive overseas. Similarly, the drop in oil prices hurt OPEC and other oil-producing nations, while at the same time significantly benefiting many oil-consuming nations. By holding a diversified portfolio of loans to foreign countries, the currency risk associated with the portfolio will be less than the sum of the individual currency risks.

Yet it is important not to overestimate the benefits of portfolio diversification for international loan portfolios. For example, it is usually assumed that Brazil, a major oil importer, benefited greatly from the drop in oil prices. But Brazil is also a major

exporter to OPEC nations. When oil prices dropped, Brazil's import requirements declined, but so did its OPEC exports. As a result, the net effect on Brazil of lower oil prices was much less favorable than a superficial analysis would seem to indicate.

Banks try to reduce the riskiness of their international loan portfolios by lending to a broad spectrum of nations. To a certain extent this strategy works; unsystematic risks are diversified away. Unfortunately for the banks, however, the systematic component of risk turns out to be far greater than anticipated. External shocks such as world recession and falling commodity prices systematically affect the ability of borrowers to repay their debts. Similarly, the advent of unexpectedly high real interest rates showed that the use of floating-rate loans, which were designed to protect banks from interest rate risk, systematically converted this risk into country risk. Further, the jump in the real value of the dollar demonstrated that dollar-denominated loans were subject to exchange risk.

Country Risk and Adjustment to External Shocks

Recent history shows that the impact of external shocks is likely to vary from nation to nation, with some countries dealing successfully with these shocks and others succumbing to them. The evidence suggests that domestic policies play a critical role in determining how effective a country will be in dealing with external shocks. Asian nations, for example, successfully coped with falling commodity prices and rising real interest rates and exchange rates because their policies promoted timely internal and external adjustment, as is manifest in relatively low inflation rates and small current account deficits.

The opposite happened in Latin America. There, import-substitution development strategies hindered the export sector, leaving the share of exports in GNP far below that of other LDCs. In addition, state expenditures on massive capital projects diverted resources from the private sector and exports. Much of the investment went to notoriously inefficient state enterprises, leading to wasted resources. Corruption drained further resources.

The decline in commodity prices and simultaneous rise in real interest rates should have led to reduced domestic consumption and a reallocation of resources toward productive investments and ex-

Asian nations successfully coped with falling commodity prices and rising real interest rates and exchange rates because their policies promoted timely internal and external adjustment, as is manifest in relatively low inflation rates and small current account deficits.

ports. But fearing that spending cuts would threaten political stability, Latin American governments delayed cutting back on projects and social expenditures. The gap between consumption and production was met by borrowing overseas, thereby enabling their societies to enjoy artificially (and thus temporarily) high standards of living.

Latin American governments also tried to stimulate their economies by increasing state spending, fueled by high rates of monetary expansion. This exacerbated their difficulties since the resulting high rates of inflation combined with their fixed exchange rates to boost real exchange rates substantially and resulted in higher imports and lower exports than otherwise. In addition, these overvalued exchange rates, combined with interest rate controls on domestic deposits and political uncertainties, triggered massive capital flight from the region—estimated at up to $100 billion during the two-year period 1981-82. The result was larger balance-of-payments deficits, necessitating more foreign borrowing and higher debt service requirements. Moreover, in an attempt to control inflation, the Latin governments imposed price and interest rate controls. These controls led to further capital flight and price rigidity. Distorted prices gave the wrong signals to the residents, sending consumption soaring and production plummeting.

To summarize, poorly managed countries will have more difficulty coping with economic shocks than well-managed countries. The message is clear: In evaluating the riskiness of a foreign loan portfolio, it is not sufficient to identify those factors, such as real interest shocks or world recession, that would systematically affect loans to all foreign countries to one extent or another. It is also necessary to determine the susceptibility of the various nations and their debts to these shocks. This requires a focus on longer-term issues involving the financial policies and development strategies pursued by the different nations.

Based on the preceding discussion, some common characteristics of country risk include the following:
1. A large government deficit relative to GDP.
2. A high rate of money expansion, especially if it is combined with a relatively fixed exchange rate.
High leverage combined with highly variable
¹s of trade.
ʰtantial government expenditures yielding
of return.

5. Price controls, interest rate ceilings, trade restrictions, and other government-imposed barriers to the smooth adjustment of the economy to changing relative prices.
6. A citizenry that demands, and a political system that accepts, government responsibility for maintaining and expanding the nation's standard of living through public sector spending. The less stable the political system, the more important this factor is likely to be.

Alternatively, indicators of a nation's long-run economic health include the following:
1. A structure of incentives that rewards risk-taking in productive ventures. People have clearly demonstrated that they respond rationally to the incentives they face, given the information and resources available to them. This is true whether we are talking about shopkeepers in Nairobi or bankers in New York.
2. A legal structure that stimulates the development of free markets. The resulting price signals are most likely to contain the correct information essential to make efficient use of the nation's resources.
3. Minimal regulations and economic distortions. Complex regulations are costly to implement and wasteful of management time and other resources.

In general, where there are clear incentives to save and invest, where the economic rules of the game are straightforward and stable, and where there is political stability, a nation's chances of developing are significantly enhanced.

Summary and Conclusions

The pattern of bank lending overseas in the post-World War II period has been one of rapid expansion, beginning in the early 1960s and sharply accelerating after the first OPEC oil price shock in late 1973. This has been followed by a sharp contraction in international bank lending on the heels of the great debt crisis of 1982.

The end of let's pretend in international banking has led to a new emphasis on country risk analysis. From the bank's standpoint, country risk—the credit risk arising from loans to a nation—is largely determined by the real cost to the nation of repaying the loan versus the real wealth it has to draw on. This, in turn, depends on the variability of the nation's terms of trade and the government's willingness to allow the nation's standard of living to adjust rapidly to changing economic fortunes. It also depends on the existence of a stable political and economic system in which entrepreneurship is encouraged and free markets predominate.

We also concluded that currency risk on a bank's dollar-denominated foreign loans is a function of deviations from purchasing power parity that give rise to changes in the real exchange rate, and the effect of these real exchange rate changes on the firm's and the nation's dollar-equivalent cash flows.

Perspectives on Country Risk

Bluford H. Putnam,
Stern Stewart & Company

Following the devaluation of the Mexican peso in 1976, Mexico adopted policies which appeared to stabilize the value of the peso and to position the country to take advantage of the country's new oil-related wealth. And with the second round of OPEC oil price hikes in 1979, Mexico's oil wealth seemed to guarantee a prosperous future. But things turned sour in the early 1980s, with the decline in oil prices serving as only the most visible sign of trouble. In 1982 the country's economy and its currency collapsed.

Major international lending institutions, in retrospect, clearly erred in their assessments of the future prosperity of Mexico. Again, with the benefit of hindsight, we can see that similar errors were made in the lending policies adopted for many other oil-producing, developing nations—not to mention the non-oil, developing countries.

What was wrong with the country risk analysis of these sophisticated, international lending institutions? What are the lessons we can learn from this unfortunate experience in international risk assessment?

In this article, the primary approach to economic country risk analysis, the "current account" approach, will be examined in light of two competing approaches: (1) the "monetary" approach and (2) the "finance" approach. Various examples from Mexico and other debtor countries will be used to illustrate the advantages of these alternate approaches over the traditional current account analysis.

To anticipate the basic conclusions, the current account approach is found lacking. First, it fails to acknowledge the role of central banks' operations as they affect capital flows, exchange rates, government fiscal policy, and domestic inflation. This shortcoming can be addressed by using a more general approach known as the monetary approach to international adjustment.[1]

Second, the current account approach fails to consider certain basic financial policy issues, such the business risk inherent in a country's development plans, how the financing plans mesh with the economic growth prospects, and how the risk of one country is associated with the risks in other countries. These problems can be alleviated simply by analyzing a country's economic prospects much as an investor might assess the value of a corporate stock and its relationship to his total portfolio.

Current Account Analysis

Most economic country risk analysis focuses on the current account. A surplus of exports (goods and services) over imports is considered favorable to a country, while deficits are viewed negatively. This view stems from the concept that the foreign exchange necessary to repay international debts must be earned through a current account surplus. If there is no surplus, then debt repayment will be endangered.

Viewing current surpluses as good and deficits as bad leads one to several policy stances. First, foreign exchange devaluations are often sought to improve export performance and discourage imports. Second, import substitution programs are designed to reduce the dependence of the country on imports. Third, trade and capital controls are introduced to prevent the importation of goods and services and the export of capital.

All of these policies are harmful to countries, even though all of them affect the current account positively, at least in the short run. The problem is that the goal of producing current account surpluses is the wrong goal—whether for economic policy or country risk analysis. It is the wrong goal for policy because it often leads to development-damaging economic decisions rather than development-enhancing decisions. It is the wrong focus for country risk analysis because it does not measure the real risks and may give the wrong signals. The

---

[1] *Monetary Approach to International Adjustment*, edited by B.H. Wilford, (Praeger Publishers, New York, 1978).

Current account deficits, in isolation, do not tell us much about either the appropriate development policy or about country risk.

fact is, current account deficits, in isolation, do not tell us much about either the appropriate development policy or about country risk.

'Competitive" Devaluation

An exclusive focus on the current account often leads policy-makers to recommend a currency devaluation. It also leads some forecasters to anticipate a devaluation. The policy perspective comes from a desire to stimulate exports by making them cheaper; the forecasting tendency arises from the surplus of domestic currency created by a current account deficit. Again, current accounts, per se, do not give much of a clue to exchange rate policy or forecasting.

Devaluations as a policy tool have two problems, only one of which is widely recognized. The first, and recognized, problem is that of inflation. As the currency devalues, imports become more expensive, which allows domestically-produced competing goods to increase in price. In a short time, inflation eats away any competitive advantage that was created by the devaluation. The best a country can achieve is one or two years of a competitive edge before the inflation rate catches, and sometimes surpasses (in anticipation of the next devaluation), the currency depreciation.

This means that devaluations may subsidize export industries for a few years, but then penalty years may follow. Another possibility is that inflation under fixed rates may erode competitiveness for several years, and then be followed by a leap-frogging devaluation. Neither situation does much good for long-range development.

In Mexico, for example, the devaluation of 1953 created a period of several years in which prices were generally lower in Mexico, on a purchasing power basis, than in the U.S.. From 1956 through the 1960s, purchasing power remained in relative parity with the United States, and the fixed exchange rate of 12.5 pesos per dollar stood fast. Then, in the 1970s, Mexican policies began to produce inflation in excess of that in the U.S. The government was able to hold the peso at the fixed rate until 1976, by which time Mexican prices had accumulated some 45 percent more inflation than in the U.S. When the devaluation came, it virtually eradicated the price differences overnight.

From 1977 through 1982, Mexico again adopted a set of government policies producing significantly more inflation than in the U.S.—more than 50 percent more over the six years. But when the devaluation came, the peso sunk much lower than purchasing power parity would have suggested. The peso did not just catch up, instead it exceeded the inflation differential. In 1982 and 1983, inflation rocketed to equate purchasing power at the much lower exchange rate.

Clearly, exchange rate devaluations, at best, just buy some time for the export industry. And they may buy the time with an undisclosed price— namely, inflation—to be paid in the future.

But there is a second problem, one that is quite long lasting. Devaluations do not affect trade alone, they also affect capital stocks and flows—negatively.

First, most developing countries cannot borrow internationally in their own currencies. Their international borrowings are generally denominated in U.S. dollars, Japanese yen, Swiss francs, or other "hard" currencies. Thus, developing countries usually have a "short" dollar position, in the language of foreign exchange traders. That is, they will take a capital loss if the dollar appreciates relative to their domestic currency. When the peso devalued in 1982, Mexico suffered such losses, making it necessary to generate huge amounts of pesos to meet just the interest payments on the dollar-denominated debt.

Second, devaluations raise the specter both of rising inflation and future devaluations. In response to these expectations, domestic currency interest rates rise, often dramatically. This rise in interest rates comes at a time when the economy is already under great strains and matters are just made worse by the aftermath of the devaluation.

Current account followers often ignore the capital account in the balance of payments. And they ignore the effects on domestic interest rates. These failures are understandable, but not acceptable.

The Monetary Approach

Economic country risk analysis must treat the whole balance of payments, not just one part. The best method to achieve this is the monetary approach to the balance of payments. This approach examines *total* international money flows—that is, capital as well as trade flows. Using this approach allows the forecast to focus on the central bank as the fulcrum of the economy, and thus to measure the pressures that may be building for a devaluation.

*Using the monetary approach allows the forecast
to focus on the central bank as the fulcrum of the
economy, and thus to measure the pressures that may
be building for a devaluation.*

For example, Mexico was on a fixed exchange rate with the U.S. dollar from 1976 into 1982 at around 22 pesos per dollar. Using a monetary approach model, and plugging in U.S. inflation and U.S. interest rates, would have yielded a forecast of large outflows of international reserves well before the crisis. But a look at the international reserves of the central bank would have shown them to be increasing even in early 1982. Some economists might reject the model, but the proper interpretation would have been to "red-flag" the tremendous foreign borrowing by the Mexican government as an early sign of trouble. Mexico was using the loans to shore up its international reserves, which is never a cure but only a temporary expedient at best.

In Venezuela, a fixed exchange rate had been in place for over two decades. A follower of the monetary approach would have noted two early warnings signs of trouble in 1980 and 1981. First, the central bank's ratio of international reserves to domestic assets began to deteriorate dramatically. Second, the changes in the domestic assets held by the central bank became associated directly with the increasing government deficits. That is, the central bank was purchasing an ever-increasing portion of the government's debt. To fund these purchases, the central bank was selling its international reserves. Prior to 1979, the central bank of Venezuela held most of its assets in the form of international reserves and did not assist the government in financing deficits. When this changed, the monetary approach analysis sent warning signals, but the current account approach did not.

These two changes occurred well before Venezuela was viewed as a problem country by international banks. The country had lots of oil and the current account was not viewed as having deteriorated too far. But the weakness in the oil markets had changed government policy for the worse, and the monetary approach model showed where and how—early.

The Good and the Bad

Are current account surpluses necessarily "good" and deficits "bad?" In 1983 and 1984, for example, the United States saw its current account deteriorate steadily toward larger and larger deficits. Across the border, Mexico moved quickly and substantially in the surplus direction. Yet Mexico is the

country trying to recover from the disaster. Current accounts more often reflect relative growth and investment prospects than current risks.

In 1983 and 1984 the U.S. was in the first stage of a booming economic expansion that outpaced performance around the world and required large new investment. Hence, as the U.S. export markets grew slowly and as the U.S. demand for imports increased, the current account moved into a large deficit.

Was this a problem? The answer is "No." The U.S. current account deficit reflected its current rapid growth and the prospect for strong growth in the future. Far from being in trouble, the U.S. is a country that attracts large amounts of overseas capital.

Mexico, on the other hand, moved toward a current account surplus after its development prospects evaporated, particularly in the oil market. Its current account surplus reflects not a healthy economy able to repay its debts, but a country that has limited growth potential (at least over the next few years) and cannot attract new capital.

In the language of corporate finance, the U.S. (1983-1984) is, and will continue to be, a negative "free cash flow" country (that is, it generates a current account deficit). But it is a country nevertheless with large quantities of investment projects expected to earn high returns relative to the alternatives available internationally. To extend this analogy to corporate finance, the U.S. is much like a high-growth company such as Hewlett-Packard: it continually needs new cash not because it is going bankrupt, but because it has attractive investment projects— much more than it can fund from internal sources.

Mexico, by contrast, is like a company on the verge of bankruptcy. The country is moving to a positive "free cash flow" position because it is not investing for its future. It has limited attractive investment projects and has made a number of capital allocation errors in the past.

The point of this analysis is that expecting countries to run sustained current account surpluses is wrong. A surplus is neither good nor bad in itself. Current account deficits can be good, if they represent a healthy economic environment with expected high returns from investment.

More important for country risk analysis than current accounts is the basic outlook for new investment in the country. Are quantities of projects available that can earn attractive rates of return? If the country's economy is healthy, the current account will take care of itself.

The U.S. is much like Hewlett-Packard: it continually needs new cash not because it is going bankrupt, but because it has attractive investment projects—much more than it can fund from internal sources.

Import Substitution

Import substitution policies are those development programs that subsidize in various ways the growth of industries that can "replace" imports. The goal is explicitly to move the current account to surplus.

These policies interfere directly with the capital allocation process and go directly against the grain of one of the oldest and most accepted theories in economics: Ricardian comparative advantage. By subsidizing industries in order to make them able to compete with imports, countries are allocating capital to those industries that are at a comparative *disadvantage*. Stated another way, in terms of corporate finance, the country is investing in projects likely to have low returns relative to returns available from investment projects in other industries.

The effect of a given capital allocation program on the current account is the wrong criterion for any investment project. The corporate finance literature suggests rather conclusively that value can be created only when investments are made in projects expected to earn rates of return above those generally available and of similar risk.

For example, Mexico's capital allocation process has suffered from the current account illusion discussed here. First, Mexico has created an industrial structure that is not nearly as competitive internationally as it should be, primarily because the wrong projects received the subsidies. Second, Mexico recently bet heavily on one industry, oil, to solve the rest of its problems. The share of oil in Mexico's exports grew from less than 3 percent in the 1960s to greater than 70 percent in the 1981-1982 period. Even more critical, during 1977-1982 the growth of non-oil exports was hurt by public policies which were oriented almost exclusively to the oil sector.

This is not to say the oil industry did not offer attractive investment opportunities and that other types of exports did. But the data is indicative of the kind of push that Mexico gave the oil industry—at the expense of almost everything else.

While this criticism of the current account method of allocating capital is directed predominantly at public policy, it does have implications for country risk analysis. Because the country is choosing investment projects on a basis that is not related to the creation of value and wealth, it can seriously damage its economic prospects. Rather, the country should look at risk and return criteria which do relate to wealth creation. This would focus attention on growth-enhancing policies.

From a country risk perspective, import substitution policies are clear signs of future trouble. They may make the current account look better in the short run, but they do not produce the long-run economic health that is needed to repay long-term international debts. International lenders should view these policies with some alarm.

Portfolio Diversification and Country Risk

While many lending institutions give lip service to portfolio diversification, the emphasis they put on current account analysis betrays them. When focusing on current accounts the global question often asked is the following: Do the individual current accounts from around the world sum to zero or, put another way, are the current account forecasts globally consistent? There is nothing wrong with asking this question, but for country risk analysis it places the emphasis in the wrong place.

Certainly, if done correctly, the current accounts of each country in the system must sum to zero. But for country risk, this method of viewing the interdependencies in the forecast is misleading. The important interdependencies involve the risks that correlate across countries.

For example, Mexico, Indonesia, Venezuela, and Nigeria all share a common risk characteristic: dependence on oil markets. Their current accounts will go up and down together with the oil market. So looking at the global current account picture may not help in terms of country risk analysis; it will just guarantee a consistent oil forecast.

In the financial world, the important global risk consideration is how much risk the addition of a new investment adds to the total portfolio. To answer this question, one cannot view countries independently. Instead, one must attempt to measure the correlation of the risks across countries.

For example, a portfolio of 100 percent gold is very risky, by any standards. But if 5 percent or 10 percent of the total portfolio is invested in gold, the portfolio is likely to be more stable than without the gold. Why? Because gold is not correlated with many economic risks and can balance a portfolio.

Adding loans to Nigeria to a portfolio already

From a country risk perspective, import substitution policies are clear signs of future trouble.

heavy with loans to Mexico, Venezuela, and Indonesia does not add African risk to Latin American risk and Asian risk. It adds oil risk to an oil portfolio.

Most international lending institutions set country limits on lending, but fail to set limits on the risks they take by industry internationally. They consider a loan to build a factory in Mexico to have Mexican risk. It may be a factory, but because Mexico has oil risk, the loan has oil risk.

Portfolio analysis has a lot to offer country risk analysis. And after the disasters of the past few years, one suspects some lending institutions will get the message.

Country Risk Analysis— After the Fall

The damage inflicted on the stockholders of international lending institutions from the excesses of the 1970s has been severe. Several major international banks have seen their stock prices fall to as low as 50 percent of book value. A few better run banks have suffered less, but even these banks were not immune.

Furthermore, banks have resisted admitting the scale of their errors. That is, accounting standards allow banks to carry loans at full value (or in excess of recoverable value) for several months after the account has moved into arrears. Then, in many cases, the banks actually negotiate a rescheduling of the loan, providing the borrower with the money to pay the overdue interest. This makes the loan "current" in an accounting sense, but may not make the

credit any less risky. Stockholders, of course, understand this and have already penalized the banks; their best guess at the amount of permanent damage is already reflected in banks' stock prices.

This failure to admit error in the accounting sense is also evident in a failure to come to grips with country risk analysis. If anything, time spent on country risk assessment is probably less now than in the late 1970s. Banks have been more interested in cutting costs (and risk assessment, of course, is a cost center) than in analyzing how they got where they did and how to avoid getting there again.

Furthermore, the emphasis on current accounts to the exclusion of other approaches—such as the monetary and finance considerations described in these pages—is still the rule. The issue can be summarized as follows: International lenders are still myopic about countries, seeing their differences rather than their interrelationships. That is, it is still easier to analyze a country by studying its institutions and special characteristics than by studying its relationships to other countries and to world markets. The former approach makes some sense; countries do differ substantially. But the risks that have proven to be the most severe are those that simultaneously affect many countries. Only the monetary and finance approaches—in essence, a market-oriented as opposed to a country-oriented approach—can guard against these broader risks.

Hopefully, lessons will be learned. International banks are still repairing the damage rather than seeking new international opportunities. There is still time to prepare for the opportunities and challenges that an increasingly integrated world will offer.

The International Banking Crisis: Measuring the Risks

by Bluford H. Putnam,
Stern Stewart Putnam & Macklis, Ltd.

In 1974 there were dire predictions of a crisis in international banking. The system, it was said, would not be able to handle the huge recycling of credit required by the OPEC price hikes. In 1979, when OPEC was again raising prices, some analysts again issued grave warnings. This time, in 1983, it is sharply *falling* oil prices—and the breakdown of the OPEC cartel—that is causing the concern. The specter of worldwide economic chaos has once again been revived by the popular financial press. There was, however, no crisis in 1974, there was none in 1979, and the likelihood of future crises in the international banking system is very, very remote. Perhaps we can lay this ghost to rest by subjecting it to the clearer light of economic reality.

The crucial issue in 1983, as it was in 1974 and 1979, is the international banking network's ability to cope with major *redistributions* of the world's wealth. In each of these cases, the proximate cause of the redistribution was, as it is now, a significant change in the price of oil relative to all other goods. In 1974 and in 1979, oil prices increased, making oil-producing countries relatively wealthier and oil-consuming countries relatively poorer. The reverse is now taking place, as the price of oil falls.

It is important to start by realizing that the net change in total worldwide wealth from changes in oil prices is not likely to be great. The issue thus is *not* whether the world as a whole has been impoverished or enriched by this latest shock from volatile oil prices. The relative wealth changes, though, are clearly very large. And as the oil price continues to fall, these changes will become even larger. The question, then, is: given that the world's total wealth remains largely intact, will this Herculean task of redistribution strain the international banking network?

Let's begin by remembering that wealth redistribution, that is, the transfer of assets (and liabilities) from one country to another, is one of the major functions of the international banking system. The evolution of the banking network into its present form, although partly the result of government mandate and control, is largely the result of bankers' collective experience in responding to strong market-supplied incentives. The banking system, like most private enterprise, has proved remarkably resourceful when allowed to confront problems with-

out undue interference (and distortions) imposed from outside authorities. And though it will have to withstand some shocks in the near future—mainly in the form of reductions of short-term profitability—the system is fundamentally sound.

To understand why such massive, oil-based shifts in relative wealth are not likely to cause the banking network to collapse, we need to look more carefully at what a banking system does, and how it makes its profits.

Banks as Intermediaries

Bankers are quintessential middlemen, channeling money and credit from original lenders to borrowers farther down the credit pipeline. Banks purchase funds—their raw materials—from a variety of sources, repackage those raw materials, and then sell them at a higher price. The profit comes from the spread between the price received from the buyer (borrower) and the costs both of purchasing and repackaging those materials (funds).

In the international banking system, the pricing of these two economic functions is very explicit. Banks can borrow funds in the Eurocurrency interbank markets at a given interest rate, and they charge their borrowers that same rate plus a spread or mark-up on the base interest rate. If the maturity (for purposes of repricing or adjusting the rate) is identical for the bank as borrower and as lender, the bank faces no interest-rate risk.

The bank also charges separate fees for processing and packaging the loan. The fees, which are received up-front, plus the spread, which is earned over the life of the loan, are intended to cover the bank's costs of repackaging the funds, and to provide profits for stockholders. The expected profit must be sufficient to provide an acceptable return on invested capital, one that compensates investors for the risks of default or delayed payment.

In theory, the primary risk in the financial intermediary business is the possibility of default by the borrower. The borrower's failure to repay principal means a loss of capital—and interest payments missed are foregone operating income—for the lending bank. Because the market for lending money is a highly competitive one, banks cannot pass through the consequences of default, or missed payments, to the ultimate lenders. Indeed, one of the most important services of intermediaries is to bear just this kind of risk. It is worth noting, moreover, that interest rates incorporate an implicit premium for bearing this risk of default.

In practice, though, defaults in international banking are very, very rare. They are more common among corporate borrowers in an industrialized country like the U.S., than among international borrowers. Even delayed payments of interest and principal by international borrowers, though more common, are infrequent.

Delayed payment, however, is very different from default. This is an important distinction. If its payments are suspended, a bank admittedly loses the opportunity to change its investment position; it is stuck with the present borrower for a while longer than originally expected. International banks, however, generally can change the *terms* of the loan agreement to compensate for the delay and the increased risk of default. This is called 'rescheduling' and, contrary to popular belief, it is profitable. Rescheduling allows banks, in effect, to adjust their perception of the probability of default risk, and to reprice their loans accordingly. (Domestic bankers do not often have this luxury.)

A rescheduling of debt does not of course eliminate the ultimate risk of default, but nor does it usually "forgive" any part of the debt. Rescheduling is profitable, in part because banks must expect to earn higher returns to compensate their stockholders for the increased risk of their loan portfolio. The higher returns are achieved in two ways. In any rescheduling, there are fees charged for the additional repackaging. These are due and payable immediately. Secondly, the spread over the base rate (or cost of raw materials) is increased, often dramatically. So, if the payments are eventually made, the profits are quite high. And the higher spread is accruing even throughout grace periods. If the loan is finally repaid, banks do very well—they simply have to put up with the inconvenience of a few years' delay.

In typical domestic corporate banking, there are a number of options for rescheduling. For example, if a corporation falls behind in interest and principal payments, it can go into bankruptcy proceedings and, in many cases, receive some forgiveness of the debt. Or corporations can negotiate equity-for-debt swaps with their bankers.

In international banking, the borrower is often a national authority or government agency. Sovereign borrowers cannot turn to bankruptcy courts or issue equity for debt. With such borrowers, it is simply a case of rescheduling or default. But, to repeat this obvious, yet crucial point, only default brings losses to a bank. Rescheduling brings higher returns—returns expected to compensate the lender for the increased risk of default. *The expected rate of default, then, not the expected rescheduling rate, is the best indicator of the of the international banking system.*

cted rate of default is always much lower than the rescheduling rate. Default by one sovereign borrower is not likely to trigger defaults by others. Though falling oil prices will certainly affect many borrowers simultaneously, each tends to have different resources on which to draw. Because of this built-in diversification— which exists even among the most oil-concentrated national economies—the odds of a domino-like chain of defaults are quite low.

Banks themselves also make it a point to diversify their lending portfolios (although some clearly do a better job of it than others). This diversification, combined with the generally higher spreads earned in all reschedulings, should cushion the effects of an increased rate of default across the entire banking system's portfolio.

Default Risk and Wealth Redistribution

There is little question that a worldwide redistribution of wealth increases the general risk of default. From the perspective of international bankers, this increase in risk is particularly important, especially for their near-term outlook for profits.

Banks, and indeed all international lenders, find themselves in an asymmetric position because of their status as creditors rather than equity holders. The redistribution of global wealth makes some of their customers poorer and some wealthier, and the risk of default by the now wealthier set of borrowers falls while that of the poorer set rises. International banks lose in this process because they are prevented (either by domestic or local law, or both) from taking an equity stake in a sovereign borrower. Their potential gains from the wealth redistribution are thus limited to the interest contracted for in the initial loan agreement. Their expected losses, however, are increased since they are now exposed to the complete or partial loss of their investment in the event of default by newly impoverished countries. Thus, wealth redistribution will have serious consequences on the *profitability* of international banking, at least over the next few years.

But, as argued earlier, a temporary reduction in bank profitability does not mean that the entire system is on the verge of collapse. The redistribution of the world's wealth caused by falling oil prices is, in mathematicians' terms, a "zero-sum game." Though banking is, on net, more risky, the risks to the international economic system are not significantly greater.

Back to Individual Bank Profitability

Some international banks, then, will have loan losses and increased pressure on profitability during the upcoming period of massive wealth redistribution. Indeed, one of the less recognized risks to profitability occurs when a few banks get hit—whether because of bad luck or bad management—with more than their share of defaults. In such cases, the creditworthiness of those banks is brought into question by the market, and they must pay more for their raw materials. These added costs cannot, in general, be passed through to the bank's borrowers. This kind of credit classification has happened before in the Eurocurrency interbank markets—in 1974, for example, after Bankhaus Herstatt failed.

Banks that must pay premiums for purchased funds can be squeezed quite badly on profitability. Most Eurocurrency loans are on a LIBOR-plus basis, where LIBOR is an average of several banks' offered rates on Euro-deposits. When a lending bank is forced to pay a premium, its cost of funds can even exceed the base lending rate (LIBOR) to which the loan spread is added.

The crisis, then—if crisis there is—will be faced only by certain banks, not by the system as a whole. If the creditworthiness of the entire network were in doubt, then Eurocurrency interest rates would increase relative to interest rates on relatively riskless investments, such as U.S. government short-term securities. In this case, however, all banks would pay the same, though higher rate for their purchased funds (deposits), and then pass on the cost through a base rate-plus-spread lending contract. The interest spread, though, and hence the profitability of banks in general, would be unaffected.

In penalizing only under-performing banks by charging them a premium for funds, the international money markets also provide a stern deterrent to poor credit management. *In fact, the long-term health of the system depends on banks being made to bear the consequences of bad loans or improper diversification.*

How Much More Risky?

The risks of individual banks do add up to an international banking system that is, in some respects, riskier than before. But, the question is, how much riskier? Put another way, how many defaults are necessary to do irreparable damage to the system?

The resilience and durability of the banking system depends on a number of factors, but three come to mind most readily. Relying on these three measures of profitability and capital adequacy, we can feel reasonably assured that the total level of risk confronting the international banking system is quite manageable.

First, the *total* profits of banks in any one year provide a major cushion. International banks normally earn between .04 and .07 percent on their total assets. Second, the equity of international banks generally equals 3 to 4 percent of total assets. Third, risks are broadly diversified throughout the system, which means that a few defaults cannot trigger a general collapse. Thus, one-year's profits, plus equity, plus loan loss reserves, amount to 5–7 percent of the total (asset) size of the international banking system. This cushion, combined with the benefits of diversified lending portfolios, should do much to dispel the popular intimations of mortality now surrounding our banking system.

To bolster the case, these figures cited should be weighed against an amount considerably less than the book value of loans to oil-producing countries. Many of these loans are offset by substantial deposits from the same sovereign borrower. The size of the total world bank portfolio at risk is thus much smaller than a casual look at the numbers would suggest.

In sum, though the system is more risky, collapse is far from imminent. Drawing attention to the problems of individual banks, or individual borrowers, is missing the forest for the trees. Certain species are endangered, but the forest is merely undergoing another round of the evolutionary process. The survivors become ever more durable.

Policy Implications

The soundness of the international banking system does not rely in any important way on the intervention or support of central banks or governments. Nor does it depend, despite the recent clamor of international bankers and developing country governments, on an increase in the subsidies to poorer nations administered by the International Monetary Fund (IMF).

The issue of worldwide income redistribution will inevitably involve industrial country governments and international authorities. But, it should be recognized that what is really fueling the rhetorical fireworks is *not* some disinterested concern about the health of the world economy. As always, the subjectivity of a fairly narrow self-interest can be counted on to sound the alarm loudest and longest. If industrial countries want to provide financial aid to countries made poorer by the fall in oil prices, they are certainly free to do so. Governments may choose to do the same through such international institutions as the IMF. But, such institutionalized charity should be identified for what it is—the taxpayers' gift to international banks and developing countries alike.

The international banking system is not endangered. Driven and disciplined by profit incentives held out by world capital markets, the system has repeatedly demonstrated its efficiency in channeling capital around the world. The system's resourcefulness was displayed in 1974, in 1979, and it will show itself again in 1983.

Competitive markets work because of a reliably consistent system of rewards and penalties. When these are set aside by government decree, the system functions less efficiently. Subsidies to banks trying to avoid the system's penalties for accepting bad credit risks, or improperly diversifying their portfolios, do not strengthen the system. They simply provide a small measure of very temporary security. And this is provided at the much greater cost of weakening the incentives of international bankers to lend—and international governments to spend—wisely. *The real danger to the international banking system is that international governments may try to "fix" a system that already works.*

Index